ISBN 978-0-331-32204-0
PIBN 11202143

1 MONTH OF
FREE
READING

at

www.ForgottenBooks.com

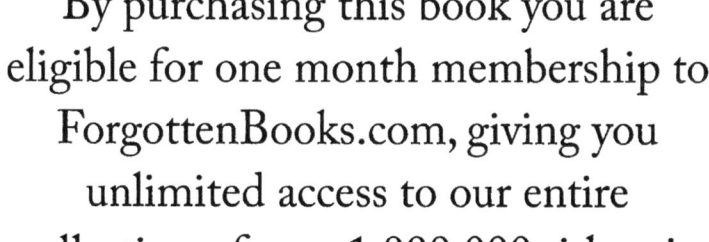

By purchasing this book you are eligible for one month membership to ForgottenBooks.com, giving you unlimited access to our entire collection of over 1,000,000 titles via our web site and mobile apps.

To claim your free month visit:

www.forgottenbooks.com/free1202143

English
Français
Deutsche
Italiano
Español
Português

www.forgottenbooks.com

Mythology Photography **Fiction**
Fishing Christianity **Art** Cooking
Essays Buddhism Freemasonry
Medicine **Biology** Music **Ancient**
Egypt Evolution Carpentry Physics
Dance Geology **Mathematics** Fitness
Shakespeare **Folklore** Yoga Marketing
Confidence Immortality Biographies
Poetry **Psychology** Witchcraft
Electronics Chemistry History **Law**
Accounting **Philosophy** Anthropology
Alchemy Drama Quantum Mechanics
Atheism Sexual Health **Ancient History**
Entrepreneurship Languages Sport
Paleontology Needlework Islam
Metaphysics Investment Archaeology
Parenting Statistics Criminology
Motivational

LAPWORTH CHURCH

FROM THE SOUTH

CHURCH

FROM THE SOUTH

MEMORIALS OF
A WARWICKSHIRE PARISH

MEMORIALS

OF A

BEING PAPERS MAINLY DESCRIPTIVE
OF THE RECORDS AND REGISTERS
OF THE PARISH OF LAPWORTH

BY

WITH A LARGE-SCALE MAP OF THE PARISH,
PLAN, AND 17 ILLUSTRATIONS

Ay, now am I in Arden
As You Like It

36 ESSEX STREET W.C.
LONDON
1904

TO

J. H.

EDITORIAL NOTE

*R*OBERT HUDSON *was born in* 1834 *at Pocklington,
in Yorkshire.   At the age of twenty-seven he came to
reside in Lapworth, and here he remained until his death
in* 1898.

*A resident in the parish for nearly forty years, one of
its Churchwardens for twenty years, Chairman of its latter-
day Parish Council, and one of its Charity Trustees—all
that pertained to Lapworth, whether past history or present
duties, had for him a keen and abiding interest.   Thus it
came that he explored the old chests in our church, and
gave his leisure for many years to the happy labour of
deciphering their time-worn contents.   What he discovered
from his examination, how he made the scraps of yellow
parchment to yield up their story, is (with much else relating
to the parish) set forth in this volume.*

*The MS. was almost finished when the Author died, and
the book now appears practically in the form in which he
left it.   Some few additional facts have been noted here and
there, mainly because they seemed helpful in bringing the
record up to the present time.   If mistakes are found (and
it is vain to suppose that no mistakes have crept in), the
blame for them attaches to the Editor alone, who, with little
knowledge of parish history and small fitness for his task,
has sought as best he may to fill up blanks and determine
marginal queries which were found now and again in the
MS., and has finally, after a delay which no one can regret
so much as himself, seen the volume through the press.*

Criticism on one point may perhaps be forestalled by a sentence as to why the book contains no general index. To furnish a complete index would add enormously to the bulk of a volume made up so largely of proper names. An abridged index, omitting these names or giving only a selection of them, would be of little or no value. Besides, the two main Appendices (Nos. I. & II.) in some sort serve the purpose of indices, since they give the date under which every name appears in the deeds and registers, and should thus enable reference to be made to the various sections of the book wherein such person or family may be expected to figure.

Apart from this prefatory note, the Editor himself is responsible for one additional page. He believes, with a confidence little removed from knowledge, that in dedicating the volume to her whose initials stand on that page, he writes only what his father would have written, in his own minute and beautiful hand, if the working-day had been but a little longer.

LAPWORTH, *June 20th*, 1904

CONTENTS

NOTE.—*It was originally intended to append to this book a complete Calendar of the Deeds of the Lapworth Charity Trustees* (circa 1190–1502), *with full notes and elucidations. But to do this would have added so much to the bulk of the volume that it has been determined instead to present the Author's MS. of the Calendar of Deeds to the Reference Department of the Birmingham Free Library. It will be available there for all time to anyone who, after reading this book, desires fuller information as to the Lapworth Deeds.*

LIST OF ILLUSTRATIONS

*The views marked * are from photographs taken by Mr. F. S. Reynolds of Olton, near Birmingham, to whom the Editor here expresses his warm thanks and great indebtedness.*

The sketches of the seals, parish chest, deed box, and stone in churchyard wall were made for this book by Ernest W. Hudson.

INTRODUCTORY

There is not an acre, I think I may say, in England, certainly there is not a parish or a manor, that has not its place in English history . . . and there is not, I think, an intelligent person in England who is not in one way or another a sharer in such interests of tradition if he would or could realise it. By realising your own personal connexion with these, you realise your historical relation to the progress of your country, and, by working out the details of the local or personal history in which you are so interested, you may yourselves largely contribute to the ascertaining of historical truth in detail. Every parish must have a history, every parish has a register, every person has a parish.

STUBBS. *Mediæval and Modern History*

INTRODUCTORY

LAPWORTH, situated in the heart of what used to be called the "Forest of Arden," and just within the parliamentary division of South Warwickshire, having no railway station of its own,[1] and no main road passing directly through it, is in the enviable position of being

> Not wholly in the busy world, nor quite
> Beyond it.

It is near enough to the railway to make the neighbouring towns of Birmingham, Warwick, Leamington, and Stratford-on-Avon easily accessible, and far enough away to retain its own quietness. It has probably undergone less change in recent times than most of the rural villages of Warwickshire; and, except that it begins now to be dotted here and there with the red brick of the modern country-house, it remains a parish of cottages and farmsteads, so widely scattered and isolated that strangers still, quite innocently, ask the way to Lapworth when they are in the middle of it. Even by the church there are only some three or four houses within sight of each

---

[1] Since this was written, Kingswood Station, on the Great Western line, has been changed in name to Lapworth Station.

other. The "semi-detached" house is almost unknown to us. We stand practically on the same
level as the centre of Birmingham, about 450 feet
above the sea, and the graceful spire of our church
forms a conspicuous landmark. Through our parish,
indeed, extends one of the central watersheds of
England, so that we find streams quite near to each
other, of which the one sends its waters, by way of
the Lapworth and Henley-in-Arden brooks, to the
Alne, the Arrow, the Avon, the Severn, and so into
the western sea, while the other goes eastward to the
North Sea by way of the Blyth, the Trent, and the
Humber.

The parish has an area of 2,984 acres, and a
rateable value (1895) of £6,775.[1] By the census of
1891, it had 617 inhabitants, whereas in 1831 it had
656, so that its tendency for at least the last half-
century has been to decrease.[2] The evidence of its
parish registers goes to show that for the last two
centuries it has been almost stationary. It is not
known to have been the birthplace of any noteworthy
person, or the scene of any remarkable event. If,
therefore, the village that has no annals is, like the
nation in similar case, happy, it should be an ideal
place to live in ; and, as a matter of fact, there would
be no difficulty in finding parishioners ready to main-
tain that it is so.

This book is not an attempt to give the parish any
annals. It does not profess to be a history. Its aim

---

[1] In 1904 the rateable value was £7,182.
[2] In 1901 the population is set down as 723. A good number of new
houses had been built in the parish during the preceding decade.

is the more modest one of setting out, under the
name of *Memorials*, a sort of parish scrap-book, by
means of which may be retained in something like
order and legibility, and securely fastened down as it
were, the village records and the odds and ends of
papers (very fragmentary many of them) which in the
course of seven centuries have accumulated, and,
by the providence which watches over things least
cared for of men, have survived in our parish chests.
In the lapse of so long a time, no matter how placidly
the current of village life may ordinarily have flowed,
it would be strange if there had not been exceptional
seasons when relics were cast ashore which are still
worth picking up and looking at.

It has been mentioned in books of local history
that Lapworth possessed parish records which went
further back than those of most other Warwickshire
parishes, but certainly it has not been known that
they went back into the twelfth century—the earliest
of them belonging to the reign of Richard I.—and
that from that time forward there is hardly a score of
years at any time which has not left some trace of
itself. No systematic examination of these has previously been made by anyone. If the task which
has now been undertaken by a parishioner, quite in-
experienced in such work, should be found to be, as
he fears, performed very imperfectly, and be wanting
in what an expert would have supplied, he will still
hope for lenient judgment. It is certain that intimate
local knowledge is very desirable, if not indeed absolutely necessary, for the performance of such work,
and the possession of that qualification may to some

extent counterbalance the want of others. A very long residence in the parish, and the circumstance of his having for many years filled the office of church-warden, and been permitted, by the courtesy of the trustees of the parish charities, free access to their papers, have afforded the writer facilities for his in-quiries which must have been lacking to a stranger, however otherwise better qualified. Further, he has done, whether well or ill, what no one else had any inclination to do.

Some readers may think that he has given too much space to, and perhaps dwelt at tedious length upon, the deeds of the pre-Reformation period, con-cerned, as they are for the most part, with trivial buyings and sellings, exchanges and bequests of little plots of the parish lands. He has, however, in this been largely influenced by the belief that labour which extends our knowledge, in any detail, to the period before the establishment of parish registers, and tells us, even if it be no more than the names, of those who lived here in the centuries that had then already passed into the darkness, is not bestowed in vain. He thinks, indeed, that all names which can be rescued from the preceding time are so much clear gain. Between the parish register and the genera-tions that passed away unregistered (*ignotique longâ nocte*) there is in nearly every parish a great gulf fixed. In this parish, at any rate, there have been brought into the light and fairly written down some four hundred names of men and women who lived here, or were more or less intimately connected with Lapworth, in the course of more than three centuries and a half before, in 1561, that record was begun. And a careful study of their names and of the bits of land they owned has now and again, as will be seen, brought to light little pieces of family history probably quite as extensive and interesting as any that will survive of most of us when we shall belong to a past as distant as theirs is from us.

It is surely of interest to see the long continuance of names here in the pre-Reformation period, and their final disappearance; to see that it has been no uncommon thing for families to take root here and abide their two, three, or even more centuries, and leave no trace of themselves except on some bits of parchment now at last deciphered, or in the name of a field or a lane, of which name the significance has long been utterly forgotten; or again to see from the comparatively modern parish register how the old order has changed, how it is no longer the landowner in our parish whose name has long continuance, but names of humbler families, descended, perhaps, from those who were his serfs. We have not in the parish now one single landowner whose family record here goes back a century, while of the labouring class we have several who bear names, and those not common names, which have appeared steadily and without intermission in the parish register for well-nigh the whole time of its existence.

This point of view will be illustrated by two of the appendices, in which are set out—

1. A list of all the names that occur in the pre-Reformation deeds (1190–1502), arranged in the order of precedence, as to dates, in which they are found.

2. An index showing in tabular form every surname that occurs in the parish registers (1561–1860), and indicating the respective decades of each century in which the name appears.

The latter is of curious interest in giving at a glance the duration of families in the parish, showing what families were here together, how names have disappeared for a longer or shorter time and then reappeared, indicating doubtless in many cases the return of descendants to the home of their fathers, and in many other ways is very suggestive. It is believed that such an arrangement has not been set out for any other parish.

The increased interest which is now taken in parish registers and the organised efforts that are being made to further the printing of them, gratifying as they are, will require many years to produce any sensible impression on the enormous mass of such registers, and we may suppose the tendency will be to print the more important registers first. But, as an interim arrangement, such an index as ours is a good deal better than nothing, and much more easily and cheaply produced than a complete print. It also shows much that the complete print itself would not show.

If neighbouring parishes were similarly treated, each would add immensely to the value and the interest of the other. If what has now been done for Lapworth in this particular should stimulate anyone who has access to the registers of his own parish, and more especially any of the neighbouring clergy, to do the like, the writer can assure such fellow-labourer that he will find his task by no means wanting in interest.

One word more in closing these introductory remarks. Much that follows, in what has almost unconsciously grown to be a book, was cast at first into the form of lectures, and delivered here to the writer's fellow-parishioners. Lapworth people naturally took a warmer and more appreciative interest in matters relating to Lapworth parish than strangers can be expected to take. None the less, there is matter in the volume which may well interest even those whose ill-fortune it is to be unrelated to our parish. The directness of address which the form of lectures involved has been purposely retained to a considerable extent, notwithstanding that such lectures have been enlarged by the addition of much new matter, and that documents are here printed entire which were then only described or given in brief extract.

Seal of deed, 1337
Thomas Purfreẏ to Henry Bossebẏ
(with a reference to land of William Stẏkemon)

p. 27

FROM THE EARLIEST OF THE PARISH
RECORDS (*circa* 1190) TO THE
TIME OF THE BLACK DEATH (1349–50)

. . . from the dust of old oblivion raked."

HENRY V.

MEMORIALS

OF A

WARWICKSHIRE PARISH

CHAPTER I

FROM THE EARLIEST OF THE PARISH RECORDS (*circa* 1190) TO THE TIME OF THE BLACK DEATH (1349–50)

IN undertaking to tell my fellow-parishioners and neighbours something about "Bygone Lapworth," I have ventured to assume that there is a desire amongst most people to learn what may be learned about the history of the place in which their own lot happens to be cast, and that we of Lapworth are likely to have more interest in the past of our own village than in that of neighbouring villages. These other villages may be quite as interesting in themselves, but they are not so interesting to us. The fact that we walk these lanes, and wander about these fields and beside these brooks, and worship in this church which has looked down upon so many generations, creates and encourages a wish to know something of those who did so before us in the centuries that are gone—something, even if it be no more than their names.

Now there happens to have been preserved in our parish an exceptionally large number of parchments and papers which hitherto have never undergone any careful examination, and it is of these that I wish to give some account. I think, indeed, that anyone who undertakes such a work performs a pious office for his parish, and though I have discovered nothing of a very exciting character, I have yet found so much which seemed at least worth notice, that my embarrassment has been to know what to reject.

The Parish Registers begin with 1561, when Elizabeth had been on the throne three years ; but we owe it to the accident of our having " parish charities " that records have survived, connected therewith, which go back to a much more distant period. The earliest of them has been pronounced on high authority to be fully seven hundred years old. It is a time so distant that, when we read descriptions of village life in those days, we can hardly realise that we are living in the country which they describe. If it were possible for any of us to be dropped down into the Lapworth of seven hundred years ago, we should see that the church—a church, at any rate—stood then where it stands now. This is certain, because the very earliest deed we have tells us who was then rector of it ; but it is also pretty clear that it was a church without spire or tower—a smaller, lower, and altogether more in-significant-looking building than our church is now. We should find the roads, if we could recognise them as roads, taking generally the course they take to-day, and the brooks flowing in precisely the same beds, though not through enclosed, but through open fields. But, apart from these main features, all would be strange to us : the poor mud-built hovels, without chimneys or windows, which had to serve as human habitations ; the teams of eight oxen dragging their small ploughs ; the half-clad labourers, their wives and children, with less of comfort about them than the cattle of to-day—all would seem, indeed, incredible.

And yet there have survived from these distant times some few things which are absolutely unchanged; old parchments, namely, which were handled, written, read by, and were subjects of lively interest to, the parishioners of Lapworth of those days. These we can still decipher and to some extent understand if we have patience enough.   There is, indeed, something solemn in the thought that these relics of our predecessors (whose bones crumbled into dust in our churchyard centuries ago) have lain unknown, but sheltered by the same roof, close beside generation after generation of churchgoers, waiting to be looked at and spoken to, and able to speak feebly back again. There can be little doubt that ever since these deeds became the property of the parish they have been kept inside the church.

Probably few small rural villages possess such a long series of documents relating to their own parish. These documents fall naturally into two groups—first, those before the Reformation, and, second, those which follow that great event.

The earlier group consists of about a hundred and twenty small parchment deeds.   They nearly, but not

quite, all relate to sales, gifts, or other dealings with
land in Lapworth, Nuthurst, or the immediate neighbourhood, and although no longer of any value as
evidence of title, there is no doubt that the larger
number of them refer to land which still belongs to
the Lapworth Charity Trust, or to land which at some
former time did belong to it or to the church.   Some
few, however, are not of this character, and it is difficult
to understand how they have come to be preserved in
the parish chests.   These hundred and twenty deeds
or thereabouts are spread, as to date, over nearly all
the reigns from (it is believed) that of Richard I. up to
the latter part of the reign of Henry VII., a period of
over three hundred years.   There are, for instance
(admitting that the years of the earlier and undated
deeds are to some extent conjectural)—

of Richard I. .	1
of John .	1
of Henry III. and of Edward I.	7 [1]
of Edward II.	4
of Edward III. about	50 [2]
of Richard II.	9
of Henry IV.	4
of Henry VI.	22
of Edward IV.	10
of Henry VII.	9

At the period to which the very earliest of these
belong, it was not customary to date deeds of this

[1] It is very doubtful to which reign one or two of these belong.

[2] This large number is, of course, to be accounted for mainly by the
fact that Edward III. reigned for fifty years.

Sciant presentes et futuri quod ego B. de Agnecfall' uffaunif et conceff[i] et hac presenti carta mea
confirmaui Galfrido fil' Alexandri vnam dimid' virgata[m] terre in Lapplthorp' cu[m] oib; p[er]tinenc'[iis] p[re]dcte dimid' virgate terre [con]uenienc'[ibus]... habendam... t[enen]dam... de me et de her[e]dib; me...
... qui cum... Boftul hue... venit...
ill[e] et heredef fui L[ib]e... quiete et honorifice... t[enen]do fide... in ut heredib; mea ille
vel heredef fui... fol'... B. et heredef fui... Dro hac [con]ceff[i]one... [con]firmac[i]one d[omi]no m[e]o
... et B. B. affociata... et B. p[er]t[i]n[e]nc[i]a[m]
... R. god' p[r]incipal[is]... Dro hac [con]ceff[i]one... [con]firmac[i]one
et fol' in r[e]cog[n]it[i]one... B. et... vffaunf... et heredef mea... v[e]nu[m]... [con]uenienc[iis]
... p[re]dco fin[e]... faluo s[er]uicio
fuuo d[omi]no Reg... Ego uo... hac [con]ceff[i]one et [con]firmac[i]one... s[er]ta fui... p[ro]babil'... hac carta figilli
mei mu[n]imine [robor]aui. Hijs teft'[ibus]... S[imone] de... et... eccl[es]ie... Willelmo... Jotte de Ludimu...
... d[e] capellano de pakill[es]...
franco[ne]. Ricardo Baffett... Fred[er]ico... Will'o... hurt... et aptio. A...

description. We can only make out the date approximately by the character of the writing, a matter which has, however, been so closely studied that most of such deeds can be assigned almost as well as if they were dated. It was not till the reign of Edward II. that it became the custom to put a date. Earlier dated deeds are exceptional. We have nine before that reign which are undated ; all of them, it is thought, either prior to the year 1300, or immediately after.

Although they are many in number, they are not large in bulk. The average size of a deed conveying, it might be, a goodly estate was not more than nine inches by three inches ; sometimes a good deal less, sometimes a little more. They are all in Latin, and the writing is so full of abbreviations and arbitrary signs that it is a kind of shorthand, and, until one has got some practice in it, it is rather difficult to read. Parchment, on which they are written, was very expensive in those days, and this was probably one reason why the lawyers exerted themselves to get so much into so little room, instead of going, as they do now, on a totally opposite principle. They seem to have had, too, some secret for making their ink, which we have lost. On the earliest of these parchments, for instance,[1] which is over seven hundred years old, or contemporary with the Third Crusade, the writing is almost as clear and black as on the day it was written. The beauty of it, too, is remarkable ; it is so accurate and uniform that it will bear examining through a powerful magnifier, and even then show hardly more irregularity than a printed book. It is curious and

---

[1] See illustration opposite.

interesting to note that several of these old deeds have the seals tied on with rushes, and such rushes remain flexible at this time, though I should not like to attempt to untie and tie them again. The use of rushes in this way has been thought to be connected with an old form of land tenure known as the *traditio stipulae*, the rush representing an actual delivery by the grantor of the produce of the soil.

It happens that our deeds begin at a point where Dugdale admits himself, as regards our parish, to be deficient. "From hence," he writes, under Lapworth (meaning from the period of the Conquest), "till King Henry III.'s time having no light of record to guide me, I must by what appears afterwards only guess at the probable course of its succession"; that is, of the succession in the lordship of the manor. Our records seem to show that the succession was not exactly what he surmised, but that there were links in it of which he had no trace. The first of our deeds would have told him of a new family, that of the Marshalls (who seem to have held the manor for at least two or three generations, and were important people here from the time of Richard I. to 1349), and a new rector (about 1190), of whose existence he did not know.

This oldest of our deeds, which, as I have said, belongs doubtless to the reign of Richard I., is a grant of half a virgate of land, with a dwelling-house thereon, from Ralph Marshall (or Ralph "the Marshall"), who was at that time lord of the manor of Lapworth, to Geoffrey, the son of Alexander. That is all the description which is given of Geoffrey; his surname is not mentioned, but a later deed shows

him to have been a Prat. It was a time in which
not everybody possessed a surname, or, at any rate,
if a man had one it was not thought necessary to mention it always. Now the virgate of land differed as to
its extent in different parts of the kingdom, and it did
not mean a compact piece of land, but a number of
acre and half-acre strips scattered in the open fields,
often wide apart from each other. The word "virgate,"
indeed, meant simply "a bundle of strips." The whole
subject of ancient land measures is one on which
authorities are much at variance, but in this part of
Warwickshire the virgate seems to have been about
sixteen acres. Dugdale calls it so in speaking of
Lapworth. This was, therefore, a grant of about
eight acres with a house, and Ralph Marshall says
that for such grant the said Geoffrey has paid into
his hands 40s. by way of recognition (this being, no
doubt, the fine customarily levied by the lord on a
change of tenancy by death or otherwise), and that he
is to pay annually to him or his heirs 2s. 6d. at three
terms of the year, namely, 10d. at the feast of St.
Michael, 10d. at the feast of the Purification of the
Blessed Virgin Mary, and 10d. at Pentecost. This
payment of rent at three periods of the year, instead
of quarterly as now, was customary then and for
centuries later. Half-a-crown a year was the rent to
be paid for these eight acres and a house, but, although
it is estimated that a shilling at that time was fully equal
in purchasing power to a pound at this time, we must
not understand rent in anything like the same way as
we do now, for these tenures under the lord of the
manor were always accompanied by some substantial

services in the way of labour beyond the money payment.   Subject, however, to entrance fine, rent, and
services, the son had practically as indisputable a claim
to succeed his father as if the occupation were his own
freehold.   Seebohm, the greatest authority upon the
conditions of the old English village community, says
that virgates or half-virgates of land were held only
by tenants of the rank of villein.   He gives also
many illustrations from the Hundred Rolls and from
the Gloucester Chartulary of the time of Edward I.,
nearly a hundred years later than this deed, showing
that the labourer's wage for all kinds of farm work was
even then only $\frac{1}{2}d.$ a day (Seebohm's *English Village
Community*).   This, therefore, indicates to us the
servile position of the tenant holding under the
present deed.

The land is described as being situated in Lapworth,
and all of it "ad Boscum," at the wood.   The words
"all of it" have reference to the strips making up
this half-virgate, which, as I said, were frequently
scattered about.   The Conqueror's *Domesday Book*,
compiled about one hundred years before this deed,
says, under "Lapworth": "There is a wood two miles
long and one mile broad."   The deed says this half-
virgate was also subject to certain customary services
to our Lord the King.   This description of "at the
wood" might perhaps indicate that it was at Kingswood, and that Kingswood was not then the meaningless name it is now, but was mostly covered by a forest
belonging to the King, as that of Bushwood belonged
to the bishop of the period.   It is not easy for us to
locate in our parish this *Domesday* wood "two miles

long and one mile broad," but probably Bushwood, Kingswood, and Chesset Wood all joined on to each other with little break, so making one continuous forest. I find Chesset Wood called "Chasse-Wode" in some of our later deeds, as if it were then more especially a hunting wood. The deed ends with the names of no fewer than ten witnesses who were present at the sealing of it. The first is that of Nicholas, rector of the church of Lapworth (spelt as it is now except that it has no "o," and pronounced probably "Lapputh," as our labourers pronounce it to-day), followed by John de Luddinton, Walter (then chaplain of Packwood), Simon de Charlecote, William Pakeman, Walter his brother, Roger Franceis, Richard Hatecrist, Geoffrey feisant, Robert Prat, and after all the names are given, the words are added, "and many others."

This Nicholas, rector, is the first Rector of Lapworth of whom there is any record. Dugdale gives a list of all the rectors whose names and dates he had ascertained from the Bishops' Register at Worcester, but the first on his list is about a hundred years later than this deed. There is another deed about a generation later, in the reign of John, in which this Nicholas appears again as a witness under the description "parson of Lapworth"; so that he would seem to have held the living a long time. Simon de Charlecote, who is another of the witnesses, belonged to a family which in the reign of John (1204) changed its name to Lucy, and the Lucys have lived at Charlecote from that day to this. The "de Luddinton" family have their place in Dugdale, and took their name, no doubt, from the pretty village of Luddington, near Stratford-on-Avon. The mention of Walter as chaplain of Packwood tells us, at any rate, that there was then also a church at Packwood. The curious name of Hatecrist reappears under slightly varied spellings on several other deeds, but does not seem to have continued in the parish later than the reign of Henry III. or Edward I. Robert Prat, another of the witnesses (and no doubt a relative of the Geoffrey of the deed), was of a family who were residents and landowners here for nearly three hundred years, and whose name survives under that of our familiar " Prat's Pit," which has borne that name for probably at least seven hundred years. It will be seen, therefore, that altogether this first of our deeds has afforded us many subjects of comment.

In Henry III.'s reign Geoffrey, the son of the before-named Ralph Marshall, describes his father as " of Alveston," and confirms to Henry Prat, son of Geoffrey Prat (thereby giving us the surname which Ralph Marshall, of his haughtiness, withheld on the first deed), land which the father of the one had demised to the father of the other, another holding apparently from that of the first deed, together with four selions (or lands as we now call them) in a field named " Wetecroft." For this confirmation he says that Henry Prat has paid him 20s. sterling ; the rent is to be 3s. 6d. a year, payable as before at three terms, and the grantor describes himself as *dominus vir iste terre*, thus telling us that the Marshalls were then lords of the manor.

It is in John's reign also, probably soon after the

year 1200, that we find a deed which is interesting to us, because it relates to land still belonging to the Charity Trust, and calls a certain field by a name that with very little change it has borne to the present day. It is a conveyance from one Luke Sorel to William le Oiselur, and the description is—

that land which is called Vlelega and extends from Selewines land which he holds of me up to the high-way which is between Bellũ Desertũ and Burmĩgehã [*not dissimilar spellings from the Beaudesert and Birmingham of to-day*] and thence towards the house of Roger the son of the Smith to the length of 35 perches and thence towards the house of Richard the son of Orm to the width of 5 perches and thence up to the corner of the ditch of the land that William the son of Lofric held of Simon Bagot for his homage and service.

How suggestive this string of names is! None of the people have surnames. It is simply " Roger, the son of the Smith "; " Richard, the son of Orm " (a Scandinavian name of which we have a survival in the Orm's Head); and " William, the son of Lofric" (an old Saxon name, the same as was borne by Godiva's husband of Coventry). This field at the Birmingham road[1] was then about nine acres, and it was to be held "with the right of pannage and tollage" (*i.e.* the right of running swine, with other privileges), together with other lands in Lapworth (in all, about fourteen acres, as far as I can make out), for the annual rent of 3*s.*, to be paid in equal sums of 1*s.* at three terms as in the former cases; but in addition to these three payments the tenant was to pay between Michaelmas and Christmas *quatuor widecocs* (four woodcocks), and for this grant Luke Sorel says that

[1] In the hands of Mr. Lyndon in 1904.

William le Oiselur has paid into his hands the sum of one mark of silver (equal to 13s. 4d.). Probably in our day the four "widecocs" would be more difficult to pay than the money rent. In a later deed, however, the land is described as *croftum sive grovam*, being probably mostly coppice, to which these birds would naturally resort. Among the witnesses to this deed are Simon Bagot and Luke Bagot, members of the family that then owned and gave their name to Preston Bagot and Morton Bagot. "Vlelega," the name of this field, was probably pronounced "Uleleya," *V* being then used as the capital form of *u*, and in later deeds it takes the French form of "Lullayes," later still becoming "Ulley" and "Ulleys," then "Hullis," "Hullies" ("Big" and "Little," it having been divided into two fields), and in quite recent schedules of the charity estates appearing as "Hollys," which probably after a while will be corrected into the politer form of "The Hollies."

Of deeds of the reigns of Henry III. and Edward I. there are some half-dozen containing names and references of interest. They make mention of other members of the family of Marshall; of William de la Harecourt and Yvee Pippert, who were joint lords of the Manor after the Marshalls; and of Sir Hugh de Brandestone, who held the Manor in the time of Edward I., and is known to have died in 1299. Sir Edmund Truscel, of Nuthurst, also appears in this reign, the first we find of a family that continued to be connected with Nuthurst and Lapworth for more than three centuries.

When we reach the reign of Edward II. the deeds,

as I said, begin to be dated, and the manner of dating in those days is that they generally give the day of the week and say which saint's day is next to it, before or after. A very large number of these deeds are dated on the Sunday, and after the names of a string of witnesses (seldom less than six or seven) they nearly always wind up with the words, "and many others." Anything in the way of a transfer of or dealing with land was a serious business, and advantage was probably taken of the gathering of the people at church to have such deeds witnessed after service was over. So much was Sunday the favourite day for executing such deeds, that out of seventy-seven of our Lapworth deeds on which the day of the week is recorded, no fewer than thirty are dated on that day. Only one is dated on a Friday, which was counted an unlucky day, then as now. It is clear, too, that it was considered a distinction to witness these deeds. The same families witness them generation after generation, the names being usually those of the principal landowners of the parish and neighbourhood, so that by their help we trace the existence of families here for long periods.

I said these old deeds did not all relate to land. In the reign of Edward II., for instance, there is a very interesting little parchment, by which Walter at the Hethe says that—

Being of sound mind and moved by hearty affection he gives and confirms to his son Walter and Agnes his wife all his existing goods and chattels movable or immovable except only such draught-horses colts oxen for the plough and heifers as may by their labour sustain him in honour and comfort so long as he shall live.

There is a curiously human touch about this which compels one to hope that the young people were good to this village Lear of ours for the rest of his days.

The family of Hethe, under various forms of prefix, as "de la," "atte," "o' the," was here about two centuries, its members being apparently land-owners of consideration.

In working through these old records few incidents are more interesting than coming across names explanatory of the existence of other names in our parish, which would otherwise be meaningless to us in the present day. Thus, in 1323, we get the name of one John de Brocsawe, whose family was here to 1349, and left land to the parish; not one of them seems to have been here later than 1349, but their name remained behind them for a little while in "Brocshawe Lane," that which runs parallel with the Birmingham road, from what used to be called Ford Lane to what we now call Wharf Lane, and adjoining which there is a field, which on our Tithe Map bears the name of "The Brockshire" at this day. In Richard II.'s time (1395), this road bears the pretty name of "Nuthele (= Nut-hill) Lane"; and in our own day we know it as "Periwinkle Lane," from the abundance of wild periwinkle—or, perhaps it will be safer to say, the late abundance, for our visitors from Birmingham and elsewhere seem determined to tear all the periwinkle up by the roots, and so compel us to find for the lane yet another name.

Again, in a deed of Henry IV. (1408), which I read at an early stage of my investigations (for it was a work of time to get these deeds in order of date),[1] I found mention made of "a messuage called Stikemones place, with a croft called Stikemones feld," and was inclined to imagine some murder to account for a name so evil-sounding; but it was rather a dis-appointment to discover that it was only a family name, as shown by the attestations of William Stike-mon and others to deeds. Perhaps many a grim legend that attaches to, and is tenderly cherished in connection with country pits and fields and lanes would be disposed of as unromantically if the neces-sary bits of parchment would turn up. But here again the remarkable thing is that, nearly five hundred years after the last of the Stikemons passed away, we still have " Stickman's Meadow " and " Stickman's Close" amongst our recorded field-names.

The Feisants, one of whom is a witness to our first deed, seem to have been a Packwood family, settled there from Richard I.'s time to at least 1349, when we get our last entry of them. There is enough resemblance in the name, spelt as it sometimes is " Feysaunt," and bearing in mind that *y* was already in use for *th*, to prompt the inquiry whether they might possibly have been the forebears of the Fether-stons of Packwood,[2] who were certainly settled there about a century later.

. It is, however, more probable that the immediate predecessors of the Fetherstons at Packwood House were the Prats, already mentioned in connection with the same deed. Their ownership of " Prat's Pit " on

---

[1] " Land of William Stykemon " is referred to in a deed of 1337 which has a quaint seal showing the busts of two men with hands crossed, illustrated on p. 10.

[2] "1468. Joh'es Fedurston et Emotta uxor ejus de Pakwood." (Register of the Knowle Guild.)

the Fetherstons' (late Arton's) estate, points in that direction, and one of the members of the family of whom we have mention (in Henry III.'s reign) is called "Sýmone Prat de Pacwode." They owned land in Lapworth, Packwood, Kingswood and Nuthurst.

Many of the names that occur at this period are Norman, and can be found in the Roll of Battle Abbey. Their owners were probably the immediate descendants of some of the "twenty thousand thieves," as a distinguished writer has called them, who came over with William the Conqueror, and among whom he divided the lands of England.

Such were the Marshalls and the Trussells already mentioned. Such were the Sorels, who, though not appearing in our deeds later than the time of Henry III., would seem to have been connected with the parish much longer, as a Chancery suit of the time of Elizabeth relates to " Sorell's fields."

We had Roger Franceis as a witness to our first deed. In later ones the name occurs as "le franceis," and speaks for itself. "Ankertill le fraunceys" would be to his Saxon neighbours simply "Ankertill the Frenchman." The family continued here from Richard I. to the latter part of the reign of Edward III.; about two centuries. Towards the end of that time they appear to have dropped the "le" altogether.

Scut or Scot, as it was variously written (appearing first in John's reign), has a more native sound to us. The Scuts were here just about the same period as the last named, the latest trace of them being in 1370, but lands which had been theirs were called " Scutteslond " in the parish for centuries later.

The name of "le Oiselur," mentioned in connection with the field called "Vlelega" (*circa* 1190), was
perhaps found awkward in English mouths, and therefore abandoned in favour of an English equivalent.
There seems to be little doubt that one "Robertus
dictus ffaukener de Henleẏ," whom we meet with
in the reign of Edward I. (*c.* 1290), is of the same
family (he used a seal which bears a falcon with out-
spread wings), and as little doubt that Thomas le
fouler, of about the same period, and Walter le fouler,
of some fifty or sixty years later, were also of the
same family—a family which dies out with this Walter
in 1349. There is a curious confirmation of this, which
might otherwise seem only a fanciful surmise, in the
apparent identity of their holdings. It has been
mentioned that the land which passed to William le
Oiselur in John's reign called "Vlelega" (with other
land simply described as *in villa de Lappeworth*) was
subject to the reserved rent of 3*s.* a year, payable to
the lord at three terms, together with a further obligation of "four woodcocks to be paid between Michaelmas and Christmas." The deed of "Robert, called
the Faukener," has relation to land close to "Vlelega":
whilst the last mention we have of Walter le Fouler is
in a deed of one John le Weyn, or le Sweyn, of Eder-
ston (now Edstone), who seems to have been one of
his heirs (1349), and speaks of "all that moiety of the
land and tenements in the town and fields of Lapworthe which was Walter le fouler's of the same, and
which fell to me by heredity," and in disposing of it
he declares it to be subject to an annual rent to the
lord of 1*s.* 6*d.*, payable at three terms, and two wood-

cocks to be delivered (*equis porcionibus dividendis,* *i.e.* one at a time) between Michaelmas and Christmas. Here, therefore, we have one-half the land charged with one-half the rent and one-half the woodcocks, payable in exactly the same way as double these charges were payable in regard to the entire holding some 160 years earlier. We know how these rents payable to the lord passed unaltered from father to son for long periods of time, and I think this goes far to make it probable, if not certain, that the Walter le Fouler of Edward III. was of the family of William le Oiselur of the time of John.

Walter passed his land, as mentioned above, to "le Sweyn," and "le Sweyn" to one John Hardyng; and in 1374 we find John Jory, Chaplain of Lapworth, who had been enfeoffed by this John Hardyng, dealing with part of it under the name of "le foulers," which name continues to be used in documents for at least two centuries later, and in our Tithe Map we still have "Fowler's close" and "Fowler's meadow."

Names originally derived from employments or occupations continued almost invariably to be so marked in those days. We meet with no instance in which they are without the "le." Thus we have Johannes le Archer (1346) and Thomas l'archer (1363) witnessing deeds dated at Nuthurst. These were Archers of Umberslade, ancestors of Sir Simon Archer (the antiquary and friend of Dugdale) and of the family which was raised to a barony by George II. under the title of "Lord Archer of Umberslade." In Dugdale and in Hannett's *Forest of Arden* a full account of them is given. They appear to have been closely connected with Lapworth for a long period.

We have John le Harpur (1343) and John le Shepeherd (1360). We have Cooks in great variety of spelling, thus—

Walt' le Kooc de L. . . .	1320
Joh' Coci de Henleye . . .	1330
Radulphus le Cok de L. . . .	1341
Caleb le Cooke . . .	1343
Ric' Coccus de Henley . . .	1361
Thomā Koce . . .	1361

It is not unlikely that our Lapworth Cooks, the first of whom is a Walter, may have been connected with the Walter Cook, canon of Lincoln, who founded the Guild of Knowle at the close of the fourteenth century.

Of the great family of Smith, which has since over-run the world, our record is—

Ricardus filius fabri . .	(*temp.* John)
Walter faber	1337
Thomas le Smȳth de Thoneworth .	1341
Richard le Smȳth	1343
Will' le Smȳth de Pacwode . .	·1361

The name is always written with the dotted ẏ.

The greater part of the prefixes of our surnames are, however, derived from places of residence or origin, and very few names are without a prefix of some kind.

A family calling themselves indifferently " de la Coppe " or " atte Coppe " were prominent landowners here 1323–61. They have left their name to our

Cop Green, on the Bushwood side of the parish—
which before their day is called "Pratte's Green,"
from the still older family of Prat already mentioned.

Robert de Wenhal, who witnesses a deed of 1341,
and who is called at a later date "de Oowenhale,"
probably preserves for us something like the pronunciation of Ullenhall at that day, as he seems to have
been lord of the manor of that place.

The name of Attwell, as it has ultimately become,
appears first with us in the time of Edward I. (c. 1280).
We have as witnesses—

Roger' ad Fontem	. . .	(c. 1280)
Will' ad Fontem	. . .	,,
Will' de Fonte	. . .	1322
Roger' de Fonte	. . .	,,

These two forms were no doubt used indifferently by
the same men. By 1342 the name has begun to be
written "atte Welle," and later also sometimes "atte
Wẏle," and so continues to Edward IV. (1462), when
we have the last of them in "John atte Welle Gen.
de Lappeworthe": the last, that is, in this series;
but they continued here, and are seen in connection
with parish trusts, etc., up to Elizabeth's day. They
would seem, therefore, to have been of local importance for about three centuries. They do not, however,
appear in the Parish Register. This family furnishes
almost the latest instance we have of the Latinisation
of surnames. The practice does not appear to have
prevailed after the time of Edward II.

The "de fulwode" family seem to have been
in great demand with us as witnesses, the deeds

which bear their names being usually dated at Nuthurst. They lived at Clay Hall, near there, and were principal people of Tanworth, some of their tombs in Tanworth Church being figured by Dugdale. The first we have is Richard de F., *temp.* Edward I. They are always styled "de Fulwode" (with unimportant variations of spelling) up to 1388. When we next meet with them in 1435 they have dropped the " de," our last entry previous to that year being Richard Fulwode de Toneworthe, *armiger.*

In 1320 we have Margery ate Bache, daughter of Robert ate B. de Thoneworth. There are Beaches at Tanworth still as landowners; but how far their connection with the village dates back I do not know.

John ate Lee de Thoneworth also appears with us 1320–46, but in these deeds not later. Three hundred years after, the name of Lea (variously written also as Lee, le, and Leigh) begins to be of frequent occurrence in our Parish Register, and from 1620 to 1850 there are only two decades in which it does not appear. The family is frequently distinguished as " of Tanworth." There would seem to have been two or more families of the name, settled respectively there and at Lapworth; both of them burying, baptising, etc., at Lapworth, and perhaps descended from this John ate Lee of Edward II. The window at the west end of our north aisle was given to the church some twenty years ago by the Misses Lea of Tanworth.

The Aylesburys appear first with us in Philip de Aylesbury, 1361–70; but the name occurs no more till nearly a century later, 1455–80, and then as John Aylesbury, *tout court.* Their name survives in Ayles-

D

bury House, in Packwood parish, where they lived till the latter half of the eighteenth century, and their monuments are many in Packwood Church. This John now mentioned is, however, sometimes styled *de Etyngdon*, so that they would not appear at that time to have been settled at Packwood. He stands in the Register of the Knowle Guild with his name disfigured (1460) as *Johes Elysbery de Etynton et Eliz: uxor eius.*

Richard de Barre, Lyndraper, 1329–62, I mention because he has the almost unique distinction of having a trade attached to his name. His family seem to have continued here about a century. He conveys land which is described as lying between certain land called Hethcroft and the King's highway leading towards "Burmy̅nghm̅." This family, I think, has survived in field and place names, for we have "Barr's meadow," "lane," and "close"; and "The Bare House Farm" (miscalled "Bear House") probably derives from them. The family were connected also with Rowington.

We find the names of several who were chaplains here. There seems to have been always a chaplain as well as a rector. The chaplain was, of course, not like a modern curate, appointed by the rector and holding office during his pleasure, but had apparently a much more secure tenure. He would appear to have been more actively engaged with parish affairs than the rector. Secular matters were probably left chiefly in his hands, and his name is, therefore, met with frequently, while that of a rector is comparatively rare.

The first Chaplain of Lapworth mentioned in these records is Sir Walter de Brynkunhul, in a deed of 1337.

In the long reign of Edward III., which lasted fifty years, we have about fifty deeds,. and amongst them there is a very curious group. For a hundred years or more before this time there had been a family owning land in the parish whose name was written first " in Lone." The earliest was a Thomas in Lone ; then the name began to be written " in the Lone " or " in the Lane," for Lone is only the old way of spelling Lane. About the beginning of the fourteenth century the head of the family was one " John in the Lone," who dying left a son, another " John in the Lone," who, with Agnes his wife, seems to have had a large family, and amongst them yet another son John. It is almost, though not quite, certain that there were thus once three persons named John in the Lone living here at the same time. John the third, at any rate, took Holy Orders, and became Chaplain of Lapworth in the lifetime of his father, mother, and brothers, ministering in the church of the parish in which, no doubt, he was born. He has frequently, though not always, the title " Sir," usually given to the clergy in those days. He is " Sir John in the Lone, chaplain " (*Dns Johannes in the Lone, capellanus de Lappeworth*). The various forms in which the name of members of the family appears are : " in Lone," " in ȝe Lone," " in ye Lone," " atte Lone," " in le Lane," " in the Lone," " in the Lane " ; but the favourite form is " in the Lone,' which in its setting of Latin context is somewhat striking.

This John the Chaplain evidently busied himself very much in the affairs of the parish, and had the confidence and regard of the people, for in the

twenty-third year of the reign of Edward III. we
find that there are more than a dozen deeds, all dated
very near to each other, to all of which " John in the
Lone, Chaplain," is a party.   Several are executed
on the same day, and various members of two families
more especially are found to be conveying their
property to the chaplain absolutely, without any
expression that such property is to be held in trust ;
but by-and-by we find him reconveying sometimes
the whole and sometimes portions of such properties
to their widows or children, or back again to themselves.   The explanation seems to be that this year,
1349, was the year of the awful pestilence called the
" Black Death," which swept over the land, and,
indeed, over all Europe, and formed so memorable an
epoch in the history of England.   It is estimated by
historians to have carried off half the people of this
kingdom, thereby giving rise to altered conditions of
labour which went far to put an end to the absolute
serfdom which had previously existed.   It is very
probable that the people here were dying on all
hands, and that in a sort of panic those who were
not yet struck down turned to the chaplain, as to
one in whom they knew they could confide in their
extremity.

At this time John in the Lone had been Chaplain
of Lapworth about six years, namely, from 1343 ; he
probably succeeded Walter de Brynkunhul.   The
last mention we have of him as still alive is in a
power of attorney executed by him—dated on the
" Wednesday following the feast of St. Barnabas "
(June 11th) in the twenty-third year of Edward III.—

to Walter atte Welle, to put Paulinus de Brome, John le Mareschal, and two others, in possession of all the lands, tenements, and rents which he held in feoffment from Geoffrey atte Heth and Thomas Prat ; together with lands and tenements belonging to himself.

He would seem to have been putting his own affairs in order. To him might fittingly be applied the lines of Richard Baxter :—

> " I preached as never sure to preach again,
>   And as a dying man to dying men."

There is little doubt that he died immediately afterwards, for the next mention we have of him is as " late chaplain of Lapworth " (*quondam capellanus*) ; and not only so, but we learn at the same time that Paulinus de Brome and John le Mareschal had died soon after him, leaving as heirs none but young children.

The very significant deed by which we learn this bears date in September of 1350, and is executed by Sir Hugh de Brauncheston, Knight, at that time Lord of the Manor, and a grandson of the Sir Hugh mentioned previously under Edward I. By it he makes over to Thomas Scut what he describes as all the lands, rents, and tenements which had fallen to his custody by the death of Paulinus de Brome[1] and John le Mareschal, by them held *ex dono et feoffamento Joh'is in la Lane*, late Chaplain of Lapworth—which lands, etc., Thomas Scut is to hold until the full coming of age of the children of the said Paulinus and John.

[1] This Paulinus de Brome is described in a deed preserved in the Record Office as " asserens se esse fil : et heredem p'pinquiorem Rob'ti de Brome de Lappeworthe." (Inq. P.M. 19 Edw. ii.)

In that same memorable year of the Black Death, 1349, it is recorded by Dugdale that there was also a change of rector at Lapworth. It seems probable, therefore, that Ivo Pipard, who had been rector here from 1322, fell a victim to the great plague, as did the chaplain also. It is said to have been specially fatal to the clergy because they were compelled to come so much in contact with the people.[1]

The seal of John in the Lone,[2] more or less approaching completeness, remains on two or three of the charters, and putting these portions together we are able to make out that it bore the device of an ass under a tree. Some such device was used in those days to typify the "Good Samaritan." And these old deeds of ours seem to suggest, if we expand the little hints they give us, that our John in the Lone of so many centuries ago not only used this emblem for his seal, but made the Good Samaritan the exemplar of his own life and practice, setting him forth *non loquendo tantum sed vivendo.*

His chaplaincy evidently extended from 1343, or perhaps a little earlier, up to June, 1349. His father and mother were living here, at any rate at the beginning of it. He had also three brothers, Robert, William, and Richard, all of whom appear from time to time as witnesses of deeds. None of them, however, appear after that fatal year of 1349, nor is there

---

[1] Geoffrey le Baker, a clerk of the abbey of Osney, near Oxford, whose *Chronicle* gives a vivid contemporaneous account of the ravages of the Black Death, says : "Of this disease, few of the first rank died, but of the common people an incalculable number, and of the clergy and cleric class a multitude known to God only."

[2] See illustration, p. 42.

anything to show that one single member of this old
family of "in the Lone" survived the visitation of the
Black Death.

In looking over this group of deeds with which
John in the Lone is so closely connected, and seeing
the quaint old English name stand out so curiously
amid the crabbed Latin shorthand, one cannot help
wondering who wrote them. They are for the most
part beautifully written, and apparently by the same
hand, upon parchment of a uniform consistency, in size
generally about nine inches by three inches, or sometimes a little larger. Did the people in their hour of
need have to send away in haste to fetch a lawyer
from elsewhere? Hardly, I think. Then who was the
village scrivener? The most probable supposition is
that we have here the handiwork of John in the Lone
himself. At any rate, there is a distinct change of
handwriting in our deeds immediately after his death,
with new methods of abbreviation, punctuation, etc.

It is sufficiently proved, I think, by what has been
already said that some of what is now land of the
Parish Charity estates can be identified as having
become so, with other land no longer identifiable, at
the time of, and probably by reason of the panic
caused by, the Black Death.

How much reason there was for such a panic, and
how much our parish suffered from the awful pestilence, is indicated not unimpressively by these old
deeds. We have already seen that rector and chaplain both died, and that Paulinus de Brome and John
le Mareschal, whom the chaplain had enfeoffed immediately before his death, died immediately after

him, and that the three brothers of John in the Lone disappear at the same time; but, beyond this, careful observation soon shows that 1349[1] has become for us a distinct line of demarcation between old and new; families that had been in the parish for long periods are seen no more after that year; surnames of other families appear with new Christian names, showing the father to have been succeeded by the son or other kinsman; and lands with whose ownership we have become acquainted have passed into other hands. Here are examples of such changes :—

John le Archer, our neighbour: died, according to Dugdale, 1349.

Richard Aleyn, first appears 1329: last seen in 1349.

John de Barton, appears very frequently between 1319 and 1349: not afterwards.

Margery de Brokchawe, the last of her family, conveys lands to the church in 1349: not mentioned later.

Agnes de Corveser, appears 1343–8: conveys her lands in the latter year.

Simon Dene, owned land in Lapworth 1337–48; was living in the latter year; in 1349 deeds witnessed by Roger, probably his son. Neither of them appears afterwards.

ffeÿsond, family settled at Packwood from 1190 to 1349: no trace left after the latter year.

[1] The Black Death may be said to have extended over three seasons in the British Isles—a partial season in the south of England in 1348, a great season all over England, in Ireland and in the south of Scotland in 1349, and a late extension to Scotland generally in 1350. . . . The great mortality came to an end everywhere in England by Michaelmas, 1349. (Creighton's *History of Epidemics in Britain.*)

Geoffrey atte Heth and Agnes his wife : appear in several deeds in 1349, but not after.[1]

Walter de Notehurst, a frequent witness from 1300 to 1349 : not later.

Walter le Fouler : shown to have died between May and July, 1349.

Walter Page, appears as witness 1342–9 : not later.

Pakemon, family here from 1190 : last appearance in 1349.

Thurstan, here from *temp.* Edward I. to 1349 : not mentioned later.

John Prat, conveys his land to John in the Lone, 1349 : not mentioned later.

Thomas Prat, conveys his land to John in the Lone, 1349 : shown by a deed of the next year to be dead.

John Pymmyger, witnesses many deeds 1348–9 : appears no more.

Robert Scut, witnesses deeds 1330–48 : appears no more.

William Stikeman, witnesses deeds 1338–48 : last appears October, 1348.

Robert de Toppesford, whose family were here from the time of Henry III. to 1349 : conveys land in this last-named year, and his name ceases.

William atte Well, active here 1342–9 : appears to have been succeeded by (? his son) Walter in the latter year.

Thebaldus Wilkyn and Edith his wife, appear from 1319 to 1349 : not later.

---

[1] In 1344 Geoffrey atte Heth, junior, conveys all his goods to John in the Lone by a deed which remains in excellent preservation. The seal bears the quite recognisable device of the Virgin with the infant Christ. (See illustration, p. 134.)

Non-appearance after this year is, of course, only negative evidence, but it will be admitted that the disappearance of so many names at the same period out of the limited number of the land-owning class who chance to be mentioned in our records points very strongly to death as the cause of such disappearance. If out of that limited upper-class so many were taken, what must the ravage have been amongst the labourers, their wives and children, of whom no sort of record remains? Probably they died wholesale and there was not a cottage without its dead; and what was happening here was happening in all the villages round about.

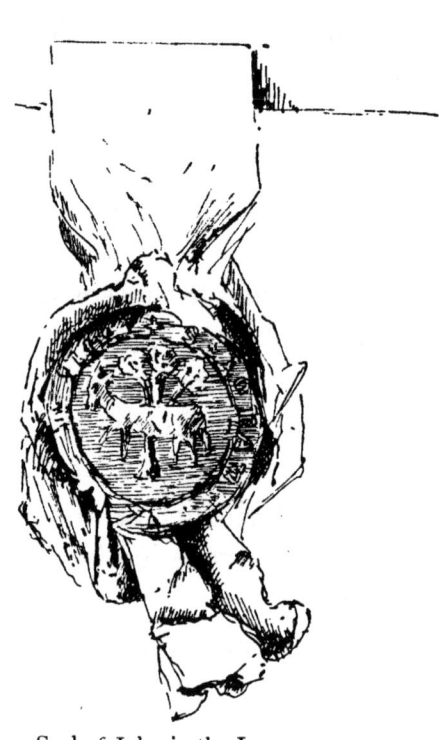

Seal of John in the Lone
Chaplain of Lapworth
1343–49

p. 38

FROM 1350 (*et circa*) TO THE END OF THE
PRE-REFORMATION DEEDS (*circa* 1502)

" . . . some smack of age in you, some relish of the saltness of
HENRY IV., Part 2

CHAPTER II

FROM 1350[1] (*et circa*) TO THE END OF THE PRE-REFORMATION DEEDS (*circa* 1502)

LEAVING John in the Lone, whose name has become so familiar to us, we find ourselves, after the ravages of the Black Death, for the most part amongst new families.

The Trussells, as we have seen, were, however, of those who came over with the Conqueror, and whose names are to be found in the Roll of Battle Abbey. They were Lords of many Manors, and amongst others of the Manor of Nuthurst. Their principal place in this neighbourhood was at Billesley, and the fine old house called Billesley Hall probably goes back at least to their later days. The first we have of them is that Edmund " Truscel" already mentioned under Edward I. They continued at Nuthurst, appearing in our Lapworth deeds and registers for about three centuries and a half, and lived in a house which stood where Nuthurst House now stands. In 1349 Sir William " Trussel" executes a deed relating to land which still belongs to the Charity. He was a very notable man and a very truculent ruffian in

---

[1] Some of the families to be mentioned originate with us, as will be seen, *earlier* than 1350.

his day.   He took an active part in the wars between
Edward II. and his wife and son, and when the
unfortunate King fell into the hands of his wife's
army, and was shut up a prisoner in Kenilworth
Castle, it was this Trussel who went as spokesman
at the head of a deputation of nobles, and addressed
the monarch in brutal and violent language, re-
nouncing on their part and his own their allegiance,
and announcing to the King his deposition.   Most
of the old chroniclers dwell on this scene, and record
Trussel's speech :—

"I, William Trussel, in name of all men of the land of
England, of all the Parliament procurator, resign to thee,
Edward, the homage that was made to thee sometime, and
from this time forward now following, I defy thee and prive
thee of all royal power, and I shall never be tendant to thee
as for King after this time"—which being done, Sir Thomas
Blunt, Knight, Steward of the Household, by breaking his
staff resigned his office.   (*Speed.*)

Soon after this the fallen King was taken off to
Berkeley Castle, and there murdered.   This Sir
William Trussel, who doubtless often trod our lanes,
seems to link Lapworth in a small way with the
broad stream of English history.

The next we have of the name is more than a
century later, when John Trussell, of Nuttehurst
(*nuper de Billysseley, arm.*), under date of 19 Edward
IV., 1480, makes an exchange with "Nicholas Slye,
of Lapworthe, yomon, and Thomas Underwood of
the same, Churchwardens" (*gardiani ecclesiæ
p'ochial'*), by which he receives "two parcels of
land called Cordemore, with one parcel of meadow

land annexed thereto, lying within the demesne of Nuttehurste," and the churchwardens receive "a meadow called 'ffurdon,' lying at Issundeforde brugge between a lane there called 'le ffurde lane' and a rivulet there called 'Issundeforde brok' in width, and extending in length from land of St. Mary the Virgin of Lapworthe called 'le ffurden' up to another road leading from Henley towards Burmyngeham."

"Furden" would seem to have been a general name given to land lying alongside the brook, as we have in this deed two pieces in Lapworth bearing that name, while a third, also so called, is separated from them only by the highway, which at that time was the boundary at this point between the parishes of Lapworth and Nuthurst. The last named (in Nuthurst) still bears its old name of "Forden," all three being bounded by the Lapworth Brook, here called by the curious lost name of "Issundeforde brok"; while also "Issundeforde Brugge," which bounded the field on the west, tells us that our brook, where it crossed the Birmingham road, had already been bridged in 1480. In Sir Edmund Truscel's deed of Edward I., before noticed, mention is made of certain land as lying "at Es'eneford within the town and territory of Notehurst." This also doubtless was land lying by the same brook, and the names are connected.

The field given to the churchwardens by this exchange is readily identifiable, its boundaries being still as described, except that it no longer extends westward to the Birmingham road, because in 1794 that road was diverted at this point to some little distance westward, and what was the old road now lies between the present road and the field. The field also no longer belongs either to the charity or to the church ; neither is there anything to show how · it was lost.

The Trussells continued at Nuthurst until about the middle of the seventeenth century. After the Parish Register was begun in 1561, they soon became contributors to it and furnished many entries, Lapworth being the burial-place for Nuthurst. The last of such entries is in 1621. They are always entered with some mark of distinction, and remained, no doubt, the principal family of Nuthurst to the end.

The Bromes, or "de Bromes," as they for a long time called themselves, were in their day (which was a long day) a family of much importance in Lapworth, and, indeed, outside it. Their name still survives in the interesting old house called Brome Hall, where they resided. We trace them from the time of Edward I. for at least two centuries and a half, witnessing, buying, and selling. There seem to have been three John Bromes here in succession, the first appearing frequently in our deeds between 1361 and 1408, about which latter date he became, according to Dugdale, the first member of Parliament for the borough of Warwick; his son, John the second, acquired the ownership of Baddesley Clinton and went to live there ; while *his* son, the third John, was killed in London in 1468, in the porch of Whitefriars Church, being stabbed by a steward of the Earl of Warwick in a quarrel about a lawsuit. His death was avenged by his son Nicholas, who, after many years, slew, at Longbridge, this steward, Harthill, who had killed his father. Nicholas was then living at Baddesley Clinton. Manslaughter seems to have come easy to him, as he is further accused of causing the death of his chaplain at Baddesley, whom he "found chucking his wife under the chin." (This also is Dugdale's story.) By way of penance for his crimes he was (not hanged, as he would have been in our day, but) enjoined by the Pope to rebuild the steeple of Packwood Church, as also that of Baddesley Clinton, on which latter his name still remains, recording that he did build it in the reign of Henry VII.

The family appears to have ceased about that time to have much connection with Lapworth, for in the reign of Henry VIII. we find Brome Hall was the residence of the Slyes. In 1578 we have, however, Jhone Brome as witness to a deed poll of Edmund Catesbie. There are no Bromes in our Parish Register.

The "le Persones" first appear in one Thomas le Persones de L. in 1330, and the name occurs very frequently, the "le" being dropped occasionally, from that time to the latter half of the fifteenth century (1461). They are shown to have continued in the parish after we lose sight of them in these deeds, for ,when the Parish Register is established they appear early, and continue, with one or two long breaks in the seventeenth century, almost up to the present day. Probably they were continuous in descent from the old family of the time of Edward III. Towards the end of the fifteenth century, some of them begin to be described as of Tanworth. Possibly the last of the

E

old stock here was a Parsons, who in a drunken fray shot his uncle, a Hildick, some thirty years ago, and immediately afterwards shot himself and fell dead in the road before this uncle's cottage door. This Parsons (who was buried at night in our churchyard without any funeral rites) was said to be of an old local land-owning family.

Le Corveser (= the Shoemaker), a French name, which was adopted into old English and was for some centuries the usual designation of a "shoemaker," appears with us in 1343. "Agnes, the widow of John le Corveser, of Henleye," appoints her beloved in Christ Walter de Hereford her attorney for giving to her son Richard full and peaceful seisin in all her lands, tenements, etc., in the towns and in the fields of Lapworth, Kingswood, and Packwood. From this description of her property as lying in these three places we infer that her husband had not really been in the shoemaking business personally, but that she was a widow of substance. There is a seal attached with the motto " I' espere," the device being a very neatly designed anchor. (See illustration, p. 72.)

Her deeds, in all probability, came into our chest as evidence of title of *Richard dictus le Corveser*, her son, who by deed of 1361 left lands in trust to the parish. In another deed (1363) he is further described as *clericus, de Henleye*. He, therefore, seems to have been a man of considerable wealth, owning lands "in the common fields" of many parishes round about Henley.

The land which he gave to the parish seems to have been in quantity about seven acres, though no longer identifiable. Subsequent dealings with it show how unalterable a rent became when once fixed in those days, and throw a little light on customs then prevailing. In 1425 a lease of it is granted to George Assheby for three lives, a blank being left in the lease with permission to him to fill in, after his own name, at such time as he likes (whensoever and whomsoever) the names of two other persons, the lease expiring only on the death of the longer liver of these two. This granting of a lease in blank was, of course, calculated to prolong its duration greatly, as the holder would defer inserting the next name as long as he could. The rent was 3*s.* 6*d.* a year, about 6*d.* an acre. The lease thus created seems, however, to have run out in 1462, so that the lives had proved to be but short. Then a fresh lease is granted to Thomas, the son of Richard Assheby, for his life at the old rent of 3*s.* 6*d.* Probably the same rent had existed from the time of the bequest in 1361. The grantors this time describe themselves as "Richard Browne and Thomas Slye of Lapworthe, collectors this year of the rents of all the lands and tenements belonging to the Church of the Blessed Mary of Lapworthe, with the assent and consent of all the parishioners of the said town." The land is described further as "two crofts called Corveser's crofts belonging to the said church." It was not land applicable to other than church uses, though apparently all the church lands were dealt with by something like a parish meeting, and 6*d.* an acre seems to have been the rent with which the parish was satisfied for several generations.

The family of "de Toppesford" were here as landowners about one hundred years.[1] The "de" having been dropped, the old name became Topesforde, Top- forde, and then Tapford. And what we now call Tapster Lane, running down from the church towards Cop Green, is written in the Overseers' books as Tapsford Lane and Tapford Lane as late as the beginning of the nineteenth century.

That branch of the great family of de Montfort which had its castle on the hill at Beaudesert sent us some of its offshoots. Richard de Montfort, who was an illegitimate son of Peter de Montfort of Beaudesert, by one Laura de Ulnehale (who died a nun at Pinley Abbey), describes himself as "Lord of a moiety of the Manor and town of Lapworth." He also owned land in Nuthurst.

One of the witnesses in 1364 of a deed of this Richard is Roger atte grene, who was one of the co- founders, some ten years later, with him and others, of our curious and interesting west chantry,[2] which is supposed to have been used also as a relic chamber. We have nothing amongst our parish papers bearing on the building or endowment of the chantry in ques- tion, nor, indeed, is there anything bearing on ancient structural dealings with any portion of the church.

Rose, wife of Richard de Montfort, was a daughter of Sir Hugh de Brandestone, on whose death the lordship of the Lapworth Manor had been divided between her and a sister who married Philip de Ayles-

---

[1] The last appearance of the de Toppesford family, associated so directly with life in Lapworth to-day, since one of our lanes perpetuates their name with only a reasonable measure of corruption, was in a deed of 44 Edw. III. This deed has a seal with the very clear impression of two birds, shown on p. 200.

[2] See further on p. 248, and illustration at same page.

bury, already mentioned. It was through her that Richard de Montfort became Lord of half the Manor. Her first husband was Nicholas Dyrvassel (himself a witness here in 1361), whose soul is one of those that were stipulated to be prayed for when her second husband settled lands upon the chantry. She herself survived in second widowhood many years, and in 1399 (22 Richard II.) we have an indenture of hers (dated at Notehurst on the Sunday next after the feast of St. John *ante portam Latinam*), in which she styles herself "Lady of Codbarewe," and grants to John Prat of Notehurst and Alice his wife three fields called Longefeld, Pylorislond, and Nothershethpece, for the term of their joint lives, at a rent of 5*s*. 4*d*. She is even shown to have been living as late as 6 Henry V. (1419), in which year she executes a deed conveying the Manor of Lapworth to John Catesby of Ashby Leger, in whose family it remained till Elizabeth's day (Dugdale). This, however, is not one of our deeds.

Nothing now remains of Codbarrow save the moat near the east entrance to Umberslade Park, but it indicates for us where stood, no doubt, at that time a fairly large house, in which the Lady of Codbarrow affixed her seal in red wax to this bit of parchment, still very distinct and legible after some fifteen generations have passed away. The names and arms of this Richard and Rose still remain in the west window of the nave of our church, above the chantry which they founded—probably the oldest piece of glass left in the church. In Dugdale's day it was in the west window of the south aisle. The case-

ment in which the shield was fixed was blown out in
1891 in a high gale of wind, and fell to the ground.
Fortunately it was but little injured, and, after being
well repaired, it was put back, and may last now as
long again as it has lasted already, if only it escape
the hands of the restorer.

We have no Montforts in this series of our old
deeds after Richard and his wife, but on the introduction of the Parish Register we find the name one
of the commonest. None of them, however, are
mentioned with any special mark of distinction. They
seem to have belonged to the yeoman class, frequently
filling the usual parish offices and feoffeeships. There
are only one or two decades in which the name does
not appear up to the end of the seventeenth century,
when it entirely dies out. The farm called Mountford
Farm derives its name from this old family.

In 1361 we find the Chaplain of Lapworth was one
John Jory, who before coming here had been Chaplain
of Wootton. Between John in the Lone, who died in
1349, and this John Jory there was probably another
chaplain of whom we have no trace. The two Johns
must have been personal friends, because we find mention in some of the deeds of their having both been
members of the parish trusts at one and the same time.

When Richard de Montfort and his co-founders
built and endowed the chantry in 1374 they appointed
as the first chantry priest this John Jory, who had
then been chaplain here for some years. During his
chaplaincy we have evidence of his activity in secular
affairs in two deeds creating separate trusts of the
parish lands, such trusts consisting respectively of five

and nine of the principal people of the parish or neighbourhood.

The revenues of the Lapworth chantry thus created appear to have been derived from

two messuages, two carucátes of land, twelve acres of meadow, and sixteen shillings rent (all lying in Toneworth), for maintenance of a priest to sing mass there every day to the honour of the Blessed Virgin, St. Thomas the Mártyr, and all saints ;

and Dugdale gives a further account of the settling of these on John Jory, and a list of all those for whose souls or good estate prayers were to be made. He adds that the yearly value of these lands in 37 Henry VIII. was £5 3s. 9d. We have no such lands now, so doubtless they were confiscated under Henry VIII. as being devoted to superstitious uses. They must have been of considerable extent, probably not less than two hundred acres. We cannot tell what quantity the carucate represented. It was, says Seebohm,

the land cultivated by a plough team, varying in acreage according to the lightness or heaviness of the soil, and according to the strength of the team. In some cases the carucate seems to be identical with the normal hide of 120 acres, but other instances show that it varied in area.

The value of the Lapworth living (apart from the chantry) was given in 26 Henry VIII. as only £9 9s. 7d., so that the chantry priest must have been in importance a formidable rival of the rector. He had also, we may suppose, in addition to his income as chantry priest, a separate income as chaplain, though from what sources a chaplain was paid we have no knowledge. The chantry had always its own patrons, and was never in the gift of Merton College, as was the living of Lapworth. From the de Montfort family it seems to have passed into the gift of the Earls of Warwick, and thus we get in the list of its patrons (given in Thomas's *Dugdale*) two names famous in history :—

1450.   Richard Nevill, Earl of Warwick (known as " the King-maker ").

1473.   George, Duke of Clarence, brother of King Richard III. (Shakespeare's " false, fleeting, perjured Clarence "—tradition's hapless victim of the malmsey butt).

The next Chaplain of Lapworth with whom we make acquaintance is William Hȳkones. In 16 Richard II. (1393) Roger atte grene, who must then have been well stricken in years, enfeoffs him, together with John Brome and Richard Persones, in parish lands in the towns of " Lappworth, Notehurst and Henleȳe," which he had of the gift and feoffment of John in the Lone and . . . (seven others). The parish, therefore, at that time owned property in Henley which it has long since lost.

Two years later this chaplain is concerned with two others in granting a lease for three lives of certain land called " collerudynges," at the annual rent of 7s. 6d. I do not know the meaning of the name " collerudynges," unless it has reference to the land lying as it does on a slope of rising ground. The name has undergone vicissitudes since the time of Richard II. By an easily understood misreading it appears at one time as " Colerndinges." In the early part of Elizabeth's reign it has become "Cold Rudding." In a schedule of 1699 it, having been divided, stands described as "Little Cole redding" and "Great Cole redding." In the latest list of the Charity properties it is "Little Cold Ridding" and "Big Cold Ridding," and the present tenant knows the fields as Little Redding and Big Redding, the word "Cold" having dropped out—a curious instance of how old names are changed and lost. The quantity at the present day is 12 a. 0 r. 39 p., so that the rent was about 7½*d.* per acre, and it being church land the further services to the Lord of the Manor were probably very inconsiderable.

The only other Chaplain of Lapworth whose name occurs in this series of deeds is John of Aston, who in 1408 is enfeoffed by Sir Robert Horton (parson of the Church of Lapworth, acting as attorney for John de Brome), and put at the head of a new trust, just as we have seen the three preceding chaplains, John in the Lone, John Jory, and William Hỳkones, were at the head of trusts in their times. This confirms the opinion previously expressed that the chaplains took more especial charge of the secular affairs of their parishes. It is rarely that the rector appears in any of these transactions.

With the Greens, or "atte Grenes," we first made acquaintance in Roger, co-founder of our chantry under Edward III. The family appear to have taken firm root here. Through the sixteenth century we find them, after this series of our old deeds comes to an end, filling parish offices, feoffeeships, etc. After the institution of the Parish Register (1561), with the exception of a rather long break from 1570 to 1610, they are steady contributors thereto, without omission of a single decade, up to 1850–60. The name is, of course, so far a common one that we could not draw any positive conclusions from the surname alone. But the constant recurrence of the same Christian name points to heredity. Their continued holding, also, of parish offices and trusts shows them to have been principal parishioners and landowners. When the Stratford-on-Avon Canal was constructed through the parish a hundred years ago, Isaac Green was one of those from whom land had to be acquired both here and in the parish of Tanworth. He was the last of many of the same Christian name, and his iron-railed tomb stands by our south porch, recording that he died in 1805 at the age of ninety-four. There is in the Register also the entry—

1712. Isaac ye son of Isaac and Mary Green.
       Bapt. Sep. 9th.

Probably he lived in our village during the whole of the interval between those two dates, and it does not seem unreasonable to suppose that he may have come in direct descent from old Roger atte Grene. Five centuries is a good record, but the stock seems now to be worn out.

The parish "table of bequests," under date 1454, records that—

Elenor Ford, widow, gave two closes and a meadow (called the Ford Fields) to this church.

Her family first appear here in the time of Edward III., 1360. Deeds of that date seem to have been lodged in support of her title ; and her grants of 1454 still remain in good preservation. They show also that her name was not Elenor, but Ellen—in Latin Elena.

Incidentally these evidences of the widow Ford's title throw some curious light on the simple ways of the time. There are three deeds bearing date 1360 (evidently there should be four), and from them we learn that at that date one Theobold atteford was a widower at Nuthurst ; his son, Thomas, being at the same time settled at Lapworth. At the same time was living at Lapworth one Isabella, the widow of Thomas le Ro. By mid-July, 1360, the widow had, it appears, found herself ready to marry again, and Theobold of Nuthurst being also willing, they agreed together. But with a prudent desire that each one should keep control of his or her own property—for they both owned land in Nuthurst—their first step was to take measures to that end. And the way they set about it was for each of them to execute a deed of feoffment to Thomas le Persones and Walter atte Welle, feoffees of parish trusts in Lapworth.

Accordingly by this deed (dated at Nuthurst on the Monday within the feast of St. Margaret the Virgin —July 20th) Theobold grants and concedes to the before-mentioned Thomas and Walter "all his lands and tenements in Notehurst which fell to him by heredity," and which are fully described ; to which grant five of his principal land-owning neighbours bear witness.

At the same time (though the deed does not survive) Isabella conveys to the same Thomas and Walter "all her lands in the town of Notehurst."

Whereupon we may assume the marriage took place without further delay, inasmuch as we find about three weeks later two deeds bearing the same date (namely, at Notehurst on the Sunday next after the feast of the Assumption of the B.V.M.—August 15th) from the above-named feoffees to Theobold atte ford of N. and Isabella his wife. In the one they grant to the newly wedded pair all the lands of which they had been enfeoffed by Theobold, and in the other all those of which they had been enfeoffed by Isabella, inserting in each deed respectively a provision that if it should happen to them, the said Theobold and Isabella, to depart this life (*discidere in ¹fata*) without heirs of their bodies lawfully begotten, then in the one deed what had been Theobald's property should pass to his heirs, and in the other what had been Isabella's should pass to her heirs. It was a friendly arrangement to keep the respective properties in their own families. The oddity of it is that it should be effected in this simple way through the medium of their neighbours. If the latter, as I am inclined to believe from other deeds, were also churchwardens, then though they did not do this in their official capacities, they would seem to have been regarded as general utility men, and employed in a much greater variety of business in the parish in those days than churchwardens are to-day. These bits of parchment, about nine inches by four inches, covered each with some six or seven lines of writing, were much simpler and much cheaper than marriage settlements are now, and probably were found to be quite as effectual.

The witnesses of this last pair of deeds are five of the principal local people. These five, on that Sunday morning in August, after they had heard mass in Lapworth Church (which served for Nuthurst also), we may perhaps, without any great stretch of imagination, suppose to have walked over to the house of Theobold, where the deeds were dated, and there, with Thomas le Persones and Walter atte Welle, churchwardens or not, completed the business, and joined the feast of the newly wedded pair.

Theobold's descendant, the widow " Elena atte fford," in 1454, really left two separate bequests to the parish, which, through similarity of names, became by lapse of time confused. " Le ffordefeldes," the name of which did not long adhere to the land, were left absolutely to the church (*ad opus ecclīe p'ochial' beate Marie virginis de Lappeworth*). " Le ffordes," which still bear the name of " Forden," were not so left, but the churchwardens were to pay thereout "yearly to God and the Church of the B.V.M. of Lapworth eight shillings sterling." The quantity of " le ffordes " out of which this rent was to be paid was then probably from 15 to 16 acres, so that we arrive again at 6*d.* an acre as about the average rent of those days. The rent reserved to the church was thus about its full value; but the parish might thereafter, it would seem, apply increased rental to other charitable uses. The quantity of this land now is 14 a. 3 r. 4 p. (there having been about an acre taken from it by deviation of the Birmingham road before mentioned towards the end of the eighteenth century), and instead of 8s. it brings in £17. The road passed then to the east of the small farmhouse called the Brook House, at the corner of the road leading to Lapworth Church, instead of, as now, to the west.

The Ford bequests altogether were about 28 acres. The description in our table of bequests is incorrect; instead of two closes and a meadow, Elena Ford gave in all four fields and two meadows, all of which still belong to us.

The lane which runs from the Birmingham road to Lapworth Church used to be called Ford Lane, perhaps from this family,[1] perhaps from its being entered by a ford across the brook before a bridge existed, or perhaps we may need to go back further still, seeking the origin of the name in the fact that our village itself was Lapford before it was Lapworth, and is so written in *Domesday Book*. Ford Hall, in Tanworth parish, and not far from Nuthurst, may not improbably have been called from this old family. Whether " Forden," as the name of the fields beside the brook, preserves the name of the parish benefactor, or is due to the fields being bounded by the brook, we cannot say. Perhaps both influences have worked.

One John Barnturst, whom the widow Ford made her attorney for executing her bequests, was more properly Barnethurst. The name was subjected to numerous vagaries of spelling, as Barneshurst, Banhurst, etc. This John was a very important

---

[1] The seal is given on p. 227 of a deed of 1435 whereby " William vorde " makes over certain lands (which he had of the gift of his father) to his mother, " Ellen at yᵉ vorde." " Vorde " probably preserves for us the then pronunciation of " Ford."

person in the parish in those days, and has *parcarius de Lappeworthe* appended to his name when it occurs as witness, being Henry VI.'s keeper of the Royal Park here, still held in remembrance by the farm called "Lapworth Park." That farm, and the adjoining land to the extent altogether of 452 acres, is tithe free at the present day, the exemption arising, doubtless, from its having been Crown land, and the Crown not paying tithe. The area thus exempt probably indicates the extent of the former park.

John Barnethurst's seal bears the letter ḅ with a crown over it. (See illustration, p. 250.) He seems to have founded a family that was here about a century and a half, the name being of frequent occurrence in the Register up to about 1590, but not appearing later.

Of the Slyes we get the first entry in 1388. They were a family destined to very long continuance and importance in the parish, lasting, indeed, to almost our own day. A Nicholas Slye, as mentioned before, was churchwarden in 1480, and the chalice still used in Lapworth Church bears the inscription (without date) *ex dono Nicholas Slye.* It was, however, as shown by the hall-mark, the gift of a later Nicholas of the Commonwealth period. Of Roger Slye, who left lands to the parish in 1527, and whose will of that date survives, we shall have more to say later.

William Kettill, who seems to have been joined in trusts here, 1408–32, is called "of Snetfield" (Snitterfield), to which place he had removed from Lapworth, but is only noticeable, perhaps, because his seal appears to have been a kettle. (See illustration, p. 222.)

The table of bequests says that "George Ashby,

senr., gave lands for the maintenance of this church in 1440." The first mention we get of the family is of Thomas, the father of this George, in 1425; and of the latter we have many indications, in feoffeeships and as witness, from that date to 1469. But the deeds by which his gift to the parish was made have not survived, nor have we anything which indicates for us the extent or position of the lands. Dugdale describes them as having been of no less extent than 106 acres, in Lapworth and Nuthurst, left to the then rector, Ralph Perot, and his successors, to provide a lamp to burn in the church and for other charitable uses. They would appear to have been confiscated to the Crown as being devoted to superstitious uses, and ought not to stand in our table of bequests, which is supposed to record only what we still possess. It seems, indeed, to err in both directions, omitting what we do possess as well as recording what we have lost.

The Asshebys appear to have been numerous here to the end of the fifteenth century, the name also contributing many entries to the Register from its commencement in 1561 until about 1660. Their record in Lapworth, therefore, was about two centuries and a quarter.

Sir John Hill (*D'ns Johannes Hylle*) was rector here from 1456 to 1488—thirty-two years. Our table of bequests says :—

1479. John Hill, Rector of this parish, purchased of Thomas Pratt lands and tenements, lying and being in Lapworth, Nuthurst and Beaudesert, for the maintenance of this church.

The deeds, five in number, which still survive show unmistakably that this statement is incorrect. Rector Hill did not purchase the lands. The parish benefactor was Thomas Pratt himself, of the old family that we know to have been here at the close of the twelfth century. Moreover, the lands in question were, along with others, the subject of a parish suit, just about a hundred years later (of which more hereafter), in which suit they are properly described as lands "of which Thomas Prat, deceased, did in the law of charitable devotion enfeoff one John Hill, John Aylesbury and others for the maintenance, sustentation and reparation of the parish church of Lapworth for ever." Parish documents of still later date also speak of this as "Prat's bequest," and it is difficult to understand how the truth could have been so entirely lost as to lead to the gift being ascribed to Rector Hill.

The lands thus bequeathed by Thomas Prat escaped confiscation after the Reformation, and are still part of the Charity Estates, about 20 acres in all. One of them is the "croft or coppice called Ulley," of which, under the name of Vlelega, we heard three hundred years earlier. Another portion comprised "eighteen selions lying dispersed in Cleycrofte, with the parcels or doles of meadow land thereto belonging, as per marks and boundaries there placed."

This Cleycrofte, which still retains its name, is interesting as the sole visible survival in the parish of the old system of dividing the open field into strips, which were owned alternately and cultivated by the jointly contributed labour of the village community. The plan of it[1] shows how it is divided into two parts

F   [1] See plan at p. 312.

(separated now by a hedgerow), representing respectively the old arable, cut up into selions or ridges (the "lands" with which we are everywhere familiar), and the meadow "thereto belonging." It will be seen that we have four strips traversing what are now the two fields, the intervening strips belonging to a private owner, and with no defined boundaries between the two properties. But in the lower field, that is, in the old meadow land, there may still be found two of the old boundary stones (*metas et bundas*), of which there must have been eight at first. They project a foot or more above the ground,[1] and have probably been there since the days of Thomas Prat and Rector Hill. In the arable portion such boundary marks were unnecessary, as the variously owned strips were divided from each other by unploughed balks. The headland which gave common access to the strips and "doles of meadowing" is still well defined. We cannot, however, count up in "lands" anything like our eighteen selions, which must have been of irregular size. Our quantity is precisely the same now as it was in 1699, when a new survey was made of these, then called the Town-lands, the area of each strip being put down separately. The term "selions" had then apparently gone out of use, but mention is made of Big lands and Little lands, the whole said to be "lying dispersed in Cleycroft, with the meadow doles thereto adjoining," and it is put on record for the benefit of posterity (in the Parish Register) that "in 1709, John Grene divided y^e meadow in Claycroft from y^e arable by the cutting of a ditch."

[1] A photograph of one of these stones is given opposite.

BOUNDARY STONE IN MEADOW CALLED "CLEYCROFT"

MARKING DIVISION OF LAND INTO "SELIONS"

The rather striking name of Morteboys occurs as that of a witness in 1472, described as of " Pakwode." The name does not occur again in this series of our old deeds, but the family had evidently settled in our neighbourhood, perhaps remaining at Packwood for some time as their chief place. On the institution of the Register the name appears in the last decade of the sixteenth century and the first of the seventeenth, then after a little break reappears 1650–9, and continues, without intermission of a single decade, for two hundred years. It may still be read on gravestones in our churchyard. The family owned land in Nuthurst as well as here, and are often described in the Register as of that place. In 1701 Isaac Morteboyes of Nuthurst leaves 5s. a year to the poor of this parish. The last of the Morteboyes who resided here was the parish schoolmaster within the memory of some still living in the parish who were his pupils. He was not only the last of his line, but of the old order of schoolmasters, his pupils being taught, before the erection of the present school buildings, in one of the cottages which were removed from the churchyard in 1892. He (John Morteboyes) had £20 a year for teaching school, and £5 a year for keeping the books and collecting the rents of the Charity Estates. He lived in, and owned, the house near the canal bridge, the garden of which house has long been noticeable for its quaintly clipped old yew trees, of which he was very proud. In 1844 he died, at the age of eighty-three, perhaps ending a line which had continued here nearly four centuries. Further, I cannot abstain from telling how, as recently as in 1896, the then occupier of this

same house had a call made on him late at night by a
poor old parishioner, whose business was "to ask Mr.
Morteboyes to write her a letter." More than fifty
years after the old schoolmaster had been laid to rest
in our churchyard, she, having outworn her wits, still
remembered how he had written letters for her when
she was a young woman.

There seems to have been, towards the end of the
fifteenth century, rather a spirit of emulation in the
parish as regards benefactions. Contemporary with
Thomas Prat were the Skynners and the Underwoods, both of whom bequeathed lands. Symon
Skynner belonged to a family of importance here,
and at Little Alne, Sambourne, and elsewhere
(according to Dugdale). Thomas Underwood is
described as "Baxtere," and was also churchwarden.
The lands they left still belong to us.

Some of the deeds which have survived through
all these centuries concern themselves with very
trivial matters. One grants a right of way ten feet
in width alongside a certain field, the grantor binding
himself and his heirs, under penalty of a hundred
marks, not to obstruct the same. Another grants a
hedge, and a mere next thereto lying, in "bodde-
brokes croft," and gives the exact measurement of
length and width in feet and paces.

There are also several small parchments which
take the shape of stays of action against the feoffees
and churchwardens in respect of causes of complaint
which the litigants (as they express it)
have had, have, or might be thought to have, from the
beginning of the world (*a pryncipio mundi*) up to the day of
making these presents.

One of these is dated at Banbury (1425). The Charity Trust at the present day includes a house at that place, though no record exists as to when or how it was acquired. There can be little doubt that it belonged to the parish at this date, and that three of the feoffees, whose names appear in the document, had journeyed to Banbury to settle some dispute which had arisen.

But perhaps the most curious of all these miscellaneous parchments is a little one of Henry IV.'s time (1412), being a power of attorney from William Amyson, "baxtere" (or as we should now call him, baker), and Alice his wife, of "Colleshull" (that is, Coleshill), to John Prat, of Lapworth, to collect for them a debt of 4*s*. 4*d*. from John Couper, of Packwood, "which he owes" (says the instrument) "to us for food purchased and had from us in time past." And John Prat is authorised to sue for the recovery of the same before any of the judges he thinks best, and to give a receipt and acquittance "as if we ourselves were present." Whether this 4*s*. 4*d*. was ever collected we shall never know, but it is certain that William Amyson must have been very angry about it. It is an odd little bit of history to have survived nearly five hundred years in our parish chest.

And with this memorial of William Amyson's unpaid bread bill of 4*s*. 4*d*. we close our examination of these ancient deeds. Extending as they do over more than three centuries (from *c.* 1190 to 1502), they furnish to amateurs a curious and interesting study in palæography. The variety of handwriting which we get within this period is very great. Some

of the oldest deeds are the easiest to read, and their
ink the best preserved. We soon learn that though
certain forms and rules of contraction are characteristic of certain definite periods, the extent to which
these are used depends much upon the temper of the
scribe. In this respect, however, our Lapworth
deeds are, of course, different in no way from others.
On the whole, they have been wonderfully well preserved, many of them being remarkably bright and
clear, and as specimens of caligraphy quite perfect.
They have probably never until now been the subject
of any thorough examination. The condition of
many of them when first inspected suggested that
they had not been unfolded for centuries. They
have been kept in six or seven small boxes, and these
again in an iron chest which is much too full. The
oldest box [1] is probably not less than four or five
centuries old—a circular box of oak turned out of the
solid, height $3\frac{3}{4}$ inches, diameter 5 inches, with a lid
formerly tied on with leather thongs, of which only
one remains. This ancient deed chest now, indeed,
suggests a receptacle for tobacco rather than parchments. The others are chip boxes of quite modern
appearance ; yet some of them are inscribed in handwriting apparently of the Elizabethan period. Each
box has clearly been at some time appropriated to the
deeds relating to such properties as were named on
the lid ; but explorers who have taken the deeds out
have found themselves unable to identify them and
put them back again—which is the less surprising
as in many cases the internal description of land is

[1] See illustration, p. 228.

only that it is *in campis de Lappeworth.* The result has been that each box has been tightly refilled with such deeds as came first to hand. They were all without endorsement, folded to a size of about two or two and a half inches by one inch. On the back of each I have now marked the date, so far as ascertainable.

With all their faults and their severe demands upon one's patience, a student leaves them with regret, for at any rate they are parchment, and to pass from sound parchment to paper decayed and ragged, and from the carefully formed letters of these old scriveners to the handwriting of the time of Henry VIII. and Elizabeth, is grievous to flesh and spirit. On the other hand, there is a new interest in the latter, inasmuch as they begin to be, for the most part, in English.

Seal of deed, 1343
Agnes, widow of John le Corveser
to Richard, her son

p. 50

FROM THE TIME OF THE REFORMATION
(*circa* 1527) TO 1688

"... *written down old with all the characters of age.*"

HENRY IV., Part 2

CHAPTER III

FROM THE TIME OF THE REFORMATION
(*circa* 1527) TO 1688

OF the reign of Henry VIII. not much has come
down to us in our chest except the Will of
Roger Slye, who stands in the table of bequests as
having left in 1527 (18 Henry VIII.)

> a cottage and lands to the poor and highways.

It consists of two sheets of paper stitched end on
end, thus forming one continuous face of writing,
30 inches by 12 inches, and is clearly a contemporary
copy supplied to the parish by way of title to the
bequest. We strike in it a more distinctly personal
and human note than we have had before. It contains many quaint and simple touches characteristic
of its period, and is of further interest as showing the
intimate relations subsisting between the testator and
the families of Ferrers of Baddesley Clinton, the
Catesbies, and the Lucys of Charlecote. It is,
indeed, one of the most interesting of our memorials,
and runs thus :—

THE WILL OF ROGER SLYE. (1527)

✠ In Daye nomyne. A men. yᵉ yere of owre Lord MVc
& XXVII yᵉ XXIIJ day of . . . I Rogere Slye of wholle &

p'fytte mynde make this my laste Welle & Testam^t ase here afeter followeth. forst I be qwethe my sowle to Alle myghtie God & to owre lady saynte Mary & to alle ye blessyd compene of hevyn & my body to be beryed in ye chercheyerde of lape worthe be my father & mother & there to be dolte at my beryalle to pore pepolle xl^s peny dolle. Allso I be qwethe to ye psone of lape worthe for tythes forgotton xij^d & to ye mother cherche of Worseter iiij^d [1] I wylle that my wyfe shalle have alle my landes in kyngeswode for terme of her lyfe & after her deycesse I wylle y^t she assyne some onyste man to have occupashon of thys lande telle ye tyme y^t Rogere Slye ye sonne of Ollyver Slye come to ye ayge of xxiiij yeres & ye profyt thereof to go to George Rogere & Margere Whelplay chelderyn of Margere Whelplay. Allso y^t she have parte of my porchesyd land in Lapeworthe gret Topes-forde w^t a medowe lyeing thereto in lyke manar & forme ase she hathe othere landes before spessyfyed & ye remaynder thereof to ye s^d Rogere before mencyoned & to ye ayeres malle of hys body lawfully begoton & for lake of ayeres malle of hys body lawfully begoton to remayn to Robert Slye & to ye ayeres malle of hys body lawfully begoton & for ye lake of ayeres malle of hys body lawfully begoton to remayne to James Slye & Richard Slye afeter ye forme aforesayde. And yefe alle these aforesayd dye wetheowte ayeres malle of there bodyes lawfully begoton that then ye s^d landes I wylle to be sowlde & ye mone thereof to goe to ye fynding of a pryst to syng at Saynt Caterynes awter in Lapeworthe Cherche to pray for ye sowles of Nycholas Slye Ellyne Rogere Margaret hys wyfe & Ollyvere. It: I wylle y^t a cottage cawllyd Dyghtenes w^t iij croftes & ij orchard plekes & vij landes in ye owld fyld a crofte lying wythe in Syans fylde & a long slyng joyning thereto goe to soche usys ase here afeter foloweth: forste I wylle y^t a tapar be fownde be fore owere lady at ye West ende of ye cherche of Lapeworthe of v^{li} waxe & y^t ye p'son & ye chawntreprest kepe a urbbete wonce in ye yere & thay to have for ther labore iiij^d a pese & ij^d for ye lyghte of ye herse & a peny for ryngyng ye grete belle & a masse peny allso I

---

[1] These bequests for "tithes forgotten" were common in wills of the period.

wylle y^t iij^s iiij^d be dawlte a pone good fryday to ye pore
pepulle of ye same paryshe be ye dyskreshon of ye cherchemen
for there tyme beyeng. Allso xx^d to ye mayntenyng of y^e
rodelyghte Allso to ye myndyng of ye hye wayes be twene
Harbere hethe & Lapeworthe cherche yerely xx^d & y^t to be
done be ye cherche wardynes for ther tyme beyeng to make
ther a cownte be fore ye paryshe at ye cownte day & to have
for ther labore viij^d Allso I wylle y^t ye rest of ye rentes be
dronken at ther cownte day & pray for owere sowlles &
alle Krystyn sowlles so 'y^t owere ladyes tapar be kepyd
& mayntened for wythe v^{li} of wexe for evarmore.

Thes be ye fefares y^t be fefyd in thes landes be fore namyd
to soche usys ase be fore be expressyd forst Sir Edward ferys
kynghte Master Rychard Cattesbe ar. Wyllm̄ lewse hary
ferys John bewfoo Nykolas Knyghte John Lodebroke John
Oldnalle Wyllm̄ Asheby Robard banethrost Rogere Waw
. . . John Raye. It: I welle whene viij of thes fefares be
dede y^t ye iiij y^t be . . . shalle make a newe fefement be y^e
vyse of ye p'son & ye parysh . . . & thay to make so mene
a gene & so to conetenew for evare. Allso I wylle y^t my wyfe
have my takyngs y^t I have & howld of Master Cometon to
her & to her asynars Allso my takyng of Rowle I wylle she
have ye terme of her lyfe & she to do her best therewyth at
her owne plessar Allso I welle y^t yerdly have my beste cotte
a chamalate jackate a doblate of red sylke a payere of allemen
revates a bowe & a shefe of arowes Allso to George Whelplay
my best foryd gowne & a blake satyn doblate

It: to Elsabeth my servante a stere & a hayford of ij yeres
ayge a pese & a wether shepe It: to Wyllm̄ mawdele a stere
& a hayford of ij yeres of ayge a pese It: to Thomas my
servante ij yerelyng cavys ij shepe in ye wolle It: to Jeffere
trentames wyfe a shepe in ye wolle and to her dowter a nother
shepe in ye wolle. It: to Margyte lenard a nother good shepe
in ye wolle Allso John my servante a shepe in ye wolle Allso
to yong M thomas lewse a lytylle amblyng horse of a yere
ayge & ye resedewe of my shepe I gyfe & be qwethe to
Margere Whelplay It: to Allys Slye my brotheres wyfe a
hayford of ij yeres ayge It: to her three dowteres a cawfe
a pese of a yere ayge It: yefe my wyfe dye be fore ye sayd

Rogere Slye Ollyver Slyes son come to ye ayge of xxiiij yeres y^t Sir John in wode John lodebroke John Oldnalle John Ray have ye orderyng & lettyng of alle my forsayd landes & ye profytes of theme remayne to ye ewse of George Whelplayes chelderyn un to ye forsayd Rogere come to ye ayge of xxiiij yeres fully complyght provydyd alle ways y^t ye reprayshene of ye howsyng be yerly mayntaynyd w^t ye profytes of ye rentes at ye dyskreshon of ye sayd Sir John in wode John Oldnalle John Ray. Farthe I wylle y^t ye forsayd John John & John at alle tymes conevenyante have ye fyshynge of my polles & ye mete feshe of theme to have theme at ther plessares levyng ye sayd polles sofyshantely storyd & to gyfe to Master ferys some tyme a deshe of ye beste feshe ther takand. ye resedewe of my gudes une be qwethyed my dettes payd I gyfe & be qwethe to Margyte my wyfe whome I make myne exekewtor Sir John in wode John lodebroke John Oldnalle George Whelplay joynte exekewtores w^t my wyfe & ye sayd Sir John in wode to have for hys labore a joynyd tabulle y^t wase Sir thomas Slyes & ye sayd lodebroke for hys labore xiij^s iiij^d & to John Oldnalle a blake bulle of iij yeres of ayge and George Whelplay my grete gray gyldyng Allso Sir Edward ferys knyghte & my lady lewse of ther charges to be myne ovarseares of thys my last wylle yefe yt plese theme of ther goodenys & charyte to do so moche for me & ye sayd M. ferys to have for hys labore a bay gyldyng of iij yeres of ayge & my lady lewse for her payne a namblyng horse foole of a yere of ayge & thys beryng wetnesse John Raye Nykolas Knyghte John Slye carvar John grysseowld Wyllm̃ horsseley & Richard Slye.

(It may be noted that, in this will, "f" is always written, whether initial or not, in the form which we usually denote by "ff"; but as it is quite certain this was merely a form of "f" then in use and not intended to represent its duplication, it is here printed single. The forms which we usually print "y^e" and "y^t" for *the* and *that* are not written with "y," but

with a distinctly formed Saxon letter "thorn" (þ).
The true "y" is always well made in its present form.
Of capital letters, though here used for facility of read-
ing, there are hardly any.)

In Daye nomyne, with which the will begins, preserves probably the pronunciation which the testator
had been accustomed to hear from the priest.

The Sir Edward Ferys, Knight, who heads the list
of the twelve "fefares" whom Roger Slye appoints to
administer his trust, was the first of the line of Ferrers
of Baddesley Clinton. "hary ferys" we should have
supposed to be his son, but for the difficulty that
Dugdale shows a son of that name as dying a year
before this will is dated.

"my lady lewse," who was to have "a namblyng
horse foole of a yere of ayge," was the widow of the
second Sir Thomas Lucy of Charlecote, and mother of
"Wyllm̃ lewse" and of "yong M. thomas lewse," who
was also to have "a lytylle amblyng horse of a yere
ayge." By a previous marriage with George Catesby
she was also mother of "Rychard Cattesbe," esquire
(then Lord of the Manor of Lapworth, and knighted
about 1537), so that the latter was half-brother to the
two Lucys. Sir Richard Catesby was also member
for Warwickshire in the famous Parliament of 30
Henry VIII. (1539), by which the monasteries were
confiscated. In the year following he was made Sheriff
of the county (Bridges' *Northamptonshire*).

Old Lady Lucy, indeed, was a dame of very
notable connections. Daughter-in-law through her
first husband of that William Catesby, Esquire
(Shakespeare's "Sir William," though not apparently

knighted by anyone else), who ended his career with
Bosworth field, she became through her son Sir
Richard Catesby the great-great-grandmother of
Robert Catesby the conspirator, while her son
William Lucy became the father, and she the grandmother, of the third Sir Thomas Lucy, Shakespeare's
and everybody's " Justice Shallow," between whom
and the Catesbys there was thus a certain definable
amount of cousinship.

" John bewfoo " (= Beaufoe, of Emscote) was son-
in-law of Sir Edward Ferrers, having married his
daughter Ursula. Altogether we see that the "fefares" were to a great extent a family party.

Of other names mentioned in the will, " Robard
banethrost" would no doubt have been more cor-
rectly called " Barnethurst," of the Lapworth family
of that name. " John Oldnalle" and Isabell his wife
are buried in Rowington Church, their monument
still remaining, though subjected to ill-treatment in
Puritan times. " Sir thomas Slye," whose "joynyd
tabulle" was left to Sir John in wode,[1] the chaplain,
had himself been Chaplain of Lapworth.

The condition that when eight of the feoffees were
dead the four that were left should make a new
feoffment " be ye vyse of ye p'son and ye parysh and
thay to make so mene a gene and so to conetenew
for evare," is the earliest trace we find of the mode of
appointment of trustees of the Charity Estates, which
continues to this day, except that the parish has long
ceased to have any " vyse " in the matter.

---

[1] " In wode" becomes " Hynwood " in Hannett's *Forest of Arden.*

The fish pools, from which " Master ferys" was to have a dish of the best fish saved for him by the chaplain and his companions, were and still are at Brome Hall, where Roger Slye had succeeded the Bromes.

One would like to know why "Margyte lenard" was to have "a good shepe in ye wolle," whereas the others were only ordered to have "a shepe in ye wolle." The pair of *allemen revates* (German rivets) which Yerdly was to get, formed a piece of steel armour, a corslet or a cuirass, with sleeves and a headpiece, made of plates constructed to slide over each other with the bending of the arms and body. It protected the chest, arms, and neck, and was made in two pieces, and hence called "a pair."[1]

The will shows us further that in Roger's day there was a large image of the Virgin at the west end of the church, life-size probably. The five stones which still remain as projections from the wall were doubtless the supports (or are renewals of what were the supports) of this figure.

Our church had at that time three altars—namely, the high altar of St. Mary the Virgin at the east end; that of St. Katherine in the chapel on the north side of the chancel; and that of St. James at the east end of the south aisle, the piscina of the last named still remaining in the south wall.

The oldest of our bells, of pre-Reformation date, bears the inscription, *Sancta Katerina ora pro nobis.*

---

[1] "Almain-rivets. A kind of light armour, first used in Germany, in which great flexibility was obtained by overlapping plates sliding on rivets." (*New English Dictionary.*)

G

In the course of the general restoration of the interior of the church, which was carried out in 1872, when the plaster was stripped from the north wall, nearly opposite the font, there was revealed another memorial of the same period in the very recognisable remains of a large figure of St. Christopher bearing on his shoulders the infant Christ. Unfortunately this old wall-painting faded very quickly, and no sketch of it was made, but portions of faint colouring, indicating its position, still remain upon the wall.

Altogether the hints we get from this will may help us, without drawing too much upon our fancy, to realise Roger Slye as a bluff and hearty old English gentleman of his day, familiar with the best people of the neighbourhood, living in a patriarchal way down at Brome Hall, and remembering his servants by their Christian names : a rather stately and picturesque figure with his furred gown and his doublets of red and black satin, his martial accoutrements of steel and his bow and arrows. The good man did not know that within ten or twelve years of the time at which he then left his money and his land for the taper to burn before this image of our Lady, "and so to conetenew for evare," for the rood light, for the priest to say prayers for him and his relatives at St. Katherine's altar, all such bequests were to be confiscated to the Crown as being for superstitious uses. That portion of his bequest which was devoted to the poor and the highways was, however, probably preserved, though the land cannot now be identified with certainty. It will be noticed that his bequest for the highways was confined to those which lay between his house and the church, Brome Hall lying on the border of what he calls Harbere Hethe. His name appears in the Register of Members of the Guild of St. Anne, of Knowle, under 1506, with that of his relative, Sir Thomas Sly :—

Rogerus Sley et Margareta uxor ejus de Lapworthe
D'ns Thomas Sly Capellanus Cantarie de Lapworthe.[1]

Some of the papers of this period are hopelessly decayed and imperfect. One which bears, in a modern hand, the discreet and non-committal endorsement, "Mutilated document," may still be made to give up the further inscription :—

Inquisitio post mortem Thome Pratt Anno
XXVII Henrici VIIJ (1536)

It has been repaired by having a leaf of a child's copybook pasted on the back, which leaf may be perhaps a century later than the inquisition itself. The "copy" is repeated about fourteen times, and runs :—

Because that word and faithe with no degree wille stande,
Therfore, the Lawer saithe take writinge of there hande.

This was the sort of moral precept instilled into the young idea at Lapworth school. "Don't trust a man's word, but have his promise in writing."

This Thomas Pratt may have been son or grandson of the Thomas Pratt who left lands to the parish, as before described, in 1480. Enough can still be deciphered of the inquisition to show that it relates to lands formerly held by him of the respective Manors

---

[1] Thomas Sly had only two successors as chantry priest—(1) John in Wode, before mentioned ; and (2) Roger Coke, who, on the suppression of the chantry in 1553, was awarded a pension of £5 a year.

of Lapworth, Nuthurst, and "Bewdesart," and, in the description, we get the names of the Lords of such Manors and the then reputed values of the parcels of land.   Thus he held of Rycharde Catysbye, *armiger* (who has been mentioned in Roger Slye's will), as of his manor of Lapworthe, land subject to a yearly payment of two shillings and two pounds of root ginger, and then "worth by the year, free of all outgoings and repairs, ten shillings"; of Alurede Trussell, *armiger*, as of his manor of Nuthurst, land under a yearly payment of four shillings, and then "worth by the year, free of outgoings &c, ten shillings"; and of Sir Edward Aston, Knight, as of his manor of "Bewdesart, land subject to homage only, of the net yearly value of twelve pence."

The document is so imperfect that further details cannot be made out, but it seems to have been in some way connected with a suit which arose at a later period regarding parish lands.

When we see upon an Ordnance Map[1] how the lands belonging to our Charity Estates are dotted about all over the parish (and on its borders) the fact is brought home to us very pointedly that such lands have been left by parishioners for parishioners.   And, indeed, there is not one instance in which the lands have been left to the parish by an outsider, nor one in which lands have been left at all since the reign of Elizabeth.   The fountains of benevolence in that particular shape seem to have practically dried up at that time.   And doubtless this was in no small degree due to the ruthless way in

---

[1] See map in pocket at end of volume.

which charitable bequests had been then recently appropriated by the Crown.

I apprehend there are few rural parishes which can show a map so remarkable.

There can be little doubt that the first step towards amalgamation of the older trusts was made under Henry VIII. immediately after the Reformation. At that time the parish lost, as we know, various portions of its property as being land devoted to superstitious uses, and some of the trusts being thus broken up, it is most likely that the remainder were united under one body by higher authority.

An examination of the old feoffment deeds and leases of Elizabeth's reign impresses one with the idea that ponderous machinery was employed in those days to effect very small results, and illustrates the extreme tenacity and jealousy with which the parish, and we may suppose parishes generally, clung to such bequests.

A deed of feoffment constituting a new trust in 1563 is the earliest (unless we can consider Roger Slye's will to be such) that has survived in the form which, with little variation, has continued to this day. By it William Ashby, who describes himself as the sole survivor of an earlier trust body which had been enfeoffed by one Anthony Brome, at a date not mentioned, himself grants and enfeoffs to Humphrey Gower, *generosus*, and twenty-one others all the parish lands which had been held by him and his deceased co-feoffees. The list of the several properties gives the names of nearly all those with which the older deeds have made us familiar, and mentions others which we cannot now identify. Of the twenty-two persons thus enfeoffed all save one, Roger Edgworth, of Warwick, *generosus*, appear to have been parishioners of Lapworth, of the yeoman or husbandman class.

But notwithstanding the creation of this large new trust body of 1563, we find that only four years later (1567) another entirely new trust of seventeen members is established by John Collett to take charge of a bequest then made by him. He describes himself in his deed as "of Nuthurst, yeoman." But as his house adjoined the Birmingham road, where the blacksmith's shop now stands on Lapworth hill, he was only just outside our parish. He describes all the seventeen whom he enfeoffs as "husbandmen," fourteen being of Lapworth and three of Nuthurst. Ten were members of the body described above, but seven were not. He was not minded to trust his gift to any but men of his own class and his own choosing, though it was but one field. He seems to have selected it because it joined on to other land already belonging to the parish. He bought it from John Trussell of Byllesley, *armiger*, for £6 13s. 4d., as is attested by the said John Trussell's power of attorney, still existing. As the quantity was 3 a. 0 r. 14 p., the price therefore was about £2 4s. per acre. The field lying immediately behind his own house and being previously in his own occupation, he knew it, no doubt, for a bit of good land. (The valuation of 1814 put it at 36s. per acre per annum rental.)

He allowed considerable latitude as to the employment of the proceeds of his bequest, defining his

wishes by a schedule in English which is appended
to his Latin deed of feoffment.   He says :—

The intent and meaning of this my present feoffment is
that my said feoffees shall from henceforth stand and be
seised to them and to their heirs for ever of and in the said
close or croft of land with the appurtenances mentioned in
the said feoffment : Provided always notwithstanding that
the issues, profits and revenues arising, coming or growing
in, of or upon the said close or croft of land shall for ever be
yearly levied and taken by the churchwardens of the parish
church of Lapworth and their successors for the time being,
and so being by them levied, received and taken the one
moiety thereof to be converted, bestowed and employed to
the behoof, sustentation and relief of the poor people and
needy inhabitants of Lapworth, and the other moiety to be
delivered to the churchwardens of Nuthurst and their successors for the time being, to be by them given and employed
in like manner to the behoof, sustentation and relief of the
poor people and needy inhabitants of Nuthurst.   The Gift,
distribution and dispensation of the value of the same rents
and other profits coming and growing of the premises aforesaid to be made, divided, dealt and given by the said churchwardens amongst the said poor people yearly on the Friday
next before Easter Day, commonly called Good Friday; or
else to convert and employ the rents and profits aforesaid
towards the reparation and maintenance of the churches of
Lapworth and Nuthurst; or else towards the repairing and
mending of the common highways within the said parishes,
according to the discretion and appointment of both the said
churchwardens and their successors: Moreover the will and
desire of the said John Collett is that when it please
Almighty God to take out of this world all the said feoffees
except four persons, then the said four persons so overliving
their cofeoffees shall within one half year next after the
decease of the overliver of the same other feoffees deceased
by their deed sufficiently in law, with a like schedule to the
same to be annexed, enfeoff as many other persons or twelve
at least, parishioners of Lapworth or others, to the same
purposes and intents as are contained in this present feoffment.

The church of Nuthurst, for reparation of which John Collett thus made provision in 1567, had a much more important bequest made to it in the same year (according to Dugdale) by Edmund Fulwood, of Tanworth. It afterwards, but at what time is not known, fell into entire decay, and in the early part of the eighteenth century had become a ruin. It is not now known with certainty where it stood, but most probably the ruins were removed to make room for the existing (but disused) mortuary chapel near the obelisk.

Cumbrous as these numerous trust bodies appear to us (and we shall find there were others existing here along with these), there was probably little difficulty attending their ordinary working. The actual control, letting and management of the several pieces of land, etc., were left in the hands of the churchwardens or of collectors appointed on behalf of the parish from year to year. It will be remembered that in 2 Edward IV. (1462) Richard Browne and Thomas Sly describe themselves as "collectors for this year of the rents of all the lands and tenements belonging to the church of the Blessed Mary of Lapworth, with the assent and consent of all the parishioners of the said town." The feoffees existed only for the purpose of making it difficult, and, indeed, well-nigh impossible, to alienate the parish properties, and the larger the trust body the more difficult such alienation was supposed to be.

That the risk of alienation, notwithstanding all these precautions, was a real and serious one is apparent from particulars that have survived of a parish suit of the time of Elizabeth. The papers are without date, endorsed " Bill into the Chauncery v'sus Thomas Grymshawe," but the application is made to Sir Nicholas Bacon (father of the famous Sir Francis Bacon, afterwards Lord Verulam), whose Lord Keepership extended from 1558 to 1578. They show that the angry passions of the parish were roused to the extent of bringing forth much strong language, which is now so toned down by time as to have become amusing, and the record of it worth preserving :—

[Case and application for a Writ of Sub-poena against Thomas Grymshawe, of Packwood.]

To the right Honorable Sir Nicolas Bacon, knight, Lord Keeper of the great Seale of England.

In most humble wise complayning shew unto your honorable Lordship your daily orators Humphrey Gower, William Ashbye, George Walker, Thomas Slye, Willm Latchford, Willm Walton, John Smyth, Thomas Mountford, John Wheler, John Green, Willm Bosworth, and other of the poor parishioners of Lapworth in the Co. of Warw^k, that whereas one Thomas Prat, deceased, and others about an hundred years past by several conveyances in the law of charitable devotion did enfeof one John Hill, John Ailesbury and others of and in certain lands, tenements and hereditaments sett, lying and being in Lapworth aforesaid, to th' use and intent that the said feoffees and their heirs should stand seised to the use and intent following, that is to say that the said feoffees and their heirs should employ all the profits of the said lands to the maintenance, sustentation and reparation of the parish church of Lapworth for ever, as that may appear by a certain deed of feoffment of trust made unto certain feoffees of the same, which said land and hereditaments so given and granted to the uses and

intents aforesaid have been continually from time to time
always by the said feoffees and others having the said lands
to the uses aforesaid employed in and about the reparation
of the said church accordingly, now of late, so it is (right
Honorable good Lord) that Thomas Grymshawe of Pacwode
in the said Co: of Warw^k, yoman, one of the feoffees of the
said lands to the uses and intents aforesaid, and certain of
divers and sundry other feoffees being put in trust by the
parishioners of the said parish of Lapworth, being often
moved, requested and solicited by your said orators to make
a lawful conveyance of the said lands unto such other feoffees
as your said orators should know to be honest men of good
reputation and void of corruption, for further reservation and
continuation of the said lands to the uses, purposes and
intents above specified, hath, contrary to the trust and confidence to him in that behalf committed, hitherto refused so
to do But of corrupt conscience, covetous practice and
unjust dealing, and tendering only his own private lucre
and commodity, hath, contrary to the good-will of all your
said orators, made a lease of the said lands unto his son
Nicolas Grymshawe for the term of 21 years, and hath
received a sum of money of the said Nicolas by the name
of a fine for the same to his own proper use and behoof, and
hath also, upon the expiration of the said lease of 21 years
made to the said Nicolas, made an other lease of the said
land for many more years, the certain term whereof your
orators as yet know not:

Whereupon your said orators, understanding the injurious
and corrupt devices of the said Thomas G. and mistrusting
lest he of his malicious and covetous mind would wholly
convert and alyene the right and title of the premises to
some other use and intent (studying only his private profit
and gain) then the same have been hitherto and of right
ought hereafter to be employed, have by all gentle means
they could requested the said Thomas G. to demean himself
in this behalf according to the trust to him committed, which
said Thomas notwithstanding hath of late openly and in the
hearing of divers in divers and sundry places by way of
manasinge threatened your said orators that whereas he was

the survivor of the feoffees, and that the whole right and title of the premises remained in him only, he would not only lett and sett the same at his pleasure, but also would sell the same unless we, your said orators, would for his good-will in yielding to make a new deed of feoffment give him such a sum of money (to his own use) as he might demand, your said orators therefore, willing rather to purchase quietness at their common charge at home than to molest and trouble this Honorable court in enforming the same of the unjust dealing and odyous demayner of the said T.G., were contented to rempermytt the matter to the arbitrament and order of four honest men, Willm Ashbye, George Walker, Thos Busby, and Hugh Avern, who concluded and agreed that we your said orators should content and pay unto the said Nicolas Grymshawe, son of the said Thomas, for his lease x^{li} vj^s viij^d in consideration whereof the said Nicolas promised to all your said orators that he would be ready at all times to do all and every act and acts that the counsel learned in the law of your said orators should direct or advise in the assignment of the same, whereupon xl^s was paid forthwith to the said Nicolas by your said orators, and for the viij^{li} vj^s viij^d rest of the said sum of x^{li} vj^s viij^d the said N. G. hath a bond of debt made, sealed and delivered to him by the said Wm Ashbye and Geo: Walker, two of your said orators, which for default of payment he, the said Nicolas, hath put in suit to the great vexation and trouble of your said poor orators, refusing utterly notwithstanding to yield up his said lease or to make any assignment over of the same, according as he promised to the said arbitrators and to your orators. And the said Thomas G. the father also utterly refused to seal any new deed of feoffment unless we your said orators would give him iiij^{li} more in present money, which we your said orators have already paid him, yet nevertheless he still refuseth to seal any such feoffment.

Whereupon your said orators by way of complaynte made humble suit unto the Right Honorable the Lord Wyndsore, being then in that country, that it would please his Lordship to call the said Tho: Gry: before him and to examine him of the cause of his delays and covetous dealings, which his Lordship did accordingly, who proving upon the examination of the matter the crafty practices and untollerable corruption of the said Tho: Gry: thought rather then he should deal therein to refer the matter to the consideration of this Honorable Court, when good order might be taken for the punishment of such heynous crimes to the example of all other the like offenders. We therefore, your said humble suppliants and poor orators, tendering chiefly the commodity of the church and fearing lest by the sinister meands and practices of the said Tho: Gry: the said lands given to the same should be alyened and sold from the same for ever, most humbly besechen your good Honorable Lordship that it now please the same to grant a writ of sub pena out of this Honorable Court to be directed to the said Tho: G: calling him into the same to answer unto the premises: and we your said poor orators shall most humbly pray unto Almighty God for the preservation of your good lordship in prosperous estate.

To these charges Thomas Grymshawe, who describes himself as " beinge olde and impotent," makes answer at great length, substantially denying all that is brought against him, and avowing himself to be vexed at heart through being made the subject of such "unjust and malicious slanders, troubles and charges in law."

Further he declares he hath " of his own free and voluntary will, for the discharge of his conscience and performance of the trust reposed in him, already by his deed of feoffment " conveyed the lands in question to Edmunde Catesby, Edward Catesby, and John Catesby, gentilmen, and seventeen others (whom he names, parishioners of Lapworth), "being men all honest and most worthy of trust of any in the said parish in the judgment of the defendant"; but admits that he had refused to enfeoff some of the plaintiffs "because he did not think them to be worthy of trust, suspecting them covetously to seek their own private gain and not the continuance of the pious uses and intents." [The fact was he had made a show of executing such feoffment after the complaint was lodged.]

Further, he more especially denies having ever received money to his own use, and "prayeth to be dismissed out of the right Honorable court with his reasonable costs herein wrongfullie sustayned."

Then follows " The replicacion of Humphrie Gower, Willm Ashbye and others to the aunswer of Thos Grymshawe," in which they reiterate their charges and enforce them with unpleasant additions ; namely, that Nicolas the son had confessed " in the hearing of ten or twelve honest men " that his father had had from him the money paid for surrender of the lease, and

also they sayen that the said Thomas G. was not sick or under any infirmity of body, but in very good state to travel, and could have attended the Honorable Court in person if he had been so minded. And without that that[1] the defendant hath untruly alleged in his answer that he hath enfeoffed the said lands to the persons whom he names to their proper uses and intents. All which the said complainants do again aver and will prove as this Honorable Court shall award.

Finally, there has survived the actual assignation of his lease (8 Elizabeth, 1565) by Nicolas Grymshawe, to William Ashby and others, of the lands in question,

---

[1] This curious phrase, meaning "further," with which nearly every paragraph of the pleadings begins, is a literal rendering of the customary forms used in the older Latin pleadings, *Et absque hoc quod.*

the consideration money being £10 6s. 8d., " whereof the said Nicolas enologyth himself to be satisfied and paid."

There seems, therefore, to be no doubt that the charges against crafty old Thomas Grymshawe were fully proved, and that the parish narrowly escaped losing these lands.

That this suit was the cause of great excitement in the parish may be well imagined, but it would appear to have interested a wider area, and accordingly we find by an indenture of lease dated a few years later (namely, in 1573) that the lands which had thus been the subject of contest had become vested in a trust body of theretofore unheard-of extent and notability. The parish and neighbourhood had apparently determined that this particular bequest should, at any rate, run no further risk of being purloined.

At the head of this new trust we get " Sr Thomas Lucye, Knight" (thus connecting the Charlecote Justice of the Peace with us in a way not previously known); and whereas other feoffments seem to have been jealously confined, or nearly confined, to parishioners of the yeoman class, this, owing doubtless to what had gone before, includes a large number of the chief landed gentry of the neighbourhood. Among his colleagues are Henry, Lord Compton (raised to a Barony in the year previous); two of the Throckmortons of Coughton Court; three of the Somervilles of Edston, namely, John the elder, John the younger, and William his brother, afterwards knighted; William Catesbye, esquier, then Lord of the Manor of Lapworth (afterwards Sir William, and father of Robert the conspirator), and with him no fewer than five other Catesbyes—George, Richard, Edmund, Edward, and John, whose relationship amongst each other we cannot make out, though (from the pedigrees given in Dugdale and in Bridges' *Northamptonshire*) some of them were probably sons of the Sir Richard Catesby mentioned in connection with the will of Roger Slye. Besides these there was Thomas Dabridgecourt, of a noted family of Solihull ;[1] Roger Edgworthe of Warwick, gentleman ; Richard Veele, clerk ; after whom come the names of twenty-three others, mostly, but not all, parishioners of Lapworth, including many who had been concerned in the antecedent suit, and members of the Ashby trust of 1563.

Nearly all the more important people who are thus shown as the associates of Sir Thomas Lucy in this parish trust of ours were of families noted for their zealous adherence to the old religion, and it is not unlikely that his kinship with the Catesbyes had induced him to accept the position. Ten years later, when Sir Thomas was known rather as a zealot of the new religion than the old, there was a much less happy connection between the knight and John Somerville the younger, his co-feoffee, for he is seen to be then instrumental in the arrest and sending of the young man to London under a charge of treasonable conspiracy against the life of Elizabeth the Queen. Somerville, who, by the accounts that have survived, seems to have been quite crazy, was, with several

---

[1] The monument of Thomas Dabridgecourt named above is figured by Dugdale, and still remains in Solihull-Church, with a quaint inscription. He was Lord of the Manor of Chilvers Coton, in George Eliot's land.

others, condemned to suffer death at Tyburn, and escaped that doom only by strangling himself in his cell. His wife, who had been convicted and sentenced with him, was pardoned.[1]

The indenture of lease witnesseth that the said Sr Thomas Lucye and the others, "by the assent and consent of the more part of the honest men parishioners of Lapworth, have graunted and do graunten, demysen, setten and to farme letten" to Symon Baldwyn of Packwood the lands in Nuthurst, Lapworth and Beaudesert, which had been the subject of the suit before named, for the term of twenty-two years, he "yielding to the said Sr Thomas Lucye (& his co-feoffees) or to the churchwardens of the parish church of Lapworth for the tyme being the some of Twentie & four shillings . . . at thre times of the yere . . . by even porcions."

The rent being of the same amount as in Nicolas Grymshawe's lease, and made payable as above either to the feoffees or to the churchwardens, we may conclude the management was really left in the hands of the latter.

We get a trace of the great upheaval and overthrow which, under Henry VIII. and Edward VI., had taken place by the confiscation of monasteries, chantries, guilds, etc., in the shape of certain Articles of Enquiry, undated, addressed to the parish some time during the earlier years of Elizabeth's reign. The estates of the great abbeys and monastic institutions having been dealt with, the time had arrived for look-

---

[1] These facts were set out by Mrs. C. C. Stopes in the *Athenæum*, February 8th, 1896.

ing up the smaller endowments and properties which
had hitherto escaped attention. The parish is ordered
forthwith to make a return to the Crown of all concealed lands or properties. By "concealed lands"
was meant any lands which had formerly belonged to
a monastery or other religious corporation which had
been dissolved by the Act passed in the twenty-seventh
year of the reign of King Henry VIII., or Acts subsequent, and had not been delivered over to the
Crown.

It will be seen that the Articles are so searching and
minute that little could escape them. There is nothing
to show from whom the document proceeded or to
whom it was addressed, there being no heading or
signature. Probably it was a common form sent to
parishes throughout the kingdom :—

Fforst you shall enquere of all lands tenements meadows
pastures woods underwoods reversions & hereditaments within your parisshe which heretofore did belong or apperteyn to any late monasterie or priorie
& were reputed & taken as parcell or member of the
same which before this tyme ought to have come to
hands and possession of the late King of famous
memorie King Henry the eighth or King Edward the
sixth Quene Marie or to the Quene's Majestie that
now is by the dissolution of the same by force of two
several Acts of Parliament made at Westminster in the
27th and 30th yeres of the said late King Henry the
8th which have been or be concealed & wrongfully
detayned from her Majestie her said father borother
& sister of what yearly value the same is and in whose
tenure and occupacon

Item   of all colledges chaunteries free chapels chapels of ease
within your parisshe having been within 5 yeres next

H

before the 4th daie of November Anno primo Regis
Edwardi sexti and of all manors lands tenements Rents
tythes pencons porcons and other hereditaments to
them or any of them belonging which ought to come
to hands of the quenes ma^{tie} by force of any acts of
p'liam^{t} made for the dissolution of the same in the
first yere of the reigne of the said late King E. or wh:
by any weis or meanes were dessolvyd or extinguysshed
sythe the 4th daie of Februarie in the 27th yere of King
Henry the 8th being yet conceled from her highness
& so have been from her said brother and syster

Item   what lands & tenements & hereditaments were appoynted to the finding of a priest for ever & wherewith
eny prist hath ben maynteyned or found at eny tyme
within the said fyve yeres wh: were not in the reall
possession of the late King E the 6th nor quene Marye
nor yet become to the quenes ma^{tie} that now is

Item   what annuall rents proffitts or emoluments at eny
(time) within the said 5 yeres have ben demised (?) by
eny towards the finding of eny stypendarie priest
entended by eny acte or wryting to have contynuance
for ever yet conceled from her hyghnes have been conceled from her graces said father brother & sister

Item   what lands tenemts & hereditmts proffitts & other
things have been by eny conveyance appoynted to the
finding of a priest for yeres & wherewith eny priest
hath been found within 5 yeres lykewise conceled from
her highness as before is said

Item   what lands tenemts & hereditmts have been appoynted
wholly to fynding of eny rosarie (?) obit lyghte lampe
or eny other lyke entent or purpose for ever wh: have
ben kept within the said 5 yeres yet concealed have
ben concealed from her graces brother & sister

Item   wheras parte of th'issues of suche lands were appoynted
to thentents aforesaid for ever that then you do enquere
what the greatist some of money hath ben emploied
about the entents aforesaid in eny one yere within

5 yeres abovesaid yet concealed from her highness and have ben concealed from her graces said brother and syster

Item you shall enquere what somes of money & proffitts by eny manner of conveiaunce were appoynted to have contynuaunce for ever & what was the gretist some that in eny one of the said 5 yeres were emploied by eny corporacon fraternytie companye or felowshipp of mysteries or crafte towards the fynding of eny priest eny rosarie (?) lyght lamp or other lyk thing yet concealed from her highness and have ben concealed from her graces brother & sister

Item how many brother heds, guylds & fraternyties not being felowships of mysteries or craftes be within your said parisshe & what lands tenemts & hereditmts belonging to eny of them yet conceled from her highnes & have been concealed from her graces said brother & sister

Item what goods cattels plate jewels ornaments or other movables late belonging to any of the said colledges chaunteries free chapells or stypendarie priest for the furnyture of their severall fundacons are yet withholden from her ma^{tie} by whom & of what value

Item of all lands tenemts hereditmts goods & catels wh: ought to come to the quenes ma^{tie} by reson of any attainder or forfaiture of eny person or persons by treson felony or murder of or suche lyke offense or offenses wh: are concealed from her ma^{tie} or have ben concealed

Item of all lands tenemts & hereditmts wh: ought to come to the quene's ma^{tie} hands by waye of eschete vid^t if eny person or persons being borne without the quenes domynions dying (?) within the same gave eny man lands or tenemts to them & their heires foren without the speciall license of their prince or us eny person or persons holding any lands or tenemts of the quenes ma^{tie} have died thereof seased without heires generall or speciall whereby the same lands ought to eschete to her highnes or graces progenitors & are conceled or wrongfully deteyned from her ma^{tie} & her said progenitors

Item   you shall enquere generallie of all lands tenemts & hereditmts gyven by eny of the quenes ma^{ties} most noble progenitors to eny person or persons for terme of liese or lyves or in tail wh: ought to revert & come to her highnes hands by eny manner of meanes or weys in reversion or . . . & have ben or be concealed & wrongfully deteyned from her highnes or from her graces most noble progenitors & yf eny suche be . . . then to enquere where the same do lye & in whose possession the same is & to what use the same was furst gyven and appoynted toguyther with the clere yerely value thereof & who taketh proffitt of the same

Item   you shall enquere of all lands & tenemts commonly called towne lands or church lands & certifie to what uses the same were first gyven and by whom & by what conveiance & of whom the same lands are holden & by what rent or service & whether the uses have been chaunged & altered or not

What reply was made by the parish authorities to these Articles of Enquiry we have no means of knowing, but they appear to have been connected with a suit in which the parish was involved, and which was before the Court of Exchequer from time to time during the three years 18, 19 & 20 Elizabeth (1576–8).

The proceedings are interesting because in them is made repeated mention of a " Guild or Fraternity of the Holy Cross of Lapworth," of the existence of which there is at present, so far as I have been able to discover, absolutely no other evidence. The papers that have survived form a considerable bundle, but are so mutilated, decayed, and incomplete that they fail to yield a connected story.

They are endorsed in an old hand, " Walton's suit about the Town land " ; are all in Latin ; and from the opening statement of the Attorney-General it will be seen that Lapworth's small delinquency is conjoined, for what reason never appears, with more important alleged delinquencies of Birmingham and Edgbaston touching lands of Lench's Trust and lands now, perhaps, of King Edward's Grammar School, Birmingham :—

EXCHEQUER COURT: HOLY TRINITY TERM: AN: XVIII. REG: ELIZ:

Memoranda, that Gilbert Gerrard Esq, now Attorney General to our Lady the Queen, who on behalf of the same our Lady the Queen conducteth the present prosecution, attendeth in his own person in this Court on the 8th day of July ; and on behalf of the same our Lady the Queen he hath given to the Court this intelligence and information. That is to say, that all those parcels of lands, meadows, feedings, pastures & hereditaments lying and being within the town, parish and fields of Birmingham and Bordesley in the County of Warwick, that is to say 6 acres of land and 6 acres of pasture with the appurtenances in Birm^m aforesaid and 20 acres of land & 20 acres of pasture with the appurten^s in Bordesley afores^d, now or lately in the tenure or occupation of Willm Paynton or his assigns, formerly given & granted by Willm Lynche & Agnes his wife for the support and maintainance of an obit lamp, lights, a priest celebrant & other superstitious uses in the parish church of St: Martin in Birm^m afs^d and other religious rites there to be had & celebrated ; and all those parcels of land & pastures with the appurt^s in Edgebaston in the afs^d co: of Warw^k, namely 20 acres of land & 20 acres of pasture now or lately in the tenure or occup^n of Robt Middlemore or his assigns, lately

belonging or appertaining to the Guild or Fraternity of the
Holy Cross in Birm^m afs^d : together with a cottage and the
appurtenances thereof lying and being in Lapworth in the
said County of Warw^k, now or lately in the tenure or occupation of William Walton or his assigns, and formerly
belonging and appertaining to the Guild or Fraternity of the
Holy Cross in Lapworth aforesaid ;—were on the 20th day
of January in the first year of our Lady the Queen that now
is, and before and afterwards, in the hands and possession of
our said lady the Queen and sh^d be now in her possession as
in right of her crown of England by reason & force of a
certain Act of Parliament made & enacted in the 1st year of
the reign of King Edw: VI. for the dissolution of chantries,
colleges & other confiliations as in the records, rolls and
memoranda of this Court more fully appeareth.   Which notwithstanding, one John Harrison, Richard Middlemore and
William Walton, lieges of our Lady the Queen, have since
the said 20th day of January in the year first above written
into & upon possession of the said premises entered and
intruded & taken the profits thence proceeding to their own
proper use, & this their transgression hath continued to this
time & doth still continue in contempt of our said Lady the
Queen & contrary to her laws.   Considering which things
the Attorney of our Lady the Queen on her behalf asketh
the interference of the court in the premisses and prayeth
that the said John, Richard & William may come here and
answer to our Lady the Queen in the premisses.

Two days later the summons is issued to the three
defendants, over the signature of C. T. Saunders,
K^t, Westminster, returnable at Michaelmas term
following.

The Lapworth papers are, as before stated, very
imperfect and. in many parts illegible, and do not
appear to have ever included any statement of
evidence ·given.   No further mention is made in
them of the Birmingham defendants, but we gather

that there were many hearings spread over about three years. William Walton seems to have become disagreeably familiar with London, as the phrase frequently recurs " at which day the same William came here in his proper person," only, it would seem, to hear of fresh adjournments. He would appear to have pleaded that as regards the Lapworth property he was blameless, inasmuch as, before the date of the intrusion and transgression charged against him, a certain William Ashebie was seised of and in the aforesaid messuage with its appurtenances, and that he (Walton) held the same from him under a lease for a term of years, by written indenture which he would produce.

Some of the proceedings seem to have taken the shape of inquiries remitted to local juries at Warwick. On one occasion the name of Sir William Catesby is mentioned as making return of such a panel, and on another Sir Thomas Lucy (1579) reports to the Barons of Exchequer how another jury had made or ordered a distraint that had proved ineffectual on the goods and chattels of the said Walton. The papers end half-way, apparently in a decree of further distraint. It would seem that he had lost his case, at any rate for the time, and been unable to pay his costs.

The Lapworth papers give no further light on the matter, but a contemporary document relating to the same suit has been preserved in connection with the Birmingham properties.[1] It is only a memorandum

---

[1] It is through the kindness of Mr. Joseph Hill of Birmingham that a copy of this document is supplied.

of the nature of the charges against the three
defendants with short notes of the way in which
it was intended to meet them, and does not carry
the story so far as any positive hearing. The
actual informer (or "follower," as he is called)
seems to have been one "Nicholas Bayly." The
defence as regards the Birmingham properties is
immaterial to us here. As regards Lapworth the
line of defence is indicated by brief memoranda as
follows :—

William Walton pleads as to the messuage &c in Lapworth that Willm Ashby leased this to him for . . . years
and traverses that there is not any cottage in Lapworth in
his tenure belonging to the Guild in Lapworth.

A witness (Thomas Slye) to prove no Guild there.

Memorandum : "The jury know this."

To produce copy of an inquisition by virtue of a writ
ad quod damnum before the Escheator that the land was
given to feoffees for the reparation of the church of Lapworth.

Also a feoffm^t in 6 Eliz: by Wm Ashbye, heir of the survivor of the feoffees, for the reparation of the church and
highways and relief of the poor.

Memorandum : "The church coffer robbed forty years
past," &c.

The defence, it will be seen, was simply that the
Guild of the Holy Cross of Lapworth was a myth—
that there had never been any such guild.

And much as I should like to have established the
interesting fact that there was a guild here, as at
Knowle and at Henley - in - Arden, it seems almost

beyond doubt that the defence was a true one. The remark, " The jury know this," points to the fact being of common notoriety.

The witness, " Thomas Slye," was one of the parish feoffees.

The inquisition to be produced may have been that already described as bearing date 1536. Ashby's feoffment of 6 Elizabeth has been previously described, and mentions what seems to be the land in question as parish property.

Further, it is hardly conceivable that had such a guild existed we could have failed to find the name of some one or more of its masters as witnesses of parish deeds. Dugdale's silence, too, is significant. On the whole, the reasonable conclusion seems to be that Lapworth never had a guild, but that Nicholas Bayly, the informer of the Crown, had discovered a mare's nest.

One would like to know what papers disappeared in the robbery of our church coffer here mentioned. They might, perhaps, have helped us to clearer knowledge of this business.

How, with such an answer as is indicated above, the case could go on for three years, and end, as it did, adversely to Walton, it is difficult to understand. We must conclude there were weak points in the conduct either of the parish or of Walton with which we are not acquainted. The latter has left a rather pathetic record in the shape of one of his bills of charges, which runs thus :—

The charges of Willm Walton towchinge the informacon
made ageynste hym in the eschequer Teris Michis Anno
xviii Elizabethe Regine.

Imprimis for the Warden of the ffleete his ffee	ij^s iiij^d
Itm for the Atturneys ffee	iij^s iiij^d
Itm for recordinge his appurance	iiij^d
Itm for his Baile wth suerties	ij^s viij^d
Itm for a copie of the Declaracon	vi^d
Itm for the counsellors ffee	x^s
Itm for the order of the courte	ij^s
Itm given to Mr. Eaton my Lorde chiefe Baron his man for his advyse	x^s
Itm to Wr Bothe for solicitinge the said matter	ij^s
Sum total	xxxiij^s ij^d

Whych I have lane uppon myne one charge when I wase
at London iij wekes & iij days.

And with this record of his ineffectual though
liberal fee to "My Lorde chiefe Baron his man"
William Walton disappears from the suit, but only to
reappear again presently in another capacity. It is to
be feared that the parish left him to bear on his own
shoulders so much of the burden of costs that he was
impoverished, for when we next meet with him he
appears in the humble capacity of hirer of a parish
cow.

The churchwardens here, as in many other parishes
at that time, kept cows on behalf of the parish, and
let them out at low rentals to poor parishioners.
There have survived three copies of agreements
which illustrate rather quaintly this practice, so long
discontinued and forgotten. I do not know if the
text of such an agreement showing the nature of

HIRE OF PARISH COW

AGREEMENT BETWEEN THE CHURCHWARDENS OF LAPWORTH AND WILLIAM WALTON, 1580

the transaction has been elsewhere printed or preserved.[1]

This is the one, *in extenso*, to which William Walton was a party in 22 Elizabeth (1580) :—

Noverint universi per presentes me Will'us Walton de Lapworthe in Com' Warr' yoman teneri et firmiter obligari Thome Slye et Thome Mountforde in quinque marcis bone et legalis moneti Anglie solvend' eisdem Thome Slye et Thome Mountforde aut eor' alter' executor' vel assign' suis Ad quam soluc'onem bene et fideliter faciend' obligo me hered' executor' et administrator' meos firmiter per presentes Sigillo meo sigillat' Dat' tricesimo die Marcij anno regni d'ne Elizabethe dei gratia Anglie franc' et hib'n Regine fidei defens' &c. vicesimo sc'do

The condic'on of this obligac'on is suche that whereas the above named Thomas Slye & Thomas Mountforde Churchwardens of the p'ish churche of Lapworthe in the countie of Warr' the daye of the date hereof have sett & delivered unto the above bounden Willm Walton one cowe of the price of thirtie three shillings & foure pence parcell of the goods & cattelles of the parishioners of Lapworthe aforesaid to take the proffitts of the same cowe fore one whole yere from the date hereof if the said Willm Walton his executors administrators & assignes doe at any time hereafter within one yere next ensuyinge these presents uppon demande hereof made, aswele paye or cause to be payed unto the saide above named Churchwardens there successors and assignes Churchwardens of the p'ishe church of Lapworthe aforesaid the some of sixtene pence of good english moneye for the hyre of the said cowe to the use of the poore people of the same p'ishe as also doe at the ende & determynac'on of the said yere redeliver ore cause to be redelivered agayne unto the said Churchwardens there successors & assignes the same cowe saffee & sownde ore els doe paye to the said Churchwardens & there assignes at the end of the same yere the some of thyrtye three

---

[1] This one was set out by the writer in *Notes and Queries*, May 5th, 1894. An illustration of it is given opposite.

shillings & forepence of good englyshe money fore the pryse
of the same cowe at the ellecc'on & coyse of the said Churchwardens there successors & assignes without fraude ore gyle
that then this obligac'on shalbe voyde & of none effecte ore
els shall stande & abyde in his full strength & virtue.

(Seal)

Endorsement :—

Sealed & d'd in the p'sence of Wm Bothe Nich^s Slye
Rychard Peper Sampson Shilton Jhon Slye.

It would appear from these numerous witnesses that
the letting of one of the "cattelles" of the parishioners
was a sufficiently important business to require a parish
meeting.   There is nothing to show whether this particular transaction ended in the cow being returned or
paid for.   But on two other bonds similarly worded,
and where in each case the obligation is "in quinque
marcis," there is a footnote, added at the end of the
term, "Receaved uppon this obligac'on 33s. 4d. the
price of the Cowe and for the hyre of the cowe xvi^d"
(in the one case), and in the other case "xx^d."   While
the value of the cow, therefore, is expressed to be the
same in all cases, the rent seems to have varied,
perhaps according to the means of the hirer, and
4 per cent. in two cases out of the three was deemed
a fair charge.

It will be seen that while the bond is taken for five
marks (£3 6s. 8d.) the cow may be paid for by one
half the amount, or £1 13s. 4d.   The bond was what
was known as a penal bond, devised so as to give the
churchwardens a firm hold upon the hirer in case of
breach of faith.

The convenience of hiring a good cow on easy

terms by giving security for its value (and 33s. 4d. was doubtless the value of a first-class beast in Queen Elizabeth's day [1]) was probably found to be a very useful form of charity.

The churchwardens seem to have acquired their cows not always by purchase, but sometimes, at any rate, by bequest. One of our later parish documents (about 1615) makes a curious reference to a bequest of this kind. It is the copy of an impeachment by the parishioners of a misbehaving feoffee into whose conduct an inquiry was being made by a commission. In the interest of this subject of the Parish Cow I set out one of its articles, which runs thus :—

William Ashby deceased gave ij kyne to be let after the decease of his heire by y[e] churchwardens at 20[d] a cow by the yere the one 20[d] unto y[e] mending of y[e] heighway betwixt prats pit & the pinfold & y[e] other unto y[e] poore of Lapworth. William Askewe [the feoffee complained of] maried his widow that had these kyne in ano 1595 in Julij

---

[1] As illustrating the value of farming stock in this neighbourhood at the period in question, the following extract, furnished by the kindness of Mr. J. W. Ryland from a document preserved in the Rowington parish chest, is of interest :—

Inventorie of the goods and cattell of Margaret Cryar of the parish of Rowington, late deceased, praysed by Will[m] Saunders, John Reve and Rob[t] Collyns (15 June VI. Edw: VI).

THE CATTELL.

First, v kyne & ij yerelyngs p[i]sed to . . .	iiij[li]
It[m] iij beasts of ij yeres olde	xxx[s]
It[m] a mare and a colt	x[s]
It[m] one weynynge calffe . . .	iij[s] iiij[d]
It[m] two suckynge calves . . .	vi[s] viij[d]
It[m] vj shepe	xij[s]
It[m] v stoare swyne	x[s]
It[m] all the pultre	xx[d]

These prices arrived at by three valuers seem to be much lower than the value set on the Lapworth Parish cow.

since wch time there hath bine no money payed unto the heigeway nor yᵉ poore nor the kyne delivered unto yᵉ church-wardens to be lett unto poore men upon suertie according to the donors will.

This devotion of the proceeds of a cow to the repair of a specific bit of road is interesting. Prat's Pit is, of course, the pool which is known by the same name still. "The pinfold" has been lost to us within quite recent years by enclosure, but we all know where it stood. The piece of road between the two is hardly half a mile in length. No doubt Ashby, living there, had found the inconvenience of foul roads. It will be remembered that Roger Slye in the same way limited the application of his bequest for highways to the road between his house and the church.

How long these cow charities lasted in the parish I cannot tell. The last trace I get of them is, how-ever, about a hundred years later, namely in 1704, when an entry appears in a rent list of the Charity Estates :—

Recᵈ of John Kendall Senʳ for his year's rent for his land and Cow, £2. 8s. 0d.

As the two charges are lumped together we cannot from this entry alone say positively what was the rent of a cow at that time ; but no doubt it had greatly advanced. A year earlier Kendall stands as tenant of land only for £1 10s. The quantity which he held was 3 a. 0 r. 34 p., the average rent of the Charity lands being at that time 10s. an acre. Here we have the literal "three acres and a cow" supplied by the parish for £2 8s. a year. Parish Councils, therefore, have before them an undeniable precedent.

A correspondent of *Notes and Queries* (April 21st, 1894) mentions a case in which it appears by church-wardens' accounts that, in 1711, sheep were let out to poor people in the parish of Preston Candover, Hampshire, at the rate of 4d. each. Another corre-spondent (May 26th, 1894) says that "in the district of West Kirby, Cheshire, the 'Cow Charity' was dispensed up to very recent years." The conditions and methods seem, however, to have been quite different from those shown by the Lapworth agree-ments, being rather in the shape of advances of money, on security, for the buying of cows.

We get an intimation of the rental value of land in the parish in Elizabethan days from a lease dated 1587, by which Thomas Sly and eleven others, sur-vivors of the trust of 1563, grant to Nicholas Sly for twenty-one years a close called "Thachams or Thacchames" for 10s. a year. In 1826 when the Charity Commissioner made his report he called it "Thatham's," but all trace of the old name is since lost and the field is now scheduled as Church Close. The acreage is 2 a. 2 r. 6 p.; the rent was therefore hardly 4s. an acre.

It is curious that, though the Catesby family were, as Lords of the Manor and in other ways, for a long period intimately connected with Lapworth, no member of the family is either witness of or party to any deed of bequest or feoffment that has survived in our parish chest. It is still more curious that in 1894, three hundred years after its own date of

36 Elizabeth (May 1st, 1594), a deed connecting them with such parish trusts should turn up in the hands of a bookseller in Birmingham, having apparently at some distant period been abstracted from our chest. It is a Latin feoffment deed on parchment, which being abridged says :—

To all Christ's faithful people to whom this present writing shall come, William Catisbie of Asbie Legers in the County of Northampton, knight; Thomas Leighe of Stoneley in the Co: of Warwick, knight; Thomas Spencer of Claverdon in the sd Co: of Warw^k, esquire; and Robert Catisbie, son and heir apparent of the aforesaid William, desire health everlasting in the Lord. And know that we . . . in performance of a certain agreement bearing date of this present deed, between us and Robert Lawrence alias Clarke, of Lapworth, yeoman, have enfeoffed and confirmed to him . . .

—lands described at length as being then in the occupation of John Mountford and John Palmer. The names of closes are given as Tounecrofte, Sladefielde, Toppe of the Hill, Middle Fielde, ye olde Fielde, Uppfielde, together with two meadows called Longe Meadowe and Homefielde; a tenement called Myttons, three fields called Smithes-croftes and three pieces of meadow, with six acres of meadow or pasture land existing in Churchfielde, and one acre of land and meadow in a field called Merrells. Many of these names are familiar to us in connection with ancient parish bequests, but others are new and cannot be located with certainty. "Know further," the instrument proceeds,

that we the aforesaid William Catisbie, Thomas, Thomas, and Robert have made and appointed, and by this present writing put in our own place, our beloved in Christ John

Lytton and Thomas Slye as our true and lawful attornies to give full and peaceful possession, etc. etc.

In testimony of which we have appended our seals.

The signatures remain of Sir William Catesby, Sir Thomas Leigh, and Thomas Spencer, but their seals are cut away. In the case of Robert Catesby the signature is cut away with the seal. Probably the desire to possess the autograph of that eminent criminal was the motive for stealing the deed from us, and it is, perhaps, not the only one of our deeds which has disappeared for the same reason.

The instrument bears endorsements (of strangers) witnessing the signatures of Sir William and Robert Catesby, apparently at Ashbie St. Legers, where both father and son were then living, and those of the other two parties, probably at their own residences. The witnesses to the delivery and taking possession are all well-known Lapworth men, feoffees of the united parish trusts. Robert Catesby would be then in his twenty-first year and "Gunpowder Treason" still eleven years distant, and, notwithstanding all traditions connecting Lapworth with that event, there is absolutely nothing in the parish records to suggest his having ever resided here after he had grown up to man's estate.

John Lytton and Thomas Slye, to whom the power of attorney is given, were then respectively rector and churchwarden of Lapworth; and "Robert Lawrence alias Clarke" was the other churchwarden. (He is described with his alias in the Parish Register.)

It is thus clear that this deed is a surrender of a trust in order that it might come under the control

of the larger body of trustees of the parish properties.

In the feoffment deed of the united trust next in
order of date which has survived, namely, 1652, we
find several of the field-names mentioned above.
Many of these names seem to belong to fields which
now form part of what is called the "Drawbridge
Farm," formerly "Milborn Farm," from a tenant
"Armill Milborn" at the beginning of the eighteenth
century. Deeds of Edward III. (1349) give it, or
that part of it at least which lies about the homestead,
the name of "Ponke land."

It is a pity that this Catesby deed should not be in
our chest, but the trustees did not feel justified in
spending money to acquire it, especially as its owner,
despite its mutilation, set a high price upon it.

Robert Catesby, it will be remembered, married
the daughter of Sir Thomas Leigh, who is party
with him to the deed. The Thomas Spencer of
Claverdon, who is also party thereto, lived, no doubt,
in the house called "the Stone house," great part of
which remains at Claverdon, and which had been
built by an earlier Thomas Spencer (son of Sir John
Spencer of Althorp) who had died a few years
before. This is another case of our parish trusts
being held by people of high degree.

Before passing away from Elizabeth's reign we
transcribe a few odds and ends which have reference
to the rates and taxes of the period, and are now
curious.

For instance, the levying of county rates would
seem then to have been done in detail, which would

be difficult in practice now. There is a rescript for the repairing of Barford Bridge which runs thus (bearing no date, but being endorsed in an old hand "temp: Eliz:"):—

To the Constable of the parish of Lapworth.

These are to require you imediatly upone the syght hereof to levie and gather up of the inhabitants of yr p'ishe of Lapworth iiij^s iiij^d so ordered to be gathered in y^r said p'ishe by the Quens highnes Justices within the Com of Warr: for the repayringe of Barford Bridge and upon receypte of the same to make payment thereof to Richard Barret of Ulnall not faylinge hereof as you will aunswere at y^r p'ill.

Bromham Farm	. . 4^d	R^d Grimshawe	. . 2^d
Irelands Farm	. . 4^d	Nich^s Slye	. . 2^d
Humph^y Gower, Gentil .	4^d	John Shotyswell	. 1^d
Wm Ashbie	. . 3^d	John Tafte	. . 2^d
Thos Slye	. . 3^d	Rob: Tayler .	. 1^d
Wm Lathwait .	. 4^d	Rog^r Bate	. 1^d
Wm Walton	. . 2^d	Nich^s Robins .	. 2^d
Thos Mountford	. . 2^d	Wm Bosworth	. 1^d
John Bent	. . 2^d	Thos Fewister	. 2^d
Nich^s Lucett .	. 2^d	John Grene	. 1^d
John Ashbie .	. 1^d	John Jennyns	. 1^d
Wm Byssell	. 1^d	John Mountford	. 1^d
Phil: Barnehurst	. 2^d	Richard Haywoode	. 1^d
			4s. 4d.

The twenty-six assessments here recorded may be taken to have been of the principal householders of the parish at that time, the cottagers not being assessed at all. The rateable value put to some of the same names recurring in the next demand suggests that this Barford Bridge assessment was 1d. in the £.

For the following subsidy it would seem only four parishioners were held liable :—

To the Constable of Lapworth (*1568*).

Thies ar to will and require you and in the Quens M^{aties} name to charge and com'and you to levy and gather all suche somes of money rated and taxed upon the heads of every suche p'son hereunder wryten for the . . . payment of the subsedy granted to her hightnes in her parliament and mak pament thereof to me? at Warr^k the xvi day of March wherefore fayle not as you will answer to the contrary on your apparrell.

      p Richard Griffin. Collector.

Humfrey Gower in terris	.	.	iiij^{li}	.	v^s iiij^d
Thomas Slye in terris	.	.	xl^s	.	ij^s viij^d
Willus Ashbye in bonis	.	.	v^{li}	.	iiij^s ij^d
Willus Latchford in bonis	.	.	v^{li}	.	iiij^s ij^d

The assessment in this case would seem to have been at the rate of 1s. 4d. in the £ on lands, and 10d. in the £ on goods.

Another rescript, dated July 12th, 1568, is as follows :—

To the Constable and inhabytants of Lapworth.

In the Quenes M^{aties} name and by vertu of a warrant to me dyrected this shall be to charge one of you to appere at Warwyke the xxiiijth day of Julie next recommynge there and then to make p'sent payment to me the some of iij^s iiij^d for the provysion of her graces houshold according to and (*sic*) order in that behalf of late taken.

  From Oxhill the xijth day of Julie 1568.

     By Symon Walweyn. Collector.

On January 4th, 1594, there is another levy, of which the acquittance runs thus :—

Receaved the daye & yeare above said of the Constable of Lapworth for the dischardge of the third and foweth ffifteenes and tenthes due within his constabulary granted unto her mātie in the last Sessions of Parliamt the some of £6 os. 4d.   Willm Peyto.

The tax called " fifteenths and tenths " was one which was levied from a very early period, and continued till finally superseded by the Land Tax under William III.

From the time of Grymshawe's suit and Walton's suit, already spoken of, there would seem to have been a period of peace in the parish for about at least one generation.   But in 1615 there were again great convulsions, and the cause, as before, was alleged misconduct in connection with the Charity Trusts.

The parishioners seem at that time to have come to the conclusion that they could and would bear no longer with the iniquities of one William Askew, a feoffee of the day, who had the whole parish under his thumb.   On petition there appears to have been some Commission appointed and sent down to inquire into certain facts that were alleged, and there has survived, in very imperfect condition, a curious document in which the parishioners put before this Commission the charges which they made.   These occupy seven sheets of paper, each more or less mutilated and mouse-eaten.   There are indications also that three other sheets are missing.   What are left preserve for us about thirty-five different articles of impeachment against this William Askew and others implicated with him, and to each of these charges are appended the signatures of those parishioners who undertook to make good the same. Some are signed by half a dozen, some by three or four, some by two or only one. It will be seen that they supply curious and interesting information on conditions and customs which have long since passed away. The paper has never seen the light of publicity before, but in Thomas's *Dugdale* one item is mentioned, that namely which refers to the churchyard cross, and to this Dr. Thomas adds a note: "ex cartis & relatione Reverendi doctissimiq: viri Edv: Welchman R. de Lapworth." There is no doubt this is the MS. which Dr. Welchman, who was Rector of Lapworth in Thomas's day, showed him.

On the back of the document appears the endorsement (in writing of much later date) "Statements by Wm Askew and o^{rs}"—a not very illuminating description of the contents. There is no heading or anything to indicate the status of the body for whom the impeachment was prepared. It plunges at once *in medias res* :—

1. Imprimis George Ashbie was Lycensed by the king as apearreth by a graunt under the great seale of england to purchase & to endow the church of Lapworth wthall Lands worth fower markes a yeare wch Lands so purchased the sayd George gave unto the parson of Lapworth then being and the churchwardens then being & their successors ye parson and churchwardens of Lapworth for ever to be lett & sett by them and their successors to the benefit of the church in such manner as by the will and gift of the said donor apeareth

    William Lathem   Thomas Shotswell   Francis Robbins
    John Price   William Askewe   Richard Booth

2. We think their feofment is not good because it was made
   w^{t}hout the consent of the parson & some of the better
   sort of the towne besydes and when they had made
   this new feofement they put out by William Askewes
   meanes such of the old feofees as they thought good
   & put in Askewes sonnes & sonnes in law wch he can
   over rule by wch meanes the towne land is like to be
   lost & the woodes destroyd & the church stoock mis-
   imployed wch we humbly crave may be redrest as to
   your wisdomes shalbe thought fit & meet

   Roger Smith   William Lathem   Edward Price

3. In a tenement that one Glover howldeth there is a percell
   of ground taken away from his house and layd unto y^e
   land of William Ashbie & Glover payeth the whole
   rent & Asbie nothing for this xv or xvi yeares it hath
   bine so houlden & would have bine lost if this commission had not com downe. this Ashbie is a feofee
   & Askewes sonn in lawe /   William Lathem

4. William Ashby houldeth a cloase of the parrishes worth
   . . . a yeare for fyfteen shillings a yeare & had also . . .

5. William Askewe did carry away out of the churchyard all
   the stones of a verie fayer cross built wth arches wherin
   a dosen men might have stood dry if occation had
   served and was a verie convenient cross for a preacher
   wich stones William Askewe did groundsill his house
   with /   William Lathem

6. William Askewe hath taken away from a tenement wch
   Edmond Sly houldeth a peece of ground wch tenement
   is of the gift of George Asbie above mentioned & is to
   be lett by the parson & churchwardens & Askewe
   houldeth it wthout rent paying therfor, & Sly payeth y^e
   whole rent notwthstanding moreover William Askewe
   houldeth a peece of ground in a cloase that is cauled
   Merrill geven unto the clarke to find rushishes for the
   church wthout rent paying also /   William Lathem

7. Williā Askewe · did fell five tymber treese of Georg
   Shotswells tenement being church land to build a
   house wherin John Palmer now dwelleth being Askewes
   own land /   Gregorie ffowler   John Ashbie

8. When the churchfeeld was encloased ther was certaine
land of Shotswells tenement encloased iiij dayes woorke
at the least of errable ground ; since wich incloasuer
William Askewe & Richard Mountford have alotted
him ij dayes work & a halfe in lew of fower dayes
work & have deteined it this xvi yeares when this
ground was allotted Shotswell John Rawson found
fault wth them & said it was not sufficient Askewe
& Mountford mad answer saying it so faulleth out now
he both must & shalbe contented for he must have no
more & yet he hath nothing abated of his rent /

William Lathem

9. William Askewe sould an acker of yᵉ sayd land unto
John Rawson & entered into bond of fowertie pound
for warranty & quyet enioying of the same as his own
land for ever Rawson being then a feofee him selfe . . .

10. William Askewe did cause to be felled of Shotswells
ground since this matter was in question twentie & six
treese notwithstanding he was discharged by Shotswell
wth the consent of the parson and churchwarden all
wch trees he caused to be feched away & converted
them to what uses he thought good himselfe yᵉ land &
trees belonging unto the church /   William Lathem

11. William Askewe hath taken in unto his own land a
meare belonging unto Shotswell's land about iij or
fower yardes in breadth wch meare lyeth in church-
feelds & is dicht & quickset into Askewe's land & hath
held it so this 10 yeres /   William Lathem

12. William Askewe hath taken into his own land & unto
his own use & possession certaine land belonging unto
the church & long hath held it wthout rent paying
therefore as we thinke & now it is put over unto his
sonn Robert Askewe who houldeth it in the sam kind
& in a ground caulled Merrill & an other cauled Flame
feeld all the woodes are felled worth as he that did
faule them (sayeth) five or six pounds & William
Askew hath stoked down yᵉ meares & bounds of yᵉ
church grounds & lands so that it cannot be discerned
from his own land & will in time be lost if redrese be
not had /   Umber Sley

13. William Ashby deceased gave ij kyne to be let after the decease of his heire by ye churchwardens at 20^d a cow by the yere the one 20^d unto ye mending of ye heighway betwixt prats pit & the pinfold & ye other unto ye poore of Lapworth. William Askewe maried his widow that· had these kyne in ano 1595 in Julij since wch time there hath bine no money payed unto the heigeway nor ye poore nor the kyne delivered unto ye churchwardens to be lett unto poore men upon suertie according to the donors will   William Lathem

14. William Askew & John Rawson did com into the house of Shotswell & did take . . . & from a sawpitt . . .

15. William Askewe did take in unto his own land a lane that shoots from the church feilds unto the churchend & stocked downe ye hedges and meares & bankes & hath layd them levell with his own ground & held it for 16 yeres at least & since this commission it is layed open againe / [1]

16. William Askewe caused halfe a poore mans land to be taken from him ; his name is Glover that had his land taken from him wch land did ly in ollfeeld it hath bine deteined this 16 yeres we humbly desyer it may be restored & that it may (be) knowen by what rent Askew houlds it / one Sly gave this land unto ye parrish
William Lathem

17. William Askew hath taken a peece of ground from ye tenement wch Edmund Sly houldeth & is ye church land & of Asbies gift & layed it unto his ground called Stickmans wch we desyer may be restored & that it may be known by what rent Askew houlds it /
William Askewe [2]

18. William Askew took away from ye tenement Bauld^n Short doth hould certen ground & layed it unto Cox his tenement being Askewes frehould & another percell & layed it unto his sonn Robert Askewes land in Merrill both wch we desyer may be vewed vallewed & restorred & restitution for ye wronges /   William Lathem

[1] No signature to this charge.

[2] This William Askewe is one of the six persons who append their signatures to the first of the charges brought against his namesake.

19. William Askew took from Weales tenement certen
    ground lying in flamefeild now in the occupation of
    Robert Askewe in wch lands wthhoulding Askew
    wthstandeth the whole parrish it is thought to be worth
    fowertie ij shillings viij^d p ann We do entreat it may
    be made known how long it hath binn so held & by
    what rent /   William Lathem

20. There was twentie or sixteene poundes taken for a fine
    of . . . his land in ano 1588 & two other great fines
    taken . . . was spent by . . . in defraying their . . .

21. William Askew did take a secreat brybe of old Cook as
    he reported for to help hime unto Symmonds his land
    besyds the finne he gave unto the ffeoffees we desyer
    to know how much it was / [1]

22. Richard Mountford being churchwarden did forceably
    enter upon the ground wich Shotswell held & did fell
    cut & carry away many kyds of gorse & j load of
    underwood of hasell & thorns & John Raws^n did at
    ann other tyme take away one other load of the like
    underwood wch we crave may be redrest /
                                   William Lathem

23. John Leuset by Askewes consent as he sayd did fell a
    goodly tree of Shotswells living worth five nobles at
    the least wch we desyer he may make restitution for /
                                   William Seale

24. John Leuset the same yere did fell out of a ground thats
    cauled St Mary grove being psell of Shotswells living
    five treese to the great defaceing of ye church land &
    ye church tymber when need shall requier /
                                   William Seale

25. There was faullen out of a ground cauled Thachams in y^e
    occupation of Peter Sly & is psell of Shotswells tene-
    ment about twentie trees well grown we desyer to know
    how they were imployed   William Lathem

26. John Bent being constable caused to be felled & carryed
    away five trees of Shottswells ground we desyer to know
    how they were imployed /   William Lathem

---

[1] No signature to this charge.

27. 28. 29. (Missing.)

30. There is vi^s viij^d given for ever to be bestowed on ye mending of the heighwayes yerely the one moyity to be bestowed on the way betwixt Hockley Heath & Kingswood & ye other moyity upon ye way toward Lapworth park corner /   William Lathem

31. There are divers others wch have bine benefactors unto this church & parrish wch we know not of; both in land & money & wee entreat your warships that they wch now are or heretofore have bine feoffees may be examined upon their othes whether they have imployed ye same according to the donors will yea or no & that they may shew their bills (?) for the same /[1]

32. Further we desyer your worships that ower parrish land may not remayne & be in these ffeoffees hands or occupation nor of William Askewe for if it be wee shall have ye woods utterly destroyd wich is in efect already don and that you will displace these ffeoffees & place better for worse we cannot have /[1]

33. Further we desyer to know what ffynnes & rennts they or any of them have receaved this thirtie yeres & how much & how ye same hath bine bestowed & imployed /[1]

34. Further we desyer that ower parrish rents & stooke may not be and remayne in ye churchwardens hands to be wasted & consumed as heretofore it hath bine but that ye parrish rents . . . be receaved by the fefes successively at . . . given by them to ye churchw . . . & by them yerely . . .

Further we desyer that all the tenants wch hould the parrish lands now or have don heretofore may be examined what ffynnes they & every of them have geven in money unto these ffeffees that now are or heretofore have bine & unto whom & how much for everie several fyne or unto any churchwarden now being or that heretofor hath bine & who rec[eaved] the same & how much, and whether any of them have geven any brybe in money or moneyes worth or in lending of money to obtain their good wills & how much & who received the same /

---

[1] No signatures to charges Nos. 31, 32, and 33.

Further we desyer your worships that the booke of the
church accounts may be looked into & cast up that it
may apeare how much ye church & parrish is wronged
by the feefes & churchwardens that now are or heretofore have bine for this thirtie yeres / it is sayd that
Robert Clarke in his accoumpt this yere past being
churchwarddn wrongd the parrish three pounds at y^e
least what amends is made we know not, for this many
yeres all their accoumpts are mad emongest Askews̄
allyes so that ye rest of the parrish may look on but not
know what is don / & moreover Robert Clarke being
churchwarden did lette work of ye church unto poore
men at hard ratts & in his accoumpt put down more
than ye poor labourers had & [thus] it hath bine from
tyme to tyme /   john West

These are certainly grave charges, and there are
many phrases and passages in the document which
refer to conditions that we can hardly realise now or
understand. The "four days work at the least of errable
ground" which was taken from Shotswell, and for
which he had back only "two days work and a half,"
conveys no intelligible idea to us, but there is no doubt
"a day's work of land" was then a well-defined
measure of quantity, having relation, when arable land
was in question, to the system of co-operative plough-
ing which was then general, and under which a man
furnished his quota of oxen to the parish team of eight,
for they always ploughed with eight oxen, the day's
work being brought into the parish account on some
well-understood basis. It is of interest in connection
with this subject to find that we have on our Tithe
Map as field-names at this day—

	a.	r.	p.
No. 72. Four days work (arable	3	3	32)
„ 73. Eight days work (arable	9	2	7)

from which we might infer that a day's work of arable land was about an acre, varying, doubtless, according to the quality of the land. Then there is the close called "Merrill" which the clerk held rent free on condition that he found "rushishes for the church." It was the custom then at the principal feasts to strew the floors of the churches with straw or with green rushes, according to the season of the year.

The charges of felonious cutting down of large quantities of trees and woods point to the parish having then been much more thickly wooded than it is now. At that time, the "Forest of Arden" was, doubtless, something more than a name.

The "two kyne" which were left to the parish, and which Askew intercepted by marrying the widow to whom they had fallen, have been already referred to in connection with the cow-letting agreements (p. 109).

We have further instances of bequests for repairs of roads being confined to specific portions of such roads.

What we find it hardest to forgive William Askew of all the offences charged against him is the pulling down and carrying away from the churchyard of the "verie fayer cross built with arches." It stood, no doubt, south of the church porch, and the expression that it was "a verie convenient cross for a preacher" suggests that it was occasionally so used, and that in fine summer-time the parson may sometimes have delivered his sermon there in the open air. Such crosses were often of very great antiquity. Some writers believe that they were often older than the churches themselves, marking preaching places which existed before the parish had a resident priest.

There is nothing to show what was the result of these complaints, or whether the Commissioners did anything. But it is probable that the inquiry had as an effect the helping to bring the Charity Trusts under better government.

Towards the end of Elizabeth's reign, despite the progress made towards unification, there seem to have been still about half a dozen separate trusts in the parish. Probably, however, the principle had been established that, as these minor trusts died out, they should merge in the general trust of the parish estates; but it is not till the time of the Commonwealth that we find this had been completely effected.

It has always been a charge against the trustees of charities who worked under no practical control that they showed favouritism or were guilty of corruption by granting long leases for inadequate rents, or (as it was suspected) for so-called fines which were often omitted to be brought into account; and it has been seen that this feeling found strong expression among the indictments formulated by the parishioners in 1615.

These long leases were quite the rule in Lapworth. In 1605 the then feoffees grant a lease of a messuage and lands, which we can identify as comprising about 45 acres, for ninety-nine years or three lives, namely, "to Thos Shatswell or Jane his wife or Thomas his son if they or any of them soe longe shall lyve," at the annual rental of £10 a year; and there is no mention of any fine or money consideration for the granting. But there is no reason to suppose any corruption in this case, and we may assume that the rent (about 4s. 6d. an acre) was near the ordinary rent. "Thachames" we saw was let for about 4s. an acre.

In 1615 a lease was granted for a similar term to William Weston the elder of Banbury, tallow chandler, and his heirs absolutely, without restriction to any lives, of a messuage or tenement therein described, at 50s. a year, the consideration being that he has paid to the feoffees "the sum of Ten shillings of good and lawful monie of England towards the repayringe, new casting and mending of the Tennor or greate Bell of Lapworth, being broken." This is the first distinct mention we have of the Banbury house, which still belongs to the Charity Estates and now lets for £35 a year. By whom it was bequeathed to the parish there is nothing to show, but there is no doubt it belonged to us in the fifteenth century (see p. 69). This lease appears, however, to have been broken, as the feoffees are found dealing with the property again in 1653 at a lower rent.

In 1622, again, a lease for two lives or "fourscore and nineteen years" is granted of what must have been a considerable holding, as it is described as a messuage or tenement called Ilens, with its "orchyard" and garden, "three parcells of ground adjoining the said messuage, and one Broume close lying within Flamesfielde, with a slinge and footinge along a ground called St. Marie Grove, and all houses, barnes, edifices and buildings thereunto belonging." And all this is let on lease nominally for ninety-nine years, but really for two lives of husband and wife, for the annual rent of £2 13s. 4d., payable in equal portions half-yearly to the feoffees or to any six, five, four, three, or two of them. This refers, I think, to property that has been lost to the parish.

There is a long break in the series of feoffment deeds. None exist between that of 1563 and 1652, though doubtless the lineal succession was duly kept up. In the latter year the feoffees had been again reduced to a point perilously near extinction, namely two persons, William Ingram, Gent: and John Smith, yoman : both of Nuthurst. They created a new trust of eleven persons, amongst whom their own names are not included. At the head of this trust were Benjamin Lovell of Lapworth, clerk, and Salathiel Lovell, Gent:, his younger son. The father was at this time what is usually called the "intruded Rector" of Lapworth, having taken the place of John Doughty, Rector, a strong Royalist, who had been turned out of the living at an early period of the troubles which preceded the Commonwealth. We shall have something more to say of these Lovells when we come to deal more particularly with the Parish Register (pp. 159–62).

There is evidence that Benjamin Lovell made himself active in parish affairs, and was a man of capacity, but he seems to have been unable to prevent his co-trustees from bringing themselves into discredit almost equal to that of any of their predecessors. Such bodies, one after another, appear to have displayed a wonderful capacity for getting themselves into hot water, and when the Protectorate had come to an end, and Lovell had made way for a new and legitimate rector, the parish estates were apparently found to be

in such disorder again that yet another Commission
was needed to order them aright.

In October, 1668, or, as the documents call it, "the
20th year of the reign of King Charles the second"
(counting from the day on which his father was beheaded), this Commission sat at Warwick, the members being Sir Robert Holt, Bar^t; Sir Henry Pucker-
ing, al^s Newton, Bar^t; Ja^s Prescott, Esq; Sir Chas
Lee; Thos Rawlins & Wm Purefoy, Esq^s. They were
styled "Commissioners for the due execution of a
certain Statute of the 43rd Elizabeth," entitled "An
Act to redress the misemployment of lands, goods and
stocks of money heretofore given to Charitable uses,"
and they conducted their inquiry with a jury of fifteen
persons.

They found, after long inquiry and examination of
witnesses :—

1. That Benjamin Lovell and the others had never
   been enfeoffed in proper form and that all
   their proceedings were invalid. (The Commission always speaks of their enfeoffment as
   being under a deed of 1649, and of the feoffees
   as fifteen in number; but the deed itself still
   exists, and is dated 1652, and enfeoffs eleven
   persons only.)

2. That all the surviving members of the trust of
   1649 had been either active or passive in misemployment of the parish funds, or else had
   not troubled themselves at all about their
   trust, and (in the Commissioners' words)
   forasmuch as it appeareth unto us that there is not a
   convenient number of persons now living within the

K

parish of Lapworth to be made new feoffees other
than the said persons who have as aforesaid neglected,
misemployed or misgoverned the trust reposed in
them: and for that it doth not appear to us that
such feoffees ought necessarily to be men of the
parish of Lapworth, according to the true intent of
the legators and donors, Therefore, We do hereby
order and adjudge and decree that the said pre-
tended indenture of 1649 and all grants, leases, &c.
made under the same shall be absolutely null and
void.

And that the said Benjn Lovell (and others) being
the survivors of the so-called trust of 1649 or any
two or more of them shall before the first day of
August next ensuing convey and confirm (the parish
lands, &c.) unto the following, namely,—

Foulke Greville of War-
wick, Esq:
Sir Robt Holt of Aston,
Bart:
Thos Archer of Tanworth,
Esq:
John Fetherston of Pack-
wood, Esq:
Thos Fetherston of Pack-
wood, Esq:

Edwd Feild of King's
Norton, Gent
Robt Charnock of Good-
rest Lodge, Gent
john Powell of Lap-
worth, Clerk

This meant that, whereas from time immemorial
the parish lands had been managed by parishioners
and freeholders of Lapworth, the new trust was made
up entirely of landed gentry of the neighbourhood
and of the rector of the parish for the time being.
Except the latter, the only one named who had any
direct interest in the parish was Sir Robert Holt, who
was Lord of the Manor.

The decree was that all deeds and papers should be

forthwith delivered over to the said Foulke Greville and the others ; that all tenants should before the said first day of August deliver up their leases and tenancies to the new feoffees, who might in their discretion grant new leases or refuse them.

Further, a practically new scheme of administration was set out, the effect of which was that the actual management of the parish properties was to be left in the hands of the Rector, Churchwardens, Overseers, and Surveyors of Highways, who should once a year at Whitsuntide submit and render full accounts to the feoffees.   In other words, whereas the feoffees had hitherto been accountable to the parish, the parish should henceforth be accountable to the feoffees : on the face of it a very sagacious and excellent change— from the point of view of the feoffees.

Thomas Slye, one of the survivors of the condemned trust, was adjudged to pay to the new trust for moneys misemployed by him the sum of £80 8s. 4d.; and John Robbins, another of the survivors, was similarly amerced in £48 14s. 9d.   These were, of course, large sums at the time.

The parish, at whose instance the Commission had been set in motion, would appear, therefore, in this decree, to have got a deal more than they had asked for or desired.   It was no part of their object to be overruled by outsiders in the administration of their property.   But they, as well as the survivors of the old trust, seem to have been equal to the occasion. Benjamin Lovell, and Salathiel his son, and others had gone away ; and no survivors were left in the parish but Thomas Slye and John Robbins, who simply did nothing whatever. None of the notables were ever enfeoffed at all in the Lapworth properties, and Thomas Slye, indeed, seems to have waxed rampant in his defiance of authority, whereof there remains a curious record, thus :—

In 1653 the Lovell trust had granted a fifty years' lease of the Banbury house and toft to one Matthew Cave, brasier. In 1677 this had still twenty-six years to run, and we find Thomas Slye (describing himself as the last survivor of the Lovell trust, which seems to have been incorrect) granting to the said Matthew, with consent of the freeholders and inhabitants of Lapworth, a new lease for ninety-nine years at 30s. a year, to commence from the expiry of the lease then running, which would have carried the tenancy on to 1802. The lease is said to be granted in consideration of the said Matthew Cave having paid to the said Thomas Slye the sum of £16 for the repair of the parish church of Lapworth. Slye himself would appear, however, to have had some misgiving that he was thus carrying matters with too high a hand, and so we find on the back of the lease this endorsement in his own hand :—

if the fefees her after question this lease bee cause it was granted by Mr Slye hee beinge the last surviving fefee then answer them that thayr own leses or some of them (were) granted by him a lone & sum by to of the fefees, as William Ingram for on & Isak Green & Clemment Green.

Three months later (August 31, 1677) Slye, who had perhaps described himself as the last survivor because the others had gone away or otherwise become disqualified, joins with Benjamin Lovell, of Bow Brick-hill in the Co: of Bucks, clerk; Salathiel Lovell of Northampton, Esq.; John Askew of Barkswell, and John Robbins of Lapworth in enfeoffing William Ingram, John Camden and ten others, all of them "inhabitants within the parish of Lapworth," in possession of the parish charity estates, and so ended the attempt to rule the parish *ab extra*. The Commission seems to have been better able to promulgate decrees than to enforce them.

Slye's proceedings in regard to the Banbury lease were the cause of immediate bickerings between him and the new trust, which were only terminated in 1683 by a reference to the arbitration of "Joseph Carter, of Packwood, clerk," who amerced Thomas Slye in £16 compensation to the Banbury tenant and ordered the lease to be given up to the feoffees, thereby accounting for its existence in our parish chest. The award suggests very strongly that the £16 paid for the repair of the church had never found its way any further than Thomas Slye's own pocket.

In 1688 Cave's widow stands on a rent list as occupying the house and toft at 26s. a year, the rent having been reduced, perhaps in consideration of the cancelling of the lease granted by Slye.

In most parish histories the "Churchwardens' Accounts" furnish entries of interest. In Lapworth parish no such accounts have come down to us, and, indeed, even to the present time none have been kept

in any separate book. The reason for this is that,
from time immemorial, the normal church expenses
have been borne by the funds of the Charity Feoffees
and the record of them has merged in those of that
body.

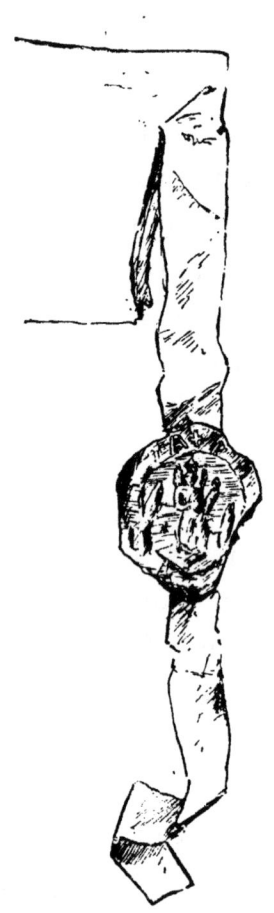

Seal of deed, 1344
Geoffrey atte Heth, junior, to John in the Lone

p. 41

THE PARISH REGISTERS

The simple Annals of my Parish poor;
What Infant-members in my flock appear,
What pairs I bless'd in the departed year;
And who, of Old or Young, or Nymphs or Swains,
Are lost to Life, its pleasures and its pains.

CRABBE

CHAPTER IV

THE PARISH REGISTERS

OF these there are thirteen volumes, the contents of which are :—

Vol.			
1.	1561 to 1749.	Baptisms, Marriages, and Burials.	
2.	{ 1750 to 1754.	„ „ „	
	{ 1754 to 1810.	Baptisms and Burials.	
3.	1754 to 1812.	Marriages.	
4.	1754 to 1794.	Banns of Marriage (neglected apparently from 1794 to 1823).	
5.	1811 to 1812.	Baptisms and Burials.	
6.	1813 to 1853.	Baptisms.	
7.	1814 to 1837.	Marriages.	
8.	1813 to 1870.	Burials.	
9.	1854 to present time.	Baptisms.	
10.	1870 to present time.	Burials.	
11.	1823 to 1895.	Banns of Marriage.	
12.	1837 to present time.	Marriages.	
13.	1895 to present time.	Banns of Marriage.	

Parish Registers were first instituted in England by an injunction of King Henry VIII., published by his Vicar-General, Thomas Cromwell, in 1538. Mr. Chester Waters in his learned and interesting book entitled *Parish Registers in England: their History and Contents*, quotes from the injunction :—

The curate of every parish shall keep one book or register, which book he shall every Sunday take forth, and in the

presence of the churchwardens, or one of them, write and record in the same all the weddings, christ'nings and burials
made the whole week before; and for every time that the
same shall be omitted, shall forfeit to the said church iij^s·iiij^d.

In many parishes the order was received with dis-
like and suspicion, and the clergy neglected to comply
with it.   Only a small proportion of the registers now
in existence go back to 1538.   Our own begins with
1561.

PARISH REGISTERS, VOL. I., 1561–1749.

The first volume[1] covers the period from 1561 to
the end of 1749.   From 1561 to 1600 all the entries
have been made at one time, being copied from some
earlier record.   In this respect nearly all registers
of the period are the same.   At first they had been

---

[1] A word or two may be permitted as to its externals.   It is a parchment book, in its original vellum binding.   Size 12 in. × 6 in.   It has had
two pairs of leather thongs for tying, but only a portion of one thong remains.   It contains 113 leaves, written on both sides, of which two at
the beginning and three at the end are, or were meant to be, fly-leaves.
Some of these have been used as a scribbling ground for the exhibition
of penmanship, and "John Wight, Schoolmaster, 1662," has sent down
his name to us in this way.   On the *verso* of the first leaf is written in a
well-formed hand—

Registrum Ecclesiæ Parochialis de Lapworth,

and above this, and again below it, the rather trite lines :—

Sic transit Gloria mundi
Life is a jest and all things show it,
I thought so once and now I know it,

the couplet being by Gay.   Page iv is filled with entries of baptisms and
marriages of 1749, the volume having at that time got filled up, and a
new one not been provided, so that the year last named overflowed first
on to a little blank space under 1588, and thence to the beginning of the
volume.   The fly-leaves at the end, like those at the beginning, have
also been used as scribbling ground, and one rector has made memoranda there of interest.   As to condition, it is rather dilapidated; but
there is no reason to think that any portion of it has been lost.

kept in paper books, often of a very cheap and flimsy kind.[1] This defect had been amended by an ordinance of 1597 that "every parish shall provide itself with a parchment book, in which the entries from the old paper books shall be fairly and legibly transcribed."

The Register proper begins with the heading :—

Año Dm 1561
Tempo : Henrici Sadler rectoris de Lapworth

and it is remarkable that this first line should furnish an addition to Dugdale, as, in the list of Lapworth rectors given by him, he omits this name. Neither is it supplied in Dr. Thomas's edition, nor in any other list which I have seen.

Henry Sadler has left no further trace of himself in our register or in any other of the parish records, and his name does not occur in Foster's *Alumni Oxonienses*. He appears to have resigned the living in 1584.

The first entry in the register is—

> Dyonysius Gaston sonne of Henry Gaston was baptized the first daie of September in the yeare aforesaid.
>
> [This full style of entry continues to be maintained to the end of the century. The name of Gaston recurs frequently for many years, but dies out before the seventeenth century.]

The first page has also—

1561. Nicholas Slye and Jone Mountford (Marr^d Jany 18th)
> [These Slyes and Mountfords were, as we know by older parish papers, important families here.]

The entries for this year are five baptisms, one burial, and one marriage.

---

[1] Mr. Chester Waters says : "The Churchwardens' accounts of St. Margaret's, Westminster, contain this entry, '1538. paid for a book to registre in the names of buryals, weddings, and christ'nings, 2^d.'"

1562. [Has six entries, all baptisms.]

1563. John Baker of Bromihille Farm (Bur^d Decr 7th)
[This would be the farm attached to Brome Hall.]

1564. William Shorte and Alice Shackespere (Marr^d Oct. 15th)
[Our first entry of a Shakespeare.]

1566. John Shotswell sone of Jone Shotswell (Bap^t. Jany 6th) being a bastard.

1567. John Tofte and Eliz: Wian al^s Walker (Marr^d July 14)

1568. Richd Darlison and Alice Wyan al^s Walker (Marr^d June 20)

1569. Willm Heynes and Margerie Walker al^s Wyan (Marr^d Oct 26)

[These were evidently three sisters called indifferently Wian, Wyan, or Walker. The prevalence of such aliases in old registers is well known, but not clearly explained.]

1568. Averye Hopkins al^s Pyp (Bur^d July 14)

1571. Margaret the d^r of Richd Robarts and Alice Tyler. (Bapt. Jan. 6th) being a bastard.

[It seems to have been the rule always to record illegitimacy and to give where possible the name of the reputed father.]

1574. Ursula the daughter of Edmund Catesbie was baptized the seaventh daie of July in the yere aforesaid.

1577. Mr. Richard Catesbie was baptized the one and twenty daie of Julye in the yere aforesaid.

[These are the only Catesby entries that appear in our register. Biographical notices of Robert Catesby, the conspirator, speak of him as "born at Bushwood Hall, Lapworth, in 1573," but, his father Sir William Catesby being a Catholic, the son was not likely to be baptised in our church. Of the Edmund Catesbie named in the first of these entries there remains a Deed Poll with his signature, dated 1578, relating to lands in Lapworth and Nuthurst, but the document is defective and does not tell us where he lived. The second entry, namely, of the baptism of "Mr. Richard Catesbie" in 1577, is a singular exception to the almost invariable practice of giving the parents' names. The prefixing of

" Mr." to the names of infants of the more important people was not unusual in registers of the period. But in this case I am of opinion that the record is of an adult baptism. Dugdale in the Catesby pedigree (under Lapworth) has (1578)

Ric. Catesby æt 42. an 20. Eliz:

Probably this is the Richard of our entry, and he and Edmund were brothers, sons of Sir Richard Catesby, who died 7 Edward VI. and has been mentioned in these records before as the first husband of Lady Lucy. Both Edmund and Richard are parties with Sir Thomas Lucy to a parish trust before noticed.[1] They may not unlikely both have been recusants.]

From 1561 to 1564 baptisms, marriages, and burials are mixed. From 1564 to 1574 we get first all baptisms within that period; then a similar ten years of marriages, followed by the same ten years of burials. This suggests that they had been kept in separate books, or separate divisions of the old paper book. With 1575 the register reverts to the system of mixed entries.

1573. Clement ffisher and Margaret Shorte (Marr^d May 2nd)

1577. Willm Dickenson, sonne of Thomas Dickenson alias Fewster (Bap^t Mch 22)

John Alderman of Draygton & Margarett Lucett (Marr^d Jan. 17)

1578. Ulpian ffulwell of the p'ishe of Nawnton within the countie of Glocester & Marie Whorewood of this p'ishe (Marr^d April 14)

John ffisher the sone of Clement ffisher (Bapt. May —)

[The Lucetts were one of the principal families of Nuthurst. This Clement Fisher is not unlikely to have been of the Packington family, with whom that Christian name was a favourite. A Clement Fisher was one of the bearers of the coffin of the Earl of Leicester when he was buried at

[1] See p. 95.

Warwick in 1588. Clement Fisher, Esquire, is mentioned as member of a Special Commission sitting at Warwick in 1603–4.[1] Another (Sir) Clement was prominently concerned in the escape of Charles II. after Worcester fight, and the late Tom Burgess in his *Historic Warwickshire* is satisfied that the escape would take the fugitive uncrowned King through our lanes and past our church until he struck the Birmingham road at Lapworth Bridge. If so, it seems to be the only royal visit our parish can claim.]

For the first two decades contained in the register the entries are as follows :—[2]

	Baptisms.	Marriages.	Burials.
1561 to 1570	90	19	44
1571 to 1580	86	18	48

1580. Humphrey Gower, gen^t (Bur^d Decr 9th)

[He had been an active man in the village trusts, etc., and his name appears in the suit against Thomas Grimshaw which is described at length earlier.]

1584. [In this year Dugdale (Dr. Thomas's edition) has the entry in his list of Rectors: "Joh: Litton. Cler. 30 Oct 1584. v. p. res."]

It is only by this entry that we know that at this time Henry Sadler resigned the living. The register itself gives no indication of the change.

Foster's *Alumni Oxonienses* says :—

John Litton. B.A. from Merton College 9 March 1579–80. M.A. 4 July 1582. Rector of Lapworth, co. Warwick, 1584.

Perhaps consequent on this resignation, and on John Litton not having come to reside here immediately thereafter, the entries of the next year or two indicate that the register was neglected. In

---

[1] *Records of Rowington*, by J. W. Ryland.
[2] See also pp. 171 and 190.

many instances Christian names, and even surnames, are omitted, thus—

1584. Willm Grimshawe and Alice ... his wyffe (Marr^d April 7)
Thomas Grimshawe and Alice . . . (Marr^d May 4)
Richard Grimshawe, being lunatic (Bur^d Oct 31)

1585. Twoo infants of Wm Grimshawe (Bur^d Feb 7) not baptised.
Auphilus Thacker (Bapt^d)
One infant of Willm Cooke, dead born (Bur^d Mch 20)
Richard . . . (was Bapt^d April 18)
Twoo poore women were buried the sixt daie of Julie.

1586. Xxofer Dracke and Margarie Bawdwyne (Marr^d April 20)
The wyffe of Thos Durie (Bur^d Nov 13)
The daughter of Raphe Seale (Bur^d Nov 20)

1587. The wyffe of Xxofer Dracke (Bur^d Mch 19)

The year 1588 is omitted entirely. At the end of 1587 a blank of about two-thirds of a page has been left, with the intention doubtless of filling in 1588 when the entries should turn up. But they never did turn up, and the blank space was utilised for five entries of baptisms under the date of 1749, the register having at that time been quite filled up and no new volume obtained to go on with.

1591. Katherine Woodhurst daughter of Thos Woodhurst of Woodhurst (Bur^d May 17th)
Wm Parsons the sone of Thos Parsons dwellinge at the boxe-trees (Bapt: Mch 16th)
John Davyes s. of John Davyes dwellinge in Oxford (Bur^d Mch 4)
John Lovett, s. of Thos Lovett, Gent. & Eliz: his wyffe (Bapt July 7)
[There is no Woodhurst in this neighbourhood, or elsewhere than in Huntingdonshire, so far as I know. The " boxe-trees," no doubt, is that part of Hockley Heath still so called. The Lovetts were an old Nuthurst family.]

The headings of each year begin in 1592 to be given with much formality, thus :—

Anno Dm̃ 1592   Año incipiente in feste annunciationis beatæ Mariæ virginis scdᵐ computacionem eccliæ Anglicanæ.

1592.   Anne Litton, widdow, was buried the 19ᵗʰ July.
[This would be the rector's mother.]

1593.   *Johẽs Litton fillius Johĩs Litton Rectoris hujus p'ochiæ baptizatus fuit quinto die Decembris Año Dm scdm cõputaciõem Eccliæ Anglicanæ 1593.*
[Nothing but Latin was good enough for the rector's eldest son: for others English sufficed.]

The remaining entries of his family are :—

1594.   Richard Litton s. of John Litton & Katherine his wiffe (Bapt Janʸ 22ⁿᵈ)

1597.   Henry Litton (Bapt Janʸ 23ʳᵈ)

1601.   Thomas Litton (Bapt. May 23ʳᵈ)

Katherine Litton the wiffe of Mʳ John Litton (Burᵈ Mch 5ᵗʰ)

This rector, John Litton, may be of some speculative interest to us as a possible acquaintance of Shakespeare. Major Walter in his *Shakespeare's True Life* says : "Old Roman Catholic families associate the Vicar (*Rector*) of Lapworth with other neighbouring clergy, namely the Vicars (*Rectors*) of Beaudesert and Wootton Wawen, as friends of Shakespeare in early youth and as having met frequently together at Shottery Chantry." But no definite authority is given for this statement.

John Litton's incumbency here did, however, just cover the period of Shakespeare's active life, and the two men must have been of about the same age. As Litton took his B.A. degree at Merton in 1579–80, and that degree was usually taken in those days about the age of twenty-one, he probably came here as rector when he was only about twenty-four or twenty-five, Shakespeare being then (in 1584) twenty. Litton continued rector here till his death in 1613, and could hardly be ignorant of the greatness of his near neighbour. In the scarcity of intellectual companionship he may even have sought and been fortunate enough to obtain his acquaintance. Beaudesert is four miles, and Wootton Wawen six miles, from Lapworth on the way to Stratford, and the rectors of the three places were sure to be well acquainted with each other. But I should like more precise data for associating Shakespeare and Litton, and for supposing that they may have exchanged visits.

Going back to the register, we have :—

1591–2. Elizabeth Grissold the wyffe of Robert Grissold (Bur^d 13th Febr^y)

1592. Robt^e Grissold and Gillian Smyth (Marr^d Nov 12th)

1593. Julian Grissold the wife of Robt^e Grissold (Bur^d Oct 5)

1594. Robt^e Grissold and Margerett Smith (Marr^d April 30)

[The second wife "Gillian" becomes "Julian" at the end of her short wedded life, the first being probably the correct form of her name (although Julian was formerly used as a female name), and the widower is soon comforted by a third marriage to yet another Smith.

These Grissolds under a great variety of spellings furnish many entries to the Parish Register from its commencement till towards the end of the seventeenth century. They never have any prefix or affix of distinction, but they were, no doubt, a branch of the family of the Greswolds of Solihull. The will of the above "Robert Gryssould," dated July 29, 1616, and proved at Worcester, July 22, 1617, directs his body to be-buried in Lapworth Churchyard ; and the will of the above-named Margaret, his third wife, dated 1621 and proved at Worcester June 12, 1622, directs her body to be buried there also "by her husband." But there is no entry of burial of either of them in the Register, which omission suggests its having been badly kept.[1]]

1593.   Jone Grene of Bromingrome a poore woman going abroad died in childburth & was buried (June 20th)

Willm Batyer, the sone of James Batyer a poore France man was baptized (Oct 14th)

["Going abroad" means, we may suppose, only "on the tramp."]

1595.   Elizabeth d^r of John Shackespere & his wife (Bapt June 19th)

1597.   John Hodgkins and . . . were married (Oct 16)

[Another instance where they had not preserved the woman's name.]

Between the last two entries the register was neglected. The latest entry in 1595 is of the 20th July, and two-thirds of a page are left blank as if for further entries. For 1596 a page is headed in the elaborate manner before described, but it remains blank. The first entry for 1597 is of the 10th April. •There is, therefore, a period of upwards of twenty months for which the register is deficient.

1597.   Mr Robt^e Holt the sone of Mr Thomas Holt esquier was baptised (Nov 14th)

1598.   Katherine Holt the daughter of Thomas Holt esquier was baptised (Mch 4th)

---

[1] The oldest of the altar tombs in our churchyard (standing near the porch) bears a shield with three greyhounds, and has been commonly supposed to be the tomb of a Greswold. But the arms of that family show two greyhounds only. It is more likely that the shield bears the arms of the Hardings, a very old family who were here before the Greswolds.

[This Thomas Holt, father of the two children registered above, was, there can be little doubt, then living at the Manor House, Bushwood Hall, where the Catesbys had lived before him. He acquired afterwards the Lordship of the Manor of Lapworth, but must at this time and for some years afterwards have been merely occupying as the tenant, first of Sir William Catesby and then of Robert Catesby. The statements that are made as to the sale and resale of the Manor can hardly be reconciled in any other way. Thus Dugdale says :—

which William (being likewise a knight, and residing much at Bushwood) had issue Robert and other sons, which Robert having sold this lordship to Sir Edward Greville of Milcote,[1] of whom Sir Thomas Holt of Aston-juxta-Birmingham purchased it, etc. etc.

Elsewhere I find the date of Sir William Catesby's death given as 1598, and the date of Robert Catesby's sale to Sir Edward Greville as "in the time of James I." Robert Catesby owned the Manor, therefore, from 1598 to (at least) 1603, and it is probable that Greville held it a very short time. Meantime Thomas Holt, being of a very old and notable family, was in the way himself to become a very notable Warwickshire man. The *Dictionary of National Biography* gives the date of his birth as 1571 ; and also says :—

In 1599 he served as sheriff of Warwickshire. On 18th April, 1603, he was knighted by James I., having gone as one of a deputation to meet and welcome him on his way to England upon his accession to the throne. Ten years later he was made a Baronet. In July, 1608, he had obtained damages against one Wm Astgrigg for a slanderous statement made by him "that Sir Thomas Holt took a cleaver and hit his cook with the same cleaver upon the head, and clave his head so that one side thereof fell upon one of his shoulders and the other side upon the other shoulder, and this I will verify to be true." On appeal, however, by Astgrigg against the damages given it was ingeniously argued that altho' it had been stated

---

[1] Dugdale (under Milcote) gives a very gruesome account of a murder committed by Sir Lodovic Greville, the father of this Sir Edward, and of his putting an accomplice into the bed of the murdered man to dictate a fraudulent will : for which crime he was sentenced to be, and was, "pressed to death," at Warwick ; probably the most terrible mode of execution then known.

that the halves of the cook's head had fallen on either shoulder, no averment had been made that that was what the cook died of, or that Sir Thomas killed him, and the judgment of the King's Bench was given in favour of the appellant.

Sir Thomas Holt's chief claim to be remembered now is that he was the builder of Aston Hall, which he left in about the form in which we now see it. The inscription which he put upon it still remains, recording how he began to build it in 1618, came to dwell in it in 1631, and did finish it in 1635. *Laus Deo.*

He was a very zealous Royalist, and suffered much in the cause of King Charles I., as all local histories recount. The *History of the Holts of Aston,* by Alfred Davidson (Birmingham, 1854), gives much information of interest concerning him and his family. He lived to the age of eighty-three, and his tomb is with those of his fathers in the Church of Aston-juxta-Birmingham. Both the children who were born at Lapworth appear to have died young. (Davidson says he had fifteen children, and survived them all.) It is probable that he had ceased to reside here before he acquired his title, and lived mostly at his Manor of Duddeston. Whatever may be the exact date at which he acquired the Lapworth Manor, it remained in his family for many generations, passing on the death of the sixth Baronet, Sir Charles Holt, in 1782, by descendants in the female line, to the Holt-Bracebridge family of Atherstone.[1]]

1598.   James Mortiboyes & Anne Ashbie (Marr^d June 24th)

[This is the first occurrence in the register of the name of Mortiboyes, which had first appeared in the parish in 1472, and continued to be of frequent recurrence until the middle

---

[1] The Historical Manuscripts Commission (Appendix to 6th Report, p. 40, a.) gives the following note about Sir Thomas Holt, which is perhaps worth preserving :—

Calendar 1644. Petition of Richd Horton of Yardley in the co: of Worcester : complains that he was drugged in an ale-house by Thos Haddon, bailiff to Sir Thomas Holt, and there made to sign an acknowledgment that he owed £28 to Sir Thos Holt and £20 to Haddon. During the course of subsequent proceedings Haddon has died in prison, and petitioner, a countryman, aged and illiterate, is likely to be ruined. Prays for redress against Sir Thos Holt. (No record of any action on such petition.)

of the nineteenth century. The name of Ashbie, which appeared frequently in the pre-Reformation deeds, also continues to be of the commonest in the register up to the beginning of the eighteenth century.]

At the end of 1598 an entry which extended to four lines has been carefully erased with a knife.

The transcript has now ended. With the first entry in the year 1600, we get a new handwriting.

1600. George Lucette the son of John Lucett (Bapt Mch 30th)

1602. Eliz: Slie the d^r of Peter Slye (Bapt April 28th) & the same Eliz: was Bur^d Apl 29th

[When a child dies shortly after baptism the burial is often added as a note.]

1604. Richd Digbye the sonne of Mr Thos Digbye (Bapt July 28th)

1605. Elzabeth Wedger the daughter of Roberte Wedger, a stranger (Bapt May 27th)

[The name of Digbye never occurs again. He, too, was perhaps a stranger, but apparently of more importance than Wedger.]

1608. Fulke Bellars & Ursula Yomans widdowe were married the 22th of July

[Up to this time dates have oftenest been written in words. Now they begin to be in numerals, sometimes Roman, sometimes Arabic. Such forms as 21th, 22th, 23th, etc., are common. The affix "*th*" seems at this time to have been made applicable to all numerals. It is not until much later that we meet in the register with 21st, 22nd, etc.]

Elizabeth Wilye, spuria, was baptised the 15th Sept^r.

[This poor little waif had neither father nor mother recorded.]

From November 26th, 1611, to June 11th, 1613, there are no entries. . For a period of nearly nineteen months the register again had been entirely neglected. Within the time John Litton, who had been rector here twenty-nine years, had died. Perhaps he had been incapacitated by infirmity for some time before his death, and that may account for the gap in the register. There is no record of his own burial, but that he was buried here where his wife and mother had been buried there can be little doubt.

1613. Clement ffisher Buried Jany 28th.[1]

Thomas's *Dugdale* enters in the list of Lapworth rectors :—

Joh: Moreley: Cler: in Art: Mag^r: ult: Maii 1613. v. p. mort.

and Foster's *Alumni Oxonienses* gives us the following :—

John Morley of Somerset, pleb St Mary Hall, matric 17 Oct
   1600 aged 18. B.A. 17 Dec 1604. Fellow of Merton College
   1605. M.A. 20 June 1609. Rector of Lapworth 1613, and
   of Wootton Courtney, Somerset, 1613; Vicar of North
   Petherton, Somerset, 1615, Canon of Wells 1616, and B.D.
   4 June 1616.

John Morley would seem, as it were, to have merely called at Lapworth on his road to promotion elsewhere. He was here only a little more than four months, and the few entries which we may ascribe to him are in a very scrawling and almost illegible hand.

Thomas's *Dugdale* gives us again as his successor—

Joh: Elly.   16 Oct. 1613.   (v. p. res.)

Probably this new rector did not take charge at once, as the register is again neglected from the above date for several months, entries being made without

---

[1] See under 1573, p. 141.

dates as if only put in from memory at a later period ;
thus :—

1613.. Edwd Kerby the sone of Wm Kerby was bur^d in the
        yere above wrytten.
      John the sonne of John Saunders was Baptised in
        lente in the yere of our lord god first above
        wrytten.
      Geo: Warde was buryed the yeare aforesayd.
      Matthew Parker in the yeare aforesayd.
      Annet Kerby the daughter of Willm Kerby was buryed
        in the yeare above mencyoned.
      Mr Clive Price (Bur^d Feb 20th)

At the last-named date, being nearly at the end
of the year, a more exact record had been re-
gained.

It is a curious circumstance that when the above-
named John Elly came to be rector here in 1613,
another John Elly (not improbably a relative) was
Rector of Beaudesert.   Our John Elly was rector
here from 1613 to 1633.   The Beaudesert John Elly
was rector there from 1606 to 1636, so that for twenty
years these two adjoining parishes were held by rectors
of the same name.   This has very naturally led to the
supposition that the two livings were from 1613 to 1633
held by the same man, and it is only by the pains-
taking work of Mr. Foster that I am saved from
that error.   His record of the two men, and of a son
of the first in order, is as follows :—

John Elly of Co: Worc^r pleb: Exeter Coll: Matric 26 June
  1590 aged 17.   B.A. 5 July 1594.   M.A. 14 July 1598, then
  "literis incumbens" in the household of the Bp. of Worc^r,
  perhaps Rector of Beaudesert, Co: Warw^k, 1606–36, father
  of John 1630.

John Ellye of Co: Worc^r pleb: Exeter Coll: matric 19 May
1598 aged 17 (subscribed his name Elleus) Fellow of Merton
Coll: 1602. B.A. 27 Jan 1601–2. M.A. 10 Feb 1606–7
B and D.D. 19 July 1633. Rector of Lapworth, co:
Warw^k, 1613; Vicar of Elham, Kent, 1612–14. Canon
of Windsor 1623 until his death 1639.

John Elly, s John of Beaudesert, sacerd: Oriel coll: matric
11 June 1630, aged 17. B.A. 17 Oct 1631. M.A. 11 June
1634. Vicar of Isleworth, Middlesex, 1637.

John Elly seems to have aimed at introducing
better order in the register by putting " Weddings,"
" Burialls," and " Baptisms " under separate headings.
He also began to make the entries in Latin, but after
a few years the former practices in both respects were
reverted to.

The next two entries have reference to himself :—

1618. *Johannes Ellie Rector ecclesiæ de Lapworth & Katha-
rina Lawrence matrimonio copulat' fuer' decimo
septimo die Augusti.*

1624. John the sonne of Mr John Elly *rectoris ecclesiæ* was
baptised the 22th day of July.

   [The spelling of his name seems to have been a matter of
   indifference to him. There were three John Ellys before:
   now we have four, here and at Beaudesert, all living at the
   same time, as each rector had called a son after his own
   name.]

1616. *Jhoanna Younge uxor Johāis Younge sepulta . . .
Novem^r.*

1617. *Johannes Shackspur et Maria Lucett matrimonio
copulat': fuerunt Decimo sexto Februarij
Jocosa filia Edmond: Sley baptizat: proximo die Marcij
et sepulta vicesimo die Maij.*

[Shackspur and Sley falling thus together call up a vision of
Christopher Sly, the immortal tinker. There were at this time, as
shown by the register, certainly not fewer than four families of Sly
in the parish, so that the name is one of the commonest. We have,
however, sought in vain for a Christopher.]

1619. *Anna filia M^gri Thomas Trussell de Nuthurst fuit baptizata vicesimo quinto die Maij.*

1621. Mistriss Trussell the wife of M^r . . . Trussell of Nuthurst (Bur^d Mch 22nd)

Elizabeth, wife of Mr Thos Lovett of Nuthurst (Bur^d April 20)

[These were old Nuthurst families, then dying out. The Trussells we have seen to be connected with Nuthurst and Lapworth from *temp*. Edward I.]

1623. Edmund Right and Eliz: Shakspeare (Marr^d June 10th)

Eliz: wife of Edm: Right (Bur^d Mch 10th 1623–4)

1624. Alice, wife of John Shakspeare (Bur^d 21th July)

[Our register has many entries of Shakespeares about this time, and the name, under about ten forms, continues to be a common one for more than a century later.]

Eliz: d^r of Thos Chambers of Kingsnorton borne at Nuthurst. (Bapt: Oct 20th)

Robt Baker of Bewdesarte and Brigett Fetherston of Balsall by virtue of a license from Worcester were here married (Jan 24, 1624–5)

[The first entry of a marriage by licence.]

1625. Elinor the daughter of Roger Bendall vagabond (Bapt Dec 20)

1626. Anne the daughter of Strange Peacock (Bapt May 16)

1626–7. Richard, sone of David Joanes, a vagabond, born at Nuthurst (Bapt Mch 12)

1627. Robert the sone of Edw: Steavens, borne at Bushwood Hall (Bapt April 1st)

1628. Mr Thomas Mason Clarke & Eliz: Slye (Marr^d Aug 24)

[This entry gives the first instance of a double Christian name.]

1629. Anne . . . the daughter of . . . a pore man (Bapt Decr 27th)

William Askew was buried (Nov 4)

[This would be the man against whom the parishioners made such grave indictments, of removal of the "churchyard cross," etc., in 1615. See p. 117 *et seq*.]

1630. John the son of John Smith of Kingswood was both baptised and buried the 7th day of May.

[There are other entries similar to this.]

Thos Morse a stranger late of Hayworth Ingram (?) in the Co: of Lincoln (Bur^d Aug 26th)

1632. Jone the wife of john Bradshaw Gent: (Bur^d Apl 2nd)

Eliz: d^r of Mr Spooner of Nuthurst (Bur^d May 9th)

1633. John Bradshaw & Katherine Mecock, widow (Marr^d Nov 6)

jane Bennett al^s Houma of Packwood (Bur^d Mch 5)

It is in this year that we get the first mention of a family, that of the Ingrams, which settled at Nuthurst, and continued there till our own times :—

1633. Wm Ingram of Nuthurst and Susanna Mountford (Marr^d April 30)

Susanna the wife of Wm Ingram of Nuthurst (Bur^d Nov 15)

1635. Eliz: d^r of Wm Ingram of Nuthurst (Bapt Sep 27)

1636. Eliz: d^r of Wm Ingram of Nuthurst (Bur^d Oct 31)

1637. Eliz: the wife of Wm Ingram Gent (Bur^d April 10) being of the parish of Nuthurst.

Rebekka ye daughter of William Ingram of Nuthurst was baptise: the 27th of September:

1640. Isaac the sonne of Mr Wm Ingram of Nuthurst (Bapt Nov. 3)

[The first of the Ingrams, therefore, who settled at Nuthurst would seem to have been thrice married. The successive heads of the family took an active part in our parish trusts, etc., for many generations, and there are nine of their tombstones in the floor of our church. The last of the family to be buried there was Miss Hannah Ingram, in 1853, aged ninety. With her the Nuthurst stock died out. The Ingrams lived in what is now called Nuthurst House, which probably stands on the site of the old house of the Trussells.]

In 1633 John Elly, who had then received the degree of D.D., resigned his living and went to Windsor, of which place he had been made a canon ten years previously. He held the canonry till his death in 1639.

Just at this time the register has half a leaf cut away, but as the entries are continuous as to dates it is probable that the piece of parchment was cut off because wanted for some other purpose.

1633. Willm son of Frank Grissold Bapt: May 5.

Mr. W. B. Bickley, of Birmingham, having been engaged in researches respecting the Greswolds on behalf of a descendant in America, has been good enough to supply me with the following copy of a certificate given on behalf of the parish of Lapworth to the parish of Birmingham, on the occasion of the removal of this William Greswold in 1688. It shows the Lapworth branch of the family to have fallen to very low estate, and is of interest as illustrating the watchfulness of the Birmingham folk, who required the certificate to guard against the Greswolds becoming a charge upon their new parish. The name of Greswold never occurs in the register after the date of this certificate. It would appear, therefore, that this family of paupers did not return :—

(*Endorsement*) WILL: GRESWOLD OF LAPWORTH.
CERTIFICATE 1688.

Wee the Minister Churchwardens & Overseers of the poore of Lapworth in the County of Warwicke; Doe certifye whom it may Concerne That wee doe acknowledge & owen William Grissold with Elizabeth his wife & Children of Lapworth aforesaid to be Inhabitants within our said p'ish of Lapworth. And that wee will receive them as such when ever they shall bee sent to us by the Inhabitants of Birmingham and doe farther promise that wee will save harmlesse &

keepe Indempnifyed the Inhabitants of Birmingham of &
from all and all mañer of Charge or Trouble which may
happen to Come growe or arise by reason of the stay and
aboade of the said William Grissold his wife and Children.
Witness our hands the sixth Day of Aprill Añoqᵉ Doɱ 1688

Th: Cole Rectʳ   Thoˢ Sly senior
John Camden   John Whitfoote
Samuel Mountfort
Thomas Sanders
Thoˢ Sly
William Askew
Henry Leea Churchwarden

Thomas's *Dugdale* gives the entry of John Elly's
successor thus :—

Joh: Doughtie. Cler. 13 January 1633. (for 1633-4.)

Foster gives unusually full particulars of his preferments, etc., thus :—

John Doughty of Dowghty. Subscribed 30 April 1613.
   B.A. from Brasenose Coll: 4 Nov. 1616. Fellow of
   Merton Coll: 1619. M.A. 11 July 1623. D.D. 19 Oct
   1660. Proctor 1631. (removed by the King 23ʳᵈ Aug.)
   Rector of Wood Norton, Norfolk, 1616; of Ruchock, co:
   Worcester, 1631; of Lapworth 1634-46, and of Beaudesert
   1636. Lecturer of Salisbury St. Edmund's; Canon of
   Westminster 1660; and Rector of Cheam, Surrey, 1662;
   died 25 Decʳ 1672, aged 75; buried in Westminster Abbey.

How many livings he held at once we do not know.
It was a singular circumstance that, after succeeding
one John Elly at Lapworth in 1633-4, he should
succeed the other John Elly at Beaudesert in 1636,
and it is certain that he continued to hold these two
livings together until the troubles of the Civil War
became so acute that he, being a very zealous
Royalist, abandoned them both to avoid sequestra-

tion and imprisonment, and joined the King at Oxford. He shared the misfortunes of the House of Stuart till the Restoration, when he was rewarded with the Westminster Canonry. Anthony à Wood (*Athenæ Oxonienses,* vol. iii. p. 976) adds :—

He died at Westminster, after he had lived to be twice a child, on the day of the Nativity of our Saviour 1672, and was buried in the Abbey Church of St. Peter there, near to the body of Dr Brian Duppa (on the North side of Edward the Confessor's chapel).

Wood also gives the titles of several works of polemical divinity which he left behind him, and says he was "much frequented for his edifying sermons."

In *Churches of Warwickshire,* under "Beaudesert," is preserved this extract from one of the Staunton MSS. destroyed by the fire at the Birmingham Reference Library in 1879 :—

The following petition presented to the House of Lords about 1640, by the parishioners of Beaudesert against the Rev. J. Doughty, rector of that parish, and also rector of Lapworth, exhibits a striking specimen of the puritanical feeling then so widely spreading itself through the country. After accusing him of neglect of duty and other delinquencies, it concludes with these charges :—

The said John Doughty is a common resorter to the houses of Popish recusants, a favourer of them and their religion, and a scoffer of goodness and good men.

The said John Doughty preaching at Lapworth about Mich^s last upon Matth. viii. 13. affirmed that it was not necessary for the Minister to prove his doctrine by Scripture, but the people ought to believe it on his authority ; and further said that there is now a generation of men sprung up that will believe nothing but what is proved by Scripture, insisting that turning and tossing over the leaves of the Bible is a disturbance to the congregation, with other words to that effect.

The said John Doughty, speaking of the new Canons, said there was nothing in them to be disliked, and further that he did verily believe in his conscience, that if St. Paul had been there and made them, the Parliament would have condemned them, or words to that effect.

1634.   Eliz: the daughter of John Shaxpeare. (Bapt Aug 18)

1636.   Henry Queiney the son of John Quiney (Bur^d May 16)

[The name of Quiney is frequent in the first half of this century.

The John Shaxpeare named above left, in 1637, two shillings a year to Lapworth and Packwood to be distributed in penny loaves at the parish church of each place on All Souls' Day, "to add to the poor people's feast that day." The distribution appears to have been still made here when the Charity Commissioners' Inspector reported in 1826, but the charity has been since lost.]

About this time we enter upon a period of very bad handwriting and spelling, the entries having been left probably to the parish clerk, who was quite illiterate.

1640.   Aless the dauter of Mr Edward Tressell, babtised (July 28)

[The last entry we have of the old Trussells.]

The next year is headed 16401, but it is only the clerk's way of expressing 1641. In that year he records that—

Edward . . . the sonne of . . . was babtised (Sep 1)

There is great confusion and uncertainty also as to whether the year shall begin as of old with Lady Day or with January 1st. Thus 1643 is treated as of nine months only, and we get these entries :—

1643.   Stfen the sone of Stfen Rogers of Tanworth, babtised Decr 10th

Eliz: dauter of Elias Cent (Kent) babtised the last day of the old year.

and Mari the dauter of Thomas Dison babtised the 1st. day of Jany 1644.

There was a clear intention here to alter the old order, but the change only continues for the year 1644. 1645 is made to consist of fifteen months, and

1646 begins with Lady Day. Constant watchfulness is needed therefore in January, February and March to know to what year an entry really belongs. This state of uncertainty continues for a long period.

1644. Leander (?) daughter of Francis Grisell bapt. 18 August.

The register has no trace of the eccentric Christian names that were in use in the high days of Puritanism,[1] but we get this one, which proves afterwards to be a sign of the times.

1647. Salathiel the sone of John Saxspor of Tanworth was babtised the 7 day of November.

[Saxspor is, of course, one of the many variants of Shakespeare.]

1648. Audrie Coke. (Bur^d Nov 4)

[Audrie is rather frequent as a Christian name.]

Suannæ the dauter of William Cambden (Bapt Feby 8) of nitgh [? at night].

With 1649 the beginning of the year is again made January 1st, and we get the entry, in a very neat, small hand :—

Mary the daughter of Thomas and Joane Goodwin was baptised January 21th Año Dm̃ 1649 p' me Beniamin Lovell min: ibid:

It was 1648–9, just nine days before King Charles was beheaded at Whitehall. Benjamin Lovell, who thus signs himself "resident minister," was the successor to Dr. Doughty, and had taken charge of the parish under Commonwealth auspices. He was apparently (to use the term which was applied to such cases after the Restoration) the "intruded rector."

---

[1] The Rowington Register has :—

1649. God hathheard, son of John Palmer, bapt.

He was, however, a regularly ordained priest of the Church of England, and had been Rector of Preston Bagot from 1636. There still remains a stone tablet, sunk into the north wall of the chancel of the church there, with the inscription :—

Here lieth the body of John Lovel, third son of Benjamin Lovel, Parson and Pastor of this church, who died in the fourth year of his age and was buried Septr 19th 1639.

It is probable that Lovell came here soon after Dr. Doughty's flight in 1646. That he was here in 1647 is rather curiously suggested[1] by the baptism of John Saxpor's child as "Salathiel," for Benjamin Lovell had a son of that name, then a youth of fourteen or fifteen, and doubtless living at home with his father. It has been mentioned in connection with the parish charities that both father and son were made feoffees in 1652. The father probably continued here as minister till 1657. (He appears as holding parish offices in 1654.) It is likely also that while at Lapworth he continued to hold the living of Preston Bagot. The record of incumbents of that place does not give the date of institution of his successor. He had clearly left us in or before 1658, and seems to have gone to Leckhampstead, Bucks, in the register of which place is the entry (quoted in *Notes and Queries*, 8th S. vol. i. 131, as from Browne Willis's *History of Buckingham*) :—

Lekhampstead. Burials 1658 Sep. 1. Mrs. Lovel wife of M^r [Benjamin] Lovel [intruded] Rector.

---

[1] Since the above was written the author finds, in an abstract of title relating to property in the parish, mention of "Benjamin Lovel, clerk," as farming land here of Dame Alice Lucy (widow of the third Sir Thomas) in 1647.

to which, in the *History*, is appended the note :—

N.B.—She was mother to Sir Salathiel Lovel, a judge, who was clerk to an attorney at Buckingham.

While resident at this place he seems to have married again some two years later.

Foster (*Alumni Oxon.*) gives the following record of him and a son, Robert :—

Lovell, Benjamin ; B.A. from Merton College 11 April 1627, M.A. from St. Edmund Hall 8 July 1630. Rector of Preston Bagot, co: War: 1636. Licensed 15 Decr 1660 (then of Leckhampstead, Bucks, widower, aged 52) to marry Mary Grace Williams of Low Leyton, Essex, Widow; Rector of Tooting Graveney, Surrey, 1661 ; Vicar of St. Albans, St. Stephen's, 1663 ; of Marlborough, St. Mary, Wilts, 1663 ; Vicar of Langley Abbotts, Herts, 1664; of Great Missenden, Bucks, 1670, and Rector of Bow Brickhill, Bucks, 1671 ; father of Robert 1650.

Lovell, Robert ; B.A. from Christ Church 16 Dec 1650, M.A. 21 June 1653 (s. of Benjamin, Rector of Lapworth, co: War:). An excellent botanist, professed physic and had some practice therein at Coventry, where he died ; buried in the Church of the Holy Trinity 6 Nov 1690.

It will be seen that while the record of the father omits mention of his connection with this place, that of the son calls him " Rector " here. His numerous and rapid preferments seem to indicate that he continued in favour after the Restoration. The latest note we get of him is from our own papers before quoted (p. 133), where he is described as of Bow Brick-hill, Bucks, clerk, as late as 1677 : at which time also his son Salathiel is described as of Northampton, Esquire.

This Salathiel would appear to have gone from Lapworth to London to enter on the study of the

M

law, and to have prosecuted it very successfully. The register of admissions to Gray's Inn has the entry :—

1648 June 26: Salathiel Lovell, son of Benjamin Lovell, of Lapworth, Co: Warwick, clerk.

An account of him is given in Foss's *Judges of England*, which contains some curious inaccuracies. It speaks of him as born in 1619, entering on his legal studies late in life, namely, at the age of twenty-nine, being made a judge of the Exchequer Court when on the verge of ninety, and dying at the age of ninety-five. In all of these figures there seems to be an error of fourteen years. His monument exists in Harleston Church, Northamptonshire, recording that he died in 1713, at the age of eighty-one. He would therefore be in his sixteenth year when he entered at Gray's Inn, and his seventy-sixth when made a Baron of Exchequer to Queen Anne in 1708. The other incidents of his life given by Foss may no doubt be taken as correct, namely, that he was Recorder of London in 1692 ; knighted the same year on carrying up the address of the Corporation to King William III. on his return from abroad ; became a judge on the Chester circuit in 1695, but being afterwards in disfavour with the King obtained no further advancement until the next reign. "He was distinguished," says Foss, "principally by his want of memory, so that, while Recorder of London, he received the nickname of '*Obliviscor* of London.'"

He seems to have kept up his connection with Lapworth after he left it, and continued to own land here while he lived in Northampton.

In 1654 we find the dates of birth and not of baptism begin to be recorded.

1654. Josef the sone of John Marteboyes and his wife was borne the 8th of February.

1655. Thomas the sone of Thomas Miler was borne (July 28)

An Act ordering the "register" in every parish to make this change had been passed in the Parliament of 1653 ("register" being at that time used both for the person making the entry and for the book).[1]

The change was of very brief continuance at Lapworth. We find baptisms are again recorded in 1656, and thenceforward.

During the greater part of the Commonwealth and Protectorate periods the entries in the register are so ill-written, ill-spelt, and made with such bad ink that many are quite undecipherable, and others can be made out only with the greatest difficulty.

1656. An the dautor of Robord wip (Bur[d] June 8)
        Hneri ors and hana Glofr ware mar[ed] (Oct 8)
        M[r] Monfort widdow (Buried Oct 8)

The last entry means, no doubt, "the widow of Mr. Montfort." "Glofr" may have been intended for "Glover." "Strofer" is a spelling that occurs for "Stratford"-on-Avon.

On one of the fly-leaves at the end of the register

---

[1] A.D. 1653. Now came in force a goodly act made by the usurper Cromwell's little Parliament, or the Parliament of Saints, as they called it, that is, of all manner of dissembling hypocrites and filthy hereticks, who ordered not the baptism, but the birth of children to be recorded in the Parish Register, thereby insinuating that children ought not to be baptised, and encouraging people to withhold their infants from the sacred ordinance. (Note in "Register of Maid's Moreton, Bucks," quoted by Mr. Chester Waters in his *Parish Registers in England.*)

someone has written, in a hand of about this date, the
lines :—

> He buries the dead
> Who writes not to be read
> Better write not at all
> Than make such blind scrawl

This rhymer may have had to make searches within
the years we speak of.

A family of Cambden or Camden show themselves
in the parish at this period, and continue for a long
time, evidently as people of consideration. We have
already noted one entry in 1648.

165$\frac{0}{1}$. Mary the daughter of Mr. John Camden (Bapt 4 Feb)
1653.   John the sone of   „   „   („   7 Sep)
1656.   Henry the sone of   „   „   („   22 Apl)

The burials of these two brothers do not occur till
well into the next century, and their tombstones are
the oldest we have left in the church. The family
seems to have been here nearly a century (p. 179).

1661.   Eliz: the daughter of Thomas Crannor and Aliss his
         wyfe (Bapt: Nov 16)

> [The family of Cranmer, under various spellings, has con-
> tinued in the parish to this day. This seems to be the
> earliest occurrence of the name.]

Benjamin Lovell appears to have been succeeded by
William Caudwell, of whom we get the first trace by
this entry :—

William Caudwell, rector of Lapworth, and Anne Colmore
of Yerdington were married April ye 6. 1659.

This was the year of Richard Cromwell's protectorate, but Caudwell probably came here in 1657,
as it is not to be supposed the parish would be left
long after Lovell's departure without someone in
charge.

Foster's entry respecting him is brief :—

Wm Caldwell or Caudwell. B.A. from New Inn Hall 17 Decr 1654. M.A. 8 June 1657)

He probably came here, therefore, as a young man of twenty-four or twenty-five. The entry of his marriage quoted above is evidently in his own hand-writing, as are the following :—

Elizabeth ye daughter of William Caudwell was born March 14th 1659. (1659–60)

Elizabeth ye daughter of William Caudwell was baptised April 10. 1660.

Richard Lowe & Deborah Colmore [1] were married November ye eight one thousand six hundred & sixty.

These entries are all made by William Caudwell himself and do not stand in exact order of date, having apparently been inserted in odd spaces at a later period.

The further entries relating to him are :—

1664–5. M̃ Elisabeth Cadell (Bur^d Jan 23)
Anne daughter of M Willm Caudell & Anne his wife (Bapt^d Feb 1)

1666. M William Caudell was buried the xxvth day of July.

This is the rector himself. The clerk, whose entry is almost illegible, did not know how to spell the name.

During the whole of William Caudwell's time he and the clerk seem to have been at issue as to when the year should begin. The rector counts from March

St. Martin's Register (Birmingham) has the entries :—

1637. Dec. 10. Bapt^d Deborah dr of Ambrose & Anne Colmore.
1642. Mch. 27. Bapt^d Anne dr of Abraham & Ann Colmore.

Wm. Caudwell would therefore seem to have married a wife of seventeen,—for there can be little doubt that the two Colmores of our Lapworth marriages were those whose baptisms are thus recorded, and members of the family which has so long been influential as landowners in Birmingham.

25th, and the clerk from January 1st, with the result of great confusion.

1661. Mr Henrie ford of the parish of Bromicham and M Rebeka Ingram of Nuthurst were married the 13 day of December.

> [The settlement made on the occasion of this marriage still exists, the parties to it being Henry Ford (described as of Winson Green in the parish of Birmingham), yeoman, William Ingram of Nuthurst, Yeoman, and Cornelius Ford of Kings Norton, yeoman.[1] This Cornelius, presumably a brother of Henry Ford, was the father of Sara Ford, born at Kings Norton 1669, and married in 1706, in Packwood Church, to Michael Johnson, of Lichfield; their son being Dr. Samuel Johnson.
>
> It has always been unexplained why the marriage of Dr. Johnson's parents took place at Packwood, with which place neither of them had any connection. The explanation is not improbably to be found in the intimacy of the families of Ford and Ingram. Sara may have been visiting at her aunt Rebecca's paternal home of Nuthurst and been married from there, only two miles distant from Packwood. The wonder then becomes that they were not married at Lapworth, the church of the Ingrams. It may even have been a runaway match. Boswell's remarks are so brief that it is clear Johnson never told him more than just his mother's name.]

Thomas's *Dugdale*, although not giving William Caudwell in its list of rectors, has the entry :—

John Powell, cler, A.M. 6 Sepr 1666 (vac. p. mort. Gul: Cawdwell ult: rector)

Foster's record of Powell is :—

Powell, John, s Rich^d of Standon, Herts, cler; scholar of Gonville & Caius Coll: Cambridge, 7 Feb 1625-6, aged 15; B.A. 1629-30, M.A. 1637; incorporated 4 May 1649 from Pembroke Coll: Oxford; fellow of Merton Coll: Oxford, 22 Dec 1649; Rector of Lapworth, ço: Warw^k, 1666-74; admon. at Oxford 17 Mch 1673-4.

---

[1] For the abstract of this settlement the author is indebted to Mr. W. B. Bickley, of Birmingham.

In December, 1666, we get a welcome change of handwriting. John Powell had probably come to reside here. The writing is beautifully clear and distinct. His year begins with Lady Day; except where the clerk forbids.

1668. Richard Sly of Kingswood Brook in Rowington Parish (Bur^d Nov 12)

1668–9. Wm Walton of Packwood, aged about 75 (Bur^d Jan 20)

John Clark of Lapworth and Eliz: Harding of Hampton-in-Arden with a certificate of Banes thrice published (Marr^d Jany 28)

Eliz: the second wife of Mr Wm Ingram was bur^d Feb 24, St Matthias' Day.

Old Willm Grafton of Bals-Hall in Hampton (Bur^d Mch 18)

1669. Henry Welchman of Tanworth and Joyce Morris married with license from Worcester-court directed hither May 9.

Thomas Edkins of the Park (Bur^d Oct 10)

1670/1. Mary the wife of John Palmer of Harbery Bank (Bur^d Feb 5)

[We still have the "Park Farm," the name having reference, it will be remembered, to the Royal Park which was situated on the south side of the parish. Harbery Bank is a name that is fast dying out with us, but in the earlier half of last century the old Roman encampment so called could be very well defined. Hannett gives a plan of it in his *Forest of Arden*. The construction of the Stratford-on-Avon Canal did a good deal to obliterate it, one of the locks being dug across its north-eastern corner, and a small reservoir being partly within and partly without its lines.]

Our old enemy the illiterate clerk reappears for a short time, and asserts himself by making entries of baptisms and burials for January under a bold heading of 1672; whereupon the rector follows with further entries for January and February under the heading of 1671, which is continued to the 25th March.

1672. Thomas Tunkes, a Traveller, dying at Widdow Fisher's house, was bur^d Decr 28th.

1673. John the son Esak Grene wase babtised the iij day of June.

And with this entry the clerk disappears for ever.

John Powell resigned the living in 1674. The sole mention we have of him in regard to parish affairs is that his was the only name of a parishioner placed on the list of new feoffees appointed by the Warwick Commission of Enquiry in 1668, which list was rejected absolutely by the parish and never took effect, as has been shown before (pp. 129-33).

The next rector was Thomas Cole. The entry in Thomas's *Dugdale* is :—

Thom: Cole cler: A.M. 14 April 1674. v.p.r.

The same work preserves the inscription on his tombstone, described as a flat stone within the chancel rails.

Foster has no fewer than twelve Thomas Coles, but does not name Lapworth in his record of any of them. Ours is probably one whom he mentions as matriculating at Oriel College, in 1615, in the thirteenth year of his age : this would agree closely with the age at which he died, as shown below.

The inscription on the tomb ran :—

Depositum | Thomæ Cole A M | Ecclesiæ hujus rectoris | Avo, patre, Theologis | Doctis, Piis, Orthodoxis | [Utrisq ; Ecclesiæ Anglicanæ causâ | Exulibus | Hoc | A Penatibus & Aris | Nupero rebelli Sæculo | Illo | Etiam a Patriâ | Cruento Mariano] Oriundi | Verum propria Eruditionis laude | Docti | Morum integritatis & Pietatis | Boni | Quibus innotuit, omnibus | Commendatissimi | Obiit | Maii 19. 1688 | An: Æt: 86. |

The register contains the entry :—

1688. Mr Thomas Cole, Rect^r was buried May 21.

He would seem, therefore, to have come here at the age of seventy-two, and had then fourteen years before him. His interesting monument was to be seen " within the chancel rails " as late as 1860, when it disappeared in the course of the restoration of the chancel, which was then carried out under the direction of Mr. G. E. Street, who seems to have been very callous in regard to the monuments existing in the church, and been accorded much too free a hand in respect to them, both then and in the more extensive restoration of the fabric of the church generally, which was also carried out by him, in 1872. We can scarcely suppose, however, that he would be so ruthless as to have it broken up, and it is likely that it still exists beneath the tiles with which the chancel was at that time paved.

The following are from the register during Thomas Cole's incumbency. It is probably owing to his age that we get frequent entries showing the offices of the church to have been performed by strange clergymen.

1674. Hanna the daughter of Humphery Field and Mary his wife (Bapt: May 1st) by Mr. Walkman.

Samuel the sonn of Thomas Cranmer and Ann his wife (Bapt: Aug. 25th) by Mr Carter.

Catharen the d^r of Humphrey Shakespeare (Bapt Nov 2)

Thomas ye sonne of Thomas Taylour of this parish and of Katharine his wife was baptised at Rowington on the 9th day of this present month of March by Mr John Field Vicar of the s^d church of Rowington.

[The formality with which this baptism, performed elsewhere, is recorded in our register is singular.]

1675. Philipp the daughter of Thomas Clarke and Joan his
       wife was bapt^d June 18 by Mr Wilson.

       George Hadley, a traveller on the way, and servant to
       Thos Smith of Ilminton in ye countie of Warwick
       (Bur^d Aug 15)

       Thomas ye sonne of Samuel Maunder (Bur^d Sep 16)

       [This is the first entry of the family of Maunder (often
       spelt Mander), which continued in the parish up to our own
       times, its members filling the usual parish offices and trusts. •
       From the time of the above-named Samuel the family
       occupied Ireland's Farm, Bushwood, from father to son
       for fully two hundred years.]

       John Grizold bur^d Sepr 13 by Mr Carter.

       [Another spelling of the old Greswold name.]

       Elie the bastard son of Eunice Cowper was baptised
       Oct 3. by Mr Willm Southerne.

       The sayd Eunice Cowper was buried Oct 21.

       [This is a very brief record of a village tragedy.   William
       Southerne became Vicar of Rowington in 1684, and con-
       tinued to rent land of the Lapworth Charity for many years.]

1676. John Parkhouse of Stratford-upon-Avon and Susanna
       Hobday of Henley were married with a license
       July 23.

1677. Thomas Walford of Binton and Sarah Parker of
       Claverdon were married with a license Nov 19.

1678. . . . John Smith & Harriet his wife (Bapt^d Mch 2)

       [A case in which the sex of the child was not known.]

1681. Martin Alesbury of Nuthurst (Bur^d June 4).

1681-2. Jan 28.   Robert Barnes of Norton Lindsay in the
       co: of Warw^k & diocess of Worcester and Esther
       Bates of Shirley Street in the parish of Solihull in
       the s^d county but diocess of Lichfield & Coventry
       were married according to the tenour of a license
       obtained from the consistory at Worcester
                    p. me. Th: Cole, Rector.

1682. Jonathan & Job ye sons & Grace ye daughter of John
       Smith & Frances his wife were born at one birth &
       baptised Sept 29.

1682.   Jonathan & Job ye sons of John Smith were bur^d Oct 8.

Grace ye daughter of John Smith was buried Oct 16.

[This is the only instance of triplets that occurs in the register.]

1687–8. Uriah Waring.   Buried Feb 4.

[The name of Waring appears in the sixteenth century, very early after the establishment of the register. It is frequent through the seventeenth and eighteenth centuries, bearers of it being often described as of Tanworth. Dugdale names the Warings as principal people of Tanworth *temp.* Edward III. Waring's Green in that parish is named from them.]

For some years before the death of Thomas Cole in 1688 we find many and violent changes of handwriting, numerous entries being hardly legible. Some are made under the heading of wrong years, the true year being added at the end, thus indicating that they were not inserted at the proper time.

For the purpose of comparison with the entries of a century earlier, I give here the number which occur in the two corresponding decades of the seventeenth century. They are as follows :—[1]

	Baptisms.	Marriages.	Burials.
1661 to 1670	125	17	122
1671 to 1680	129	14	106

It will be seen that the burials have increased in a much larger proportion than the baptisms, while the marriages are fewer than in the sixteenth century.

Thomas Cole was buried May 21, 1688, and Thomas's *Dugdale* enters his successor :—

Joh: Edwards. Cl. A.M. 5 Oct 1688. v.p. mortem Th. Cole.

---

[1] See also pp. 142 and 190.

Foster's record of him is :—

Edwardes, John, s John of Rochester, Kent, minister. Trinity
coll: matric, 8 Mch 1669–70. aged 16, B.A. from Merton
coll: 1674, fellow 1676, M.A. 1678 ; rector of Lapworth, co:
Warwick, 1688–9, and of Cuxham 1693 until his death
1717.

He continued rector here only about a year.   In
Brodrick's *Memorials of Merton College* it is stated
that he resigned in 1689, but the exact date or that of
the admission of his successor, Edward Welchman, is
not given.   There is nothing to show that he took up
his residence here.

This memorandum in the register would be in his
time :—

1689.   June 23.   Collected in the parish of Lapworth in the
county of Warwick to yᵉ Brief for the Irish Protestants the sum of one pound, eleven shillings &
nine pence.   Sam: Ainge: Minʳ
                 Walter W Wilson
         p. sign: Churchwarden

Samuel Ainge is shown as Rector of Haseley in
1685 (*Churches of Warwickshire*).

1689.   Wᵐ the son of Wᵐ Whitmore of Weightmar & Anne
his wife (Bapt July 6)

There is another brief for the same purpose as the
preceding in the following year, the exact date not
being given :—

1690.   Collected to yᵉ 2ᵈ Brief for yᵉ Irish Protestants in
Lapworth 1. 17. 0 one pound seventeen shillings.
                              Paul Low: Cu:

Such collections were being made in those years all
over the kingdom under the royal briefs or mandates.

The Irish Protestants were then suffering great hardship under the ascendency of James II., who still held his ground in Ireland.

Edward Welchman is the last of the rectors given in Thomas's *Dugdale* (edition 1730), he being still living in Thomas's day. The entry is simply :—

1689. Edwardus Welchman Cl: A M: v.p.r.

Foster has a full record of his career :—

Welchman, Edward, s of John of Banbury, Oxon, gent: Magdalen Hall matric, entry 7 July 1679, aged 14. B.A. 1683, fellow Merton coll: 1684, M.A. 1688; chorister Magdalen coll: 1679–82, Rector of Lapworth, co: Warw^k, 1690–1739; Archdeacon of Cardigan 1727, Chaplain to the Bishop of Lichfield and Canon 1732, Rector of Solihull, co: Warw^k, 1736, until his death 19 May 1739.

There is a discrepancy of a year between Dugdale and Foster as to the date of his becoming rector here. It is probable Foster's record is right, and that he took charge early in 1690, being then a young man of twenty-five, and having before him a reign of fifty years. He made his home here during all that time until Solihull was added to his other preferments three years before his death, when he removed to that place, leaving Lapworth to a curate. We may assume that the duties of the Archdeaconry of Cardigan were not onerous, as they could be performed from Lapworth.

He appears to have been twice married and had a large family. I transcribe from the register the entries which refer to him, or seem to refer to his immediate relatives :—

1691. Melicent the daughter of Edw: Welchman, Rector of this parish and Elizabeth his wife was Baptised and Buried March 29th.

1693.   Anthony Smith & Susanna Welchman, both of the parish of Bishop's Hampton (Marr^d June 5)

1696.   John ye son of Edward Welchman, Rector, and Mary his wife (Bapt^d July 7)

1698.   Edward ye son of Edw: & Mary Welchman (Bapt: April 27)

1699.   Elizabeth ye daughter of Mary Welchman (Bapt: August 17)

Richd Cook of Haseley & Mary Welchman of Bishop's Hampton (Marr^d Nov 16)

John Roberts of Hatton & Anne Cooke of Haseley (Marr^d Nov 16)

1700.   Melicent ye daughter of Edw: & Mary Welchman (Bapt Dec. 29. Bur^d Jan. 6)

1704.   Nathanael son of Edw: & Mary Welchman (Bapt April 2)

1706.   Mary daughter of Edw: & Mary Welchman (Bapt Aug. 12)

1708.   Samuel son of Edw: & Mary Welchman (Bapt Nov. 5)

1711.   Thomas son of Edw: & Mary Welchman (Bapt Nov. 18)

1714.   Anne daughter of Edw: & Mary Welchman (Bapt Sep 22)

1715.   Edw: Welchman Junr and Susanna Askew both of this parish were married June 6th.[1]

1716.   Richard the son of Edw: and Mary Welchman (Bapt Dec 27)

1718.   Constance d^r of Edw: and Mary Welchman (Bapt Jan 21)

[1] This son Edward was married, it will be seen (at the early age of seventeen), to one of the old Lapworth Askews. Quite recently there has come into the possession of the writer's family an old parchment deed, dated 25 March, 1720, being the assignment of a mortgage, by direction of this same Edward Welchman and his wife Susannah Welchman, to his father Edward Welchman of Lapworth. The deed bears the signatures of Edward Welchman and his wife Susannah, and is witnessed by two members of the Askew family.

1727. Edward the son of John Welchman, Vicar of Tanworth, & Mary his wife (Bapt March 29).[1]

1733. Samuel Seagrave, Rector of Compton Winyatt, &
Elizabeth Welchman (Marr^d Oct 27)

1734. John the son of Samuel & Eliz: Seagrave (Bapt
Decr 8)

1735. Mr Edward Welchman J^r (Buried April 9th)

A reference to the Welchman family occurs in
Churches of Warwickshire, where it is stated that—
during the last century the advowson of Preston Bagot
church was possessed by the Revd Edward Welchman, Rector
of Lapworth, and subsequently by the Revd R. Welchman,
rector of the parish. [R., however, seems to be a mistake
for W.]

There remain, in Preston Bagot Church, Welchman
monuments as under :—

On floor of chancel, " In memory of the Revd Mr Willm
Welchman, M.A. Patron and Rector of this church who
died April 30. 1744. Aged 42."

Against south wall of the chancel, " Near this place lie the
remains of the Revd Mr Will'^m Welchman, Rector of this
church, who, leaving a widow and two sons, died March 10th
1760. This stone was erected to his worthy memory by his
widow. Constantine relict of the Revd Mr Wm Welchman
died June 6. 1774. Aged 54."

The elder of these held the living of Preston Bagot
from 1731 to 1744, and the younger from 1744 to
1760. Foster shows the elder to have been a grandson of John Welchman of Banbury; they stood,
therefore, to our Edward Welchman of Lapworth
in the relationship respectively of nephew and grand-
nephew. In the closing years of Edward Welchman's

---

[1] John Welchman, who brings his child to be called after and baptised
by his grandfather, was Vicar of Tanworth from 1726 to 1764.

life the four parishes of Lapworth, Solihull, Tanworth, and Preston Bagot were thus all in the hands of members of the Welchman family at the same time.

The following are entries selected from the register during the long incumbency of Edward Welchman:—

1690. Joshua Stone of Purton in Oxfordshire & Melicent Mountfort of this parish (Marr^d July 24)

1693. Joseph the son of Wm Dowler of Claverdon & Eliz: Hemming of Ipsley (Bapt Mch 31)

  [The Overseers' accounts of 1691 show us that Elizabeth Hemming had gone wrong once before and given trouble.]

1695. Mary the wife of John Cambden. Bur^d Sepr 12th

1695–6. John Cambden Senr. Bur^d Mch 22.

1698–9. Tempest ye son of John & Elizab: Lilly (Bapt: Mch 20)

1699. Collected for ye French Protestant Refugees and Vaudois £5. 11. 3. E.W.

  [There continued to be a great influx of refugees from the religious persecutions on the Continent following the re-vocation of the Edict of Nantes. Similar persecutions at an earlier period in the century had been the occasion of Milton's sonnet, "Avenge, O Lord, thy slaughtered saints."]

About this time, but without actual date, a memorandum is made on a fly-leaf of the register under the name of Edw: Welchman, thus :—

Memorandum y^t forasmuch y^t many persons under pretence of their children being in danger of death procure them private baptism and then take no care to bring them into y^e church as y^e rubrick enjoins, all they which henceforth shall be publickly baptised or having been baptised privately shall be brought into y^e church as they ought to be, I shall register with a cross as thus [bap$\overset{+}{\text{t}}$] so that this + shall be a mark of distinction betwixt those and these who shall be baptised only in private without being so brought into y^e church.

Accordingly thereafter we find the distinction kept up, a small number of baptisms being without the +.

In this year (1699)[1] the rector took the trouble to enter on a fly-leaf of the register the particulars of the survey then newly made of the parish lands, thus preserving for us the oldest complete record of such properties which has survived.

Paul Low, who signed as curate in 1690, was apparently succeeded by "William Sanderson," who signs as curate in 1701. In Henley-in-Arden parish records, Paul Low is described as curate there in 1693.

1701.   Isaac Morteboys of Nuthurst (Buried July 20th)

> [The table of bequests mentions him under this year as having left 5s. a year for the poor of the parish. The Charity Commissioners' Report, 1826, describes it as "issuing out of the lands of Wm Ingram, Esq., who duly pays it." In 1901 this was compounded by a payment to the Feoffees of a capital sum of £10, yielding to the Charity the five shillings a year thus bequeathed in 1701.]

1704.   Susanna d^r of Joseph & Elizab: Bookley of Sotley in the parish of Bromicham's Aston bapt July 16.
         Elenor Cambden (Bur^d June 17)

1706.   Jacob the son of Thomas and Elizabeth Lapworth bapt Mch 31.

> [For about two decades at this time the name of Lapworth is frequent, but does not continue. Families of that name have, however, remained in the immediate neighbourhood.]

Mary d^r of Robert Price of Henley and Mary Luckman of this parish, bapt Decr 17 and Bur^d Decr 23.

1708.   John Morrice having been baptised in his infancy by a popish woman, & that Baptism being in ye Judgment of ye Bishop null & void, was baptised June 16th & confirmed ye same day.

---

[1] Under this year may be noted the following :—

"Edward Welchman, of Lapworth, to John Chamberlayne, F.R.S., 26 February, 1699 :—

has endeavoured these ten years to get a School for ye poor of his Parish; wch does not answer his expectation, the Houses being at such distance y^t the smaller children cannot come, and the parents cannot spare others from their work; on this head desires the advise of this Society." (*A Chapter in English Church History: S.P.C.K. Minutes and Correspondence*, 1698–1704.)

N

1709. Mary the daughter of Joshua Palmer, a married Quaker of Solihull, and Mary Ward of Bushwood. Bapt Oct 8.

1711. John Tarlton of Tanworth and Eliz: Green of this parish Married May 1st

[The first entry of a family many of whose tombs are in our churchyard, and who have buried here within recent years, though no longer residing in the parish. Some early entries describe them as of Botley.]

1712. Isaac ye son of Isaac and Mary Green ba⁺pt Sepr 9th.

[The Greens were an old land-owning family of the parish. The name has continued to be a common one through every decade from the beginning of the seventeenth century, and, indeed, with one or two short breaks, from the beginning of the register. The frequent recurrence of the same Christian name points also to continuous family descent. It is not impossible they may even join on to the Roger atte Grene of Edward III., who was one of the founders of our west chantry. The child here baptised lived to the age of ninety-three. His burial is entered in 1805, and his railed-in altar-tomb stands just within the churchyard at the top of the steps.]

Richard Bunter and Mary Purdon both of Alveston were married by license directed hither Jany 4.

1712–3. Thomas the son of Armale & Margaret Milborn bapt: Jan 1st.

["Millbourne Farm," a part of the Charity Estates, still preserves the name of this family, who then occupied it. They appear in the register through the greater part of the eighteenth century.]

1713. Eliz: Bellamy of Tanworth. Buried June 7th.

[The Bellamys continue to the present time. They are at first described as of Tanworth.]

1715. Sarah ye posthumous daughter of William Hyat a souldier in Flanders by Sarah his wife was baptised Jan 12th and buryed Jan 14th.

1716. John Cashmore of St: Michaels in Coventry & Margaret Mallery of this parish (Marr^d April 8th)

Entries of the Ingrams of Nuthurst are very frequent about this time.

1717. Job Ell and Esther Sorrell both of St. Martin's in Birmingham (Marr^d Jan 25)

1718. John Vincent aged 96 bury'd March ye 1st.

1720. Henry Cambden of Bermingham bury'd Sep 16th.

1720–1. Humphry Cambden of Henly bury'd Mch 21st.

1724. John Cambden bury'd June 23rd.

1729. Elizabeth Cambden bury'd August 16th.

These entries are the last we have of a family that seems to have been of importance here, residing at Brome Hall for two or three generations. The monuments of Henry Cambden and John his brother are the oldest in Lapworth church, which is singularly poor in monuments. Henry's is a slab in the floor at the west end of the south aisle, inscribed :—

Beneath this stone lies interred the body of Henry Cambden of Birmingham the son of John Cambden of Lapworth who departed this life the 13th day of September 1720 in the 65th year of his age.

In memoriam patris charissimi hoc saxum posuere dolentes liberi.

John's is a mural tablet fixed nearly above the last-mentioned, and reads :—

Near this stone lieth the body of John Camdẽ Lord of the Mannor of Bromham Hall in this parish who died June the 20th 1724 aged 71 years.

Elize: his wife also. She died August the 12th 1729 : aged 65 years.

These two monuments were originally at the east end of the south aisle, appropriately near what is called the Brome Hall window, so that the inscriptions on them are now incorrect. They were removed in the course of the restoration carried out under Mr. Street's direction in 1872, and at the same time (under, it is supposed, some fatuous notion of arranging them symmetrically at regular distances) every tombstone in the church was removed from its original position, with the exception only of those which are in the floor of St. Katherine's Chapel, now used as a vestry.

I have failed to obtain information as to the extent, position, or history of what is called on John Cambden's monument "the Mannor of Bromham Hall."

1725.   Isaac and Rebecca twin children of Willm and Hannah Ingram of Nuthurst (Bapt: Mch 13)

1730.[1] Willm ye son of Joseph Clarke deceased & Joyce his wife bapt Aug 18th.

1733.   Anne the d^r of John Crow of Aston Cantlaw and Anne Miller of this p'ish baptised May 27th.

1736.   James the bastard child of Sarah Harris bapt Mch 17.

1737.   Ann the d^r of Ann Harris by Thos Petty the reputed father bapt Nov 28th.

[The lantern is always held up to cases of illegitimacy, not solely in the interests of morality, but quite as much in those of the descent of property.]

Thomas Shelton and Anne Rhodes both of the parish of Salford were married with Lycence October 25th.

In 1736 Edward Welchman left us for Solihull, and though he continues rector here till May, 1739, Lapworth sees him no more. During his long residence here he seems to have taken an active interest in

---

[1] Thomas's edition of Dugdale bears date this year. In it he has the note :—

There are at Lapworth 46 houses and 30 cottages and twenty teams kept. At Bushwood, which is in the parish of Old Stratford, there are seven houses, & Sir Clobery Holt is Lord thereof; but under the Earl of Middlesex, who is Lord Paramount.

These figures, however, seem unduly low. The register for the decade 1720–9 contains 128 different *surnames*, and of these not more than about fifteen appear to belong to strangers.

parish affairs, especially as regards the charities. He had the habit of jotting down on the fly-leaves of the register the repairs which he executed from time to time at the rectory and in connection with the church, thus :—

1690. I new-floored the parlour and built the chimney on the chamber over the . . .

1693. I rebuilt the big barn.

1695. I repaired the middle part of the house.

„ (Novr 11th) I planted the orchard on the east side of the garden. Edw: Welchman.

1697. I rebuilt the bigger barn and the stables and filled the pool at the east end of the house.
[A field adjoining the rectory is called " Pool Hill."]
Memorandum that Andrew Archer esquier gave me the stone wherewith I groundsilled the lesser barn.

1702. I laid a new roof on the east end of the house and set up a seat in the chancel.

1703. I made the cellar and staircase and gate . . .

1704. I planted the ashes in the churchyard before the school.

1705. F. Luckman made the arbour towards the school.

1706. I built a round end to the upper barn and the chamber over the big kitchen.
I put up the pales betwixt the fold-yard and the way to the church.

1715. I new tiled the west end of the house.

1720. I built the lean-to on the south-side of the bigger barn.

		a	r	p
1725.	Memo: the ground in Little Pool Hill .	2	0	10
	Flax-ground in Little Church Field . .	2	0	12

Probably nothing remains of Edward Welchman's house in the present rectory, which is of much more recent construction. It must, however, have been a fairly spacious building, as a Terrier of the period [1] describes it as

A Dwelling House by estimation Six Bays, Five whereof are floord with Boards & one with Plaister.

The size of houses, barns, etc., was then reckoned by bays, and a "bay," as defined by the *New English Dictionary*, was—

The division of a barn or other building, generally from 15 to 20 feet in breadth. Applied to a house, it appears to be the space lying under one gable or included between two party walls.

[1] It is by the kindness of the Rev. K. Prescot, late Rector of Lapworth, that the Terrier above referred to is now given in full.

Extracted out of the Registry of the Consistory Court of Worcester.

ANNO DOMINI 1714.

A Terrier of Glebe Lands & other possessions belonging unto ye Rectory of Lapworth in the County of Warwick & Diocess of Worcester.

Imp^s A Dwelling House by estimation Six Bays, Five whereof are floord wth Boards & one with Plaister.

Item Two Barns and a Stable by estimation Six Bays.

It. Two Gardens & Two Orchards

It One Close called Great Almscroft by estimation Two Acres.

It One Close called Little Almscroft by estimation Three Quarters of an Acre.

It One Close called Great Pool-Hill containing by estimation Six Acres of Arable Land and three Acres & an half of Meadow Ground.

It One Close called Little Pool-Hill by estimation three Acres.

It One meadow called Brick Meadow by estimation Two Acres & an half.

It One Close called Plum Furlong by estimation Three Acres & an half at ye Bottom of which is a Fish Pond made by ye present Rector.

It One Close adjoining to Plum Furlong called Little Church Field by estimation Two Acres & an half.

It One Close called Great Churchfield by estimation Six Acres.

It There is belonging to ye Rectory all manner of Tythes in kind according unto the manner & custom of ye Parish ever used.

Edward Welchman   Rector
John Askew   Churchwarden
Walter Colier his mark Churchwarden
John Green
Isaac Green.

Examined and compared with the Original Terrier
John Clifton.   D. Reg.

This is interesting as a parish document, inasmuch as no later Terrier of the Glebe lands, etc., is known to have been lodged or to exist. It cannot be made to agree with the Glebe lands of the present day. The close of six acres called Great Churchfield appears to have been exchanged about 1802 for 3 a. 2 r. 20 p. now Glebe-land, much more conveniently situated as regards the rectory.

The "school" before which he "planted the ashes in the churchyard" was part of the buildings removed in 1892. The "arbour" or summer-house, which must also have stood within the churchyard, is a picturesque addition to our knowledge of the surroundings of the church.

The mention of the "Flax-ground" points to a cultivation that passed away with the spinning-wheel.

Edward Welchman was the author of several works of theology, of which only one is mentioned in Lowndes's *Bibliographer's Manual*, namely :—

The Thirty-nine Articles of the Church of England; illustrated with notes, &c.   London, 1740.

Lowndes adds, "there have been numerous editions."

I have also seen a copy of another little book of which the title-page runs :—

A practical Discourse on the Parable of Dives and Lazarus. By Edward Welchman, M.A., Rector of Lapworth in Warwickshire, sometime Fellow of Merton College in Oxford.

London : printed for A. & J. Churchill and for George Thorpe, bookseller in Banbury, MDCCIV.

It has a dedication in the style of that period, which we should think too fulsome now, "To the Honourable Jane Lady Bowyer," whom he describes as "a Patron that to the affluence of the one (Dives) hath joined the piety of the other (Lazarus)."

The Banbury bookseller's name on the title-page is due to Banbury being Welchman's paternal home. Lapworth must have become to him his real home, and he had hardly time to settle at Solihull before his death.   There is a well-preserved brass in the floor of the chancel of Solihull Church with this inscription to his memory ; for which, though long, a book of Lapworth memorials must find space :—

Here lieth the body of the Reverend Edward Welchman formerly Fellow of Merton College in Oxford from whence he became Rector of Lapworth. He was eleven years Archdeacon of Cardigan ; three years Rector of this church, and cheerfully quitted this life in full hopes of a blessed immortality the 19th of May 1739. Aged 75.

It would be here vain and needless to attempt the character of this great man ; the lovers of truth, religion or learning knew his worth ; his own pious and learned works do now properly speak for him and will continue to speak to the latest posterity.

To predict the duration of literary fame was hazardous then as it is hazardous now, but he remains an interesting figure in our parish history. Near to his own memorial on the chancel floor are two others, one on each side, to his son and daughter, which, as the children were Lapworth born, are also here transcribed :—

Here lieth the body of Thomas Welchman, one of the sons of the Revd Edw: Welchman, who departed this life the first day of February 1774: aged 64, leaving an only daughter who married James Dolphin : their remains are here interred, the former of whom died April 29th 1808 aged 69 years and the latter June 12th 1814 aged 80.

Here lies the body of Mrs [1] Anne Welchman daughter of the Revd Archdeacon Welchman and Mary his wife. She died April ye 16th 1759: aged 44.

Through this James Dolphin, his son-in-law, Edward Welchman kept up a sort of connection with us to our own times, for Robert Dolphin, the descendant of the said James, became Lord of the Manor of Lapworth, and continued to hold it within the writer's own recollection.

---

[1] Applied in those days to a middle-aged or elderly maiden lady.

The next rector was William Darby, of whom Foster's record says only :—

Darby, W^m, s W^m of Maidstone, Kent, Gent: Merton College, Matric. 30 March 1726, aged 18. B.A. 1729. M.A. 1732.

[In *Churches of Warwickshire* the name is given as " Darly."]

He held the living from 1739 to 1751. But his name is not appended to any entry in the register; neither does it appear in connection with the parish trusts. There is nothing to show that he took up his residence here. The register during most of his incumbency seems to have been kept very irregularly. Entries that have been omitted are squeezed in after-wards with difficulty. Many have been written with much-watered ink, and are now faded beyond re-covery. Those of 1741–2–3 are nearly all illegible. This condition of things continues with little allevia-tion until 1749, when this first volume ends. We glean, nevertheless, a few entries.

1744. Richard Fancourt son of Richard and Dorothea Susanna Iago was privately baptized July 11th and received into the Church the 26th of the same month.

[This, our second instance of a child receiving two names in baptism, his mother having two also, was a son of Iago, one of the minor poets of the eighteenth century, for whom Johnson was able to afford a few words of commendation. The above entry, there can be little doubt, is in the father's writing, and so are others until at any rate the October following. He writes his name distinctly Iago, not Jago, as it is usually printed. I conclude that he was curate here at the time this child was born, and probably occupying the rectory. His father was Rector of Beaudesert, and he himself became, in 1754, Vicar of Snitterfield, which living he continued to hold with other more valuable preferment until his death in 1781. His monument is in Snitterfield Church. His principal poem, called *Edge-Hill*, in four books, is mainly descriptive, and in it he mentions many places in our neighbourhood—" Umberslade," " Temple Balsall," " Wroxall," " Solihull," etc., but Lapworth he leaves unsung.]

1746. Under this year is the entry, evidently inserted at a later date :—

Edward Court and Elizab: Miller both of ye parish of Tardebig were by license married January ye 24th 1747/8.

1747. John Lonnen bury'd Sepr 24th
[The name of London, of which this is a misspelling, was common here in the seventeenth and eighteenth centuries.]

1749. Katherine daughter of Job & Dorothy Balamy Bur^d.
[Numerous Bellamys still remain amongst us, and Job has continued a Christian name with them.]

Ursly the daughter of Ann Rogers by Uzzil Titmosh the reputed father (Bapt May 21)
[" Ursly " probably means Ursula, but " Uzzil " I have not met with elsewhere.]

With the year 1749 this first volume of the register ends. It ought to have been discontinued a year earlier ; but when the last page properly available was filled up the entries were made to overflow, as mentioned earlier, on to a little available space under " 1587," and thence to a fly-leaf at the beginning of the book. The last entry is of a baptism under date of March 18th, when the year was close upon its end.

On a fly-leaf at the end of the volume, amongst other scrawls, stands this, which we may take as epilogue by someone who advocates a classification of entries which had never been observed for any length of time :—

Let this side o'th page your weddings adorn,
The other attest when y^r infants were born,
Let the dead by y^{m}selves also stand on a side,
For who that is living wth them shou'd abide.

PARISH REGISTERS, VOL. II., 1750–1810.

[CONSISTS of forty leaves of parchment, strongly bound in calf, 16½″ × 7″. From the beginning of 1750 to the end of 1754 it contains "Christenings," Marriages, and Burials. From the beginning of 1755 it contains Christenings and Burials only; and at the end of that year there is a note :—

Memorandum : as the Churchwardens of every parish are obliged since the year 1754 to provide a distinct register for marriages only, they will not be set down here for the future.]

From the commencement of this volume the entries are made in a distinct and small handwriting, which proves to be that of one Owen Bonnell, who became curate in the beginning of 1750, while William Darby was still rector. He came as a young man of twenty-four, and he had before him upwards of forty-five years under successive rectors (four in all), during the greater part of which time he seems to have had practically the sole charge of the parish. The last of the four rectors under whom he served is still remembered by at least one old parishioner living here at this day.

There is nothing to show whether William Darby resigned this living or died, but with the heading of 1751 we get a note in the register :—

Cha⁵ Bean, Rector
Owen Bonnell, Curate.

Foster's record of Charles Bean is brief, not giving his preferments :—

Bean, Charles, s Charles of Beaksbourne, Kent, cler; Merton Coll: matric 27 July 1727 aged 15. B A 1731 : M A 1734.

He is mentioned as Vicar of St. Mary's, Warwick, from 1750 to 1766 (*Churches of Warwickshire*), and would appear therefore to have held that living along with Lapworth from 1751 to his death. There can be no doubt that he made his home at Warwick. But there are entries in the register from time to time which show that he was here occasionally.

In 1752, under the Act 24 George II. c. 23, for adjustment of the calendar, eleven days in the month of September were dropped. What would have been September 3rd was called September 14th.

In 1752 also the legal year was by another statute made to begin thenceforward with January 1st. At the end of it in the register there are three entries under January to which the note is appended : " These three last according to the new style are in the year 1753"; and accordingly under the heading of that year they are re-entered, and from that time the uncertainty and variation as to the beginning and end of the year cease.

Amongst names that are most frequent about this time are those of Bellamy, Cranmer, Mander, Mortiboys, Ingram, Green, Lea, Tarlton, and Brawdbury.

1758.   Mary Maydew (Bur^d Oct 3rd)

[This name, under various spellings (as Maidew, and even Madue), first appeared towards the end of the seventeenth century and continued about eighty years.]

1759.   Deborah Almanack (Bur^d Decr 7)

1763.   Mary the daughter of Thomas & Elizabeth Cranmer was born (by her father's account) on Feb. 11. 1763.

[Several entries relating to this and other families are qualified in this way.]

1763. Ann y̆ daughter of Isaac and Hannah Ingram (Bapt.
Jany 21st)

[She lived to the age of ninety, and was the last survivor
here of the old Nuthurst family. Though baptised Ann, she
seems to have been known by the name of Hannah, and
under that name is buried. Her tombstone in the church
says: "Hannah Ingram, last surviving daughter of Isaac
Ingram Esq of Nuthurst House. Died on the 31st. day of
March 1853: aged 92." It would seem that her age was a
matter of doubt, and is here overstated by two years. In
a book containing "Memoranda Parochiala," Mr. Mildmay,
rector at the time of her death, writes (understating her age
by two years) :—

Miss Ingram died at the age of 88, leaving £20 to be distributed amongst the poor. She wished to be buried in the
church, and as she was the last of the family I therefore con-
sented, but charged £10 fee to prevent the recurrence of such
a request.

There can be no doubt that she was the child baptised
"Ann" in 1763. There is in the register no baptism of any
Hannah, and no burial of any Ann.

No interment has taken place in the church since this
of Miss Ingram in 1853.]

1768.   This year bears the heading—

Joseph Kilner, Rector.
Owen Bonnell, Curate.

Foster says only :—

Kilner, Jo^s, s James of Lexden, Essex, cler., University Coll:
matric. 2 July 1737. aged 16, B A 1741. Merton College.
M.A. 1744.

Charles Bean is shown in *Churches of Warwickshire* as ceasing to be Vicar of St. Mary's, Warwick,
in 1766. He ceased, no doubt, to be Rector of
Lapworth at the same time, by death. It is probable,
therefore, that Joseph Kilner became rector here at a
date somewhat earlier than 1768. He held this living
till his death in 1793, but seems never to have resided

here. During all the time of his incumbency there is no entry in any of the registers which bears his signature. In a list of lands taken for the construction of the Stratford Canal he is described in 1792 as of Cirencester. He had found Owen Bonnell curate when he took the living. Bonnell continued curate all through Kilner's time, and was the only one whom the parish knew. He remained curate when Joseph Kilner, his third non-resident rector, after twenty-five years of office, died.[1] In those days such things were possible.

1772. Theophonia the daughter of Thomas and Mary Gardner, travellers (Bapt. June 13).

[For some unexplained reason this entry has a page to itself out of order at the beginning of the volume. "Travellers" means, probably, "tramps." In 1773 we get another remarkable female name, "Apalona."]

For comparison with corresponding periods of previous centuries,[2] I again set out the number of entries that occur in the register within a period of twenty years, namely—

	Baptisms.	Marriages.	Burials.
1761–1770	116	29	123
1771–1780	129	36	94

[1] Extract from *History of Cirencester*. (No author. Rudder: Cirenc[r]. 1800.)

(*Monuments in Church*)

At the entrance, just without St. Catherine's Chapel, on a plain marble tablet:

JOSEPH KILNER

of Merton College, in the University of Oxford, sometime Fellow, and since beneficiary: after a life of infirmity most graciously alleviated and wonderfully lengthened out to more than 72 years

died the 3rd day of June 1793

Prostrate to the Will of God and to the riches of his mercy, in this End to sin and Way to immortality through Jesus Christ our Lord.

[2] See also pp. 142 and 171.

It will be noticed how singularly near some of these figures are to those of a hundred years earlier.

1786.   Mary Ann daughter of William and Susanna Avery.
        Bapt July 25.

        [This William and Susanna had a large family whose baptisms are recorded in the years following. The Averys continue to furnish many entries to the register until about the middle of the nineteenth century, and there are several of their tombstones in the churchyard. The late Alderman Thomas Avery, of Birmingham, was a member of this family.]

For some years prior to 1789 small sums of money are noted at the end of each year by way of memorandum.   At the end of 1789 we find :—

Mem: that I paid the Widow Bradford of Henley the King's duty for Births Marriages and Burials in full of all demands to the end of the year 1789.   Owen Bonnell.

    [By an Act 23 George III. c. 67, a stamp duty of 3d. was imposed on each entry of a baptism, marriage, or burial, from October 1st, 1783.   This Act was repealed October 1st, 1794.]

1789.   Thomas Chambers of the Nag's Head at Hockley
        Heath (Bapt: Oct. 28th)

        [The "Nag's Head" continues to be a public-house sign there.]

1790.   Ann, daughter of Mr. Biddle of Tanworth by his
        housekeeper (Bapt: Nov. 1)

        [Owen Bonnell, it seems, did not know the mother's name.]

At the head of this year (1790) there is also an insertion made at a later date, thus :—

June 1.   1802.   On enquiry being made respecting the birth and baptism of Maria, daughter of William and Mary Haycock, the clerk produced his rough book wherein he keeps the register, and showed that a Mary Haycock was baptised with her brother William on the 12th January 1790.

1792. There are indications of the register being kept irregularly at this time.

1793. This page is headed with the signature of a new rector: "H. A. Pye (Soc: Mert:) Rector. Æt: suæ 27 vice Kilner def:"

From the beginning of Owen Bonnell's régime we have lost the fulness of the entries to which we were accustomed in the old volume, a fulness which adds so much to its interest. In burials he usually gives simply a name and a date. Towards the end of his time, indeed, he often gives nothing more, even in baptisms not naming the parents. At the end of 1793 his neat handwriting and clear signature disappear for ever. For some time past the writing has been uncertain and tremulous. There are entries so sprawling as to suggest that he had become all but blind, and one such entry is his last. During all the long period of his curacy there can be found scarcely a dozen entries, either of baptisms, marriages, or burials, in any hand but his. In the marriage register (where from 1753 the signature of the officiating minister had to be appended), from 1768 to 1793, the whole period of Joseph Kilner's rectorship, every couple is shown to have been joined together by Owen Bonnell. There is not even one case of a strange minister.

In 1796 we get the entry :—

Burial. The Revd Owen Bonnell, curate. July 31st.

He had been curate about three years under his fourth rector, H. A. Pye, who happily was at that time resident, so that probably during those years the old man had not much of the parish work.

A slab on the chancel floor, within the altar rails, used to read—

Sacred to the memory of Owen Bonnell, Clerk, who after worthily performing the duties in this parish 45 years, died the 27th July 1796 in the 70th year of his age.

The inscription has been preserved for us in *Churches of Warwickshire*, but the slab itself is gone. It was to be seen in its proper place until the restoration of the chancel in 1860, but not later. There can be little doubt that at that time it was buried, along with Thomas Cole's slab, and perhaps others of which we have no record, and that it might now be found a few inches below the pavement then laid down. If this surmise is right it must have been so buried when Owen Bonnell was still remembered by some then living here. He seems to have been, as indeed the name suggests, a Welshman, and I find this further brief record of him in Foster's *Alumni Oxon.*:—

Owen Bonnell, s of Owen, of St: Ismail, co: Carmarthen, pleb: Jesus College, matric 28 Feb. 1743–4. aged 18. B.A. 1747.

Ten years after his own death there is the entry :—

1806. Elizabeth Bonnell. Buried Feb. 28th.

Whether this was his widow, maiden sister, or some other relative we cannot tell.

Foster's record of Henry Anthony Pye (he himself writes the name "Antony" when he first signs it in the register) is—

Pye, Henry Anthony, s Anthony of St: Andrew's, Holborn, Middlesex, arm. Merton Coll: matric. 16 Dec. 1782, aged 16. B.A. 1786, Fellow, M.A. 1789, Rector of Lapworth, co: Warw^k, 1793, Vicar of Cirencester 1805, Prebendary of Worcester 1818, Rector of Harvington, co: Worcester 1818 until his death 25 March 1839.

He thus held the living of Lapworth forty-six years, and along with it successively all the preferments named until his death. At the end of 1806 he ceased to reside in the parish (leaving a note to that effect, with his signature, in the Feoffees' minute book), removing to Cirencester, where he died; but he seems to have continued to come here occasionally, especially to attend the annual meetings of the Charity Trustees, which he rarely missed until after 1836.

It is remarkable with how few steps these successive long tenures of office carry us back to very distant times. Pye is still remembered here; yet his first curate, Owen Bonnell, came to Lapworth in 1750, and might well have known Edward Welchman, who took the living in 1689, having succeeded with an interval of a few months only (and probably himself known) Thomas Cole, who was born in 1602, while Elizabeth was still on the throne. There are only four lives thus bridging three centuries.

H. A. Pye, of Lapworth, was a relative of Henry James Pye, George III.'s Poet Laureate. There are entries of his children in the register as under :—

1797. Harriet Frances, d^r of H. A. and Frances Ursula Pye
       Born July 11. Bap^t Oct. 8.

1798. Sarah Elizabeth, d^r of H. A. and Frances Ursula Pye
       Bapt Sepr 23.

1800. Henry Anthony, s of H. A. and Frances Ursula Pye
       Born Dec 7. 1799. Bap^t July 23.

1801. Thomas Pye. (Buried June 28)
           N.B. was born Novr 1801 (*sic*) and privately
       bapt^d in the same month.

1803. Jemima, d^r of H. A. and Frances Ursula Pye (Born
       July 29. 1802. Bapt April 17. 1803.)

1805. William, s of H. A. and Frances Ursula Pye (Bapt.
        June 30)
1807. Emma, d^r of H. A. and Frances Ursula Pye Bapt.
        June 14.

The son Henry Anthony became Rector of Sapperton, Glos., in 1833, and held the living fifty years—till his death in 1883.

In 1805 we have the entry :—

Isaac Green, bur^d Decr 20th

This was the last of the old land-owning family before mentioned.   His baptism was noted in 1712.

In 1806, at the time of, or shortly before, the removal of H. A. Pye to Cirencester, James Way became curate here, and from the period of his arrival takes charge of the registers and appears to have given special attention to them.   He adds a little variety to his entries from time to time by stating the cause of death ; as "drowned in the canal" (then newly made), "died intoxicated," "killed by the bursting of a gun barrel," "scalded to death," etc.   There is the following entry in 1810 :—

Buried May 23rd Mrs. Eliz: Garrett Ross Way.

and in 1816 (in another volume)—

Buried Nov 20$^{th.}$ James Way. Lapworth Rectory. 41.
                        Charles Curtis, Officiating Minister.
    [The latter was at that time Rector of St. Martin's, Birmingham, and also Rector of Solihull.   He was a famous fox-hunter.]

An inscribed tile in the chancel floor (placed there probably in 1860 in substitution for another record) reads, "Vault of the Rev: James Way 1816"; and at the west end of the south aisle, on the south wall, a mural tablet of white marble, removed from the chancel in 1860, bears a long inscription (printed in *Churches of Warwickshire*) to his memory and that of his wife and children.   It describes him as "Rector of Adwell, in the co: of Oxford, and some years the officiating clergyman of this parish."

Foster says :—

James Way, s. James of Thame, Oxon, arm: Pembroke College, matric. 2 Nov 1792, aged 17, exhibitioner 1793, B.A. 1796, M.A. 1799, Rector of Adwell, Oxon, and Curate of Lapworth, co: Warwick, 1803 until his death in 1816.

This is not quite correct, for he only became curate here, as before mentioned, in 1806.   But it seems to be a curious case of a rector making himself an absentee in order to take a curacy elsewhere, for there is no doubt that during all the ten years that he was curate here he continued to hold the living of Adwell, a small parish since united to that of South Weston, Oxon.   The records of absenteeism probably have not many such instances.

During the twenty-three years that H. A. Pye remained absentee rector after the death of James Way, his curates were, so far as appears from entries in the registers—

1817 to 1826.   G. Childe.

[In one entry he is described as "Chaplain to the Warwick Gaol."]

1826 to end of 1838.   Donald Cameron.

[He became Vicar of Snitterfield in 1840, and held that living till his death in 1877.]

1839 (to end of October).   J. H. Wilding.

H. A. Pye had died March 25th of this year (1839), but it is not until November that we get the first entry signed by his successor, G. Tyndall.

It is in the year 1839 that we find for the first time amongst the names of occasional ministers that of R. W. Johnson, who was then entering on his long incumbency of Packwood, only terminated by his death in 1889.

PARISH REGISTERS, Vols. III. TO VII., 1754–1853.

With 1810 the end of the second volume of the registers is reached, and it does not come within the scope of these *Memorials* to examine in any detail the records of more recent years.

A few words may, however, be given to the later volumes, and first to those which bring up the marriages to the corresponding period, namely :—

Vol. III: Marriages April 16th, 1754, to November 9th, 1812.
    IV: Banns of Marriages 1754 to 1794.

In 1794 the keeping of a Banns book seems to have been discontinued, and is only resumed in a new volume in 1823.

The arrangement of the marriage and other registers in columns under printed headings began with 1754, and the title-page of the first registers printed and ordered to be used in all parishes has itself become rather a literary curiosity :—

A register book for marriages in all Parish Churches and
   Chapels, conformable to an Act of the 26th of King
   George II entitled "An Act for the better preventing of
   clandestine marriages": published according to the Act
   of Parliament by Joseph Fox, parish clerk to the House
   of Commons.   London, printed for Joseph Fox, bookseller in Westminster Hall; and Benjn Dodd, bookseller
   to the Society for promoting Christian knowledge at the
   Bible and Key in Ave-Mary Lane, near St: Paul's. 1754.

Within the fifty-eight years covered by volume iii. (1754–1812) there are 177 marriages recorded—only three per annum. In these we get for the first time an educational test for the parish so far as writing is concerned. Out of the 354 people thus united no fewer than 184 are illiterate. Of 70 couples neither of the pair could write ; of 32 the man only, and of 12 the woman only, could write. There are many instances in which not only could neither of the contracting parties write, but neither could their witnesses. The first marriage recorded by H. A. Pye, after he became rector, is signed by four marks only. The variety of marks is curious. The cross is most frequent, but some prefer to attempt a circle, some of the more ambitious try to trace a heart, some make one straight line, some two, some are able to make the initial letter of their Christian name or surname. Fifty-nine, being exactly one-third of the whole number of marriages, are by licence. From 1754 to 1793 there are, as before mentioned, probably not half a dozen marriages performed by anyone but Owen Bonnell. Then till 1807 they are mostly signed by H. A. Pye, and after him, until 1812, by James Way, curate. There are very few instances of marriages performed by strange ministers, but in 1810 one Thomas Blyth officiates, and, being perhaps a nervous man, he has entered the marriage on a blank space which happened to be left under 1768, and there it stands.

The last entry in the above-described Marriage Register is under date of November 9th, 1812.

As will be seen from the list given on p. 137, Volume v. covers Baptisms and Burials from 1811 to 1812, and Volume vi. contains the Baptisms from 1813 to 1853.

The next volume of Marriages (vol. vii.) begins with July 19th, 1814, and ends October 30th, 1837. There would seem, therefore, to have been about twenty months without any marriage to record. This volume contains 81 entries in the twenty-three years which it covers. Of these 14 are by licence and 67 by banns. The educational standard shows little or no advance from that of the previous century. There are 27 cases in which neither of the married pair could write, and 13 in which neither they nor their witnesses could do so.

Volume viii. covers Burials from 1813 to 1870, while of the remaining volumes [ix., x., xi., xii., and xiii.], all but one remain in use up to the present day.[1]

---

[1] See footnote on p. 253.

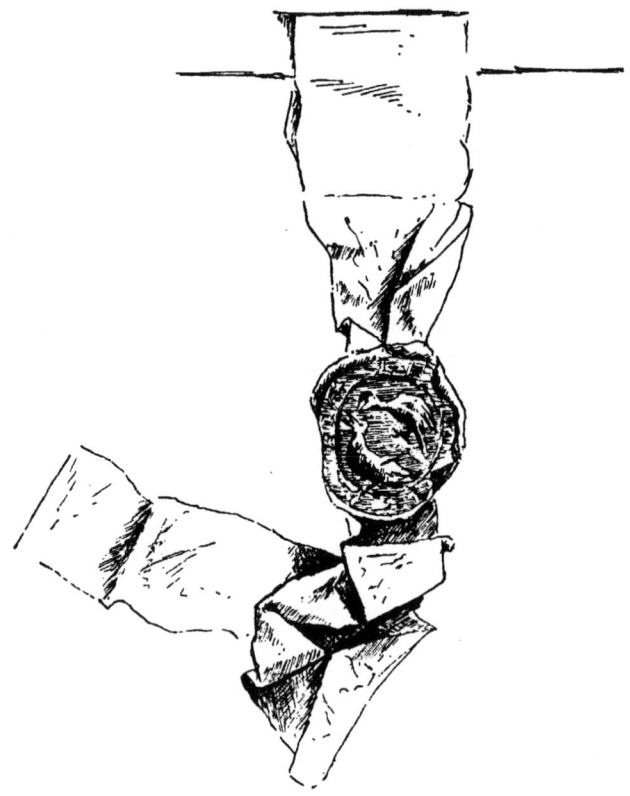

Seal of deed, 1370
Roger atte Grene & o^{rs} to William le Smẏth
(Richd de Toppesford one of the witnesses)

p. 52

OVERSEERS' ACCOUNTS

"... *the exchequer of the poor.*"

RICHARD II.

CHAPTER V

OVERSEERS' ACCOUNTS: 1688 to 1704

THERE has been preserved, not in the parish chest, but by accident, a much-decayed and mouse-eaten fragment of a book containing the accounts of the Overseers of the poor, which covers the period from 1688 to 1704.

No one year is complete except 1704. But many years are complete on the receipts side of the account ; and in most of them, though we do not get all the details of expenditure, we get the total. In the imperfect sheets we find many entries which are interesting, though only of a kind common to the period.

It happens also that just at this time (namely, in 1699) the Feoffees had a new survey made of their estates, and Edward Welchman, then rector, who had a habit of using the fly-leaves of the Parish Register as a commonplace book, entered it there, and has thus preserved for us the oldest schedule that exists of the parish properties. It gives the tenants' names, the acreage of their holdings, the names of their fields (but not their rents), and shows that the total quantity of Charity land was then 175 a. 2 r. 16 p.

In disposing of their income the Feoffees allotted

to (1) the Overseers, (2) the Highway Surveyors, and (3) the Churchwardens, not fixed sums of money, but such and such lands, leaving each of the parish authorities to make the best of their respective portions and pay their own disbursements. The Overseers seem to have had allotted to them about 43 acres and the Banbury house, from which they had an income of about £22 in relief of rates.

The survey copied in the Parish Register gives, as I have said, names and acreage, but not rent. The Overseers' accounts give names and rents, but not acreage ; so that by combining the two we learn that the Charity lands were let at this time for 10s. an acre on the average, including the houses attached to the several holdings. And as these accounts give also the amounts derived from the levies (of Poor Rates) from year to year, we have approximate data for ascertaining the rateable value of the parish at the time to have been £1,457, and that something like 10s. an acre was the outside rent of land generally throughout the parish. The Charity land was indeed let rather above than below the average.

In the years covered by these accounts, the sums raised by Poor Rates were as follows :—

Year.	Raised in Year.			Rate in £.	Year.	Raised in Year.			Rate in £.
	£	s.	d.	d.		£	s.	d.	d.
1688	18	4	4	3	1697	27	11	3	4½
1689	18	4	4	3	1698	27	11	3	4½
1690	9	2	2	1½	1699	missing			—
1691	9	2	2	1½	1700	59	14	4	10
1692	18	4	4	3	1701	27	11	3	4½
1693	13	13	3	2¼	1702	27	11	3	4½
1694	27	6	6	4½	1703	55	2	6	9
1695	22	16	11	3¾	1704	27	11	3	4½
1696	22	16	11	3¾					

1700 and 1703, as shown by the exceptionally high rates, had been years of great distress. The entries of relief given to the poor occupy about six pages in the accounts, where in other years they take up only about two.

The rateable area of the parish to-day is 2,885 acres, and the rateable value is £7,182 (1904). Probably a comparison on similar data, if obtainable in other purely rural parishes of our district, would show somewhat similar increases of value in the two hundred years.

The following are some of the entries of payments selected from these old accounts. It will be noticed that, especially as regards clothing (bearing in mind the much greater value of money in those days), the prices then paid were very heavy. The permanent poor of the parish (those, namely, who were in receipt of relief all the year round) seem in ordinary years to have been from twelve to fifteen in number.

		£	s.	d.
1688.	Paid for a paire of Stockings for Tho⁸ Palmer, he being a poore of the p'ish .		2	0
	(a shurt)			0
	(a paire of Shues)		3	4
1689.	Paid Mr Lowe for baptizing Eliz: Furley's child (illegitimate) . . .		1	0
	do: for burying Richd Peto . .			6
	do: for wrighting a certificate of buriall .			6

[Paul Lowe was curate, and the Overseers paid the burial and baptismal fees for paupers.]

	Paid to me (Walter Willson, Overseer) with a poore boy to p'ntiss . . .	6	0	0

[There are entries every year for apprenticing of children. This fee is a very heavy one for the period.]

		s.	d.
1690.	Paid to the poore of Nuthurst	12	0
	[This would be half the rent of Collett's close of 3 acres, showing it was then let at 8s. an acre.]		
	To Tho⁸ Stowe to bye him a strike (Bushel) of Corne.	2	6
	Given to John Morrell to bye Salve for his sore leg, he being a poore lame man of the p'ish	10	0
	[He has this 10s. a year for many years.]		
1691.	A new shute of clothes for Tho⁸ Palmer	11	5
	For 6 hundred of Coals for the Widd: Parrie	4	6
	For going to Ipslie and for a horse for Eliz: Hemming to ride on	2	6
	[Probably the Overseer and she rode pillion. She had been the cause of a trial between the parishes, in which much expense was incurred and Ipslie got the worst of it.]		
1692.	Paid for the charges of the marriage of Tho⁸ Slye's servant	18	6
	[The parish troubles were often brought to an end by defraying the expenses of a marriage; and the Overseers seem to have provided a good hearty meal on such occasions.]		
1693.	For 2 loads of wood for Widd: Minors she being a poore woman with several small children.	12	0
1694.	2 Hundred & half of bricks to mend Humphʸ Crandall's bricken	3	6
1695.	Given Widd: Parrie to go to the doctor with her sore eyes and for a horse to carry her	9	6
1697.	Paid Goodwife Slow when her husband was in prison		6
	For making a pair of breeches for Tho⁸ Palmer .		5
1700.	Paid Francis Mawer for going to Bromsgrove and taking Lazarus Bozward with him	6	0

		£	s.	d.
1700.	For an iron poot for Mary Croley . .		3	0
	Paid R. Jennings for going to Halesowen to seek masters for apprentices . .		1	8
	Paid Goody Pratt to buy Hall's child a coat & a surpliss & shues . . .		9	2
	Paid for 8 thrauves[1] of straw . . .		9	4
	Paid the King's duty for the buriall of Tho⁸ Satchwell		4	0

[Such entries are of frequent occurrence about this time. A tax of 4s. on each burial was payable under an Act of William & Mary, 1694. The Overseers paid it in the case of paupers. The same Act imposed a tax on Births and Marriages, but there are no entries of payment of these by the Overseers. The Act was allowed to expire soon after 1700.]

		£	s.	d.
	Paid to the third-burow[2] of Kingswood for going to take the goods of John Smith if any had bin . . .			6
	Paid for assigning a surtyvycat by to justices of Peace. . . .		1	0

[i.e. signing a certificate by two Justices.]

		£	s.	d.
	Paid Mr. Welchman (Rector) towards the money he lent for to redeem Tho⁸ Slow out of prison	1	10	0
	For going 3 times to Esqʳ Archer's on Towne business		1	6

[Probably the nearest Justice, living at Umberslade.]

		£	s.	d.
	For going to Stratford on Towne business		2	6
	Given John Kendall a strike of wheat .		3	9
	„ „ „ a strike of barley .		1	11
1704.	Paid for bread for the poor on St: Thomas Day		5	0
	Paid for a paire of breeches for Palmer's son		5	0

[1] "Thrave [Prov. Eng.] 24 sheaves of grain, set up in 2 shocks of 12 sheaves each." (*Standard Dict. of the Eng. Language.*)

[2] "I must go fetch the third-borough." (*Taming of the Shrew.*)

	s.	d.
1704. Paid for 3 weeks table for Eliz: Hall . .	4	6
Paid for cloth to make letters for the poor		6

> [Under the year 1695, there is also an entry "Paid for letters for the poor, 3s." These "letters for the poor" were badges of red or blue cloth which by an Act of Parliament of William III. those in receipt of parish relief had to wear upon the shoulder under certain penalties, and without this there was to be no relief. The badge was a large P with the initial of the parish : our poor would therefore bear the letters L.P. This provision was not repealed until 1810 (50 Geo. III. c. 52).]

At the end of each year's account a page is devoted to a list of the burials that have taken place within the year, at the foot of which is a certificate, thus :—

All which were buried in woollen only, according to the Act of Parliament in that case made, as may appear by several affidavits brought me according to the said Act.

Edward Welchman.　Rector of Lapworth.

Every parish history tells how an enactment of Charles II. (1678) provided, with a view to encourage the woollen industry of the kingdom, that the dead should be buried in shrouds of woollen only, and the relatives had to bring with them at the burial an affidavit sworn before a magistrate for delivery to the parson that this enactment had been complied with. The law was not repealed till 1815, but had ceased to be enforced at an earlier date.

Such entries are common to parish accounts of the period, but these are interesting to us as giving glimpses of Lapworth ways and conditions two hundred years ago.

VIEW OF THE INTERIOR OF LAPWORTH CHURCH

SHEWING POSITION OF ANCIENT WINDOW IN NORTH WALL OF NAVE DISCOVERED IN THE
RESTORATION OF 1872

1791–1825
(including payments made by the Treasurer of the Charity Feoffees, 1815–25)

The extracts already given from the Overseers' books were of the dates 1688 to 1704. There are no other parish books of account till about a hundred years later. The following are from the Overseers' books commencing 1791 :—

	£	s.	d.
1791. 3 Qts ale at meeting at the Bell . .		1	0
Paid J. C—— for work done in Tapsford lane		1	0

[This shows our present name of "Tapster lane" to be a comparatively recent corruption, the above form preserving much more closely the name of the old family of "de Toppesford."]

	£	s.	d.
S. Chinn. 1 lb. of wool . .			7
Widow H—— a pair of Hurd-cards .		1	6
1792. Paid Mr Bonnell for looking in the register		1	0

[Owen Bonnell was the curate who had been here then nearly fifty years.]

	£	s.	d.
Nov. 5. Gave the ringers at Gunpowder Treason		10	6

[This occurs yearly.]

	£	s.	d.
1795. April 7th. Paid for ironwork done at the stocks	1	6	0½

[They stood by the side of the road leading from Kingswood to Hockley Heath, about opposite where the drawbridge now crosses the canal to Millbourne Farm. A footpath went from there to the church, and it is said that Sunday was chosen by preference for the punishment of the stocks, perhaps that church-goers might be encouraged to virtue by the sight of the delinquents.]

P

	£	s.	d.

1795. Paid for the dole at the Church . . 4 10 0

> [At the end of 1795 there are seventy or eighty pages left blank, and the account is then resumed for 1798 only, the two years intermediate having never been entered up]

1798. Paid for a letter from Tysoe . . . 8½

> [Sundry entries for repairs, mainly of Church Bells, to the amount of about £43.]

Paid J. Smith for serving the office of Overseer . . . 10 0 0

Paid him for journey to Hungary Harbury 10 11

Paid the common fine and assigning pence for 13 years . . . 2 13 9

> [This I suppose to have been a payment of 4s. 1½d. a year from the parish to the Lord of the Manor in respect of rights of common.]

Paid for a plank to repair Kingswood Bridge . . . 4 0

> [The Kingswood brook was thus apparently crossed by a ford and a footbridge.]

Novr. Gave the ringers for Nelson's Victory . . . 18 6

> [This would be the Battle of the Nile.]

Paid for a smock frock & breeches for W. H—— . . . 7 6

1802–1806. Paid for mending Sarah Brooks's wheel 1 8

Paid for a wheel for Isabella Chinn . . 6 6

Dame Swann to buy a pair of wool-cards 2 0

> [There are many entries for the repairs of these wheels, new wheels, wool, and so on, reminding us that at the beginning of the nineteenth century every cottage still had its spinning-wheel.]

1802. Paid for bread at the Easter Meeting . 6

Paid for Ale at the Easter Meeting . . 8 0

		£	s.	d.
1802.	Paid for 20 dinners on the rent day . .	1	10	0
	„ „ ale and tobacco for do: . .	1	18	6

[The proportion of ale to bread at Easter is quite Falstaffian, and the allowance at the rent day must have been more than a gallon a man. There seem to have been also monthly meetings, for which there is always "A bottle of ale 4s. 0d." or sometimes 5s.]

1803. Paid John Maids to serve in the army of reserves 14 14 0

Paid Price to serve in the army of reserves 8 8 0

„ Wright for finding a substitute . . 26 5 0

„ the substitute's wife . . . 7 17 0

[These are, as it happens, all paid within one month. They are instances of the heavy charges which fell upon the parish and swelled the Poor Rates for many years during the continuance of the war with France. In 1804 they amount to about £60. In some years they are £70 or £80. They continue with great regularity till 1815, when relief came with Waterloo. These were large sums for so small a parish as ours.]

Aug. 24. Paid expenses endeavouring to take a man for a bastard child. 2 days, 3 persons 3 8 11

1802–5. Paid for a letter from Kenilworth . . 9½

„ „ „ from Warwick . . 9

„ „ „ from Coventry . . 1 0½

[It was, of course, the receiver who paid postage in those days.]

Pair of stockings footing for David Lock . 11¾

Gave Spragg towards a pair of mittens . 2 0

Paid Grafton & Wilks for Books for the Singers 3 16 0

1806. Gave Collett's child a Pinbefore . . 1 3

38 cwt. of Coals at 10d. . . . 1 11 8

	£	s.	d.

1807. Gave Pratt towards setting his son
apprentice   3   0   0

Consideration money for Jack Weller's
indentures   8   0   0

[Charges for apprenticing continue frequent.]

Paid for a wooden leg for T. Kendall   .   12   4

1809. Apr¹ 3ʳᵈ. Ale for the ringers at the King's
Coronation   4   8

Oct 26. Gave the ringers at the Jubilee .   10   6

[George III. entered on the fiftieth year
of his reign on that day.]

1810. Paid Mrs. Burge for doctoring Bradford's
leg   12   6

1811. Paid Mr. Green for taking the population
of the parish   1   5   5

1812. Paid John Smith's family when a Localing   8   0

1814. Feb 18. Paid for one dozen of Sparrows'
heads at 3d. a dozen   .   .   .   3

Paid for 22 doz: of ditto, old ones, at 4ᵈ a doz.   7   4

April 9. Paid the churchwarden for an
iron chest for the Registers   .   .   6   6   0

[This would be the church chest now in
use.   It most likely replaced one of oak with
three locks, which still survives¹ and probably
goes back to Elizabethan times.]

Aug. 13. Paid for ale for the ringers by
order of Mr. Edwards (Churchwarden)   1   8   0

[It is not clear what the ringing was for.
Napoleon was at that time shut up in Elba.]

Decʳ 30. Paid John Reeve 9 days by
Yard-land   4   6

1815. Jan 7. do: 3 days work by the Yard-land   1   6

[I am inclined to think "yard-land" here
means the churchyard.   Horne Tooke suggests its use sometimes in that sense.
It is rather singular that there should be
no entry of any bell-ringing for Waterloo.]

¹ See illustration, p. 266.

£ s. d.

1816. Gave Wm Carpenter's wife to free her
husband from prison . . . 3 0 0

[Many payments to her previously on
account of his being in prison. The parish
probably thought it would be cheaper to
purchase his liberty.]

Widow Woods for curing Jos: Greenhill of
the itch 1 6

The following are payments made by the Treasurer
to the Feoffees —:

1815. Paid to John Mortiboys (*i.e.* to himself)
his salary for teaching school one year 20 0 0
and for collecting the Charity rents and
keeping the accounts one year . . 5 0 0

Paid Dame Brown for teaching school 1
year 5 0 0

[John Mortiboys's school was conducted in
the school-house (a cottage) in the churchyard, pulled down in 1892; Mrs. Brown's,
for poor girls only, in a cottage by the road-
side near the "Bare House" farm. Its
ruins were removed a few years ago. Why
should not the poor also have these records
of their *Alma Mater* ?]

1815. Paid Mr. Armishaw for his valuation,
measuring & making a book of plans
and binding the same . . . 73 10 6

[This book is dated 1814. The plans are
beautifully executed by Ebenezer Robins of
Birmingham, the principal land surveyor in
this neighbourhood at that time.]

1818. Paid for a new iron chest with three locks 7 14 0

[This is the chest which the Feoffees now
use. It is not unlikely that before that time
they had used the old oak chest (mentioned
on the preceding page) in common with the
churchwardens.]

		£	s.	d.
1818.	14 dinners on the rent day . . .	1	1	0
	Ale & Porter . . .	1	14	3
1819.	16 dinners . .	1	4	0
	Ale & Tobacco . . .	2	7	6
1820.	11 dinners . . .		16	6
	Ale & Tobacco	2	3	6

[The proportion of ale per man is even greater than in the quotation given for 1802. If we deduct 4s. 8d., the then price of a pound of tobacco, the allowance at this last meeting is more than 2½ gallons a man (at 1s. 4d. a gallon). They must have qualified the ale by something stronger.]

		£	s.	d.
1818.	Paid for books for use of the church .	12	0	0
	„ „ use of the poor . .	9	0	0
1819.	A book for the singers . . .	2	2	0
	Paid Mr. Isaac Brown in part of his bill for painting the King's Arms . .	18	0	0
1820.	Paid him the remainder of his bill for painting the King's Arms & for gilding the clock face	14	6	7

[This work of art, which used to hang above the chancel arch, may still be seen in the chamber beneath the tower. It was decidedly dear at £32.]

1821.	Paid for black cloth to hang the pulpit &c at the death of the king . . .	21	11	6
1822.	Paid Thos Maids 11 days serving thatch .		12	0
	Paid C. Biddle 8 days banking & setting quick		10	8

[An illustration of labouring men's wages at that day in the parish.]

	Paid Mr. Willcox his doctor's bill . .	40	0	0

[He was the parish doctor, and must have let his bill run a long time, as I can find no other entry of the kind.]

		£	s.	d.
1823.	A suit of livery for the Biddle . .	4	9	6
	Paid Mr Job Bellamy for 26 dresses for the Charity children at 15ˢ/- each .	19	10	0
1825.	Paid for a pane of painted glass with the name of the late Thomas Fetherston upon it		8	6

[It is fixed in the west window, and bears his shield of arms: along with it are those of Henry A. Pye, the Rector, and Heneage Legge, Lord of the Manor. As there are no entries to the contrary, probably the two last named had each to pay for his own.]

June. Paid in respect of the enlargement of the churchyard . . .	21	12	0
Novr. Paid the expenses of the consecration of the additional burial ground .	26	12	0
Paid the two apparitors for attending .	2	2	0
Gave the ringers and singers at the consecration	1	0	0

[This refers to the ground gained by closing and taking in the lane which then ran round the east side of the churchyard, and insulated it. Its course is shown by the line of elm trees in the churchyard.]

Paid the expenses of Hockley House at the time Mr Harding & the Feoffees attended the Commissioners . .		12	2

[This was when the Charity Commissioners were investigating for their report of 1826.]

And finally, a little out of order, because I wished to conclude these extracts with it :—

1819. Decr 27th. Paid Thomas Baylis the remainder of his money for teaching Thoˢ Ward to play on the Violin . .	1	0	0

How much Thomas Ward's musical education had cost altogether we have no means of ascertaining, as this is the only entry relating thereto. His violin, of course, was wanted for the choir. The choir sat in the gallery, which was removed from the west end in 1872. The leader of it for many years towards the end of its existence was Mr. Samuel Gazy, whom numbers of us remember well. I am told that he played the clarionet, and that a Mr. John Hildick of that day played another clarionet. There must have been also a flute and a violoncello, but history is silent as to who played them. Then, too, there was the bassoon. It was reckoned to be the instrument which by unwritten law and precedent belonged and appertained to the parish clerk. So that when the parish clerk could play he must have had to leave his desk beneath the pulpit, gravely traverse the nave, and ascend the gallery to his instrument, and when the singing was over walk back again. But Henry Saunders, the last of the parish clerks under the old régime (a good old man, whom also I remember, and who gave one of the alms dishes of the church), could not play the bassoon, so it came about that John Ingram was the last who ever played, or probably ever will play, that instrument in Lapworth Church choir. I should much like to have heard them playing up aloft before " the old order changed, yielding place to new "; but I doubt whether the parishioners of Lapworth will ever seek to revert to the old order in this matter of their church music.

PARISH APPRENTICES

"Come hither, boy : come, come, and learn of us . . ."

TITUS ANDRONICUS

CHAPTER VI

PARISH APPRENTICES: 1680-1703

THE apprenticing of poor children of the parish was an expense which at this seventeenth-century period was regularly paid by the overseers or the feoffees of the parish charities (for instances, see pp. 205, 207, 212), and continued to be so paid up to and during the earlier decades of the last century. It is still set out as one of the objects to which under the existing deed the charity funds may be applied, but it is doubtful if any such payment has been made within the past sixty years.

The following indentures still exist, and are of interest as referring to a period of two centuries ago :—

1680. john Hollicke, apprenticed to Nicholas Green of Blocksedge in the parish of Wassall, "Spurearen," for ten years. £1 10s. 0d. paid down, and 10s. 0d. more to be paid at end of first year, "by the collector of the poor then in being."

1684. Thomas Morris to Henry Horton of Blacknell in the Co: of Stafford, "Naller": for seven years: to be taught "the art and trade of a naller." (No premium named.)

1685. Willm Palmer, son of J. Palmer, labourer, to Edw: Lichfield of Wallsall, "nayler": for seven years, "to learn the science or trade of a nayler." "By the consent of Matthew Madgett, Churchwarden, and other inhabitants of the parish of Lapworth." (No premium named.)

1700. John Clarke, son of T. Clarke, labourer, to Samuel Maunder of Lapworth, husbandman, six years from date, to learn "the art, skill and mystery of husbandry." No premium. By Edward Abbott, Churchwarden and Overseer of the poor: endorsed by the signatures of Basill ffeilding and W. Palmer, Justices.

1700. Joseph Hemmings, "a poor friendless boy of the parish of Lapworth," to Willm Moor of Ridge Core in the parish of Halesowen, Mason: until he is twenty-one;— endorsement that he is then 7½ years old. By the same Edw: Abbott and the same Justices.

1703. Wm Crandall to James Hextall of Lapworth, husbandman, till age of twenty-one. (No premium: age not mentioned.) With consent of the Churchwardens and Overseers of Lapworth and of two of her Majesty's Justices of the Peace, who sign this indenture, namely, John Clopton and Andrew Archer.

The conditions and stipulations of indentures of this period have now such a flavour of quaintness and antiquity that I preserve one of them here entire,— namely, the first on the above list :—

This indenture made the 14th day of August in the year of our Lord God 1680 witnesseth that John Hollicke of Lapworth in the County of Warwick hath by and with the assent and consent of the ffefees, churchwardens and overseers of the parish of Lapworth and the rest of the inhabitants put himself apprentice with Nicholas Greene of Blocksedge in the parish of Wassall in the County of Stafford Spurearen and affter the maner of an apprentice with him to dwell from the day of the date of these presents for and during and unto the full end and term of ten years from thenceforth next ensue-inge and fully to be completed and ended during all which term the said John Hollicke an apprentice his said master Nicholas Greene well and faithfully shall sarve, his secrets shall keep, his commandments lawful and honest shall gladly do. Hee shall not commit fornication with any woman in the house or out of the house of his master : hee shall not do nor consent any hurt to be done to his said master, but shall lett to his power or forewarn his said master thereof : he shall not hant taverns of custome or publick ale houses except it be about his master's business there to be done : at cards, dice or any other unlawful games hee shall not play : hee shall not waste the goods of his master in ordinately nor lend them without the especial leave license and consent of his said master : hee shall not contract himself to any woman in matrimony during all the said term of time : hee shall not absent himself from the sarvice of his said master by day nor by night but in all things shall behave himself as a true and faithful sarvant to his said master dewering all the term of time before mentioned ; and the said Nicholas Greene doth by these presents covenant and grant to and with the said John Hollicke his said apprentice that he shall and will teach direct and instruct him in the art and trade of a spurearen which he now followeth after the best maner that he can or may and at the end of the said term to make him free of the said trade in Wassall : in due maner to chastise him offending, and to allow him the said Hollicke, a sufficient meat, drink, washing and lodging, linens and woollens, hoase, shues, and all maner of clothes fitting for an apprentice of that calling according to the custom of the Sittey of London and at the end of the term of ten yeares to give and allow to his said sarvant and apprentice John Hollicke two new suites of linen and wollen clothes, one suit for weeke days and the other for holy days, beside those clothes he had before. In witness whereof the parties to these present indentures enterchangably have put to theare hands and sealles the day and yeare first above written.   Nicholas Green (his mark).

Witness : Willm Southerne
            Willm Ingram.

William Ingram was at the head of the parish

charity trust.   William Southerne was, to judge from entries in the Parish Register and elsewhere, probably curate here.   In 1684 he became Vicar of Rowington.

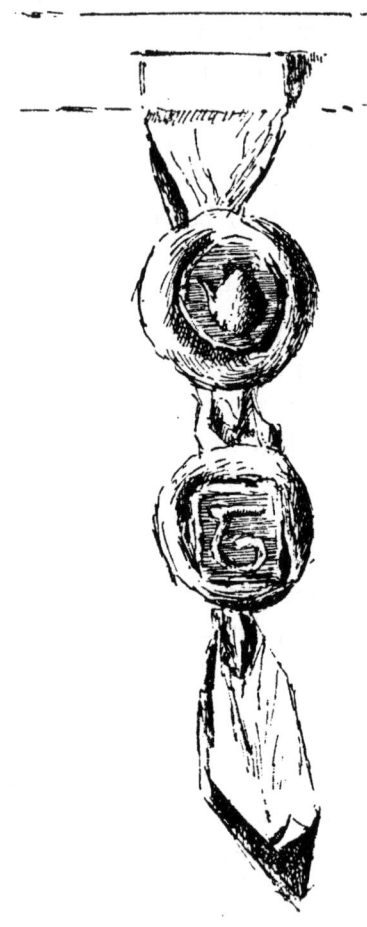

Seal of William Kettill
1408-32
p. 63

LOST PROPERTY

" Importing the surrender of those lands
Lost . . ."

HAMLET

CHAPTER VII

LOST PROPERTY

THE year 1700, closing its eventful century, left behind it in our chest the counterpart of a lease for two hundred years, which therefore only expired in 1900.

In 1699 the schedule of the Charity Estates set down by Edward Welchman on the fly-leaf of the Parish Register has the entry :—

		a	r	p
Mr. Askew.	In Merils. 4 pieces . .	2	1	28
	In Flamefield 1 Piece . .	0	3	6
		3	0	34

and the fragment of Overseers' accounts for that year shows that he paid £2 10s. a year for this land.

In 1700 (February 25) a lease was granted by Edward Welchman and his co-feoffees under which they

with the assent and consent of the Minister and Church-wardens of Lapworth in considⁿ of twenty one shillings and sixpence to them paid and of the rent hereafter provided do demise grant lease sett and to farm letten to the said Wm Askew [as follows, namely], All that arable, meadow and pasture land called by the name of: Merrills and Flamefield as it is and hath been known to be Town lands lying in five several parcels and situated in Lapworth aforesaid and now in the occupation of the said William Askew the quantity thereof being three acres and thirty four perches or thereabouts [to hold unto the said William Askew his heirs &c] from 25th March next ensuing untill the full end & term of 200 years yielding and paying yearly on the feast day of the annunciation of the B. V. M. one peppercorn if the same be lawfully demanded.

And the said William Askew covenants that he, his heirs, etc., at all times during the present demise,

will in all things order & manage the demised premises in a good sufficient and husband-like manner namely as he doth his own lands and at the end or expiration of the said term of 200 years will leave and yield up unto the said Edw: Welchman &c. their heirs assigns and successors the same in a very good sufficient and tenantable condition.

The counterpart is signed and sealed by William Askew, the endorsement being :—

25 March 1700

200
___

Expires 1900

The land thus leased was described in the feoffment of 1652 as

two sellions of land lying in a field called Merriell and four other sellions of land lying in a field called Flame-field, which said last mentioned premises were called Skinner's land.

Skinner's land, no doubt, is that which was left by Simon Skynner and Margaret his wife to Rector Hill and others in trust by a deed of 12 Ed. IV. (1473). It would be land that lay dispersed and intermixed with other lands in the before-named fields, just as the four strips of Charity land are intermixed with other land in Cleycroft to this day.

It has long ago disappeared from the list of parish properties. In the Tithe Map of the parish we still find the name of "Merrills" applied to certain land. But Flame-field has not even left its name. And though the covenant in the lease to hand over the land in the year 1900 to the Feoffees for the time being "in a very good sufficient and tenantable condition" does not seem to be contingent on the demand of the peppercorn rent, the Feoffees were doubtless wise to make no attempt to recover their own. The counter-part of the lease has, at any rate, been preserved in excellent condition, even if the land to which it relates is lost beyond recovery.

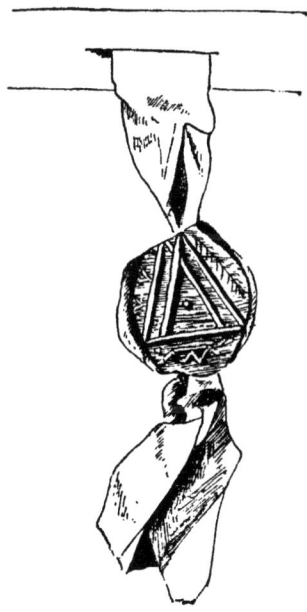

Seal of deed, 1435
William vorde to Ellen at yᵉ vorde

p. 62

The oldest of the deed boxes in Lapworth Church
5 inches in diameter, $3\frac{3}{4}$ inches in height

p. 70

THE LAPWORTH CHARITIES

"'Twere good you do so much for charity."

MERCHANT OF VENICE

CHAPTER VIII

THE LAPWORTH CHARITIES[1]

THROUGHOUT the eighteenth century, rents in Lapworth stood at much the same figure as obtained at the end of the seventeenth century (see pp. 203-4, and 225). Anything beyond 10s. an acre was exceptional, and there are cases as low as 5s. The twenty-one-year lease continued to be the rule, and such leases were renewed from generation to generation without change of rent. In 1775 (when we get the first existing schedule with rentals of the complete Charity Estate) we find an average rental of only 10s. 3½d. an acre. In 1795, under the pressure of complaints from the parishioners, this had become about 13s. In 1814 it had got as high as 17s. 6d. The average in all cases of course includes the houses attached to the lands, as it is impossible to estimate their separate value. Then in 1814, moved probably by the large profits which farmers were making during the war with France, the Feoffees had a new survey and valuation made of the

---

[1] References to the Lapworth Charities make up a great part of this book, but the reader of this Chapter (VIII.) may be referred more particularly to pp. 84-7, 133-4, 203-4, 213-15, 225-7, and to Appendix III.

Mr. R. N. Holbeche, Agent and Treasurer to the Lapworth Charity Trustees, has most kindly corrected the map showing the Charity lands, and has supplied the material for the schedule set out in Appendix III. The Editor here records his thanks to Mr. Holbeche for this valuable assistance so freely and courteously rendered.

Charity Estates, the result being that in 1816 they well-nigh trebled all their rents, the average becoming about £2 8s. per acre. Indeed, they rather over-did the thing, and presently had to make temporary reductions to the extent of about ten per cent., but most of the tenants continued to occupy at the advanced rents, showing that they must have had very good "takes" previously.

We are able to compare the gross income of the Charity Estates in successive periods, thus :—

1695	.	.	estimated	.	.	£87
1775	.	.	actual	.	.	£104
1795	.	.	,,	.	.	£127
1814	.	.		.	.	£175
1816	.	.	,,	.	.	£415
1822	.	.		.	.	£376
1826	.	.		.	.	£412
1844	.	.		.	.	£385
1892	.	.		.	.	£415

It is curious to notice that within forty-one years (from 1775 to 1816) the income is quadrupled, and that in 1892 it stands once more at the precise figure of 1816.[1]

In 1699 the acreage of the parish property as then surveyed was 175 acres. It is now 189 acres. Some pieces have been lost; but on the other hand the parish has had allotments from enclosures of commons, wayside strips, etc. Variation has been due also to some small purchases and exchanges made by the Feoffees.

Until after 1795, when the Feoffees drew up a

---

[1] For the year ending June, 1904, the gross rental was £390 10s. 9d.

case for counsel's opinion in regard to several of their difficulties, it does not appear that they kept any regular record of their proceedings or made up any yearly balance sheets.

They seem, however, in 1797, to have started a "Minute Book," which covers the period from that date to 1841. The annual meetings were of the most perfunctory kind, and the minutes rarely consist of more than a record of the names of those present (usually three or four persons) with a few lines naming what leases or other matters were considered, but without any details.

For many years in succession there is no record of any meeting being held. There is not, for example, one between 1814 and 1822. Probably the real business was transacted conversationally from time to time by some one or two of those who took the lead, and at gatherings which were of a more convivial nature than the annual meetings.

When the feoffment trusts came to be renewed, it seems to have been a chronic difficulty that there was not a sufficient number of "freeholders and inhabitants" of the parish to be found to fill up the vacancies, and that the survivors were debarred from appointing any other persons. There is no doubt that this limitation led to the appointment of unsuitable trustees.

In the volume for 1826 of the Reports of Proceedings of the Charity Commissioners is to be found the report of the Inspector sent down to inquire into the "Combined Charities of the Parish of Lapworth." He does not appear to have been shown the pre-Reformation deeds, or to have known that anything existed earlier than 1563. Indeed, after setting out the Table of Bequests he goes on to say by way of introduction : "The deeds or instruments by which these respective benefactions were made (with the exception of Collett's) are not now found among the parish documents."

He abstracts the older feoffment deeds describing the conditions of the trusts embodied in them, and is careful to preserve from them the old names of fields and properties, all of which (with many more) we have met with in what has gone before. He also appends a schedule of the rents at the time of his visit.

He does not seem to have found much occasion of complaint, but makes mention of matters of interest as to procedure, etc., which we have now no other means of knowing. The parishioners seem to have had more facilities afforded them then than now for gaining information as to their Charity Estates.

The report says :—

An annual meeting is held soon after Easter at which such of the parishioners as think proper attend. The accounts of the Treasurer for the preceding year are then produced for the inspection of the trustees and parishioners present.

The usual course is for Mr. Pye, the Minister, who is also one of the trustees, to read over aloud the several items of the account, and the book is then handed round for the individual inspection of such as desire it.

[This procedure seems to have been quite in accordance with the provisions of the old trust deeds, which distinctly aimed at a certain amount of publicity being secured both in this way and by the giving out in church of the meetings of the Feoffees. The Trustees have for the last fifty years at least held their meetings in private. But it was only after much contention that the parishioners had established so far their right to know what was done by the Feoffees.   In the Minute Book of the latter in 1814 there is the entry :—

For the satisfaction of the parish the Feoffees agree to deliver an account yearly to the parish at Easter of Receipts and Disbursements of the parish estate.   The Feoffees will also place in the hands of the Churchwardens a rental of the estate as it now stands, and from time to time correct the same and place it when corrected in the hands of the Churchwardens.

Until this time they seem to have submitted no accounts at all.]

The several cottages, being now 21 in number, are occupied by parish paupers, placed in them from time to time by order of the trustees, and they enjoy the benefit of them rent free. These cottages are estimated at the annual value of from £2 to £3 each.

The 0 a. 1 r. 1 p. appropriated for the site of a new school-house and garden was so appropriated by the trustees, in consequence of the old school-house being, as was supposed, erected upon part of the churchyard, and being then in a very ruinous condition.   The new school-house is not yet quite completed, but it is conjectured that the expense incurred by this building will not fall far short of £800.

[It really cost in the end £1,526, and there was great difficulty in working off the debt incurred (with interest at five per cent.) by annual instalments of £200, a receipt in full being given in 1833. In looking at the building one cannot help wondering how the bill could be run up to such a figure.]

For a great many years past the annual sum of £20 has been paid as a salary to a schoolmaster for teaching gratis the children of resident parishioners, without limitation of number or regard to condition, to read, write and cipher.   The number attending the school sometimes exceeds 60.   A further part of the funds is applied to the support of another school called the Charity School, at which the female children of the poor, exclusively, are taught to read, knit and sew. They are clothed every second year, and are provided with books from time to time as required.   The number of these Charity children is generally from 20 to 30.

The office of Treasurer has been filled for many years past by Mr. John Mortiboys, the schoolmaster, and a salary of £5

is paid to him for receiving the rents and keeping the books :
and one of £8 to the Clerk for his services in the church.[1]

The report describes the available funds of the
Charity as being

applied to the several purposes of the trust in proportions
varying from time to time according to their respective
exigencies.

[Apparently the Feoffees had a larger discretionary power than
they now have.]

It is further remarked that—

In the repairs of the church the chancel is included, the
parish, as we are given to understand, being liable, by pre-
scription, to repair that part.

[Recent incumbents have, notwithstanding what is said above,
recognised the repair of the chancel to be an obligation of the
Rector. In 1860 the Rev. C. A. St. John Mildmay, then Rector,
incurred an outlay of about £750, being mainly his own personal
expenditure, though aided by some private subscriptions.]

In the year 1817, several payments, amounting in
the whole to more than £400, are charged in the
accounts for law expenses, being the expenses incurred in defending a suit in Chancery which had
been instituted by some of the parishioners against the
trustees, charging them with mismanagement of this
trust estate, and with a misapplication of the funds.

[The principal charges appear to have been the corrupt granting
of leases, but it is singular that while we have so much left in the

---

[1] John Mortiboys appears to have been the first treasurer the Feoffees
ever had. In 1795 there is a marginal note upon a case that was submitted for counsel's opinion: "The grantees have for many years permitted
the overseer of the poor to receive the rents and apply them together with
the poors rates without keeping any separate account," and the question
is asked, "Are they justified in doing so, or should they appoint a
treasurer for that purpose?" John Mortiboys continued to be treasurer
and schoolmaster till his death in 1844.

way of record of the suits of Elizabeth's day, and of Charles II.'s time, there are no papers left touching this suit in the nineteenth century.   The Feoffees' solicitors, no doubt, retained them all.]

In 1841 still further discontentments in the parish came to a head, and resulted in a petition (of which also we have no copy) from certain of the parishioners, headed by the then Rector, the Rev. Geo. Tyndall, to the Court of Chancery for the promulgation of a new scheme for the government of the parish charity trusts.   It took seven years to obtain what was sought, but the application was then successful, though in the meantime Geo. Tyndall had passed away; and in 1848 the scheme under which the Charity Estates are now governed was put forward and came into operation.

This scheme has never been printed, and the parishioners have had no facilities hitherto for making themselves acquainted with its provisions.   It may be of interest, therefore, to summarise them briefly.

The new body of Feoffees was fourteen in number, the first name on the list being that of the Rev. C. Arundell St. John Mildmay, then Rector, followed by John Fetherston, Esq., of Packwood; Marmion Edward Ferrers, Esq., of Baddesley Clinton, and John Wm. Kirshaw of Lapworth, civil engineer, the remainder being all farmers and inhabitants of Lapworth.

The expenses of obtaining this new scheme and deed are mentioned in the latter as £921, the payment of which again crippled the charity funds for a long time.

After reciting at length the obligations and conditions of previous trusts, it lays down the following as the new scheme :—

1. Out of the rents and profits of the several properties vested in them the Trustees shall pay yearly "a competent sum, not exceeding one eighth part of the whole annual amount of the said rents and profits, in and about substantially repairing and keeping in good repair the Parish Church of Lapworth and insuring the same against loss or damage by fire, and in payment and discharge of the cost and expenses of and incident to the celebration of Divine Worship in the said Church."

2. They shall further "set apart yearly the sum of Ten pounds, and invest the same in their names in the purchase of a competent share of Bank three pounds per cent. consolidated annuities, and shall in like manner invest the dividends from time to time of the monies so invested until by means of such investments there shall be formed an accumulated fund of £200 like annuities, and shall apply such accumulated fund of £200 as occasion may require in or about any extraordinary repairs of the said Church which may be found necessary."
    When the fund has reached £200 the Trustees may use the dividends for general purposes, but whenever the sum of £200 Consols has been reduced by expenditure on repairs of the Church fabric, it must be made up again as before provided.

3. They shall further "yearly pay and apply such a sum as they the said trustees or the major part of them shall think proper, but not exceeding for any one year the sum of £65, in and about the well and sufficiently repairing and keeping in good repair the roads and highways of and in the parish of Lapworth."

4. They shall "from time to time as occasion shall require engage and appoint some fit and proper persons as Schoolmaster and Schoolmistress to educate and instruct at the Charity Schoolhouse, which is called the new Schoolhouse, in the Parish of Lapworth the children of the inhabitants of the said parish, both boys and girls,

in reading, writing and arithmetic and religious knowledge according to the doctrine of the Church of
England, and as regards the girls in Needlework."

They shall also allow the Schoolmaster to occupy rent free
the house and garden adjoining the schoolhouse, and shall
pay yearly "such a sum as they or the majority of them
shall think proper, but not exceeding £90," for salaries of
Master and Mistress and all other expenses whatever connected with the School, Schoolhouse, and Master's house.

5. The Parish Clerk for the time being may have rent free
the other house and garden adjoining the Schoolhouse.

6. The next charges on revenue are those of management,
administration, and collection, "and expenses of repairing & keeping in good and substantial repair and insuring against loss and damage by fire the houses and
buildings now being and standing upon, or which shall
from time to time or at any time hereafter be erected
upon, the lands and premises" of the Trustees.

7. The residue after payment of the before-mentioned charges
is to be applied "towards the maintenance and relief of
such of the aged, impotent and other poor inhabitants
of and in the Town and Parish of Lapworth as do not
receive parochial relief from or out of the rates assessed
for the relief of the Poor," for medical aid and attendance
to them, and "for and towards the binding and putting
out as apprentices and servants the poor boys and girls
educated at the Charity School aforesaid." The Trustees
may also allow poor people who come within the above
description to occupy "the small houses or cottages and
gardens" rent free or at low and moderate rents.

The remaining provisions are :—

Leases of Trust property not to exceed twenty-one years.

Trustees may set apart such land as they may think
suitable and convenient for Cottage Allotments.

Trustees may not rent for their own benefit any part of
the Trust estate.

Trustees to meet annually on the Tuesday in Whitsun
week.

Notice of such annual meetings to be affixed to the door of the church two Sundays immediately preceding the day of such meeting, and also to be sent to each Trustee at least ten days before the date of such meeting.

Treasurer to be appointed annually at such meetings, and his remuneration not to exceed five per cent. of the whole annual income of the Trust.

At each annual meeting a Chairman to be elected for such meeting only: and to have a casting vote.

A Trustee may not reside more than seven miles from Lapworth Church.

A Trustee becoming bankrupt or insolvent is thereby disqualified.

The Rector of Lapworth for the time being is a Trustee *ex officio.*

The Trustees may at any time fill up vacancies arising in their body by death, removal or other disqualification.

When the trust body is reduced to seven, it is imperative on the survivors within six months to appoint additional Trustees to bring up the number to fifteen.

The qualifications for a Trustee beyond what have been before stated are :—

1. That he be the owner of freehold estate in the parish, or
2. Occupy land in the parish to the rental of £100 a year, or
3. That he be "possessed of and entitled to a clear annual income from any source whatever of not less than £100 a year."

No Trustee may receive any remuneration from funds of the Trust.

No Trust money may be expended on dinners or other entertainments.

The record left by the Inspector in his report is, as before mentioned, that there were in 1826 twenty-one cottages let to the poor rent free. By decay, by pulling down and non-renewal, by exchange of land on which four cottages stood for land on which there was only one, and from other causes, the twenty-one cottages have been reduced to a dozen, of which few can now be said to be either rent free or let at a nominal charge. The trustees never established any sinking fund applicable to renewal of buildings, so that when cottages have become past repair and have been pulled down there has been no fund with which to rebuild them.

There is no reason to think that the scheme of 1848 contemplated the discontinuance of the old custom under which the annual meetings of the Feoffees were open to and attended by the parishioners. The provision in the Trust Deed that public notice of such meetings is to be affixed to the church door in addition to the written notice sent to each Feoffee is, indeed, a clear indication to the contrary. The parishioners, however, probably through want of knowledge of their right to attend, have for many years ceased to do so. A copy of the balance sheet of the Feoffees has, in accordance with legislative provisions, been sent annually to the Churchwardens (and been copied by them into the Vestry minute book), while another copy is sent to the Charity Commissioners.

When the Local Government Act of 1894 came into operation, one of the first steps of the Parish Council was to apply to the Charity Commissioners for their award as to the number of Trustees to be appointed by the parish through their Council. It seemed to be almost a typical case in favour of election as against co-optation, the charities being

R

ecclesiastical only in the proportion of one-third, and general as regards the remaining two-thirds. But all the parish gets by the operation of the Act is that the annual copy of the accounts which formerly went to the Churchwardens now goes to the Parish Council. The Parish Council has no power, however, to take any action whatsoever in relation to the Parish Charities. The disqualifying section of the Act, so far as concerns Lapworth parish, is the very brief one, No. 66 :—

Nothing in this Act shall affect the trusteeship, management or control of any elementary school.

An elementary school forms part of our existing charity trust, and is managed and controlled by trustees elected by co-optation : therefore the parish can have no direct representation on the trust. It seems a *reductio ad absurdum* as regards popular expectation of what was to be done by the Act for village charities.

But the alternative to abiding as we are is to make application to the Commissioners for an entirely new scheme ; and all parishes have not unlimited confidence in the wisdom of putting their properties into the crucible of the Charity Commissioners; so, for the present, co-optation continues, though admitted to be no longer in harmony with the spirit of the times. Whether it shall continue much longer, or only a little longer, the old system has, at any rate, lasted a long time, for there can be no doubt that the present body of trustees are the direct lineal successors of those who sat with " John in the Lone" when Edward the Third was King.

CHURCH RESTORATION

". . . I go to church
And see the holy edifice of stone . . .
MERCHANT

CHAPTER IX

CHURCH RESTORATION [1]

IN Mr. Pye's time, 1807, there was a so-called restoration of our church. This, it will be remembered, is the date upon the shields of arms in the west window. One incident of this restoration consisted in the bricking up of the east window. It had become much decayed, and it was cheaper to brick it up than to repair it. But a straight, narrow slit of light was left down the centre, as may be seen in pictures of the church of about 1850. It was in 1807 also that the high pews were put in, which were only done away with, at the same time as the gallery, in the later restoration of 1872. A plan of the interior arrangements of the church, bearing date 1807, still exists, showing the pulpit fixed against the eastern pillar of the south side of the nave. There were three big pews in the chancel—two on the south (which were the Rector's pews) and one on the north —and two more in St. Katherine's Chapel (now used as the vestry), which were the Fetherston pews. There were fifty-two pews in all, and with the plan is a list showing the names, not only of all the occupiers

[1] Details of much of the later repair and restoration of the church will be found in chronological order under the various rectorates dealt with in Chapter X.

of the pews, but also the names of the proprietors, for the pews were then considered as personal property attaching to the houses of the parish rather than to the people, a tradition which to a large extent obtains still, and is not a little inconvenient to church-wardens, who have to provide for the comers to new houses. It is rather a grave reminder of how fugitive and transitory we are to find that of all the names of the occupiers of these fifty-two pews in 1807, there is only one that can be fairly said to be represented now by the same family or by successors bearing the same name. The places of the other fifty-one know them no more.

In 1872 the further work of general restoration of the interior of the church, which had been begun with the chancel in 1860,[1] was carried out, again under direction of Mr. G. E. Street. The expenditure incurred was about £1,600, raised by contributions from the Rector and parishioners, aided by several outside friends, together with a donation from Merton College, Oxford (patrons of the living), and a sum of £200 set aside for the purpose by the Feoffees of the Lapworth Charities under the provisions of their trust deed. The contractors for the work were Hardwick and Son, Birmingham. The church closed for several months, during which service was conducted in the schoolroom. The reopening services were conducted on Wednesday, October 16, the Bishop of Worcester (Dr. Philpott) preaching in the morning.

The principal work carried out at this time was the

---

[1] See under 1860, p. 257.

following. From the west end an unsightly gallery was taken away, which had entirely blocked up two good lancet windows of the Early English period. High pews gave place to open seats. The stripping away of a lath and plaster ceiling from the nave discovered a fine old oak roof of open timber, which was put into good order, making the church look much loftier. The walls were denuded of accumulated plaster, and the bare stone exposed, with the effect of discovering in many parts traces of older work previously unsuspected and belonging to an early period of the church's history. In the north wall of the nave, dividing it from the north aisle, above the easternmost arch, and as it were springing from one side of it, a very curious and interesting window was thus exposed,[1] which is believed to date from Saxon times, when the wall in which it is seen was the external wall of a church without aisles. In the south aisle, at its west end, were also opened out and glazed two of the often miscalled leper windows, a little above ground level, concerning the origin and purpose of which there is so much uncertainty. In the same aisle, between the door and its east end, were also brought to light the deep recesses of two other windows, at some distant date blocked up to allow of the construction above them of the now existing windows. Here also were found a piscina and its credence table in unusually complete preservation in the south wall, the adjuncts formerly of St. James's altar at the east end of this aisle.

[1] The opening, once a window, will be noticed in the photograph of the interior of the church at p. 209.

The accommodation lost by the removal of the gallery was to some extent compensated by utilising the passage way between the north aisle and the tower, the latter up to that time having been detached from the church. Space was thus gained for seating the Sunday School children. At the same time an east window (square-headed and containing three rect-angular-shaped lights) in the chantry chapel north of the chancel (St. Katherine's Chapel, now used as vestry) was done away with to allow of the con-struction of a recess in which to place the organ—an unfortunate mistake, since the organ in a few years was superseded by a larger one which had to be placed beneath the chancel arch, leaving the recess a meaningless excrescence. The porch at the west end of the church, with small chantry chapel above it [1] (the foundation of the de Montforts and others in 1374), had been till this time blocked up on its north side, and accessible by a door on the south only, the porch itself being used as a lumber-room. The masonry on the north was removed from the ancient doorway, and a thoroughfare beneath the chapel thus restored. The two curious stone staircases which connect the porch with its superstructure were also thus brought into view. It has been supposed that one of the uses of the little room was that of a relic chamber, and that these staircases side by side were for the ingress and egress of pious visitors. This chamber, in use up to 1872 as vestry, was also connected with the interior of the church by a wooden staircase carried through one of the ancient lancet windows, and to

[1] See illustration opposite, and pages 52 *et seq.*

LAPWORTH CHURCH: THE CHANTRY CHAPEL
FOUNDED BY RICHARD DE MONTFORT AND OTHERS IN 1374

some extent concealed by the then existing gallery. This connection was cut off and the window restored to its original form.   It is, no doubt, one of the lights of the church that existed before the Montfort chantry was constructed.

Four stained-glass windows were also at this time inserted, namely, the large window at the east end of the chancel, the gift of the Rector, Mr. Eaton, and his family ; one on the south side of the chancel, the gift of Mr. John Fetherston, junr., formerly of Packwood House ; one at the west end of the south aisle, the gift of Mrs. Tyndall, widow of the Rev. George Tyndall, formerly Rector ; and a small window in the north aisle by members of the family of Kirshaw.

In connection with this restoration of the church a grievous error of judgment was committed, a great number of old tombstones hitherto standing more or less upright being then laid flat.   Inscriptions which were at that time legible are now quite lost, the change of position having caused the surface of the stone to shale and break away.   It is probably the worst thing that can be done to an old tombstone to lay it on the bare ground, exposed to the encroachment of grass and the foot of the rambler.   The tender surface, which might in its original position have retained its record for generations longer, cannot bear this rude treatment.

Seal of deed, 1461
William Persones & Elizabeth his wife to John, their son
(witnessed by John Barnethurst, Henry VI.'s Keeper of
the Royal Park at Lapworth, whose seal this is)

GENERAL NOTES, MAINLY RELATING
TO THE CHURCH AND INCUMBENTS:
1839 TO PRESENT DAY

"... *abstracts and brief chronicles of the time.*"

HAMLET

CHAPTER X

GENERAL NOTES, MAINLY RELATING TO THE CHURCH AND INCUMBENTS: 1839 TO PRESENT DAY[1]

G. TYNDALL, who succeeded to the living on the death of H. A. Pye, held it from 1839 to 1848, and is, of course, still remembered by some of the older parishioners. He was, as mentioned before, active in obtaining the Chancery Trust Deed under which the parish charities are administered.

Foster's record of him is :—

G. Tyndall, s. Thomas of Bristol (city), arm: Christ Ch: matric. 1815, aged 17, B.A. 1819, Fellow of Merton 1823–40. M.A. 1824. Dean 1824. Bursar 1827. Subwarden 1834. Rector of Lapworth 1839 until his death 23 Feb 1848.

He is buried in the north-west corner of the churchyard, and a small stained-glass window was given by his widow, as already mentioned, at the time of the last restoration. He does not appear to have had any curate, all entries in the registers being signed by himself or by occasional ministers.

[1] See pp. 196-9. (This chapter (X.) may in a sense be read as continuing the chronological record from the point reached by the chapter (IV.) on The Parish Registers.)

His successor was Mr. Mildmay, whose rectorship of Lapworth extended from 1848 to 1864.

Charles Arundell St: John Mildmay, third s. of Paulett St John Mildmay of Dogmersfield, Hants, arm: Merton College: matric. 1st Jany 1839, aged 18. B.A. 1843. Fellow 1844–9. M.A. 1846. Rector of Lapworth, 1848–64; of Long Marston, Yorks, 1864–73; of Alvechurch, co: Worcester, 1873–9; and of Denton, Norfolk, 1879–83.

(Foster, *Al. Oxon.*)

During his incumbency he had a laudable practice of putting down in volume v. of the registers (which through a change of forms had become no longer available as a register) such *Memoranda parochialia* as he thought worthy of record. Many of these are of such interest as to create a wish that the practice had been observed by his predecessors and continued by his successors. To make a clergyman the compulsory diarist of his parish might lead to the recording of many trivialities, but what would we not give for even the trivialities of the sixteenth and seventeenth centuries! Mr. Mildmay's notes were all worth making, though space will not allow of reproduction here of more than a selection from them.

1848. The late Rector, Revd Geo: Tyndall, died of an affection of the lungs, having been presented to the Rectory by Merton College in 1839. After his decease the College separated from the living the rectorial moiety of the parish of Gamlinghay, which had been held by this and one previous incumbent as a sinecure, which was thenceforth attached to the Vicar of Gamlinghay.

I was presented to the living on the 21st June of this year, and came into residence in August. The Rectory House, being of red brick and having very thin walls, was cemented and thoroughly drained. It had been considerably enlarged and improved by my predecessor, who also built the present stables and coach house.

[He expended on it about £1,000.]

On X'mas Day I presented to the church a pair of altar chairs and an alms plate of brass.

1849. Typhus fever very bad in the parish. Dr. Vaughan, Head Master of Harrow, preached here August 1st. (and again Decr 29th). Sept. 27th day of humiliation for the cholera: collection £11. 0. 6 in behalf of those visited at Bilston.

Gift from the Clerk of the parish, Henry Saunders, of another brass plate for the alms.

Nov. 15th. Day of General Thanksgiving for the removal of cholera from the land. A new church-gate and steps put up at the West End by myself.

1850. A stove given by me to the church. The Hon: & Rev: Aubrey Spring Rice appointed curate (Sepr 16th)

1851. Census: Separate occupiers 154. Inhabited houses 148. Inhabitants: Males 330. Females 333. Total 663 (including 23 m. and 5 f. on Barges and 2 in sheds). In 1841. Inhabitants 729: decrease 66.

Church computed to hold 300 besides the school. Average congregation, Morning 220. Evening 150

Scholars	95	95
	315	245

The Sunday School was commenced about 1830 under the Revd Donald Cameron, Resident Curate. We have now three unpaid male and three unpaid female teachers: average attendance 100.—Day School, average attendance for the last five years 110: in this year 108; males 52, females 56. Average expenses of the school £55.[1]

[1] In 1896 Mr. Prescot notes, under *Memoranda parochialia*, that the seating accommodation of the church is 248; children on the books of the Sunday School, 61; average attendance at Day School, 79; amount of School expenses for the year, £212.

January. I altered the entrance to the Parsonage, making the bank and small walk to the Church on the N.E. side.

October. Mr. Spring Rice resigned his curacy ·to go abroad for his health.

Packwood House: Mr. Fetherston left, and let the place to Mr. Whitehouse.

1852. Lord Cornwallis died: his estates in this parish left to his grandson, Mr. Philip Wykeham Martin.

1853. Revd J. Hungerford Penruddock ordained curate. A very bad harvest and much illness in the parish.

1854. Very severe winter: soup kitchen for the poor. Wages of Agricultural labourers 10^s/- to 11^s/- a week. Flour 13^s/6 a strike.

Mr. Penruddock left his curacy again this year.

1855. July: opening of new organ built by Nicholson of Worcester for £120: money raised by subscriptions, of which only £2 given in parish. The rest collected by me upon £40 being presented to me by two excellent gentlewomen, Miss Kirshaws, who had, unknown to me, been collecting this sum for a harmonium amongst their friends. On the day of the opening a collection of £37 6. 4 was made towards future alterations in the church, for which a sketch and plan were sent me by Mr. Street of Oxford. The organ was placed in the chancel chapel with the written consent of Mr. Miller, the Lord of the Manor.

July 31. A Confirmation was held in the Church by the Bishop of Worcester: the first known here. There were in all about 200 Catechumens.

1856. On Good Friday I was taken ill in the church, and from that time did no duty for some time. I was ordered to travel for the summer, and went to Switzerland. Rev. B. Belcher and Rev. J. P. Gell in charge in my absence: returned home in Octr and engaged Rev. J. Townsend, who lived at Hockley House, as my curate.

Barn, stables and cowhouse put in thorough repair this summer.

Mr. John Kirshaw, who lived at the Canal House, removed to Warwick to my great regret: a very great benefactor of this parish.

I left again ill, to rest, and so these memoranda were not kept up, came home again for a while and then went away for two years.

[In 1857–8, during Mr. Mildmay's absence abroad, the Rev. J. Newton Smith was curate in charge.]

1859. In the year 1859 we came back. Rev. Charles Burd became curate.

[Mr. Burd remained Curate of Lapworth till 1863. In 1867 he became Vicar of Shirley, and held that living until his death in 1900.]

1860. September: Chancel restored.

[The cost of this restoration was (the writer was informed by Mr. Mildmay) about £750, chiefly, but not entirely, his own expenditure; a certain amount of subscriptions having been derived from other sources. A great part of the work was the undoing of the work of 1807. The east window had at that time been blocked up and made into "a plastered wall displaying boards with the Creed, Commandments, &c." This was removed and a new window put in, following on the old lines as exactly as possible. A new roof was also put on the chancel, the south wall was entirely pulled down and reconstructed, the beautifully mullioned windows being carefully taken to pieces and replaced. Pews which had existed within the chancel were removed. The reredos of alabaster, representing the Last Supper, by Earp of Lambeth, and considered to be a piece of good work, was also erected at this time. The restoration was carried out under the direction of Mr. G. E. Street.]

1861. Licence to continue the work in the nave: estimated cost about £700.

[This was not really undertaken till 1872.]

1863. The porch erected and a new door.

[Part of the work of 1807 had been the removal of a south porch of open timber framework which had existed till then, but fallen into decay.]

S

1864. I was offered and accepted the living of Long
    Marston in Yorkshire. The Rev J. R. T. Eaton
    accepted this living.

    july 10. A new Bible given by departing Rector
    and Wife. Wm Ball and Wm Osborn, Church-
    wardens.

    July 12. *Vale.* C. A. St. John Mildmay.

On his resignation of the living of Denton in 1883
Mr. Mildmay ceased from active duty in the Church.
He died on March 5, 1904, having always retained a
kindly interest in Lapworth, where he is remembered
with warm regard by many of its parishioners, though
forty years have passed since he resided here.

In the same *Memoranda parochialia* is the entry:—

1864. Sep. 18. On this day I first took duty in the parish
    church, having taken up my residence in the Rectory
    the day previous. In the interval from the late
    Rector's departure the church services were per-
    formed and the parishioners visited by the Rev^d
    Bennett of Solihull and the Revd R. W. Johnson of
    Packwood.   J. R. T. Eaton, Rector.

But Mr. Eaton did not during his incumbency continue to act as parish historian.

His academical and clerical record as given by
Foster is:—

J. R. T. Eaton, s. John of Lambeth, Surrey, Gentleman,
Lincoln College, matric. 19 March 1842, aged 17. B.A.
1845. Fellow Merton College 1847–65. M.A. 1848:
Principal of Postmasters, Tutor 1848, Dean 1849, Subwarden and Librarian, Select Preacher 1863, Bampton
Lecturer 1872, White's Professor of Moral Philosophy
1874–8; Rector of Lapworth, co: War:, 1864–78; Rector of
Denton, Norfolk, 1877–9; of Alvechurch, co: Worcester,
1879–86; and of Church Lench, co: Worc:, since 1886.

To which may be added that during his incumbency of Lapworth he became Honorary Canon of Worcester, and that since the date of the publication of the above record he gave up Church Lench and returned to Denton, of which place he remained Rector until October, 1896, resigning then, and not accepting any other cure.

During his rectorship he had the following curates :—

1866–7	.	.	J. A. Farrant.
1871–2	.	.	F. J. Crosland Fenton.
1874–5	.	.	Thomas Bates.
1875–7	.	.	Julian L. Bennett.
1877	.	.	Ernest Orde Powlett.

Little more remains to be noted in our parish chronicles.

1872. The Church Restoration of this year has already been dealt with (pp. 246–9).

1873. July 26. Buried. Francis Spencer Hildick. Aged 65.
[He was shot at his cottage door by one Parsons, his nephew, who immediately afterwards committed suicide by shooting himself on the same spot. The latter was buried here at night without funeral rites and without entry in the register.]

1875. June 1. Buried. Henry Saunders 81.
[Forty years Parish Clerk.]
June 30. Buried. Wᵐ Craddock 76.
[Forty-one years Beadle.]
Nov. 6. Buried. Wᵐ Ball.
[Fourteen years Churchwarden.]

1876 (Sunday, February 27). This morning, about seven o'clock, the church was discovered to be on fire, the cause an over-heated flue. Fortunately it had taken no great hold, and was extinguished by local efforts before any fire-engine arrived. The injury was confined to the roof of the north aisle at the east end, and the pecuniary damage covered by fire insurance. In connection with the reparation of the roof consequent on this fire, Mr. Hardwick of Birmingham, builder and contractor, had a fall from scaffolding inside the church, and received injuries from which he ultimately died.

1876 (April 18). Robt Hudson[1] and Wm. Osborn, churchwardens, the former being appointed in succession to Wm. Ball, deceased.

1878. Mr. Eaton resigned the living of Lapworth, having accepted that of Denton, in Norfolk, which is also in the gift of Merton College.

The Rev. Kenrick Prescot was appointed to Lap-

---

[1] With an interval of three years, Mr. Hudson filled the office of churchwarden from 1876 until his death in 1898. Near the pew in Lapworth Church which he occupied for so many years, there is now affixed to the north wall a bronze tablet inscribed as follows :—

To the Glory of God
AND IN
AFFECTIONATE REMEMBRANCE
OF
Robert Hudson
WHO DIED 20TH JUNE 1898 AGED 64
AND IS BURIED IN THIS CHURCHYARD
HE WAS A CHURCHWARDEN OF
LAPWORTH AND A FAITHFUL SERVANT
OF THE CHURCH DURING THE
RECTORATES OF
ARUNDELL ST. JOHN MILDMAY
JOHN RICHARD TURNER EATON
KENRICK PRESCOT
AND
FRANCIS LENDON BELL
BY WHOM TOGETHER WITH A NUMBER
OF PARISHIONERS THIS MEMORIAL
WAS ERECTED

worth in succession to Mr. Eaton, and came into residence in the month of May, 1878.

Kenrick Prescot, s of Charles Kenrick Prescot, of Stockport, Cheshire, cler: Brasenose College, matric 22 June 1848, aged 17. Scholar 1848–52. B.A. 1852. Fellow Merton College 1853–64. Tutor 1854–61. M.A. 1855. Tutor Lecturer in Modern History and Law 1854. Dean 1855. Vicar of Ponteland, Northumberland, 1864–78 : and of Lapworth 1878. (Foster, *Al. Oxon.*)

Mr. Prescot had as curates :—

1879 (June) to 1880 (Feb) .	Charles Partridge.
1880 (March) to 1881 (May) .	J. M. Dixon.
1882 (May) . . .	J. Williamson.
1882 (Aug) to 1886 (April) .	Charles Partridge.
1886–9 (at intervals) . .	Alfred J. Abbey.
1890 (Jan) to 1891 (Oct) . .	J. E. Hatch.
1892 (Feb) to 1896 (Oct) . .	F. Tibbits.

1883 (March 27). Vestry Minute :—

Mr. Hudson brought forward the subject of the dangerous condition of the church spire. Mr. Chatwin, architect, of Birmingham, had been consulted, and had employed Mr. Blackburn of Nottingham, an expert in spire-work, to make a thorough examination and give an estimate. Their report was that sixteen feet of the spire would have to be taken down and rebuilt, and that the work to be done would cost £134. Ordered to be put in hand.

1885 (April). Complete statement of church spire account submitted to vestry meeting, the work of reparation having been carried out in 1883–4. More work had been found necessary than was at first contemplated, including repairs to roof of tower, etc. The total cost was £247, raised by private subscriptions, except as regards £30 drawn from the fabric fund of the Lapworth Charity estates.

In 1892 there was removed a memorial and land-mark of old Lapworth which needs some word of record here, namely, the old cottages (miscalled "Alms-houses," for they never had any endowment) which occupied the whole of the south side of the churchyard, blocking out the view both from and of the church in that direction. They were five in num-ber, of which four stood mainly within, and opened into, the churchyard, having their doors within five or six feet of the ground overcharged with interments, and being some four feet below the level of the graves. The fifth cottage was newer, opening in the opposite direction, and had been got by some structural additions to the older work. The latter dated probably from the beginning of the seventeenth century, or might even be as old as the early years of Elizabeth's reign. In pulling down these cottages a brick was found with the date 1692,[1] but there is every reason to believe they were older than that. Edward Welchman, who was rector here at that time,

---

[1] In 1893, in rebuilding the churchyard wall after the cottages had been pulled down, application was made to the Solihull authorities for the restoration of this dated brick (which had been carried away) in order that it might be built into the wall as a memorial of the cottages. The reply was an exquisite bit of officialism. It was that the brick was needed for preservation at Solihull *by way of proof that the Sanitary Authority had pulled down the cottages*, but that anyone who wished to see it could do so on application.

A memorial of another ancient cottage will, however, be found built into the churchyard wall. In 1729 Humphry Shakespear gave 20s. a year to the poor of Lapworth, issuing out of a house and land at Kings-wood. When this cottage was pulled down in 1891, a stone from over the doorway, bearing the arms (as is believed) of the Peche family, first mentioned in our deeds in the time of Edward I., was preserved and built into the south wall. See illustration, p. 284.

makes mention of them in a way which does not suggest they were then new, and the signature, " John Wight, Schoolmaster, 1662," in the Parish Register helps us a little further back. That they were built out of funds of the charity there can be small doubt, and were allowed to be built within the churchyard probably because they were from the first intended for the use of the church officers. The one next the road was the school-house, next it was the schoolmaster's ; the other two were respectively those of clerk and sexton. They continued, indeed, to be so used until the building of the new school, with houses for master and clerk, in 1828. After that date the old cottages became available as refuges for deserving poor people, generally aged or helpless, who received small weekly allowances from the funds of the charity, or from the offertory, or both. Their selection was left to the rector.

For some years, however, before the cottages were pulled down they stood empty, and had fallen into great decay, the Charity Trustees having ceased to spend money on them. The immediate occasion of their destruction was the action of the Solihull Sanitary Authority, who, failing to find anybody who would admit ownership, stepped in and pulled them down. The old cottages did not fall unmourned or without protest. There were some, indeed, in the parish and outside who subscribed money for their reparation, failing which they built one other good cottage with the money raised, and gave it to the Charity Trust. Even the Society for the Preservation of Ancient Buildings was moved to interfere, and their secretary wrote a letter of appeal. It is doubtful, though, whether any of those who wished to spare the old cottages would care to see them back again. Their removal gave to the churchyard extension which was urgently required.

Two other items of church repair may be noted.

1893–4. New dial with hour and minute hands, and additional works to clock, £25.

[The church clock is of the very old and uncommon kind called a "bedstead" clock, and is thought to date from the beginning of the sixteenth century.]

1894–5. Repairs executed to church fabric, mainly in restoration of decayed pinnacles and embattled parapets, and in connection with roof of aisles, £212 15s. 2d.

In 1896 Mr. Prescot resigned the living of Lapworth, having accepted that of Denton, in Norfolk.

In the last of some notes which Mr. Prescot added to the *Memoranda parochialia* of the Lapworth Registers he sets out that on August 13, 1896, he received from the Archbishop of Canterbury (Dr. Benson) the offer of the living of Denton, which he accepted; and that on October 13 he received the presentation to Denton, dated October 10, and signed by the Archbishop, who died suddenly on October 11 in Hawarden Church while on a visit to Mr. Gladstone.

The Rev. Francis Lendon Bell was appointed to Lapworth in succession to Mr. Prescot. He accepted the living on December 22, 1896, came into residence on March 2, 1897, and was inducted on March 7. The services had been taken, in the interval since Mr. Prescot's departure from the parish, by the Rev. Alfred J. Abbey.

Mr. Bell's record is as follows :—

Francis Lendon Bell, s. of Henry Bell of Leppington, New South Wales, cler: Merton College : matric. 22 Jan 1882, aged 17. B.A. 1885. M.A. 1887. Assis[t] priest, Wing, Bucks, 1891–93, St. Saviour, Hitchin, 1893–97. Rector of Lapworth 1897.[1]

The Rev. Albert Edward Heaton, M.A., was curate from January, 1898, to June, 1904.

The present churchwardens (1904) are Mr. A. D. Melson and Mr. W. H. Chesshire. The former is also Chairman of the Lapworth Parish Council, to which body Mr. A. H. Davey acts as clerk. The overseers for the parish are Mr. W. H. B. Wood, Mr. William Cranmer, and Mr. Jacob Dutton. The present trustees of the Lapworth Charity are the Rector, Mr. William Osborne, Mr. William Ball, Mr. William Garrad, Mr. Stephen Hattin, Mr. Frank Bowley, Mr. Edwin Clutterbuck, Mr. Frederick Huggins, Mr. Alfred Duckworth Melson, Mr. Alexander Smith, Mr. William Whitworth, and Mr. Robert Jeffery Parr. The agent and treasurer to the trustees is Mr. Robert Neville Holbeche, F.S.I.[2]

---

[1] The Editor desires here gratefully to acknowledge his indebtedness to the Rector of Lapworth for frequent help and friendly encouragement in the task of preparing this volume for the press.

[2] See footnote on p. 231.

Parish Chest
(*temp.* Eliz.) in vestry of Lapworth Church

p. 212

A LIST OF THE NAMES OF PERSONS AND FAMILIES WHICH OCCUR IN THE LAPWORTH PRE-REFORMATION DEEDS (*c.* 1190–1502)

. . . not in the roll of common men."

HENRY IV., Part I

APPENDIX I

A LIST OF THE NAMES OF PERSONS AND FAMILIES WHICH OCCUR IN THE LAPWORTH PRE-REFORMATION DEEDS (*c.* 1190–1502): ARRANGED IN THE ORDER OF THEIR FIRST APPEARANCE

** Names written in the ablative are those of witnesses only.

MARSHALL.

Radulfus Marescallus . . . Rich^d j.

Galfridus Marchal (s. of Rad. M. of
Alveston) . . . . Henry iij.

Galfrido Marescallo . . „

„ le Marechal . . . Edw. j.

Rob'to le Marchal (de L.) . . } 1322–41.
„ „ Mareschal . . }

John le Marchal . . } 1343–9.
„ „ Mareschall . . }

PRAT.

Geoffrey (s. of Alexander) . . Ric. j.

Robō Prat . . . . „

Henry (s. of Geoffrey) . . . Hen: iij.

Symone P. de Pacwode.. . . „

Geoffrey P. . . . . 1323–49.

William, John, and Thomas (sons of } 1349.
Geoffrey P.) (*William living* 1398) }

John P. of Nuthurst . . . } 1399.
Alice (his wife) . . }

Ricō Prat . . . 1387–95.

„ „ . . . . 1425–55.

Thomas Prat of Nuthurst . . 1469–80.

„ „ of L. . . . 1480.

Laurence P. of L. . . . „

Catherine P. of Henley (his d.) . 1495.

DE CHARLECOTE.
    Simone de Ch'lecote   .   .   . Rich^d j.

    Galfrido de Ch'lecote   .   .   . John.

      The family assumed the name of Lucy
in 1204.

HATECRIST.
    * Ricardo Hatecrist   .   .   . Ric. j.

      „   Hattcrist   .   .   . John.

    Sẏmone Hatecryst   .   .   . Hen. iij.

PAKEMAN.
    William Pakeman   .   .   . Ric. j.

    Walter (his brother)   .   .   . „

    William Pakemon (of L.)   .   . 1349.

FEISANT.
    Galfrido Feisant   .   .   . Ric. j.

    Johē ffeẏsaunt de Pacwode   .   . Henry iij.

      „ ffeẏsant .   .   .   . 1343.

    Johannes ffeẏsond de Pacwode   . 1349.

DE LUDDINTON.
    John de Luddinton   .   .   . Ric. j. and John.

LAPWORTH (of).
    N.,   Rector de L.   .   .   . Ric. j.

    Nich: Parson de L. .   .   . John.

PACKWOOD (of).
    Walter, Chaplain of Packwood   . Ric. j.

FRANCEIS.
    Rogero Franceis   .   . Ric. j.

    Anketil ffranceis   .   .   . John.

    Ankertill ffraunceis de L.   .   . Henry iij.

    Anketillo le franceis   .   .   . „

    Amicia (his mother)   .   .   „

    Thomas frauncey̆s   .   .   1361.

SOREL.
    Lucas Sorel .   .   . John.

    Henrico Sorel de L.   .   ,   . Henry iij.

LE OISELUR. ⎫
LE FOULER. ⎬
FAUKENER. ⎭

Will° le Oiselur	. .	John.
Thom: le fouler	. . .	Edw. j.
Robertus dictus ffaukener de Henley		,,
Walter le fouler .	. . .	1337–49.

There is reason to believe that these were all members of one family.

ORM.

Ricardus filius de Orm .	. .	John.

SCUT—SCOT.

Willmus Scut .	. .	John.
Robō Scot .	. .	1330–48.
Marion (his wife)	. .	,,
Thomas Scut .	. .	1342–70.
John ,, .	. . .	1348.
Richard (s. of Thomas S.)	. .	1361.

SMŸTH.

Ricardus filius fabri	. . .	John.
Walter faber .	. . .	1337.
Thomas le Smŷth de Thoneworth (*also spelt Smith*)	. . .	1341.
Ricō le Smŷth	. . .	1343.
Will° le Smŷth de Pacwode	. .	1361–70.
Agnes (his wife) . . . ⎫		
John, Alice, Johan, and Julia (their ⎬ children) . . . . ⎭		1370.

BAGOT.

Simone Bagot	. .	John.
Luc̃ Bagot .	. . .	,,

LOFRIC.

Willūs, filius de Lofric .	. .	John.

LA WEICTE.

Radulphus La weicte .	. . .	John and Hen. iij.
Thomas la Weyte de L. (s. of Thom: la W.)		Hen. iij.

ARSTEL.
    Thomas Arstel   .   .   Henry iij.

DE SINDBIRI.
    Sẏmone de Sindbiri   .   .   .   Henry iij.

IN ẎE LONE.
    Thomas in lone   .   .   .   Hen. iij.
    John in ẏe lone (*dead in 1337*)   .   1323–30.
    „   atte Lone   .   .   .   1337–44.
    Agnes (his wife)   .   .   „
    „   (his widow)   .   .   1346.·
    Robtō in le Lane   .   .   1337–43.
    Willō in ȝe lone   .
    „   in the lone   .   .   } 1337–49.
    John in the Lone (capellanus) (*some-
    times "Dns Johannes"; in* 1350,
    "*quondam capell:*")   .   .   .   1343–9.
    Ricō in the Lone   .   .   .   1347–9.

DE TOPPESFORD.
    Robō de Toppesford   .   .   .   Hen. iij. or Edw. j.
    Rico „   „   .
    Ricardus Topford   .   . } 1329–70.
    „   Tapford   .
    Robō Topforde .   .   .   1349.·

ALOTE.
    Thomas Alote   .   .   Hen. iij.

ATTE WELLE.
    Rogero ad Fontem   .   .   .   Edw. j.
    Willº ad Fontem   .   .   „
    Rogero de Fonte   .   .   1322.
    Willo de Fonte   .   .   „
    „   atte Welle   .   .   .   1342–9.
    Walterus atte Welle (de L.)   .   .   1349–61.
    Laurencio „   „   .   .   1360–87.
    Nicholas atte Wẏle   .   .   1361.
    Willº atte Welle   .   .   1387–99.
    Thomas atte Wẏle (de Toneworth) .   1388–93.
    John atte Welle (gener: de L.) .   .   1425–62.

STIKEMON.

Johē Stikemon	. .	Edw. j.
William Stikemon	. . .	1322.
„ Stekemon	. . .	1338–48.

PHELIP.

William Phelip de L. .	. .	Edw. j.
Emma (his wife)	. . .	„

BONEL.

Alex: Bonel of Nuthurst	. .	Edw. j.

PECHE.

Will⁰ Peche .	. . .	Edw. j.
Alice (wid: of John le P. de Notehurst)		1329.
Robtō Pech .	. . .	„
Matilda (d. of Robt. P.)	. .	1346.
Petronilla Pech (*alias* Teppẏng)	.	1349.
Johē Pech .	. . .	1387–99.

DE NUTHURST.

Hanriĉ de Notehurst .	. .	Edw. j.
Walt'o „ „	. .	„ ij., iij.
Laurencio de N.	. .	1360.
Johannes, clericus de N.	. .	Edw. j.
Roger, clericus de N. .	. .	„

BRAUNDESTON.

Hugo de Braunchestone . .⎫
  „ „ Braunstone (miles, et dns ⎬ Edw. j.
  de L., *died 1299*) . . .⎭

Hugone de Braunchestone	. .	1329–50.
Hugo de Braundeston (miles, et dns de L., *grandson of the first-named*)		1361.

TRUSSELL.

Edmund Truscel de Notehurste	.	Edw. j.
Willˢ Trussell (miles, et dns de Notehurst)	. . .	1349.
Johannes Trussell de N. (nup. de Billysseley, arm:)	. .	1454–80.

FULWODE.

Ricō de ffulwode	. .	Edw. j.
Willō de ffolewode	. . .	1320.
Johnē „ „	. . .	1362.
„ „ „ (de Toneworthe) .	1388.
Johē ffulwode	. . .	1435.
Richard ffulwode (de Toneworthe, arm:)	. . . .	1454–61.

WISTAN—WESTON.

Ricō Wistan de Toneworthe	. .	Edw. j.
Thomas Wÿstan	. . .	1341.
John de Weston	. .	1343.

HARECOURT.

Willūs de la Harecourt	. .	Edw. j.

THOURSTAN.

Henric⁹ Thourstan	. . .	Edw. j. & ij.
Thome Thy⁹stan	. .	1349.

BROME.[1]

Roger de Brome	. .	Edw. j.
Paulinus de B.	. .	1346–50.
John de B. .	. .	1361–70.
„ Brome .	. .	1388–1408.
Thomas B. .	. .	1461–85.
Robert B. .	. .	1488.

ALEŸN.

Henricus, fil: Alani de L.	. .	Edw. j.
Thoˢ Aleÿn .	. . .	1329.
Ricō A. (clerico)	. .	1329–49.
William A. .	. . .	1346–60.
Thomas A. (de Bromsgrove)	. .	1362.
Mathÿlda (his wife)	. . .	„
Alice A. de Notehurst .	. .	1398.

[1] Domina Jocosa Brome filia Johanis Brome et Priorissa de Wroxhall, obiit xxi Junii, MVᶜXXVIII (*Dugdale*).

ATTE HETHE.

Walter de la Hethe	.	.	Edw. j.
„ atte Hethe	.	.	1322–9.
Agnes (his wife)		.	1329.
Geoffrey atte Hethe	.	.	⎫
„ de la Heth	.	.	⎬ 1322–49.
„ o' th Hethe	.	.	⎭
Agnes (his wife)		.	„
Geoffrey atte H. Junr	.	.	1344.
Matilda (his widow)	.	.	„
Walter atte Heth	.	.	1349–60.
Geoffrey atte H. (s. of Walter)	.	.	1388–1433.
Margaret (his wife)	.	.	1408.
john atte H. (son of Geoffrey and Margaret)	.	.	„

The following occur only in the reign of Edward I. :—

Henry ate Slou de N.
Yvo Pippert de L.
Robō Symons de Eseneford in N.
Ricō Heremus de Linthurst in N.
Robō „ „ „
Willūs Bissop de N.
Th'me Baudrik.
Hanric le Pottere de N.
Edwardus, fil: Willⁱ, fil: capell: de N.
Walter de la Bruēre de L.

COTEREL.

Pernela Coterel of Henley	.	.	1319.

DE BERTON—BARTON.

Johē de Berton	.	.	1319–49.

WILKYN.

Thebaldus Wilkyn de N.	..	.	1319–49.
Edith (his wife)	.	.	„
Robertus Wẏlkẏnes	.	.	1363.

LEA—LEE.

    Johē ate Lea de Thoneworth . . 1320–46.

BACHE.

    Margery ate Bache (d. of Robᵗ ate B.
      de Thoneworth) . . . 1320.

KOOC—COOKE.

    Walt'o le Kooc de L. . . . 1320–41.
    johīs Coci de Henleẏe . . . 1330.
    Radulphus le Cok de L. . . 1341.
    Amicia (his widow) . . . 1347.
    Caleb le Cooke . . 1343.
    Ricō Coccus . . . 1361.
    Thoma Koce . . . „

BROCSAWE.

    Johē de Brocsawe . . . 1322–30.
    Henry Brocschawe . . . 1348.
    Margery B. (his dʳ) . . . 1349.

COPPE.

    John de la Coppe de L. . . 1323.
    Ricō atte C. (s. of William) . . 1349–61.

PORFREY.

    Roger Porfrey of Coventry . . 1323.
    Thomas Purfrey of Munsterton (his
      brother) . . . . „
    Thomas Purfrey . . 1323–38.

DE BARRE.

    Ricardo de barre (Lẏndraper) . . 1329–62.
    Johnē Barre . . . 1388–93.
    Thomas Barre . . 1408.

DE NORTON.

    Rogero de Norton . . 1329–56.
    John de Nortone . . 1349.

HARDYNG.

    Johē Hardyng⁊ . . 1329–64.
    Emma (his wife) . . 1373.
    Elena (her dʳ) . . „

LE PERSONES.

Thomas le Persones de L. . .	1330–88.
Agnes (his wife) . . .	1364.
Geoffrey le P. (s. of Agnes) . .	„
Richard le P. (s. of Thos) . .	1361–70.
Richard Persones . . .	1390–1408.
Felicia (his wife) . . .	1395.
William Persones (s. of Rich^d) . .	1395–1455.
Thomas P. (s. of Rich^d) . .	„
john P. (b. of W^m) . . .	1425–32.
john P. de L. (s. of W^m. P. de Tone-worthe) . . .	1455–73.
Alice (his wife) . . .	1455.
William P. de Toneworth . .	1461.
Elizabeth (his wife) . . .	„

DENE.

Simon Dene . . .	1337–48.
Roger D. . . .	1349.
john D. . .	1433.

LE RO.

Alexō le Ro (?) . .	1337.
Willūs le Roo . . .	1359–90.
Thomas le Ro . . .	1360.
Isabella (wid: of Thos) . . .	„

BUSSEBI.

Henry Bosseby of Coventry . .	1338.
Henry de Bussebi „ . .	„

OOWENHALE—ULLENHALL.

Robō d Wenhał . . .	1341.
Robto de Oowenhale . . .	1362.

CORVESER.

John le Corveser of Henley . .	1343.
Agnes (his widow) . . .	1343–8.
Richard dictus le Corveser de Henley, clericus (s. of john and Agnes) .	1343–63.

ARCHER.

    johnē le Archer (de N.)   .   .   1346.

    Thomas L'archer   .   .   .   1363.

AUSTẎN.

    Johnē Austẏn   .   .   1349.

    Scolastica Austeẏn   .   .   .   1361.

SHEPEHERD.

    Johē le Shepeherd   .   .   .   1360.

    Thomas Shepđē   .   .   1381–93.

    Isabella (his wife)   .   „

    Thoma Shepherd   .   .   1431.

ATTE FORD—FORD—VORDE.

    Walter atteford of Notehurste .   .   1360.

    Theobald   „   „   .   .   „

    Isabella (his wife)   .   .   .   „

    Thomas atte forde of L.   .   .   1361.

    Thomas atte ffoorde   .   .   .   1399–1435.

    Ellen at ye vorde (atte fforde : his

       widow)   .   .   .   .   1435–54.

    William vorde (s. of Ellen at ye vorde

       and Thomas)   .   .   .   1435.

DE WOTTON.

    Ralph de Wotton (parson of Beau-

       desert)   .   .   .   .   1361–3.

    Thomas de W.   .   .   1363.

HUWOTES.

    Thomas Huwotes de Kẏngeswode   .   1361.

    William, s, of Thomas H. (Yoman) .   „

    john Huwit   .   .   .   .   1393.

MARTẎN.

    john Martẏn .   .   .   1361–98.

    Walter M.   .   .   .   1387–1435.

    Richard M.   .   .   .   1425.

AŸLESBURY.

> Philippo de Aÿlesbury (*s. of Sir Roger de Aÿlesbury of Edston, and mar. to Alice, d. of Sir Hugh de Brandeston*) . . . 1361–70.
>
> John Aylesbury de Etyngdon (*great-grandson of Philip*) . . . 1455–80.

ATTE GRENE.

> Roger atte grene de L. . . . 1361–95.
>
> John atte grene . . . 1408.
>
> Thomas atte grene . . . „

DE MONTFORT.

> Ricardus de Monteforti . . . 1362–70.
>
> Rose Mountfort (D'na de Codbarewe: wid: of Rich^d) . . . 1399.

The following occur only in the reign of Edward III. :—

> Henrico de Lÿle . . 1329.
>
> Thomā Maÿdemon . . . „
>
> Willō Warde . . . „
>
> Sir Walter de Brÿnkunhul (Chaplain of L.) . . . . 1337.
>
> Waltō Onlÿ . . . „
>
> Walt'o Page . . . 1342–9.
>
> John le Harpur . . 1343.
>
> Walter de Hereford . . . 1343–61.
>
> john fflauvill . . . 1344–9.
>
> Theobald Adith de N. . . . 1346.
>
> John Pÿmmyger . . . 1348–9.
>
> Adam Bockeleÿe de Henley . . 1348.
>
> Geoffrey Bodi „ . . . „
>
> Richard Wÿbert „ . . . „
>
> Weleÿe Dÿggele . . . „
>
> Henry Weteboo . . . 1348.
>
> Caldwell, Prior of . . . „
>
> Geoffrey le Wardē . . . 1349.
>
> John le Weÿn (*or* le Sweÿn) . . . „

John Jobus de Henleẏe . . 1361–3.
John Jory . . . 1361–74.
William Ine . . . 1361.
Nicholas Dẏrvassel . . . „
Hawẏcia de Allesleye . . . „
John Hemery . . . „
„ de Hamslape . . . „
„ Porreys (?) . . . „
„ de Hasulhoẏlte . . . „
Thomas le Carpunter . . . „
Henry Selle . . . 1362.
John Pyl . . . „
„ Timmins (?) . . . „
William de ffoshẏde of Henleẏe . 1363.
„ Curchedoune (?) . . 1364.

BLYTHE.
William Blythe . . 1381–1425.
Laurence B. . . 1431–55.
john B. . . 1432–54.
Thomas Blithe . . 1462.
William Blythe . . 1476–88.

LEHULLE—HULLE.
Sẏmon de Lehulle . . 1387.
Sẏmon Huɫɫ . . 1393.

SLYE.
john Slye (*and* Slẏ) . . 1388–1425.
Thomas Slye (*and* Sley) . „
Walter Slẏ . . . 1393–1408.
Richard Sly (*and* Shly) . . 1425–35.
John S. (s. of john) . . 1425–33.
Nicholas Slye . . 1432–80.
Thomas S. . . 1461–88.
john S. . . . 1472–80.
William S. (*and* Slee) . . 1473–88.

The next we have is Roger Slye, who
died in 1527, and whose will is extant,
leaving lands to the parish.

WELBE.

    Thomas Welbe   .   .   1381.

HÝKONES.

    William Hýkones (Chaplain of L.) .   1393–5.

FFLECCHER.

    Thomas ffleccher   .   .   1393–1408.

    The following occur only in the reign of Henry IV. :—

        john of Aston (Chaplain of L.)   .   1408.
        Robert Horton (Parson of L.) .   .   „
        William Ketel (*and* Kettill, of Snet-
          field)   .   .   .   .   1408–32.
        John Morton (Tailor)   .   .   1408.
        „   Kete   .   .   .   .   „
        William Amyson (of Colleshull)   .   1412.
        john Couper (of Packwood)   .   .   „

ASSHEBY.

    Thomas Assheby   .   .   1425.
    john A.   .   .   .   .   1425–62.
    Thomas A. (s. of Rich[d])   .   .   „
    George A. (s. of Tho[s]) .   .   .   1425–69.
    Richard A.   .   .   .   .   1430–62.
    William A.   .   .   .   .   1476–80.
        This family appear continuously in the
    Parish Register from 1560 to 1660.

UNDERWOOD.

    Thomas Underwood (Chwd[n]) .   .   1425.
    Thomas Underwood (Chwd[n]) .   . ⎫
                                  ⎬ 1473–1500
    Thomas Hundurwood   .   . ⎭
    Katherine (his wife)   .   .   .   1488.
        The second Thomas and wife be-
    queathed lands to the parish.

WALTON.

    Thomas Walton   .   .   1454–88.
    William W.   .   .   .   1502.

SKÝNNER.

Sýmone Skýnner . .	1454–85.
Margaret (his wife) . . .	1473–85.
Richard Skýnner (*alias* Beer of Lytýlauen: s. of Sýmone) . .	1455–73.
Phillip S. (of Sambourne) . .	1473–6.
Alice (d. of Rich^d) . . .	1476.
Johanna S. de Toneworth (d. of Henry S. nuper de Pacwode) . .	1485.

This family left lands to the parish.

BARNETHURST.

john Barnethurst (parcarius) . .	1454–88.

His family continued here till about end of sixteenth century.

The following are confined to the reign of Henry VI. :—

William Haverell (of Banbury) .	1425.
Thomas Spenser . . .	„
Henry Henbrok . .	1425–35.
Symon Glynn . .	1432.
Margaret (his wife) . .	
Philip Brokhurst . .	1433.
Thomas Albryghton . . .	„
„ Hynton (of Henley) . .	1433–54.
William, Chaplain of Nuthurst .	1435.
Sir William Catesby (*owning land in Nuthurst*) . . .	1454.
John Hancokkes . .	„
William Halle . . .	„
Roger Childe (of Henley) . .	1455–61.
Robert Clerdon (? E'ndon) . .	1455.
John Elshawe (of Tanworth) . .	1461.
Thomas Heywarde . . .	„
John Alcokk' (of Tanworth) . .	„

The following appear in the reigns of Edward IV. and V. :—

Richard Browne . . .	1462.
William Baker (of Henley) . .	1472.
„ Bluntt (*deceased*) . .	„
Thomas Mason (Master of the Gild of the Holy Trinity of Henley in Arden)	1472.
William Reynold (of Henley) . .	„
John Deyst (of Henley) . .	„
Richard Morteboyes (of Pakwode) .	„
Sir John Hylle (Rector of L.) . .	1473–80.
Sir John Cosenar (Chaplain of the Chantry of the B.V.M. of Tanworth)	1473.
Thomas Appulbe . . .	„
Nicholas Stevyns . .	} 1473–88.
„ Stephens . .	

The following appear in the reign of Henry VII. :—

BEDULL (*alias* SCLATTER).

John Bedull, *alias* Sclatter, de Clyfford Chamberleyn-juxta-Stratford-super-Avon: (Yoman) . . .	1485–8.
Agnes (his wife) . .	„

LYNCECOMBE.

John Lyncecombe de Lyncecombe .	1485.

ROUNDE.

Richard Rounde de Knolle . .	1485.
William Rounde de Pakwode . .	„
John Rowñ de Pakwode . .	„

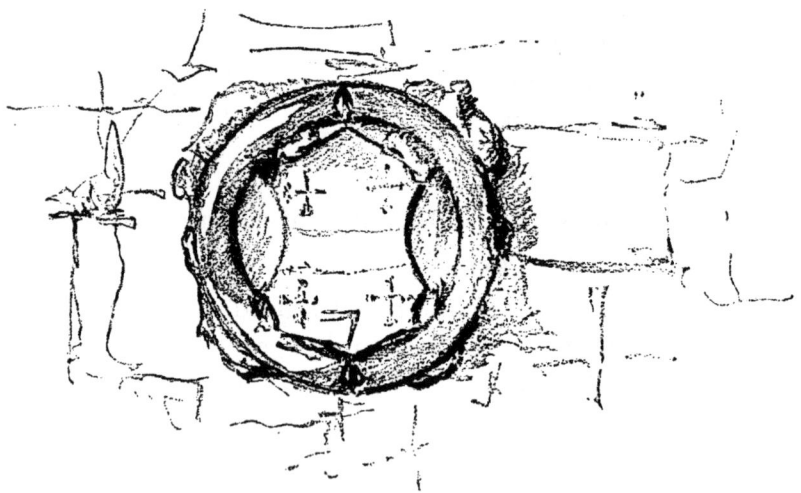

Stone built into wall of Lapworth Churchyard
from Humphry Shakespear's cottage at Kingswood

p. 262 (footnote)

AN INDEX TO THE NAMES CONTAINED WITHIN
THE REGISTERS OF THE PARISH OF LAPWORTH
FOR THREE HUNDRED YEARS: 1561–1860

. . . what the dickens his name is."
                    MERRY WIVES OF WINDSOR

APPENDIX II

AN INDEX TO THE NAMES CONTAINED WITHIN THE REGISTERS OF THE PARISH OF LAPWORTH FOR THREE HUNDRED YEARS: 1561–1860

SHOWING THE SUCCESSIVE DECADES OF EACH CENTURY IN WHICH SUCH NA OCCUR, AND THEREBY INDICATING THE RELATIVE CONTINUANCE OF FAMI IN THE PARISH

[EXAMPLE.—*In the first line of this Index it will be understood that the name "Abbern" appe only during the three hundred years, namely, between 1640 and 1650. The figure "4" does not indi year, but the decade. It shows that the name "Abbern" appears in the Parish Registers in "the fo the seventeenth century.*]

Name.	Sixteenth Century.				Seventeenth Century.										Eighteenth Century.										Ninet Cen		
	1561-9	1570-9	1580-9	1590-9	1600-9	1610-9	1620-9	1630-9	1640-9	1650-9	1660-9	1670-9	1680-9	1690-9	1700-9	1710-9	1720-9	1730-9	1740-9	1750-9	1760-9	1770-9	1780-9	1790-9	1800-9	1810-9	1820-9
Abbern									4																		
Abots [Abbots]										5				9	0	1	2										
Adams														9													
Addleton																											
Af (?)										5																	
Aikobe (?)											6																
Aisloppe					0																						
Akers																											
Albert																1											
Alderman		7																									
Aldington																											
Aldrige [-dge, -eridge]						1		3																			
Alen [Allen, -yn, -eyn]										5		7	8		0	1	2										
Alesbury													8														
Allcock [Alcock]																		3			6	7					
Almanack																				5							
Alsop [Alsb]											6					1		3									
Amphlett																											
Ancorn [-corns]																										1	
Andrews														9													
Anson																									0	1	2
Apletree			8																								
Arch																	2	3	4	5							
Archer																									0		

Name	Sixteenth Century				Seventeenth Century										Eighteenth Century										Ninet Cent		
	1561-9	1570-9	1580-9	1590-9	1600-9	1610-9	1620-9	1630-9	1640-9	1650-9	1660-9	1670-9	1680-9	1690-9	1700-9	1710-9	1720-9	1730-9	1740-9	1750-9	1760-9	1770-9	1780-9	1790-9	1800-9	1810-9	1820-9
Archpole								3																			
Arculus [Arkellus, Hercules]																									0	1	2
Ariss																											
Arnall [-owl, -old, -owld]								3	4	5	6	7	8														
Asbury																			4								
Ashbie [-bye]	6	7	8	9	0	1	2	3		5					0												
Ashmale [-mole]												7	8	9	0		2										
Ashurst														9													
Askewe		7	8	9	0	1	2	3	4	5	6	7	8	9		1	2										
Assinder [Aussinder, -ter]														9	0												
Aston																									0		2
Astley																										1	2
Atkins																											2
Attwoode	6											7	8														
Austin														9	1	2											
Averill																2											
Avern																			4	5			8				
Avery																							8	9	0	1	2
Bache															0				4								
Bacon			8	9	1						7													9			
Badger																					6						
Bailies [Baylies, -iss, -is. Balyes]			8	9											0	1	2					7	8	9	0	1	2
Baker	6						2	3							0	1		3				7					
Balden [Bawden, Baldwin, Bawdwine, Bawldwyne]	6	7	8		0						6															1	2
Ball [-e]			8					3																			
Balok											6																
Bankes							2			5																	
Bannester [Bannister, Banister]			8	9	0	1									0		2										
Bant																							8			1	
Barber					0																						
Barfoot																		3									
Barker						1	2	3	4	5				9	0		2										
Barlow [-e]		7																							0		
Barnby			8																								
Barnbrook																								9	0	1	2
Barnee												7															
Barnes													8														
Barnet [-tt]											6		8														
Barnhurst		7	8																		6						
Barnod											6																
Barret [-tt, Barte]														9	0	1	2				6		8				
Bartlam																							8				
Bate [-s]	6			9									8	9	0		2	3	4	5	6	7	8	9	0		2
Battin																											
Beach																					6					1	
Beardsmore [Berdmore]																						7					2
Beardsworth																											

Name	Sixteenth Century				Seventeenth Century										Eighteenth Century										Nineteenth Century		
	1561-9	1570-9	1580-9	1590-9	1600-9	1610-9	1620-9	1630-9	1640-9	1650-9	1660-9	1670-9	1680-9	1690-9	1700-9	1710-9	1720-9	1730-9	1740-9	1750-9	1760-9	1770-9	1780-9	1790-9	1800-9	1810-9	1820-9
Bedle					1																						
Beesley																							8				
Belcher											8																
Bele									4																		
Bellamy [Belamy, Ballamy, Balamy]																1	2	3	4	5	6	7	8	9			
Bellers					0																						
Benbrook [-e]																											
Benford [Bentford]					1		3		5	6	7	8	9		0	1											
Benlow								4																			
Bennett [-nnet, -nnit, -net]										5		7	8	9	0	1	2	3	4	5	6	7	8	9			
Bennett, *alias* Houma							3																				
Benson																											
Bent	6	7	8	9	1	2																					
Berrie					0	1																					
Bewell																											
Bicknil																											
Biddle [Biddell]											6				0							7		9			2
Biddolph														9													
Billings [Billing]																											2
Birch																2											
Bird		7										7			0				4	5		7				1	
Bishop																							6		0		2
Bissel [-ll]	6		9								8									4	5						2
Black														9	0	1											
Blacknowle			8																								
Blake								4																			
Blaydon							2																				
Bliss																		4									
Blunt															1								9		0		2
Boardsley																						7					
Bolt															0	1											
Bond																						7	8	9	0		
Bonnell																								9	0		
Boobee (?)	6																										
Boon													8														
Boot [-e]																						7				1	
Borton										5																	
Borston								3																			
Boswell [Bosell]								3		5																	
Bosworth [-e]	6	7			0	1					6	7				2											
Bot [-tt]																2	3	4	5	6	7	8					
Bowater						2					7																
Bowdler							3																				
Bowen																									0		
Bower							3																				
Bowler								4																			
Bozzard											6	7		9													
Bozzard, *alias* Palmer												7															
Bradbury [Broadbury, Brawdbury]														9	0	1	2	3				8	9		0	1	2
Bradford																						7		9	0		2
Bradley																		4								1	

U

Name.	1561-9	1570-9	1580-9	1590-9	1600-9	1610-9	1620-9	1630-9	1640-9	1650-9	1660-9	1670-9	1680-9	1690-9	1700-9	1710-9	1720-9	1730-9	1740-9	1750-9	1760-9	1770-9	1780-9	1790-9	1800-9	1810-9	1820-9	1830-9
Bradshaw								3									2	3			6	7	8	9			2	
Bragg																										1		
Breakwell																									0			
Bridges						1	2																					
Briggs		7																										
Briscoe [Brisker, Brister]																								9			2	
Bristow [-e]																												
Brittain																												
Brodhurst		7																										
Brooks [Brokes, Brookes]								3	4	5	6	7		9	0	1	2	3		5	6	7	8	9	0		2	
Broton																												
Browne [Brone]				9			2		4	5					0	1				5	6	7	8	9	0	1	2	
Brunt																											2	
Buckingham						1																						
Bufferey [-ffry, -ffery, -fery]											6	7		9	0	1	2	3	4	5	6	7	8					
Buckley [-ly, Bookly]													8	9	0		2											
Bull			8	9	0	1	2																					
Bullock											6	7	8															
Bun [-nn]														9		1	2			5	6	7		9	0	1	2	
Bunter																1												
Burdett [Borded]									4	5																		
Burge				9			2																		0	1		
Burley			8	9	0																							
Burman [Borman]																							8		0			
Burnbrook																							8					
Burr																				5		7						
Burrows																											2	
Burton				9	0		2											3	4	5	6	7		9	0	1		
Busby																							8					
Bushell																												
Butcher [Bucher]																		3	4	5	6	7		9	0		2	
Butler				9									8															
Butwell [Buttwell]																1	2	3		5	6	7	8	9	0	1	2	
Byrd [-e]						1		3																				
Byrchie								3																				
Cale		7																										
Callow													8	9			2											
Calloway																								9				
Cambden [Camden]										5	6			9	0		2											
Cameron																												
Cammell																1												
Camp																			4									
Carelesse							2																					
Carpenter [Carpinter]		7															2	3	4	5	6			9	0	1		3
Cash																												
Cashmore																1												
Castle [Castell]							2																					
Cater		7																										
Cattell																												
Catesbie [-ye]		7												9														
Caudwell [Cadell]										5	6																	

Name	Sixteenth Century				Seventeenth Century										Eighteenth Century										Ninet. Cent.		
	1561	1570	1580	1590	1600	1610	1620	1630	1640	1650	1660	1670	1680	1690	1700	1710	1720	1730	1740	1750	1760	1770	1780	1790	1800	1810	1820
Cauffen [Coffen]												7	8	9													
Cawdry, alias Cooke							2																				
Cawrow (?)										5																	
Cenninge, Canning [-e]	6	7	8	9		1		3		5														9	0	1	2
Cent [Kent]									4																		
Cendol [-e, Cendowell]										5	6																
Cerby										5																	
Chace						1																					
Chamberlayne [-lin,-lain,-layn,-laine]														9						5	6			9			
Chambers							2																	9	0	1	2
Chandler																				5							
Chatterley																								9			
Chedle												7															
Cheedon [-en]								3					8														
Chesshire [Cheshire]																			4		6		8		0		2
Childe [-s]						1																				1	2
Chin [-nn]																	2			5		7	8	9	0	1	2
Clark [-e, -erke, -erk]	6	7	8	9	0	1	2	3	4	5	6	7	8	9	0		2	3	4	5	6	7	8	9			2
Clare								3																			
Clarkson [Clarson, -s]								3		5						1		3	4	5							
Claydon																											
Clayton																											
Cleaver																							8				
Clews																					6	7	8				
Cloves																1		3		5			8				
Cogger																	2										
Coke									4		6																
Cokeley																											2
Cole													8														
College [-edge]							2				6																
Collcutt															0												
Collett																								9	0		
Colleycutt																									0		
Collins									4				8	9		1	2										
Cooles [Coles]		7	8				2	3		5																	
Cooper								3										3		5			8				
Colmore										5	6																
Cooke [Coocke, Cooks]			8		0							7		9		1		3	4	5	6	7	8	9	0	1	
Cooke, alias Cawdry							2																				
Commander																								9		1	2
Comby														9	0	1											
Congrave													8														
Connell																											
Constable																											2
Copage																											
Cope																							8				
Copperthwaite																									0		
Corbet [-tt]																	2						8				
Corte [Court, -te]								3	4	5		7	8	9		1	2	3	4		6	7		9		1	2
Cotterell [-ttrell]				9		1		3	4	5	6			9	0	1	2	3	4		6	7	8		0	1	2
Cox [Coxe, Cokex]	6	7	8	9		1	2			5					0					5	6	7	8	9	0	1	2
Cowper							2	3				7															
Craddock [Cradock]																											2

Name	Sixteenth Century				Seventeenth Century										Eighteenth Century												
	1561-9	1570-9	1580-9	1590-9	1600-9	1610-9	1620-9	1630-9	1640-9	1650-9	1660-9	1670-9	1680-9	1690-9	1700-9	1710-9	1720-9	1730-9	1740-9	1750-9	1760-9	1770-9	1780-9	1790-9	1800-9	1810-9	1820-9
Cranm (?) Crannor, Cranmer, Crammer, Cramner, Cranmore	6										6	7	8		0	1	2	3	4	5	6	7	8	9	0		2
Crendall														9	0	1	2				6						
Crooke														9													
Cros	6																										
Crow																		3									
Crowder						1																					
Crowly [-ley]														9	1												
Crump																											
Cubbage																2											
Cundy									4	5																	
Cuney								3																			
Culcup [Culcope, Kulcup]												7	8		0	1	2	3	4	5	6	7	8				
Currier																			4								
Curtis																											
Curtney				9																							
Dafforn [-ern, -on]																						7	8	9	0		
Dalby																											
Dale																					6						
Daniel [-ll]																1							8	9	0	1	2
Darbie	6																										
Darlison	6																										
Davyes [-ise, -is]			9		1																			9			
Dawes																											
Dawkins					0																						
Day [-e]																			4			7	8				
Dee [Dey]																											
Denman																											
Dennet (? Denner)																		3									
Denson																							8				
Denston [-e]																						7	8				
Dent															1												
Dickinson, *alias* Fewster		7																									
Digbye					0																						
Dipple																						7					
Dison [Dyson]								4																			
Dive						2																					
Dixton																						7					
Doley [Doly]													8	9	0	1	2	3	4								
Dolphin																											
Dolson																							8				
Dolton								2										3	4	5	6	7	8	9			
Doncalf														9													
Donsby																					6						
Dowler														9													
Downing																											
Dracke [-ake]			8	9			2	3		5																	
Duckett																											
Dudley						2																					
Duffel		7																									
Duffin [-ng]																							8	9			
Dufton																											

Name.	Sixteenth Century				Seventeenth Century										Eighteenth Century										Nineteenth Century					
	1561-9	1570-9	1580-9	1590-9	1600-9	1610-9	1620-9	1630-9	1640-9	1650-9	1660-9	1670-9	1680-9	1690-9	1700-9	1710-9	1720-9	1730-9	1740-9	1750-9	1760-9	1770-9	1780-9	1790-9	1800-9	1810-9	1820-9	1830-9	1840-9	1850-60
igard																														5
igglass [Douglas]															0	1	2													
ikes																									0	1	2		4	
inckley			8	9																										
irham								3																						
irie			8																											
itton																										1		3		
ye [Die]							2	3	4	5		7																		
ides																			4			7								
iton																												3		
iorall [Ebrall]			8																					9		1	2	3	4	5
ien [Edden]															0														4	5
igecox																											2	3	4	5
igeoak																		3								◂				
iges																											2			
ikins [-ens]								3		5	6	7	8	9			2	3	4	5	6	7	8		0				4	
iwards	6																					7		9	0	1	2		4	5
gelston																										1				
l																1														
lie [Elly]						1	2																							
lin [-en, -ens]																										1		3		
kin																														5
liott																														5
lies											6																			
ms																1														
ns [Emms, -es]								3							0	1	2													
hrington																1														
vans																						7	8	9						
vatts		7																												
ves																				5										
rr [ffares]			8	9	0	1																								
rre [Farr]																										1				
ifefold											6																			
lks [Faux, Fawkes]																	2	3	4	5		7								
intom [Fantham]																									0	1	2	3		5
irdon																													4	5
arshon (?)				9																										
arefox [fferfox]								3			6																			
helle (?)																								9						
nton																								9						
therston [Fetherstone]	6						2																	9	0			3	4	
wster			8																											
ʒld												7																		
eld												7			0		2	3					8		0	1	2		4	
lipes											6																			
ndall																			4											
ndon																			4		6									
ndon						1																								
sh												7																		
sher [-y]		7	8		0	1	2																							
sher [Fishere]										5	6																			
tter																						7								

Name.	Sixteenth Century.	Seventeenth Century.	Eighteenth Century.	Nine Cen
	1560-9 1570-9 1580-9 1590-9	1600-9 1610-9 1620-9 1630-9 1640-9 1650-9 1660-9 1670-9 1680-9 1690-9	1700-9 1710-9 1720-9 1730-9 1740-9 1750-9 1760-9 1770-9 1780-9 1790-9	1800-9 1810-9
Flechar [Fletcher]	. . . . .	. . . . . . 6 . . .	. . . . . . 6 7 . 9	
Fleetwood	. . . . .	. . . .	 9	1 2
Flyfield	. . . . .	. . . .	. . . . 8 .	
Ford	. . . . .	. . . . . 6	. . . .	.
Foster	. . . . .	. . . .	. . . .	. .
ffowler	. . . . .	o . 2 . . . . 7 . .	. . . .	. .
Fowler	. . . . .	. 1 . . . 5 . . . 9	. 1 2 9	. 1 2
Foxe	. . . . .	. . . . 7 . .	. . . .	o . .
Foxall	. . . . .	. . . .	. . . . 7 8 9	o . .
Francton	. . . . .	. . . :	. . . . 7 . .	. .
Franklin	. . . . .	. . . .	. . . . . 5	o . .
Freeman	. . . . .	. . . .	o 1 2 3	. . 2
ffulford	. . 7 8 9	. . . .	. . . .	. .
Fulford	. . . . .	. . . .	 9	. .
Fullard	. . . . .	. . . .	. . . .	. 1 .
Fuller	. . . . .	. . . .	. . . .	. .
ffulwell	. . 7 . .	. . . .	. . . .	. .
Fulwell	. . . . .	. . . . . . 5 . . .	. . . .	. .
Gaddsden	. . 7 . .	. . . .	. . . .	. .
Gardiner [-ener]	. . . . .	. . . . . . 6 . . .	. . 2	o 1 .
Garner [-or]	. . . . .	. . . . . 5 6 . . .	. . . . . 5 6 7 . .	. . . .
Garret [-tt]	. . . . .	. . . . 7 . .	o . . . . 8 .	. .
Gaston	6 . . 9	. . . .	. . . .	. .
Gaydon	. . . . .	. . . .	. . . . 7 . .	. .
Gazy	. . . . .	. . . .	. . . .	. .
Gent	. . . . .	. . . .	. . . .	. .
Gibbs	. . . . .	. . . . 8 . .	. . . . 8 .	2
Gibson	. . . . .	. . . 2	. . . .	. .
Ginkins	. . . . .	. . . . . 5	. . . .	. .
Gilbert	. . . . .	. . . .	. . . . . 5 6 7 . 9	1 2
Gill	. . . . .	. . . .	. . . .	. .
Gillert	. . . . .	. . . .	. . . . 4	. .
Glover [Glofor]	. 6 7 8 9	. 1 2 3 4 5 6 7 8 9	. . . 3 . 5	. .
Gloxtalls	. . . . .	. . . .	o	. .
Goad	. . . . .	. . . . 8 . .	. . . .	. .
Goddard	. . . . .	. . . .	. . . .	. .
Godfrey	. . . . .	. . . .	. . . .	1
Godwin [Goodwin]	. . . . .	. . . . 4	. 1	. .
Good [-e]	. . . . .	. . . .	o 8 9	. .
Gornald	. . . . .	. . . .	o	. .
Goughe	. . . . .	. 1	. . . .	. .
Gould [Gold]	. . . . .	. . . . 7 . .	. . . . . 5 . 7 . .	1
Gouren	. . . . .	. . . .	. . 2	. .
Gower	. 6 7 8 .	. . . .	. . . .	. .
Grafton [-ffton]	. . . . .	. . . 3 4 5 6 7 . 9	o . 2 . . 5 6 . 8 .	. .
Graves [Greaves]	. . . . .	 9	o . . . 4	. .
Great	. . 8 .	. . . .	. . . .	. .
Greathed [-head]	. . . 9	. . . .	. . . .	. .
Greatwiche	. 7 8 .	o	. . . .	. .
Gregge	. . . .	o 1	. . . .	. .
Green [-ene, -eene]	6 . . 9	. 1 2 3 4 5 6 7 8 9	o 1 2 3 4 5 6 7 8 9	1 2
Greenhall	. . . .	. . . .	 9	. .
Greenhill	. . . .	. . . . 8 .	o 1 2 3 4 5 6 7 8 9	. 2

Name.	Sixteenth Century				Seventeenth Century										Eighteenth Century												
	1561-9	1570-9	1580-9	1590-9	1600-9	1610-9	1620-9	1630-9	1640-9	1650-9	1660-9	1670-9	1680-9	1690-9	1700-9	1710-9	1720-9	1730-9	1740-9	1750-9	1760-9	1770-9	1780-9	1790-9	1800-9	1810-9	1820-9
Greenway																											
Griffin														9		1							8	9			
Griffiths																						7	8				
Grimshawe	6	7	8	9	0																						
Grinnell [Grinnol]																			4		6						
Grooby																		3				7	8				
Grynd [-ind]		7																									
Gryssold [Grysolde, Grisell, Grissold (-e), Grisewold, Griswold, Grysholde, Grishold, Grizold, Greswold]	6	7		9	0	1	2	3	4	5		7															2
Guest																								9			
Gurley																											2
Hackett														9													
Hackstall														9													
Hackster		7							4		7																
Hadleton [-ddleton]																											
Hadley [-le]											6	7		9	0				4	5							
Haird												7															
Hales [Hale]												6			0		2	3									
Hall [-e]							2	3	4	5	6	7	8	9			3		5								
Hamilton, *alias* Freeman																											
Hammond																											
Hancox [-cks]																			4	5		7	8	9			2
Hands [-es]												7		9													2
Hanker																										1	2
Hanson																									0		2
Harbin																				4							
Harborn [-e]																		3		5	6	7	8		0		
Harbut																								9			
Harcourt																						6					
Harcool (?)										5																	
Harden	6																										
Harding [-e]			8				2			6					0												
Hardman																											
Hardwick																						7					
Hares												7															
Hargrave				9																							
Harper																											
Harris			8												0	1	2	3	4						0		2
Harrison							2													4		7					
Hart [-e]	6																										
Harwood																	2		4								
Haselor [Haslor]							2																				
Haskins				9																							
Haslocke					1																						
Hassall																									0	1	
Hastings																						6		9			2
Hathorne										6																	
Hatton																											1
Hawkes																					5				0	1	
Hawkins																						7	8	9	0	1	

Name	Sixteenth Century				Seventeenth Century										Eighteenth Century												
	1561-9	1570-9	1580-9	1590-9	1600-9	1610-9	1620-9	1630-9	1640-9	1650-9	1660-9	1670-9	1680-9	1690-9	1700-9	1710-9	1720-9	1730-9	1740-9	1750-9	1760-9	1770-9	1780-9	1790-9	1800-9	1810-9	1820-9
Hawkwood																				5							
Hawthorne						1									0												
Haycock [-acock,-aikok,-aiecok]										5	6											7	8	9	0		
Hayles [Hailes]												7	8								6						
Haytor										5																	
Hayward				9																							
Hays [Hayes]																		3				7				1	
Heartley																									0	1	
Heath																				5	6			9	0		
Heath, alias Swanne			8	9																							
Heaynes [Heynes, Haynes, Haines]	6			9															4				8	9			
Hemming [-e, -min, etc.]	6									5				9					4	5	6	7	8				
Henley											6																
Herbert																											2
Hercules [Arculus, Arkellus]																									0	1	2
Heritage [-etage]																								9	0		2
Herrison										5																	
Hextal [-ll]														9	0												
Heyward [Hayward]									4					9	0	1											
Heywood [-e] Haywood [-e]		7			0																6	7					
Hicken [-in]																									0	1	2
Hickeson											6																
Hickman														9													
Hicks																									0		
Higgeson											6																
Higgins [-ens, -gens]		7	8	9										9			2				6			9		1	
Hikkense									4																		
Hildick																											2
Hill [-e]					0	1					6	7	8	9	0										0	1	2
Hinckley																1											
Hinkes																1											
Hiorns																			4								
Hobby [-ie]											6	7		9													
Hobday												7															
Hobley																	2										2
Hodges				9									8	9	0	1	2										2
Hodgetts																					6						
Hodgkins				9				3																			
Holden																					6	7					
Holding																									0		
Holiocke [Holyoak, etc. Twelve spellings]			8				2	3		5	6	7	8	9	0	1	2	3	4	5	6	7	8	9	0	1	
Hollands																											
Holly																											2
Holt				9																							
Holtam								3																			
Hood																								9			
Hopkins [-e]									4	5	6	7	8		0	1	2	3	4	5		7		9			
Hopkins, alias Pyp		7																									
Horley																											2

NAMES IN PARISH REGISTERS 1561–1860

Name	Sixteenth Century				Seventeenth Century										Eighteenth Century										Ninet. Cent.		
	1561-9	1570-9	1580-9	1590-9	1600-9	1610-9	1620-9	1630-9	1640-9	1650-9	1660-9	1670-9	1680-9	1690-9	1700-9	1710-9	1720-9	1730-9	1740-9	1750-9	1760-9	1770-9	1780-9	1790-9	1800-9	1810-9	1820-9
Hornsby																											
Horsley													8														2
Horton		7																		5	6	7	8	9	0	1	2
Hough																											
House [Howes, -se]					1	2			5	6																	2
Houghton [Howtyn]														9											0		
Howe																											
Howell						1																					
Howkines								4																			
Hulston [Hurlstone]																					6	7		9	0	1	
Hubbald																	2										
Hudson [Hodson, Hutson]	6	7			0	1	2			5																	
Hughes [Hues]												7	8	9	1	2					6						
Humfrays [Humphries]										5									4		6						
Hunscot																		3									
Hunt						1		3										3	4							1	2
Huson																						7					
Hutchins																											
Hutton																				5						1	
Hyat																1											
Hyons																		3									
Iago [Jago]																			4								
Ichener (?)		7																									
Ince										5		7	8														
Ingram								3	4		6	7	8	9	0	1	2	3		5	6	7	8	9		1	2
Inson																											2
Jakeman [Jackman]																							8	9	0		
James							2								0												2
Jarvis																										1	
Jeffcoat																											2
Jelphs [Jelffs, Jelf, Jelff]																											
Jencks			9																								
Jennaway	6																										
Jennings [Jenings]					0			3				7		9	0	1	2										
Jephs [Jeffs]																											
Jinkins [-enk-, Ginkense]								4									2							9	0	1	
Jewkes																							8				
Joanes [Jones]							2					7			0								8		0		2
Jobson																										1	
Johns																	2			5				9	0	1	2
Johnson			8			1		3	4								2	3								1	
Jordan [Jurdan, Jardan]														9	0	1	2	3					8	9	0	1	2
Joyner																											
Kay [Keay, Key, Keys, Keyes]																						7	8	9		1	
Kench																								9			
Kemp																	2		4	5	6	7	8	9	0		2
Kempson															0												
Kemsey																		3									
Kendal [-ll]							2				6			9	0	1	2	3	4	5	6	7	8	9	0	1	2

Name	1560-9	1570-9	1580-9	1590-9	1600-9	1610-9	1620-9	1630-9	1640-9	1650-9	1660-9	1670-9	1680-9	1690-9	1700-9	1710-9	1720-9	1730-9	1740-9	1750-9	1760-9	1770-9	1780-9	1790-9	1800-9	1810-9	1820-9
Kendrick [Kenrick]																1							8	9	0	1	
Kent [Cent]									4														8				
Keyte																											2
King							2							9				3								1	2
Kingerley [-lee]																											
Kirshaw																											
Kilcupp [Killcope, Cilcob, etc. Ten spellings]					0	1	2		4	5		7	8														
Kirbye [Kerby, Cerby, etc. Eight spellings]					0	1	2	3	4	5	6			9	0	1	2	3							0		
Knapton																			4								
Knewitt																											
Knib																										1	
Knight	6				0	1													4	5	6	7	8	9		1	2
Kylworth							2																				
Lakinge [Laykins]						1	2																				
Lamberd [-bard, Lomberd]									4	5	6																
Lambsdale																	2										
Lancaster																			4								
Lane													8										8				
Langford																											
Lapworth															0	1											
Lathame [-am, -um]	6	7				1	2	3																			
Lathford	6	7	8				2																				
Lawly																				5							
Lawrence						1														5					0		
Lawrence, *alias* Clarke				9			2	3																			
Lea [le, Lee, Leigh]							2	3		5	6	7	8	9	0	1	2	3	4	5	6	7	8	9	0		2
Leadbeater											6	7	8	9													
Leadbury [Led-]											6	7	8		0	1		3									
Leaton																										1	
Leeke											6	7				1											
Leeson [-s]																1		3	4	5	6	7	8	9	0		2
Levett																											2
Lewis [Lewes]											6		8	9	0						6				0		
Lightfoote		7																									
Lilly												7		9													
Lines																											
Lingart															0												
Lindon																											
Litlton			8																								
Litton				9	0																						
Littleford								3																			
Loble										5																	
Lock [-e]																						7		9	0		
Lofel								3																			
Lomb [Lome]				9						5																	
Long												7	8			1	2										
London [Lonnon]				9		1	2	3	4	5	6	7	8	9		1	2	3	4	5	6	7					
Louch																					6	7	8	9	0		
Lovett			8	9	0		2	3				7															
Lowe [Low]								3			6											7				1	

Name.	1561-9	1570-9	1580-9	1590-9	1600-9	1610-9	1620-9	1630-9	1640-9	1650-9	1660-9	1670-9	1680-9	1690-9	1700-9	1710-9	1720-9	1730-9	1740-9	1750-9	1760-9	1770-9	1780-9	1790-9	1800-9	1810-9	1820-9
Lucett [-e]	6	7	8	9	0	1	2	.	.	.	.	.	.	.	.	.	.	.	.	.	.	.	.	.	.	.	.
Lucie	.	.	.	.	.	.	.	4	.	.	.	.	.	.	.	.	.	.	.	.	.	.	.	.	.	.	.
Luckman [Luk-, Louk-]	.	.	.	.	.	1	2	3	4	5	6	7	8	9	0	1	2	3	.	5	6	7	8	9	0	1	.
Maget [-tt, Madget, -tt]	.	.	.	.	.	.	.	.	.	.	6	7	.	9	0	1	.	.	.	.	.	.	.	.	.	.	.
Maids [-des]	.	.	.	.	.	.	2	.	.	.	.	.	.	.	.	.	.	.	4	5	6	.	8	9	.	1	2
Mallery	.	.	.	.	.	.	.	.	.	.	.	.	.	.	.	1	.	.	.	.	.	.	.	.	.	.	.
Malthus [Mathus]	.	.	.	.	.	.	.	.	.	.	.	.	.	.	.	.	.	.	.	5	6	7	8	9	.	.	.
Mander [Maunder, etc.]	6	.	.	.	.	.	.	.	.	.	.	7	8	9	0	1	2	.	4	5	6	7	8	9	0	1	2
Manker	.	.	.	.	.	.	.	.	.	.	.	.	.	.	.	.	.	.	.	.	.	.	.	.	.	.	2
Manninge	.	.	.	9	.	.	.	.	.	.	.	.	.	.	.	.	.	.	.	.	.	.	.	.	.	.	.
Mantell	.	.	.	.	.	.	.	4	.	.	.	.	.	.	.	.	.	.	.	.	.	.	.	.	.	.	.
Manton [Maunton]	.	.	.	.	.	.	.	.	.	.	.	.	.	.	0	.	.	.	.	.	.	7	8	.	0	1	2
Manuel	.	.	.	.	.	.	.	.	.	.	.	.	.	.	.	.	.	.	4	.	.	.	.	.	.	.	.
Maris	.	.	.	.	.	.	.	.	.	.	.	.	.	.	.	.	.	.	.	5	.	.	.	.	.	.	.
Marre [Marr]	.	.	.	9	1	.	3	.	.	.	.	.	.	.	.	.	.	.	.	.	.	.	.	.	.	.	.
Marriott	.	.	.	.	.	.	.	.	.	.	.	.	.	.	.	.	.	.	.	.	.	.	.	.	.	.	2
Marshall	.	.	.	.	.	.	.	.	.	.	.	.	.	.	.	.	.	.	.	.	.	.	.	.	.	.	.
Marston	.	.	.	.	.	.	.	.	.	.	.	.	.	.	.	.	.	.	.	.	.	.	.	.	.	.	.
Martin [-e]	6	.	.	.	.	.	.	.	.	.	.	.	.	.	.	.	.	.	.	.	.	.	.	.	.	.	.
Mascoll	.	.	.	9	0	.	.	.	.	.	.	.	.	.	.	.	.	.	.	.	.	.	.	.	.	.	.
Mason [Mayson]	6	7	.	9	.	1	.	3	.	.	.	.	.	.	.	.	.	.	.	.	.	.	.	.	.	.	.
Masters	.	.	.	.	.	.	.	.	.	.	.	.	.	.	.	.	.	.	.	.	.	.	8	9	.	.	.
Mathers	.	.	.	.	.	.	.	.	.	.	.	.	.	.	.	.	.	.	4	.	.	.	.	.	.	.	.
Mathews [Matthews]	.	.	.	.	.	.	.	.	.	.	.	.	.	9	.	.	2	3	4	5	6	.	.	9	0	1	2
Maudly	.	.	.	.	.	.	.	.	.	.	.	.	.	9	.	.	.	.	.	.	.	.	.	.	.	.	.
May	.	.	.	.	.	.	.	.	.	.	.	.	.	.	.	.	.	.	.	.	.	.	.	.	.	.	.
Maydew [-ad-, -aid-]	.	.	.	.	.	.	.	.	.	.	.	.	.	9	0	.	2	3	4	5	.	.	.	.	.	.	.
Mayo	.	.	.	9	.	.	.	.	.	.	.	.	.	.	.	.	.	.	.	.	.	.	.	.	.	.	.
Meads [-des]	.	.	.	.	.	.	.	.	.	.	.	.	.	.	.	.	.	.	.	.	.	.	.	.	0	.	.
Mecock	.	.	.	.	.	.	.	3	.	.	.	.	.	.	.	.	.	.	.	.	.	.	.	.	.	.	.
Meek	.	.	.	.	.	.	.	.	.	.	.	.	.	.	.	.	.	.	.	.	.	5	.	.	.	.	.
Merrell [-ill]	.	.	.	.	.	.	.	3	.	.	6	7	8	.	.	.	.	.	.	.	.	.	.	.	.	.	.
Merrick [Merik]	.	.	.	.	.	.	.	.	.	5	.	.	8	.	.	.	.	.	.	.	.	.	.	.	.	.	.
Meryell [Meriall]	.	.	.	.	.	.	.	.	.	.	.	7	.	9	.	.	.	.	.	.	.	.	.	.	.	.	.
Meynard [-ay-, -ai-, Meyner, Maynar]	.	.	.	.	.	.	.	.	.	.	.	.	.	.	.	1	2	3	4	5	6	7	.	9	.	1	.
Milborn [-ourn, -ourne]	.	.	.	.	.	.	.	.	.	.	.	.	.	.	0	1	2	.	4	.	6	.	.	.	.	.	.
Miles [Milse]	.	.	.	.	.	.	.	3	.	5	.	.	.	.	.	.	.	.	.	.	.	.	.	.	.	.	.
Mildmay	.	.	.	.	.	.	.	.	.	.	.	.	.	.	.	.	.	.	.	.	.	.	.	.	.	.	.
Miller [-ar]	.	.	.	.	.	.	.	.	.	.	.	.	.	.	0	.	.	3	4	.	6	.	8	9	.	1	2
Millard	.	.	.	.	.	.	.	.	.	.	.	.	.	.	.	.	.	.	.	5	6	7	8	.	0	.	.
Millington	.	.	.	.	.	.	.	.	.	.	.	.	.	.	.	.	2	.	.	.	.	.	.	.	.	.	.
Mills	.	.	.	.	.	.	.	.	.	.	.	.	.	9	0	1	2	.	.	5	.	.	.	.	0	1	.
Milord	.	.	.	.	.	.	.	.	.	5	.	.	.	.	.	.	.	.	.	.	.	.	.	.	.	.	.
Milward	.	.	.	.	.	.	.	.	.	.	.	.	.	.	.	.	.	.	.	.	.	7	.	.	.	.	.
Milton [Mylton]	.	7	8	.	.	.	.	.	.	.	.	.	.	.	.	.	.	.	.	.	.	.	.	.	.	.	.
Minors [-or, -ers]	.	.	.	.	.	.	.	.	.	.	6	.	8	9	.	.	.	.	.	.	.	.	.	.	.	.	.
Mirriett	.	.	.	.	.	.	.	3	.	.	.	.	.	.	.	.	.	.	.	.	.	.	.	.	.	.	.
Mitton (?)	.	.	.	9	.	.	.	.	.	.	.	.	.	.	.	.	.	.	.	.	.	.	.	.	.	.	.
Moore [Moor]	.	.	8	.	.	.	.	.	.	.	.	.	.	.	.	.	.	.	.	.	6	.	.	9	.	.	.
Morell [-rrel, -rrell, -rril]	.	.	.	.	.	.	.	.	.	5	6	.	8	9	0	.	.	3	.	.	.	.	8	.	.	.	.
Morgan	.	.	.	.	.	.	.	.	.	.	.	.	.	9	0	.	.	.	.	.	.	.	.	.	0	.	.
Morlie	.	.	.	.	.	.	.	.	.	5	.	.	.	.	.	.	.	.	.	.	.	.	.	.	.	.	.

Name	Sixteenth Century				Seventeenth Century										Eighteenth Century												
	1561-9	1570-9	1580-9	1590-9	1600-9	1610-9	1620-9	1630-9	1640-9	1650-9	1660-9	1670-9	1680-9	1690-9	1700-9	1710-9	1720-9	1730-9	1740-9	1750-9	1760-9	1770-9	1780-9	1790-9	1800-9	1810-9	1820-9
Morris [Morrice, Maurice, etc.]											6	7	8	9	0	1	2	3	4	5				9			2
Morse								3																			
Mortiboyes [-teboys, etc.]				9	0					5	6	7	8	9	0	1	2	3	4	5	6	7	8	9	0	1	2
Morton											6																
Moseley																											
Mountford [-fort, Monfort, etc.]	6	7	8	9	0	1	2	3		5	6		8	9													
Mugg																	2	3									
Mulless [-iss]																									0	1	
Mumford																											
Murfiye								4																			
Nash [-e]												7												9	0		
Nason																	2				6		8				
Neal [-e]																								9		1	2
Needle																											
Neville																											
Newbold		7																									
Newcomb															0												
Newey																						8					
Newitt																											
Nicholls																											2
Nickes [Nix]																						0					
Normicott																											
North (?)			8																								
Norton											6				1												
Offender								4																			
Oldnall						2																					
Oliver																				5				9	0		
Olney				9																							
Onley								3																			
Orton																											
Osborn [-e] (?)		7			1										1											1	2
Overs																											2
Overton					1								8		0	1	2	3	4	5	6	7	8				2
Owen						2		4																			
Pace																											2
Pachet [Patchet, Paget]									5								3				7						
Page																								9			2
Paiton [Payton, Peyton]								4				8	9		0	1				5							
Palmer [Palmar]					1	2		4	5	6	7	8	9		0	1	2	3	4	5			8	9			2
Palmer, alias Welche		7	8	9																							
Panaken (?)																										0	
Panckes																										0	
Papster		7																									
Pardo [-oe, -y]																											2
Parke [-s]	6																										
Parker					1	2	3	4	5	6	7	8					2				6						1
Parkhouse												7															
Parmon													8														
Parsonage																											

Name.	Sixteenth Century.				Seventeenth Century.										Eighteenth Century.												
	1561-9	1570-9	1580-9	1590-9	1600-9	1610-9	1620-9	1630-9	1640-9	1650-9	1660-9	1670-9	1680-9	1690-9	1700-9	1710-9	1720-9	1730-9	1740-9	1750-9	1760-9	1770-9	1780-9	1790-9	1800-9	1810-9	1820-9
'arsons [Persons]	6	7	.	9	.	.	.	3	.	.	.	.	8	9	0	1	2	.	4	5	6	7	8	9	0	1	2
'arr	.	.	.	.	.	.	.	.	.	.	.	.	.	.	.	.	.	.	.	.	6	.	.	.	.	.	.
'arry	.	.	.	.	.	.	.	.	.	.	.	7	8	.	0	.	.	.	.	.	.	.	.	.	.	.	2
'arton	.	.	.	.	.	.	.	.	5	.	.	.	.	.	.	.	.	.	.	.	.	.	.	.	.	.	.
'aterston [Patt-]	.	.	.	.	.	.	.	.	.	.	.	.	.	.	.	1	2	.	.	.	.	.	.	.	.	.	.
'atton	.	.	.	.	.	.	.	.	.	.	.	.	8	.	.	.	.	.	.	.	.	.	.	.	.	.	.
'ayne	.	.	.	.	.	.	.	.	.	.	.	.	.	.	.	.	.	.	.	.	.	.	8	9	.	.	2
'eacocke	.	.	.	.	.	.	2	.	.	.	.	.	.	.	.	.	.	.	.	.	.	.	.	.	.	.	.
'earson	.	.	.	.	.	.	.	.	.	.	.	.	.	.	.	.	2	.	.	.	.	.	.	.	.	.	.
'eers	.	.	.	.	.	.	.	.	.	.	.	.	.	.	.	.	.	.	.	5	.	.	9	.	.	.	.
'enn	.	.	.	.	.	.	.	.	.	.	.	.	.	.	.	.	.	.	.	.	.	.	.	.	0	1	.
'enny	.	.	.	.	.	.	.	3	.	.	.	.	.	.	.	.	.	.	.	.	.	.	.	.	.	.	.
'ensill	.	.	.	9	.	.	.	.	.	.	.	.	.	.	.	.	.	.	.	.	.	.	.	.	.	.	.
'epper	6	.	.	.	0	1	2	.	.	.	.	.	.	.	.	.	.	.	.	.	.	.	.	.	.	.	.
'epy [Peppe]	6	7	8	9	0	.	.	.	.	.	.	.	.	.	.	.	.	.	.	.	.	.	.	.	.	.	.
'erlin	.	.	.	.	.	1	.	.	.	.	.	.	.	.	.	.	.	.	.	.	.	.	.	.	.	.	.
'etford	.	.	.	.	.	.	.	3	.	6	.	.	.	.	.	.	.	.	.	.	.	.	.	.	.	.	.
'eto [Petoe, Peyto]	.	.	.	.	0	1	.	3	4	5	6	7	8	.	0	1	2	3	4	5	.	.	.	.	0	.	.
'ettifer	.	.	.	.	.	.	.	.	.	.	.	.	.	.	0	.	.	.	.	.	.	.	.	.	.	.	.
'etty [-ey]	.	.	.	.	.	.	.	.	.	.	.	.	.	.	.	1	2	3	4	5	6	.	8	9	0	.	.
'ettitt	.	.	.	.	.	.	.	.	.	.	.	.	.	.	.	.	.	4	.	.	.	.	.	.	.	.	.
Phillips [Philips]	.	.	.	.	.	.	.	.	.	.	.	.	8	.	.	.	.	.	.	.	6	.	.	.	.	1	2
Phipps	.	.	.	.	.	.	.	.	.	.	.	.	.	.	.	.	.	.	.	.	6	.	.	.	.	1	2
Pinner	.	.	.	.	.	.	.	.	.	.	.	.	.	.	.	.	.	.	.	.	.	.	.	.	.	.	.
Pitt	.	.	.	.	.	.	.	.	.	.	.	.	.	.	.	.	.	.	.	.	.	7	.	.	.	.	.
Pointer	.	7	8	.	.	.	.	.	.	.	.	.	.	.	.	.	.	.	.	.	.	.	.	.	.	.	.
Pool [-le]	.	.	.	.	.	.	.	.	.	.	.	.	.	.	.	.	.	.	.	.	.	.	.	.	0	1	2
Porter [Poter]	.	.	.	.	.	.	.	.	.	5	.	.	8	.	.	.	.	.	.	.	.	.	.	.	.	.	2
Poulteney	.	.	.	.	.	.	.	.	.	.	.	.	.	.	.	.	.	.	.	.	.	.	.	.	.	.	2
Pountney	.	.	.	.	.	.	.	.	.	.	.	.	.	.	.	.	.	.	.	.	.	.	.	.	.	.	2
Powel	.	.	.	.	.	.	.	.	.	.	.	.	.	.	.	.	.	.	4	.	.	.	.	.	.	.	.
Powers [-ese]	6	.	.	.	.	.	.	.	.	.	.	.	.	.	.	.	.	.	.	.	.	.	.	.	0	.	.
Pratt	.	.	.	.	.	.	.	.	.	.	.	.	.	.	.	.	.	.	.	.	.	.	.	.	.	.	.
Preist, *alias* Hodges	.	.	.	9	.	.	.	.	.	.	.	.	.	.	.	.	.	.	.	.	.	.	.	.	.	.	.
Priest	.	.	.	.	.	.	.	.	.	.	.	.	.	.	.	.	.	.	.	.	.	.	.	.	0	1	.
Pretty	.	.	.	.	.	.	.	.	.	.	.	.	.	.	.	.	.	.	.	.	6	.	.	.	.	.	.
Prew	.	.	.	.	.	.	.	.	.	.	.	.	.	.	.	.	.	.	.	.	.	7	.	.	.	.	.
Price [-se]	.	.	8	9	.	1	2	3	4	5	6	7	8	9	0	1	2	3	4	.	6	7	8	9	.	.	.
Prior	.	.	.	.	.	.	.	.	.	.	.	.	.	.	.	.	.	.	.	.	.	.	.	9	.	.	.
Pritchard	.	.	.	.	.	.	.	.	.	.	.	.	.	.	.	.	.	.	.	.	.	.	.	.	.	.	.
Pritchet [-tt]	.	.	.	.	.	.	.	.	.	.	.	.	.	.	.	.	.	.	4	.	.	.	8	.	.	.	.
Proctor	.	.	.	.	.	.	.	.	.	.	.	.	.	.	.	.	.	.	.	.	.	.	.	.	.	.	.
Pyp, *alias* Hopkins	.	7	.	.	.	.	.	.	.	.	.	.	.	.	.	.	.	.	.	.	.	.	.	.	.	.	2
Pugh	.	.	.	.	.	.	.	.	.	.	.	.	.	.	.	1	.	.	.	.	.	.	.	.	.	.	.
Purdon	.	.	.	.	.	.	.	.	.	.	.	.	.	.	.	.	.	.	.	.	.	.	.	9	0	.	.
Pye	.	.	.	.	.	.	.	3	.	.	.	.	.	.	.	.	.	.	.	.	.	.	.	9	0	.	.
Quiney [-inie, -inney, -einey]	.	.	.	.	.	1	.	3	.	5	.	.	.	.	.	.	.	.	.	.	.	.	.	.	.	.	1
Quinton	.	.	.	.	.	.	.	.	.	.	.	.	.	.	.	.	.	.	.	.	.	.	.	.	.	.	.
Radcliffe [-t-, -tlife, -tlyffe], Rackliefe	6	.	.	9	0	.	2	3	.	.	.	.	.	.	.	.	.	.	.	.	.	.	.	.	.	.	.
Radford	.	.	.	.	.	.	.	.	.	.	.	.	.	.	.	.	3	.	.	.	.	.	.	.	.	.	.

Name.	Sixteenth Century.				Seventeenth Century.									Eighteenth Century.										Ninet Cent
	?	1570-9	?	1590-9	?	?	?	?	1640-9	?	1670-9	?	?	?	?	1730-9	1740-9	1750-9	?	1770-9	?	1790-9	?	? ? ?
Rainbow																								1 2
Rainols								5																
Raison										9														
Randal [-ll]													0 1											
Randolph										8														
Ravenhull																	5							
Rawbone [-boune]		7								9							4					9		
Rawlins [-ens, -yns]							6			9		0												
Rawson [Roson]			8 9	0 1 2 3 4																				
Rawsley (-sby ?)			8																					
Reading												2												
Reeve [-s]																				9			0 1
Reid																								2
Reynolds [Ren-]												0 1		4 5 6 7 8										0 1 2
Rhodes													3											1
Rice										9														
Richard [-s]						4 . 6								5								0	
Richardson				1 2 3													8						1
Richmond																								
Rider										9														
Right					2																			
Rightwood					2																			
Riley																								2
Robarts [-berts, -bberts]		7				4				9			3 4 5 6		9								
Robins [-bbins, -bbyns, Rawbins]	6 . 8 9			0 1 2 3 4 5 6 7 8																				
Robinson [Raubinsone, Robeson]							6 7																	
Rock																								1
Roe															8							0 . 2
Rofford					4																			
Rogers [-rse, Roggers]					2 . 4 5 6 . 8 9							0 1 2 3 4 5 6 . 8 9											
Rollings																								
Rose														6 . . 9								0 1 2
Rouse																								
Rowe														7									
Roxperrie							6																	
Russel [-ll]															9							0 . 2
Rutter					2 . . 6 . 8																		
Sabell												1 8									
Sadler			9		2 . . 5 . . 8 9				1 2 3 4 5 6 7													
Safefold (?)							6																	
Salmon												2 . 4										
Sammes (?)	6																							
Sanders [Saunders]					1 . . . 5 6 . . 9							3 4 5 6 7 8 9									0 1 2
Sandwell																					9	0 . .
Satchwell													3										
Savage													3									1 2
Sawier [Sawyior]		7					8																
Saywell																	7					
Scarlet					5 6 . 8																		
Seagrave													3										
Seale [Seal, Sele]		7 8		5										5								

Name.	Sixteenth Century.				Seventeenth Century.										Eighteenth Century.										Ninete Centu		
	1561-9	1570-9	1580-9	1590-9	1600-9	1610-9	1620-9	1630-9	1640-9	1650-9	1660-9	1670-9	1680-9	1690-9	1700-9	1710-9	1720-9	1730-9	1740-9	1750-9	1760-9	1770-9	1780-9	1790-9	1800-9	1810-9	1820-9
ealy [Seely]																											3
earle									5																		
eedaway																										1	
ergeant [-jeant, Sarjant, etc.]												7	8	9	0	1	2										
ermon																				5							
hackespeare [Shakspere, Saxpor, etc. Ten spellings]	6			9		1	2	3	4	5	6	7			1								9				
hatwell [Satwell]										5	6																
harpe																											
haw [-e]	6	7		9		1											2	3	4	5	6	7	8				2
heale					0																						
helton																		3									
hepherd																											2
hervington [Shirvinton]																											2
herwin																		3									
heward																			4								
hort [-e]	6	7	8			1		3																			
hoteswell [-ates-, etc. Seven spellings]	6		8	9		1	2	3			6	7	8		0	1	2	3									2
ilk																											2
immons [-onds, -ymonds, Simanse]				9						5							2	3	4	5		7					
keldon																										1	
lye [Slie, Sley, Sly]	6	7	8	9	0	1	2	3	4	5	6	7	8	9	0	1	2	3		5	6						
malwood																				5							
methyes							2																				
myth [-e, Smith]	6		8	9		1	2	3	4	5	6	7	8	9	0	1	2	3	4	5	6	7	8	9	0	1	2
nape	6																										
neadwell [Sned-]																									0	1	2
neth																	2										
oden																						7		9			
oley																											2
orrel															1												
penser [-cer]											6				1					5							
pire [Spiers]												6								6							
pooner						1	2	3																			
pragg																									0	1	
pry																											
tandley [Stanley]																	2			5	6						2
taples																							8	9	0	1	2
tarram [Starham]																	2	3									
teedman																											
tevens [Stephens, Steavens]							2	3																			
teward																											
tokes [Stoaks]																			4	5	6			9			
tone														9	1					6							
torer																				6							
tow													8				2	3	4		6						
tratford							2														6						
tubbs																											
ugar [Suker]							2																				

Name	Sixteenth Century				Seventeenth Century										Eighteenth Century												
	1561-9	1570-9	1580-9	1590-9	1600-9	1610-9	1620-9	1630-9	1640-9	1650-9	1660-9	1670-9	1680-9	1690-9	1700-9	1710-9	1720-9	1730-9	1740-9	1750-9	1760-9	1770-9	1780-9	1790-9	1800-9	1810-9	1820-9
Sumner	.	.	.	.	.	.	.	.	.	.	.	.	.	.	.	.	.	.	.	5	.	.	.	.	.	.	.
Swadkins	.	.	.	.	.	.	.	.	.	.	.	.	.	.	.	.	2	.	4	.	.	.	.	.	.	.	.
Swain [-e]	.	.	.	.	.	.	.	.	.	.	.	.	.	.	.	.	.	.	.	.	.	.	.	.	.	1	2
Swale	.	.	.	.	.	.	.	.	4	.	.	.	.	.	.	.	.	.	.	.	.	.	.	.	.	.	.
Swanne [Swan]	.	.	.	.	0	.	.	.	.	.	.	.	.	.	.	.	.	.	.	.	.	.	.	.	.	.	.
Swanne, *alias* Heath	.	.	8	9	.	.	.	.	.	.	.	.	.	.	.	.	.	.	.	.	.	.	.	.	.	.	.
Swinnerton	.	7	.	.	.	.	.	.	.	.	.	.	.	.	.	.	.	.	.	.	.	.	.	.	.	.	.
Symson	.	7	8	.	.	.	.	.	.	.	.	.	.	.	.	.	.	.	.	.	.	.	.	.	.	.	.
Tabberner	.	.	.	.	.	.	.	.	.	.	.	.	.	.	.	.	.	.	.	.	.	.	8	.	.	.	.
Taft	.	.	.	.	.	.	.	.	.	.	6	.	.	.	.	.	.	.	.	.	.	.	.	.	.	.	2
Talis	.	.	.	.	.	.	.	.	.	.	6	.	.	.	.	.	.	.	.	.	.	.	.	.	.	.	.
Tandy	.	.	.	.	.	.	.	.	.	.	.	.	.	.	.	.	.	.	.	.	6	7	8	9	0	.	.
Tarlton [-leton]	.	.	.	.	.	.	.	.	.	.	.	.	.	.	.	1	2	3	4	5	6	7	8	.	0	1	.
Tarplee	.	.	.	.	.	.	.	.	.	.	.	.	.	.	.	.	.	.	.	.	.	.	.	.	.	.	.
Tatnall	.	.	.	.	.	.	.	.	.	.	.	.	.	9	.	.	.	.	.	.	.	.	.	.	.	.	.
Tay	.	.	.	.	.	.	.	.	.	.	.	.	.	.	.	.	.	.	.	.	.	.	.	.	.	.	.
Taylor [-lour, -ler, Tailor, -llor]	6	7	8	9	0	.	2	.	.	.	6	7	8	9	0	1	2	3	4	5	6	7	8	9	0	1	2
Terrey [Terry]	.	.	.	.	.	.	.	.	.	.	.	.	8	.	.	1	.	.	.	.	.	7	.	.	.	.	.
Thacker	.	.	8	.	.	.	.	.	.	.	.	.	.	.	.	.	.	.	.	.	.	.	.	.	.	.	.
Thomason	.	.	.	.	.	.	.	.	.	.	.	.	.	.	.	.	.	.	.	.	.	.	.	.	.	.	2
Thomson	.	.	8	.	.	1	.	.	.	.	.	.	.	.	.	.	.	.	.	.	.	.	.	.	.	.	.
Tibett [Tibbetts, -ots, -atts]	.	.	.	.	.	.	.	.	.	5	.	.	.	9	0	1	2	3	4	.	6	7	8	.	0	.	.
Tidmarsh	.	.	.	.	.	.	.	.	.	.	.	.	.	.	.	.	2	.	.	.	.	.	.	.	.	.	.
Timmins	.	.	.	.	.	.	.	.	.	.	.	.	.	.	.	.	.	.	.	5	6	.	.	.	.	.	.
Timms	.	.	.	.	.	.	.	.	.	.	.	.	.	.	.	.	.	.	.	.	.	.	.	.	.	.	.
Titmosh	.	.	.	.	.	.	.	.	.	.	.	.	.	.	.	.	.	.	4	.	.	.	.	.	.	.	.
Tomlinson	.	.	.	.	.	.	.	.	.	.	.	.	.	.	.	.	.	.	.	.	.	.	.	9	.	1	.
Toms	.	.	.	.	.	.	.	.	.	.	.	.	.	.	.	.	2	.	.	5	6	.	.	.	.	.	.
Toste	6	7	.	.	.	.	.	.	.	.	.	.	.	.	.	.	.	.	.	.	.	.	.	.	.	.	.
Townend [-send, -shend]	.	.	.	.	.	.	.	.	4	.	.	.	.	.	0	.	.	.	.	.	6	.	.	.	0	1	2
Travers	.	.	.	.	.	.	.	.	.	.	.	.	.	.	.	.	.	.	.	.	.	.	.	.	.	.	.
Treen	.	.	.	.	.	.	.	.	.	.	.	.	.	.	.	.	.	.	.	.	.	.	.	.	.	.	.
Trotman	.	.	.	.	.	.	.	.	.	.	.	.	.	.	.	.	.	.	.	.	.	.	.	.	.	.	.
Truman	.	.	.	.	.	.	.	.	.	.	.	.	.	.	.	.	.	.	.	.	.	.	.	.	.	.	.
Trussell [Triss-, Tress-]	.	.	.	.	.	1	2	3	4	.	.	.	.	.	.	.	.	.	.	.	.	.	.	.	.	.	.
Tucker	.	.	.	.	.	.	.	.	.	.	.	.	.	.	.	.	.	.	.	.	.	7	.	.	.	.	.
Tunkes	.	.	.	.	.	.	.	.	.	.	.	7	.	.	.	.	.	.	.	.	.	.	.	.	.	.	.
Turner	.	.	.	.	.	.	.	.	.	.	.	.	.	.	0	.	.	.	4	5	.	.	8	.	.	1	2
Turvey	.	.	.	.	.	.	.	.	.	.	.	.	.	.	.	.	.	.	.	.	.	.	.	.	.	.	2
Twicross [Twycross, -e]	.	.	.	.	.	.	.	.	4	.	6	7	8	.	.	.	.	.	.	.	.	.	.	.	.	.	.
Twist	.	.	.	.	.	.	2	.	.	.	.	.	.	.	.	.	.	.	.	.	.	.	.	.	.	.	.
Tyce	.	.	.	.	.	.	.	.	.	.	.	.	8	.	.	.	.	.	.	.	.	.	.	.	.	.	.
Tyler [Tiler, -or]	.	7	8	.	.	1	.	.	.	5	.	.	.	.	.	.	.	.	.	.	.	.	.	.	.	.	.
Tyndall	.	.	.	.	.	.	.	.	.	.	.	.	.	.	.	.	.	.	.	.	.	.	.	.	.	.	.
Tyrrel [-ll]	.	.	.	.	.	.	.	.	.	.	.	.	.	.	0	1	2	.	4	.	.	.	.	.	.	.	.
Tysoe [Tisoe, Tico]	.	.	.	.	.	.	2	3	.	.	.	.	.	.	.	.	.	.	4	.	.	.	8	.	.	.	.
Underhill	.	.	.	.	.	.	.	.	.	.	.	7	.	.	.	.	.	.	.	.	.	.	.	.	.	.	.
Upton	.	.	.	.	.	.	.	.	.	.	.	.	.	.	.	.	.	.	.	.	.	.	.	.	.	.	.
Veele [Veal, -e]	.	7	.	.	.	.	.	.	.	.	.	.	.	.	.	.	.	.	.	5	.	.	.	.	.	.	.

NAMES IN PARISH REGISTERS 1561–1860

Name.	Sixteenth Century.				Seventeenth Century.										Eighteenth Century.										Nineteenth Century.			
	1561-9	1570-9	1580-9	1590-9	1600-9	1610-9	1620-9	1630-9	1640-9	1650-9	1660-9	1670-9	1680-9	1690-9	1700-9	1710-9	1720-9	1730-9	1740-9	1750-9	1760-9	1770-9	1780-9	1790-9	1800-9	1810-9	1820-9	1830-9
Vincent																1												
Viners [Vinas]																										1	2	
Wadley																						7						
Wagstaff [-e]	6																	3		5						1		
Waham																										1		
Waite						1					6																	
Waitman [Weight-, Wight-]													8	9	0	1	2											
Wakefield																						7	8			1	2	
Wakeley									4																			
Walden																										1		
Walford												7							4									
Walker	6	7																										
Walker, alias Wyan [or Wian]	6	7																										
Walle								3																				
Wallerie [Woollerie]		7				1																						
Wallington [Walin-]							2				6				0						6	7				1		
Walton	6		8	9			2	3	4		6	7	8	9	0	1	2	3	4	5	6	7		9		1		
Ward [-e]		7	8	9		1	2	3		5	6	7	8		0	1	2	3	4		6			9	0	1	2	
Wardell [-le]																					6	7	8	9	0	1	2	
Waringe [-einge, -eine, -ing, -in, -en, etc.]	6							3		5	6		8		0	1	2	3		5	6	7					2	
Warmington [Wor-]																								9				
Warner																						7						
Warrick						1																						
Waters [Warters]																									0		2	
Watton								3	4				8	9	0	1	2	3		5		7						
Watts		7																										
Wattson [-tson]																						7	8		0	1	2	
Way																									0	1		
Wayle [-æle, -eale, -eal], Whale, Wele, Weall	6	7	8			1		3			6	7										7	8	9		1	2	
Waynman	6																											
Wealde									4																			
Weaver																					6	7	8					
Webster							2																					
Wedgburie									4																			
Wedge [Wedger]					0								8															
Weekes [Wekes, Wikes, Wykes, Wicks]								3		5	6	7	8	9	0	1	2	3										
Welch [-e]		7	8																									
Welche, alias Palmer						1																						
Welchman											6			9	0	1	2	3										
Wells														9										9	0	1		
Wendicke					0	1																						
West [-e]		7	8	9	0	1		3		5																	2	
Westell								3																				
Westrapp [-rope]								3																				
Wetege											6															1		
Whaley																						7						
Wharr.																												

Name	| Sixteenth Century ||||	Seventeenth Century	Eighteenth Century	||

Name	1561-9	1570-9	1580-9	1590-9	1600-9	1610-9	1620-9	1630-9	1640-9	1650-9	1660-9	1670-9	1680-9	1690-9	1700-9	1710-9	1720-9	1730-9	1740-9	1750-9	1760-9	1770-9	1780-9	1790-9	1800-9	1810-9	1820-9
Wharum [-am, Waram, Wareham, Warham]																		3	4	5	6						2
Whateley [-ie]						1	2	3					8	9	0												
Wheeler [Wheler, Welor, etc.]	6	7	8			1		3	4	5				9	0	1	2		4							1	2
Wheret [-tt], Weret [-it]												7	8		0												
Whery																			4								
Whippe [-ipp, -ip, Wip]							2	3		5																	
Whissal [-ell]																									0	1	
Whitaker [Whytaker]						1																					
Whitanes				9																							
White [Wite]	6	7																3		5	6		8		0		
Whitehouse																										1	
Whiting							2																				
Whitmore, *alias* Weightman													8														
Whorewood		7																									
Wian [Wyan], *alias* Walker	6	7																									
Wilks																				5	6						
Williams	6			9		1	2	3	4	5	6				0	1	2			5	6	7	8	9	0	1	2
Wilson [-ll-, Walesoene]				9		1	2																		0	1	
Wilshire	6																										
Wilye					0																						
Wimlet [-tt]																								9			
Wincott															0												
Windsor																											
Witfote [-tt], Whitefoot [-e, -tt]								3		5	6	7	8	9	0	1	2					7					
Wofe										5																	
Wood [-s, Wod]								3	4	5		7								5		7	8	9	0	1	2
Woodcock														9					4					9		1	2
Woodfield																										1	
Woodhouse						1											2	3	4								
Woodhurst			8	9																							
Woodman													8														
Woodward			8			1		3													6	7	8	9	0	1	
Wooldridge																								9			
Woolley																			4								
Woolloms [Woll-]							2																				
Wotton [Wooton]																		3	4	5	6						
Wright [Right]							2							9					4	5					0	1	2
Wyatt		7																									
Yardley													8				2	3						9			
Yate [Yates]			8			1		3								1											
Yomans [Yeomans]					0																						
Young [-e]						1				5																	2
Young-Palmer																											

A SCHEDULE OF THE PROPERTY
OF THE LAPWORTH CHARITY

" Whose tenours and particular effects
  You have, enscheduled briefly, in your hands."
HENRY V.

APPENDIX III

A SCHEDULE OF THE PROPERTY OF THE LAPWORTH CHARITY, EXTRACTED FROM THE TRUSTEES' VALUATION AND SURVEY BOOK OF 1814 (FROM SURVEY MADE IN 1811 BY EBENEZER ROBINS)

MILLBOURNE FARM.

Nos.	Names of Pieces.	Quantities.		
		a.	r.	p.
1.	Homestead . . .	o	2	33
1a.	Fordrove . . .	o	o	21
2.	Greensward or Barn Close .	4	o	13
3.	Grass Pit Close . . .	2	3	10
4.	Church Close . . .	3	1	3
5.	Millbourne Hill (arable) .	4	o	10
6.	Millbourne Hill (meadow) .	2	o	16
7.	Millbourne or Little Meadow	1	1	14
8.	Two Acres or Piddock Close .	2	2	21
9.	Yard or Barn Close . .	4	o	19
10.	Three Cornered Close . .	o	3	37
11.	Navigation Close . .	3	3	3
12.	Turnpike Close . .	3	3	19
	Total	33	3	19

WARWICK ROAD.

12a.	New house occupied by a person of poverty . . .	o	o	3
13.	House and garden . .	o	o	21
14.	House and garden }			
15.	House and garden } . .	o	o	27
16.	House and garden }			
17.	House and garden } . .	o	1	20
18.	House and garden }			

WARWICK ROAD.

19.	Homestead . . .	o	2	2
20.	Home Close . . .	1	3	27
21.	Green Close . . .	2	1	32
22.	High Park . . .	1	2	22

IN TAPSTER LANE.

23.	Little Church Close . .	o	3	12
24.	Big Church Close . .	1	2	34
	Total	9	o	9

VILLAGE AND TAPSTER LANE.

Nos.	Names of Pieces.			Quantities.		
				a.	r.	p.
24a.	House and Garden	.	.	0	1	1
25.	First Close	.	. .	1	0	11
26.	Second Close	.	. .	0	3	21
27.	Third Close	.	. .	0	2	38
		Total		2	3	31

NEAR PACKWOOD.

28.	First Close	.	. .	1	0	12
29.	Second Close	.	. .	3	2	11
30.	Third Close	.	. .	3	0	30
31.	Fourth Close	.	. .	2	3	12
		Total		10	2	25

EDITOR's NOTE.—Since this schedule was drawn up in 1814, this land (numbered 28, 29, 30, and 31 on map) has been exchanged for allotment ground on the Warwick Road, near the Pound, lettered **X** on map.

WARWICK ROAD.

32.	House and garden / House and garden / House and garden / House and garden / House and garden	.	.	0	2	5

WARWICK ROAD AND COP GREEN.

33.	Garden	.	. .	0	0	19
34.	Town Close	.	. .	2	3	12
34a.	Kendalls Close .	.	. .	4	0	3
		Total		6	3	34

EDITOR's NOTE.—The land numbered 34a on map, together with No. 41, has been exchanged for the strip (surrounding No. 50) lettered **W** on map.

KINGSWOOD BROOK.

35.	House and garden					
35a.	House and garden	.	.	0	1	39
35b.	House and garden					

EDITOR's NOTE.—The land numbered 35b on map, together with No. 37, has been exchanged for the Rowington Allotment, lettered **V** on map.

36.	Meadow	.	. .	1	0	31
36a.	Waste	.	. .	0	0	30
		Total		1	1	21

37.	Allotment	.	. .	0	2	10
38.	Allotment	.	. .	1	1	36
		Total		2	0	6

EDITOR's NOTE.—The land numbered 37 on map, together with 35b, has been exchanged for the Rowington Allotment, lettered **V** on map.

The land numbered 38 on map, was sold to the Birmingham and Oxford Junction Railway Company.

LAPWORTH STREET.

39.	First Close	.	. .	2	0	21
40.	Second Close	.	. .	5	0	23
		Total		7	1	4

COP GREEN.

Nos.	Names of Pieces.		Quantities.		
			a.	r.	p.
41.	⎧ House and garden ⎫ ⎪ House and garden ⎪ ⎨ House and garden ⎬ ⎩ House and garden ⎭	.	0	2	27

EDITOR'S NOTE.—This land, numbered 41 on map, together with No. 34*a*, has been exchanged for the strip (surrounding No. 50) lettered **W** on map.

TAPSTER LANE.

42.	Big Town Field	. .	3	3	27
43.	Little Town Field	. .	2	2	20
		Total	6	2	7

HOLE HOUSE LANE.

44.	Homestall	. . .	0	1	17
45.	Little Close	. . .	1	1	16
46.	Little Hill	. . .	0	1	31
47.	Over Close	. . .	3	0	3
48.	Garden Close	. . .	2	2	21
49.	Brook Meadow .	. .	1	3	22
		Total	9	2	30

OPPOSITE WHEAT SHEAF.

50.	Big Hullies	. . .	9	3	2

LAPWORTH HILL.

51.	Homestall	. . .	0	1	31
52.	House Close	. . .	2	0	26
53.	Little Close or Little Meadow		1	2	29
54.	Great Close or Middle Field .		3	0	9
		Total	7	1	15

NUTHURST.

55.	Four Lane End Close	. .	4	1	34
56.	Big Leesons	. .	8	3	32
57.	Little Leesons	. .	4	0	37
58.	Forden Hill	. .	9	3	15
59.	Forden Meadow	. .	4	2	29
		Total	32	0	27

LONDON ROAD.

60.	Buildings, garden, etc. .	.	0	1	5
61.	Meadow and orchard .	.	4	2	33
62.	Old House Close	. .	4	0	29
63.	Brick-kiln Close	. .	3	1	28
64.	Gorstey Close .	. .	5	1	31
65.	Little Cold Ridding	.	3	3	28
66.	Big Cold Ridding	. .	8	1	11
		Total	30	1	5

NEAR BEAR HOUSE.

Nos.	Names of Pieces.	Quantities.		
		a.	r.	p.
67.	Piece	2	1	36
68.	Piece	2	3	31
	Total	5	1	27

CLAY FIELDS.

			a.	r.	p.
69.	Selions of Meadow in Clay Croft		0	1	11
70.	,, Meadow ,,		0	3	28
71.	,, Meadow ,,		0	1	17
72.	,, Meadow ,,		0	1	19
73.	Pasture ,,		0	2	35
74.	Pasture ,,		1	1	39
75.	Pasture ,,		0	1	34
76.	Pasture ,,		0	1	34
	Total		5	0	17

EDITOR'S NOTE.—See plan opposite, and references to this land on pp. 65–6.

MILLBOURNE FARM.

(STRATFORD CANAL COMPANY AND STRATFORD AND HENLEY COAL COMPANY.)

		a.	r.	p.
77.	Canal, etc., through Fordrove and Barn Close . .	0	3	15
78.	Dò., Turnpike Close . .	0	2	15
79.	Do , Navigation Close . .	0	3	30
	Total	2	1	20

EDITOR'S NOTE.—These are lands which are part of the bed of the canal or form towing-path banks, in respect of which the Great Western Railway Co. (for the Stratford Canal Company) pay an annual rent.

		a.	r.	p.
80.	Canal, etc., through Navigation Close . . .	0	0	26

EDITOR'S NOTE.—This is land forming a canal branch (for wharf) in respect of which Mr. John Dowdeswell pays an annual rent.

EDITOR'S NOTE.—Apart from the *exchanges* of land noted in the above schedule, the following have been *added* to the property of the Charity since this table was prepared in 1814 :—

The allotment adjoining the Recreation Ground at Harboro' Banks, made over to the Charity under the Harboro' Banks Enclosure Award, marked Y on map.

The land adjoining the Pound Cottages on the Warwick Road, purchased in 1857, marked Z on map.

These additions, as well as all lands received *in exchange*, will be found noted upon the large scale map, in pocket at end of volume.

The Trustees of the Lapworth Charities also own a House and Buildings at Banbury, yielding an annual rent of £35.

They further administer the interest on £300 received for the land at Kingswood taken by the Oxford and Birmingham Junction Railway Company, and the interest on £20 received in redemption of " Nuthurst " and " Thorneall's " Doles.

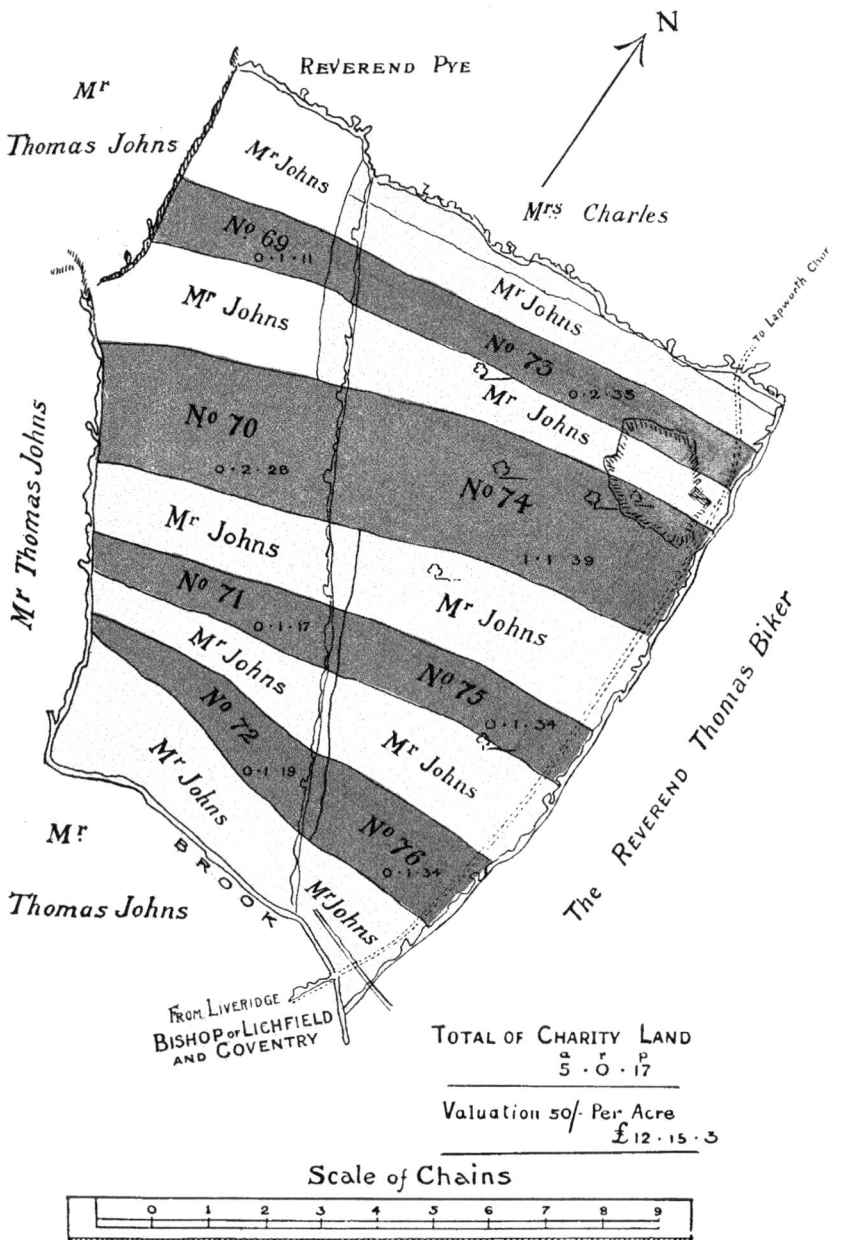

PLAN OF LAND OF LAPWORTH CHARITY, CALLED "CLEYCROFTE"
(OR "CLAY FIELDS")

SHEWING ANCIENT DIVISION INTO "SELIONS" [FROM SURVEY MADE IN 1814]

(The strips coloured red were bequeathed to the parish by deed bearing date 1479)

A CATALOGUE OF BOOKS
PUBLISHED BY METHUEN
AND COMPANY: LONDON
36 ESSEX STREET
W.C.

CONTENTS

SEPTEMBER 1904

A CATALOGUE OF

MESSRS. METHUEN'S

PUBLICATIONS

Colonial Editions are published of all Messrs. METHUEN'S Novels issued at a price above 2s. 6d., and similar editions are published of some works of General Literature. These are marked in the Catalogue. Colonial editions are only for circulation in the British Colonies and India.

PART I.—GENERAL LITERATURE

Abbot (Jacob). THE BEECHNUT BOOK. Edited by E. V. LUCAS. Illustrated. *Demy 16mo. 2s. 6d.* [Little Blue Books.

Acatos (M. J.). See L. A. Sornet.

Adams (Frank). JACK SPRATT. With 24 Coloured Pictures. *Pott 4to. 2s.*

Adeney (W. F.), M.A. See Bennett and Adeney.

Æschylus. AGAMEMNON, CHŒPHO-ROE, EUMENIDES. Translated by LEWIS CAMPBELL, LL.D., late Professor of Greek at St. Andrews. *5s.* [Classical Translations.

Æsop. FABLES. With 380 Woodcuts by THOMAS BEWICK. *Fcap. 8vo. 3s. 6d. net.* [Illustrated Pocket Library.

Ainsworth (W. Harrison). WINDSOR CASTLE. With 22 Plates and 87 Woodcuts in the Text by GEORGE CRUIKSHANK. *Fcap. 8vo. 3s. 6d. net.* [Illustrated Pocket Library.

THE TOWER OF LONDON. With 40 Plates and 58 Woodcuts in the Text by GEORGE CRUIKSHANK. *Fcap. 8vo. 3s. 6d. net.* [Illustrated Pocket Library.

Alexander (William), D.D., Archbishop of Armagh. THOUGHTS AND COUNSELS OF MANY YEARS. Selected by J. H. BURN, B.D. *Demy 16mo. 2s. 6d.*

Alken (Henry). THE ANALYSIS OF THE HUNTING FIELD. With 7 Coloured Plates and 43 Illustrations on wood. *Fcap. 8vo. 3s. 6d. net.* [Illustrated Pocket Library.

THE NATIONAL SPORTS OF GREAT BRITAIN. With descriptions in English and French. With 51 Coloured Plates. *Royal Folio. Five Guineas net.*

THE NATIONAL SPORTS OF GREAT BRITAIN. With Descriptions and 51 Coloured Plates by HENRY ALKEN. *4s. 6d. net.*
Also a limited edition on large Japanese paper, 30s. net.

This book is completely different from the large folio edition of 'National Sports' by the same artist, and none of the plates are similar. [Illustrated Pocket Library.
See also **Nimrod** and **Egan.**

Allen (Jessie). DURER. With many Illustrations. *Demy 16mo.* [Little Books on Art.

Allen (J. Romilly), F.S.A. CELTIC ART. With numerous Illustrations and Plans. *Demy 8vo. 7s. 6d. net.* [Antiquary's Books.

Almack (E.). BOOKPLATES. With many Illustrations. *Demy 16mo. 2s. 6d. net.* [Little Books on Art.

Amherst (Lady). A SKETCH OF EGYPTIAN HISTORY FROM THE EARLIEST TIMES TO THE PRESENT DAY. With many Illustrations, some of which are in Colour. *Demy 8vo. 10s. 6d net.*

Anderson (F. M.). THE STORY OF THE BRITISH EMPIRE FOR CHILDREN. With many Illustrations. *Crown 8vo. 2s.*

Andrewes (Bishop). PRECES PRIVATAE. Edited, with Notes, by F. E. BRIGHTMAN, M.A., of Pusey House, Oxford. *Crown 8vo. 6s.*

Aristophanes. THE FROGS. Translated into English by E. W. HUNTINGFORD, M.A., Professor of Classics in Trinity College, Toronto. *Crown 8vo. 2s. 6d.*

Aristotle. THE NICOMACHEAN ETHICS. Edited, with an Introduction and Notes, by JOHN BURNET, M.A., Professor of Greek at St. Andrews. *Demy 8vo. 15s. net.*

Ashton. (R.). THE PEELES AT THE CAPITAL. Illustrated. *Demy 16mo. 2s. 6d.* [Little Blue Books.
MRS. BARBERRY'S GENERAL SHOP. Illustrated. *Demy 16mo. 2s. 6d.* [The Little Blue Books.

Asquith (H. H.), The Right Hon., M.P. TRADE AND THE EMPIRE. An Examination of Mr. Chamberlain's Proposals. *Demy 8vo. 6d. net.*

Atkins (H. G.). GOETHE. With 12 Illustrations. *Fcap. 8vo. 3s. 6d.; leather, 4s. net.* [Little Biographies. Nearly Ready.

Atkinson (T. D.). A SHORT HISTORY OF ENGLISH ARCHITECTURE. With over 200 Illustrations by the Author and others. *Fcap. 8vo. 3s. 6d. net.*

Austen (Jane). PRIDE AND PREJUDICE. Edited by E. V. LUCAS. *Two Volumes. Small Pott 8vo. Each volume, cloth, 1s. 6d. net.; leather, 2s. 6d. net.* [Little Library.

NORTHANGER ABBEY. Edited by E. V. LUCAS. *Small Pott 8vo. Cloth, 1s. 6d. net.; leather, 2s. 6d. net.* [Little Library.

Bacon (Francis). THE ESSAYS OF. Edited by EDWARD WRIGHT. *Small Pott 8vo. 1s. 6d. net; leather, 2s. 6d. net.* [Little Library.

Baden-Powell (R. S. S.), Major-General. THE DOWNFALL OF PREMPEH. A Diary of Life in Ashanti, 1895. With 21 Illustrations and a Map. *Third Edition. Large Crown 8vo. 6s.* A Colonial Edition is also published.

THE MATABELE CAMPAIGN, 1896. With nearly 100 Illustrations. *Fourth and Cheaper Edition. Large Crown 8vo. 6s.* A Colonial Edition is also published.

Baker (W. G.), M.A. JUNIOR GEOGRAPHY EXAMINATION PAPERS. *Fcap. 8vo. 1s.* [Junior Exam. Series.

Baker (Julian L.), F.I.C., F.C.S. THE BREWING INDUSTRY. *Crown 8vo. 2s. 6d. net.* [Books on Business.

Balfour (Graham). THE LIFE OF ROBERT LOUIS STEVENSON. *Second Edition. Two Volumes. Demy 8vo. 25s. net.* A Colonial Edition is also published.

Bally (S. E.). A FRENCH COMMERCIAL READER. With Vocabulary. *Second Edition. Crown 8vo. 2s.* [Commercial Series.

FRENCH COMMERCIAL CORRESPONDENCE. With Vocabulary. *Third Edition. Crown 8vo. 2s.* [Commercial Series.

A GERMAN COMMERCIAL READER. With Vocabulary. *Crown 8vo. 2s.* [Commercial Series.

GERMAN COMMERCIAL CORRESPONDENCE. With Vocabulary. *Crown 8vo. 2s. 6d.* [Commercial Series.

Banks (Elizabeth L.). THE AUTOBIOGRAPHY OF A 'NEWSPAPER GIRL.' With Portrait of the Author and her Dog. *Second Edition. Crown 8vo. 6s.* A Colonial Edition is also published.

Barham (R. H.). THE INGOLDSBY LEGENDS. Edited by J. B. ATLAY. *Two*

Volumes. Small Pott 8vo. Each volume, cloth, 1s. 6d. net; leather, 2s. 6d. net. [Little Library.

Baring-Gould (S.). Author of 'Mehalah,' etc. THE LIFE OF NAPOLEON BONAPARTE. With over 450 Illustrations in the Text, and 12 Photogravure Plates. *Gilt top. Large quarto. 36s.*

THE TRAGEDY OF THE CÆSARS. With numerous Illustrations from Busts, Gems, Cameos, etc. *Fifth Edition. Royal 8vo. 15s.*

A BOOK OF FAIRY TALES. With numerous Illustrations and Initial Letters by ARTHUR J. GASKIN. *Second Edition. Crown 8vo. Buckram. 6s.*

A BOOK OF BRITTANY. With numerous Illustrations. *Crown 8vo. 6s.* Uniform in scope and size with Mr. Baring-Gould's well-known books on Devon, Cornwall, and Dartmoor.

OLD ENGLISH FAIRY TALES. With numerous Illustrations by F. D. BEDFORD. *Second Edition. Cr. 8vo. Buckram. 6s.* A Colonial Edition is also published.

THE VICAR OF MORWENSTOW: A Biography. A new and Revised Edition. With Portrait. *Crown 8vo. 3s. 6d.* A completely new edition of the well-known biography of R. S. Hawker.

DARTMOOR: A Descriptive and Historical Sketch. With Plans and numerous Illustrations. *Crown 8vo. 6s.*

THE BOOK OF THE WEST. With numerous Illustrations. *Two volumes.* Vol. I. Devon. *Second Edition.* Vol. II. Cornwall. *Second Edition. Crown 8vo. 6s. each.*

A BOOK OF NORTH WALES. With numerous Illustrations. *Crown 8vo. 6s.* This book is uniform with Mr. Baring-Gould's books on Devon, Dartmoor, and Brittany.

A BOOK OF SOUTH WALES. With many Illustrations. *Cr. 8vo. 6s.*

A BOOK OF GHOSTS. With many Illustrations. *Cr. 8vo. 6s. net.* A Colonial Edition is also published.

BRITTANY. Illustrated by J. A. WYLIE. *Pott 8vo. Cloth, 3s.; leather, 3s. 6d. net.* [Little Guides.

OLD COUNTRY LIFE. With 67 Illustrations. *Fifth Edition. Large Cr. 8vo. 6s.*

AN OLD ENGLISH HOME. With numerous Plans and Illustrations. *Cr. 8vo. 6s.*

YORKSHIRE ODDITIES AND STRANGE EVENTS. *Fifth Edition. Crown 8vo. 6s.*

STRANGE SURVIVALS AND SUPERSTITIONS. *Second Edition. Cr. 8vo. 6s.* A Colonial Edition is also published.

A GARLAND OF COUNTRY SONG: English Folk Songs with their Traditional Melodies. Collected and arranged by S. BARING-GOULD and H. F. SHEPPARD. *Demy 4to. 6s.*

SONGS OF THE WEST: Traditional Ballads and Songs of the West of England, with their Melodies. Collected by S. BARING-GOULD, M.A., and H. F. SHEPPARD, M.A. In 4 Parts. *Parts I., II., III.*, 2s. 6d. *each. Part IV.*, 4s. *In One Volume, French Morocco*, 10s. *net.*

Barker (Aldred F.), Author of 'Pattern Analysis,' etc. AN INTRODUCTION TO THE STUDY OF TEXTILE DESIGN. With numerous Diagrams and Illustrations. *Demy 8vo.* 7s. 6d.

Barnes (W. E.), D.D. ISAIAH. With an Introduction and Notes. *Two Vols. Fcap. 8vo.* 2s. *net each.* With Map. [Churchman's Bible.

Barnett (Mrs. P. A.). A LITTLE BOOK OF ENGLISH PROSE. *Small Pott 8vo. Cloth*, 1s. 6d. *net; leather*, 2s. 6d. *net.*
                            [Little Library.

Baron (R. R. N.), M.A. FRENCH PROSE COMPOSITION. *Crown 8vo.* 2s. 6d. *Key*, 3s. *net.*

Barron (H. M.), M.A., Wadham College, Oxford. TEXTS FOR SERMONS. With a Preface by Canon SCOTT HOLLAND. *Crown 8vo.* 3s. 6d.

Bastable (C. F.), M.A., Professor of Economics at Trinity College, Dublin. THE COMMERCE OF NATIONS. *Second Edition. Crown 8vo.* 2s. 6d.
                        [Social Questions Series.

Batson (Mrs. Stephen). A BOOK OF THE COUNTRY AND THE GARDEN. Illustrated by F. CARRUTHERS GOULD and A. C. GOULD. *Demy 8vo.* 10s. 6d.
A CONCISE HANDBOOK OF GARDEN FLOWERS. *Fcap. 8vo.* 3s. 6d.

Beaman (A. Hulme). PONS ASINORUM; OR, A GUIDE TO BRIDGE. *Second Edition. Fcap. 8vo.* 2s.

Beard (W. S.). JUNIOR ARITHMETIC EXAMINATION PAPERS. *Second Edition. Fcap. 8vo.* 1s. With or without Answers. [Junior Examination Series.
JUNIOR GENERAL INFORMATION EXAMINATION PAPERS. *Fcap. 8vo.* 1s. [Junior Examination Series.
EASY EXERCISES IN ARITHMETIC. Arranged by. *Cr. 8vo.* Without Answers, 1s. With Answers, 1s. 3d.

Beckford (Peter). THOUGHTS ON HUNTING. Edited by J. OTHO PAGET, and Illustrated by G. H. JALLAND. *Second and Cheaper Edition. Demy 8vo.* 6s.

Beckford (William). THE HISTORY OF THE CALIPH VATHEK. Edited by E. DENISON ROSS. *Pott 8vo. Cloth*, 1s. 6d. *net; leather*, 2s. 6d. *net.* [Little Library.

Beeching (H. C.), M.A., Canon of Westminster. LYRA SACRA: A Book of Sacred Verse. With an Introduction and Notes. *Pott 8vo. Cl.*, 2s.; *leather*, 2s. 6d. [Library of Devotion.

Behmen (Jacob). THE SUPERSENSUAL LIFE. Edited by BERNARD HOLLAND. *Fcap. 8vo.* 3s. 6d.

Belloc (Hilaire). PARIS. With Maps and Illustrations. *Crown 8vo.* 6s.

Bellot (H. H. L.), M.A. THE INNER AND MIDDLE TEMPLE. With numerous Illustrations. *Crown 8vo.* 6s. *net.*
See also L. A. A. Jones.

Bennett (W. H.), M.A. A PRIMER OF THE BIBLE. *Second Edition. Crown 8vo.* 2s. 6d.

Bennett (W. H.) and Adeney (W. F.). A BIBLICAL INTRODUCTION. *Second Edition. Crown 8vo.* 7s. 6d.

Benson (Archbishop). GOD'S BOARD: Communion Addresses. With Introductory Note by Mrs. Benson. *Fcap. 8vo.* 3s. 6d. *net.*

Benson (A. C.), M.A. TENNYSON. With 8 Illustrations. *Fcap. 8vo. Cloth*, 3s. 6d.; *Leather*, 4s. *net.* [Little Biographies.

Benson (R. M.). THE WAY OF HOLINESS: a Devotional Commentary on the 119th Psalm. *Crown 8vo.* 5s.

Bernard (E. R.), M.A., Canon of Salisbury. THE ENGLISH SUNDAY. *Fcap. 8vo.* 1s. 6d.

Bertouche (Baroness de). THE LIFE OF FATHER IGNATIUS. With Illustrations. *Demy 8vo.* 10s. 6d. *net.*
A Colonial Edition is also published.

Bethune-Baker (J. F.), M.A., Fellow of Pembroke College, Cambridge. A HISTORY OF EARLY CHRISTIAN DOCTRINE. *Demy 8vo.* 10s. 6d.
                [Handbooks of Theology.

Bidez (M.). See Parmentier.

Biggs (C. R. D.), D.D. THE EPISTLE TO THE PHILIPPIANS. With an Introduction and Notes *Fcap. 8vo.* 1s. 6d. *net.*
                        [Churchman's Bible.

Bindley (T. Herbert), B.D. THE OECUMENICAL DOCUMENTS OF THE FAITH. With Introductions and Notes. *Crown 8vo.* 6s.
A historical account of the Creeds.

Binyon (Laurence). THE DEATH OF ADAM, AND OTHER POEMS. *Second Edition. Crown 8vo.* 3s. 6d. *net.*

Blair (Robert). THE GRAVE: a Poem. Illustrated by 12 Etchings executed by LOUIS SCHIAVONETTI, from the original inventions of WILLIAM BLAKE. With an Engraved Title-Page and a Portrait of Blake by T. PHILLIPS, R.A. *Fcap. 8vo.* 3s. 6d. *net.*
Also a limited edition on large Japanese paper with India Proofs and a duplicate set of plates. 15s. *net.* [Illustrated Pocket Library.

Blake (William). ILLUSTRATIONS OF THE BOOK OF JOB. Invented and Engraved by. *Fcap. 8vo.* 3s. 6d. *net.*
Also a limited edition on large Japanese paper with India proofs and a duplicate set of plates. 15s. *net.* [Illustrated Pocket Library.
SELECTIONS. Edited by M. PERUGINI. *Small Pott 8vo.* 1s. 6d. *net; leather*, 2s. 6d. *net.* [Little Library.

Blaxland (B.). M.A. THE SONG OF SONGS. Being Selections from ST. BERNARD. *Small Pott 8vo. Cloth*, 2s.; *leather*, 2s. 6d. net. [Library of Devotion.

Bloom (T. Harvey), M.A. SHAKE-SPEARE'S GARDEN. With Illustrations. *Fcap. 8vo.* 2s. 6d.; *leather*, 3s. 6d. net.

Boardman (J. H.). See W. French.

Bodley (J. E. C). Author of 'France.' THE CORONATION OF EDWARD VII. *Demy 8vo.* 21s. net. By Command of the King.

Body (George), D.D. THE SOUL'S PILGRIMAGE : Devotional Readings from his published and unpublished writings. Selected and arranged by J. H. BURN, B.D., F.R.S.E. *Pott 8vo.* 2s. 6d.

Bona (Cardinal). A GUIDE TO ETERNITY. Edited with an Introduction and Notes, by J. W. STANBRIDGE, B.D. *Pott 8vo. Cloth*, 2s.; *leather*, 2s. 6d. net. [Library of Devotion.

Borrow (George). LAVENGRO. Edited by F. HINDES GROOME. *Two Volumes. Small Pott 8vo. Each volume, cloth*, 1s. 6d. net; *leather*, 2s. 6d. net. [Little Library.

THE ROMANY RYE. Edited by JOHN SAMPSON. *Small Pott 8vo. Cloth*, 1s. 6d. net; *leather*, 2s. 6d. net. [Little Library.

Bos (J. Ritzema). AGRICULTURAL ZOOLOGY. Translated by J. R. AINSWORTH DAVIS, M.A. With an Introduction by ELEANOR A. ORMEROD, F.E.S. With 155 Illustrations. *Crown 8vo. Third Edition.* 3s. 6d.

Botting (C. G.), B.A. JUNIOR LATIN EXAMINATION PAPERS. *Fcap. 8vo. Second Ed.* 1s. [Junior Examination Series.

EASY GREEK EXERCISES. *Cr. 8vo.* 2s.

Boulton (E. S.). GEOMETRY ON MODERN LINES. *Crown 8vo.* 2s.

Bowden (E. M.). THE IMITATION OF BUDDHA : Being Quotations from Buddhist Literature for each Day in the Year. *Fourth Edition. Crown 16mo.* 2s. 6d.

Bowmaker (E.). THE HOUSING OF THE WORKING CLASSES. *Crown 8vo.* 2s. 6d. [Social Questions Series.

Boyle (W.). CHRISTMAS AT THE ZOO. With Verses by W. BOYLE and 24 Coloured Pictures by H. B. NEILSON. *Pott 4to.* 2s.

Brabant (F. G.), M.A. SUSSEX. Illustrated by E. H. NEW. *Small Pott 8vo. Cloth*, 3s.; *leather*, 3s. 6d. net. [Little Guides.

THE ENGLISH LAKES. Illustrated by E. H. NEW. *Small Pott 8vo. Cloth*, 4s.; *leather*, 4s. 6d. net. [Little Guides.

Brodrick (Mary) and Morton (Anderson). A CONCISE HANDBOOK OF EGYPTIAN ARCHÆOLOGY. With many Illustrations. *Crown 8vo.* 3s. 6d.

Brooke (A. S.), M.A. SLINGSBY AND SLINGSBY CASTLE. With many Illustrations. *Cr. 8vo.* 7s. 6d.

Brooks (E. W.). See F. J. Hamilton.

Brown (P. H.), Fraser Professor of Ancient (Scottish) History at the University of Edinburgh. SCOTLAND IN THE TIME OF QUEEN MARY. *Demy 8vo.* 7s. 6d. net.

Brownell (C. L.). THE HEART OF JAPAN. Illustrated. *Third Edition. Crown 8vo.* 6s.

A Colonial Edition is also published.

Browning (Robert). SELECTIONS FROM THE EARLY POEMS OF. With Introduction and Notes by W. HALL GRIFFIN. *Small Pott 8vo.* 1s. 6d. net.; *leather*, 2s. 6d. net. [Little Library.

Buckland (Francis T.). CURIOSITIES OF NATURAL HISTORY. With Illustrations by HARRY B. NEILSON. *Crown 8vo.* 3s. 6d.

Buckton (A. M.). THE BURDEN OF ENGELA : a Ballad-Epic. *Second Edition. Crown 8vo.* 3s. 6d. net.

EAGER HEART : A Mystery Play. *Crown 8vo.* 1s. net.

Budge (E. A. Wallis). THE GODS OF THE EGYPTIANS. With over 100 Coloured Plates and many Illustrations. *Two Volumes. Royal 8vo.* £3, 3s. net.

Bull (Paul), Army Chaplain. GOD AND OUR SOLDIERS. *Crown 8vo.* 6s.

A Colonial Edition is also published.

Bulley (Miss). See Lady Dilke.

Bunyan (John). THE PILGRIM'S PROGRESS. Edited, with an Introduction, by C. H. FIRTH, M.A. With 39 Illustrations by R. ANNING BELL. *Cr. 8vo.* 6s.

GRACE ABOUNDING. Edited by C. S. FREER, M.A. *Small Pott 8vo. Cloth*, 2s.; *leather*, 2s. 6d. net. [Library of Devotion.

Burch (G. J.), M.A., F.R.S. A MANUAL OF ELECTRICAL SCIENCE. With numerous Illustrations. *Crown 8vo.* 3s. [University Extension Series.

Burgess (Gelett). GOOPS AND HOW TO BE THEM. With numerous Illustrations. *Small 4to.* 6s.

Burn (A. E.), D.D., Prebendary of Lichfield. AN INTRODUCTION TO THE HISTORY OF THE CREEDS. *Demy 8vo.* 10s. 6d. [Handbooks of Theology.

Burn (J. H.), B.D., A MANUAL OF CONSOLATION FROM THE SAINTS AND FATHERS. *Small Pott 8vo. Cloth*, 2s.; *leather*, 2s. 6d. net. [Library of Devotion.

Burn (J. H.), B.D. A DAY BOOK FROM THE SAINTS AND FATHERS. With an Introduction and Notes. *Small Pott 8vo. Cloth*, 2s.; *leather*, 2s. 6d. net. [Library of Devotion.

Burnand (Sir F. C). RECORDS AND REMINISCENCES, PERSONAL AND GENERAL. With many Illustrations. *Demy 8vo. Two Volumes. Third Edition.* 25s.

A Colonial Edition is also published.

Burns (Robert), THE POEMS OF. Edited by ANDREW LANG and W. A. CRAIGIE. With Portrait. *Third Edition. Demy 8vo, gilt top.* 6s.

Burnside (W. F.), M.A. OLD TESTAMENT HISTORY FOR USE IN SCHOOLS. *Crown 8vo.* 3s. 6d.

Burton (Alfred). THE MILITARY ADVENTURES OF JOHNNY NEWCOME. With 15 Coloured Plates by T. ROWLANDSON. *Fcap. 8vo.* 3s. 6d. net. [Illustrated Pocket Library.

THE ADVENTURES OF JOHNNY NEWCOME IN THE NAVY. With 16 Coloured Plates by T. ROWLANDSON. *Fcap. 8vo.* 3s. 6d. net. [Illus. Pocket Library

Caldecott (Alfred), D.D. THE PHILOSOPHY OF RELIGION IN ENGLAND AND AMERICA. *Demy 8vo.* 10s. 6d. [Handbooks of Theology.

Calderwood (D. S.), Headmaster of the Normal School, Edinburgh. TEST CARDS IN EUCLID AND ALGEBRA. In three packets of 40, with Answers. 1s. each. Or in three Books, price 2d., 2d., and 3d.

Cambridge (Ada) [Mrs. Cross]. THIRTY YEARS IN AUSTRALIA. *Demy 8vo.* 7s. 6d.
A Colonial Edition is also published.

Canning (George). SELECTIONS FROM THE ANTI-JACOBIN; with additional Poems. Edited by LLOYD SANDERS. *Small Pott 8vo, cloth,* 1s. 6d. net.; *leather,* 2s. 6d. net. [Little Library.

Capey (E. F. H.). ERASMUS. With 12 Illustrations. *Fcap. 8vo. cloth,* 3s. 6d. net; *leather,* 4s. net. [Little Biographies.

Carlyle (Thomas). THE FRENCH REVOLUTION. Edited by C. R. L. FLETCHER, Fellow of Magdalen College, Oxford. *Three Volumes. Crown 8vo.* 18s.

THE LIFE AND LETTERS OF OLIVER CROMWELL. With an Introduction by C. H. FIRTH, M.A., and Notes and Appendices by Mrs. S. C. LOMAS. *Three Volumes. Demy 8vo.* 18s. net.

Carlyle (R. M. and A. J.), M.A. BISHOP LATIMER. With Portrait. *Crown 8vo.* 3s. 6d. [Leaders of Religion.

Chamberlin (Wilbur B.). ORDERED TO CHINA. *Crown 8vo.* 6s.
A Colonial Edition is also published.

Channer (C. C.) and Roberts (M. E.). LACE-MAKING IN THE MIDLANDS, PAST AND PRESENT. With 16 full-page Illustrations. *Crown 8vo.* 2s. 6d.

Chesterfield (Lord), THE LETTERS OF, TO HIS SON. Edited, with an Introduction, by C. STRACHEY, and Notes by A. CALTHROP. *Two Volumes. Cr. 8vo.* 12s.

Christian (F W.). THE CAROLINE ISLANDS. With many Illustrations and Maps. *Demy 8vo.* 12s. 6d. net.

Cicero. DE ORATORE I. Translated by E. N. P. MOOR, M.A. *Crown 8vo.* 3s. 6d. [Classical Translations.

SELECT ORATIONS (Pro Milone, Pro Murena, Philippic II., In Catilinam). Translated by H. E. D. BLAKISTON, M.A., Fellow and Tutor of Trinity College, Oxford. *Crown 8vo.* 5s. [Classical Translations.

DE NATURA DEORUM. Translated by F. BROOKS, M.A., late Scholar of Balliol College, Oxford. *Crown 8vo.* 3s. 6d. [Classical Translations.

DE OFFICIIS. Translated by G. B. GARDINER, M.A. *Crown 8vo.* 2s. 6d. [Classical Translations.

Clarke (F. A.), M.A. BISHOP KEN. With Portrait. *Crown 8vo.* 3s. 6d. [Leaders of Religion.

Cleather (A. L.) and Crump (B.). RICHARD WAGNER'S MUSIC DRAMAS: Interpretations, embodying Wagner's own explanations. *In Four Volumes Fcap 8vo.* 2s. 6d. each.
VOL. I.—THE RING OF THE NIBELUNG.
VOL. II.—PARSIFAL, etc.

Clinch (G.). KENT. Illustrated by F. D. BEDFORD. *Small Pott 8vo. Cloth,* 3s.; *leather,* 3s. 6d. net. [Little Guides.

THE ISLE OF WIGHT. Illustrated by F. D. BEDFORD. *Small Pott 8vo. Cloth,* 3s.; *leather,* 3s. 6d. net. [Little Guides.

Clough (W. T.) and Dunstan (A. E.). ELEMENTARY EXPERIMENTAL SCIENCE. PHYSICS by W. T. CLOUGH, A.R.C.S. CHEMISTRY by A. E. DUNSTAN, B.Sc. With 2 Plates and 154 Diagrams. *Crown 8vo.* 2s. [Junior School Books.

Coast (W. G.), B.A. EXAMINATION PAPERS IN VERGIL *Crown 8vo.* 2s.

Cobb (T.). THE CASTAWAYS OF MEADOWBANK. Illustrated. *Demy 16mo.* 2s. 6d [Little Blue Books.

THE TREASURY OF PRINCEGATE PRIORY. Illustrated. *Demy 16mo.* 2s. 6d. [Little Blue Books.

THE LOST BALL. Illustrated. *Demy 16mo.* 2s. 6d. [Little Blue Books.

Collingwood (W. G.), M.A. THE LIFE OF JOHN RUSKIN. With Portraits. *Second and Cheap Edition. Cr. 8vo.* 6s.
Also a Poplar Edition. *Cr. 8vo.* 2s. 6d. net.

Collins (W. E.), M.A. THE BEGINNINGS OF ENGLISH CHRISTIANITY. With Map. *Cr. 8vo.* 3s. 6d. [Churchman's Library

Colonna. HYPNEROTOMACHIA POLIPHILI UBI HUMANA OMNIA NON NISI SOMNIUM ESSE DOCET ATQUE OBITER PLURIMA SCITU SANE QUAM DIGNA COMMEMORAT. An edition limited to 350 copies on handmade paper. *Folio. Three Guineas net.*

Combe (William). THE TOUR OF DR. SYNTAX IN SEARCH OF THE PICTURESQUE. With 30 Coloured Plates by T. ROWLANDSON. *Fcap. 8vo.* 3s. 6d. net.
Also a limited edition on large Japanese paper. 30s. net. [Illustrated Pocket Library.

THE TOUR OF DR. SYNTAX IN
·SEARCH OF CONSOLATION. 'With
. 24 Coloured Plates by T. ROWLANDSON.
3s. 6d. net.
Also a limited edition on large Japanese
paper. 30s. net. [Illustrated Pocket Library.
THE THIRD TOUR OF DR. SYNTAX
IN SEARCH OF A WIFE. With 24
Coloured Plates by T. ROWLANDSON. 3s. 6d.
net
Also a limited edition on large Japansee
paper. 30s. net.
[Illustrated Pocket Library.
THE HISTORY OF JOHNNY QUAE
GENUS: The Little Foundling of the late
Dr. Syntax. . With 24 Coloured Plates by
ROWLANDSON. Fcap. 8vo. . 3s. 6d. net.
Also a limited edition on large Japanese
paper: 30s. net.
[Illustrated Pocket Library.
THE ENGLISH DANCE OF DEATH,
from the Designs of THOMAS ROWLANDSON,
with Metrical Illustrations by the Author
· of 'Doctor Syntax.' With 74 Coloured
Plates. Two Volumes. Fcap. 8vo. 9s. net.
Also a limited edition on large Japanese
paper. 30s. net.
: [Illustrated Pocket Library.
THE DANCE OF LIFE: a Poem. Illus-
trated with 26 Coloured Engravings by
THOMAS ROWLANDSON. Fcap. 8vo. 3s. 6d.
. net. r
Also a limited edition on large Japanese
paper. 30s. net.
[Illustrated Pocket Library.
Cook (A. M.), M.A. See E. C. Marchant.
Cooke-Taylor (R. W.). THE FACTORY
SYSTEM. Crown 8vo. 2s. 6d. '
[Social Questions Series.
Corelli (Marie). THE.PASSING OF THE
GREAT QUEEN : A Tribute to the Noble
Life of Victoria Regina. Small 4to. 1s.
A CHRISTMAS GREETING. Sm. 4to. 'is.
Corkran (Alice). LEIGHTON. With
many Illustrations. Demy 16mo.'. 2s. 6d.
net. [Little Books on Art.
Cotes (Rosemary). DANTE'S GARDEN.
· With a Frontispiece. Second Edition.
Fcap. 8vo. cloth 2s. 6d.; leather, 3s. 6d. net.
BIBLE FLOWERS. With a Frontispiece
and Plan. Fcap. 8vo. 2s. 6d. net.
Cowley (Abraham) THE ESSAYS OF.
Edited by H. C. MINCHIN. Small. Pott
8vo. Cloth, 1s. 6d. net; leather, 2s. 6d. net.
[Little Library.
Cox (J. Charles), LL.D., F.S.A. DERBY-
SHIRE. Illustrated by J. C. WALL.
Small Pott 8vo. Cloth, 3s. ; leather, 3s. 6d.
net. [Little Guides.
HAMPSHIRE. Illustrated by M. E.
PURSER. Small Pott 8vo. Cloth, 3s. :
Leather, 3s. 6d. net. [Little Guides.
Cox (Harold), B.A. LAND NATIONAL-
IZATION. · Crown 8vo. 2s. 6d.
[Social Questions Series.

Crabbe (George), SELECTIONS FROM
THE POEMS OF. Edited by A. C.
DEANE. Small Pott 8vo. Cloth, 1s. 6d.
net; leather, 2s. 6d. net. [Little Library.
Craigie (W. A.). A PRIMER OF BURNS.
Crown 8vo. 2s. 6d.
Craik (Mrs.). JOHN HALIFAX, GEN-
TLEMAN. Edited by ANNIE MATHE-
SON. Two Volumes. Small Pott 8vo.
Each Volume, Cloth, 1s. 6d; leather,
2s. 6d. net. · · [Little Library.
Crashaw (Richard), THE ENGLISH
POEMS OF. Edited by EDWARD HUT-
. TON. Small Pott 8vo. Cloth, 1s. 6d. net;
leather, 2s. 6d. net. [Little Library.
Crawford (F. G.). See Mary C. Danson.
Crouch (W.). BRYAN KING. With a
Portrait. Crown 8vo. 3s. 6d. net.
Cruikshank (G.) THE LOVING BAL-
LAD OF LORD BATEMAN. With 11
Plates. Crown 16mo. 1s. 6d. net
From the edition published by C. Tilt, 1811.
Crump (B). See A. L. Cleather.
Cunliffe (F. H. E.), Fellow of All Souls' Col-
lege, Oxford. THE HISTORY OF THE
BOER WAR. With many Illustrations,
Plans, and Portraits. In 2 vols. Vol. I.; 15s.
Cutts (E. L.), D.D. AUGUSTINE OF
CANTERBURY. With Portrait. Crown
8vo. 3s. 6d. [Leaders of Religion.
Daniell (G. W.), M.A. BISHOP WILBER-
FORCE. . With Portrait. Crown 8vo.
3s. 6d. [Leaders of Religion.
Danson (Mary C.) and Crawford (F. G.).
FATHERS IN THE FAITH. Small 8vo.
1s. 6d.
Dante. LA COMMEDIA DI 'DANTE.
The Italian Text· edited by PAGET
TOYNBEE, M.A., D.Litt.· Crown 8vo.' 6s.
THE INFERNO OF DANTE. Trans-
lated by H. F. CARY. Edited by PAGET
TOYNBEE, M.A., D.Litt. Small Pott 8vo.
Cloth, 1s. 6d. net; leather, 2s. 6d. net.
[Little Library.
THE PURGATORIO OF DANTE.
Translated by H. F. CARY. Edited by
PAGET TOYNBEE, M.A., D.Litt. Small Pott
8vo. Cloth, 1s. 6d. net; leather, 2s. 6d. net.
[Little Library.
THE PARADISO OF DANTE. Trans-
lated by H. F. CARY. Edited by PAGET
TOYNBEE, M.A., D.Litt. Small Pott 8vo.
Cloth, 1s. 6d. net; leather, 2s. 6d. net.
See also Paget Toynbee. [Little Library.
Darley (George), SELECTIONS FROM
THE POEMS OF. Edited by R. A.
STREATFEILD. Small Pott 8vo. Cloth,
1s. 6d. net; leather, 2s. 6d. net.
[Little Library.
Davenport (Cyril). MEZZOTINTS.
With 40 Plates in Photogravure. Wide
Royal 8vo. 25s. net.
[Connoisseurs Library.

JEWELLERY. With numerous Illustrations. *Demy 16mo. 2s. 6d. net.*
[Little Books on Art.

Dawson (A. J.). MOROCCO. Being a bundle of jottings, notes, impressions, tales, and tributes. With many Illustrations. *Demy 8vo. 10s. 6d. net.*

Deane (A. C.). A LITTLE BOOK OF LIGHT VERSE. With an Introduction and Notes. *Small Pott 8vo. Cloth, 1s. 6d. net; leather, 2s. 6d. net.* [Little Library.

Delbos (Leon). THE METRIC SYSTEM. *Crown 8vo. 2s.*

Demosthenes: THE OLYNTHIACS AND PHILIPPICS. Translated upon a new principle by OTHO HOLLAND. *Crown 8vo., 2s. 6d.*

Demosthenes. AGAINST CONON AND CALLICLES. Edited with Notes and Vocabulary, by F. DARWIN SWIFT, M.A. *Fcap. 8vo. 2s.*

Dickens (Charles).
THE PICKWICK PAPERS. With the 43 Illustrations by SEYMOUR and PHIZ, the two Buss Plates and the 32 Contemporary Onwhyn Plates. *3s. 6d. net.*
This is a particularly interesting volume, containing, as it does, reproductions of very rare plates. [Illustrated Pocket Library.

Dickinson (Emily). POEMS. First Series. *Crown 8vo. 4s. 6d. net.*

Dickinson (G. L.), M.A., Fellow of King's College, Cambridge. THE GREEK VIEW OF LIFE. *Third Edition. Crown 8vo. 2s. 6d.* [University Extension Series.

Dickson (H. N.), F.R.S E., F.R.Met. Soc. METEOROLOGY. Illustrated. *Crown 8vo. 2s. 6d.* [University Extension Series.

Dilke (Lady), Bulley (Miss), and Whitley (Miss). WOMEN'S WORK. *Crown 8vo. 2s. 6d.* [Social Questions Series.

Dillon (Edward). PORCELAIN. With many Plates in Colour and Photogravure. *Wide Royal 8vo. 25s. net.*
[Connoisseurs Library.

Ditchfield (P. H.), M.A., F.S.A. ENGLISH VILLAGES. Illustrated. *Crown 8vo. 6s.*

THE STORY OF OUR ENGLISH TOWNS. With Introduction by AUGUSTUS JESSOPP, D.D. *Second Edition. Crown 8vo. 6s.*

OLD ENGLISH CUSTOMS: Extant at the Present Time. An Account of Local Observances, Festival Customs, and Ancient Ceremonies yet Surviving in Great Britain. *Crown 8vo. 6s.*

Dixon (W. M.), M.A. A PRIMER OF TENNYSON. *Second Edition. Crown 8vo. 2s. 6d.*

ENGLISH POETRY FROM BLAKE TO BROWNING. *Second Edition. Crown 8vo. 2s. 6d.* [University Extension Series.

Dole (N. H.) FAMOUS COMPOSERS. With Portraits. *Two Volumes. Demy 8vo. 12s. net.*

Dowden (J.), D.D., Lord Bishop of Edinburgh. THE WORKMANSHIP OF THE PRAYER BOOK: Its Literary and Liturgical Aspects. *Second Edition. Crown 8vo. 3s. 6d.* [Churchman's Library.

Driver (S. R.), D.D., Canon of Christ Church, Regius Professor of Hebrew in the University of Oxford. SERMONS ON SUBJECTS CONNECTED WITH THE OLD TESTAMENT. *Crown 8vo. 6s.*

THE BOOK OF GENESIS. With Notes and Introduction. *Second Edition. Demy 8vo. 10s. 6d.* [Westminster Commentaries.

Duguid (Charles), City Editor of the *Morning Post,* author of the 'Story of the Stock Exchange,' etc. THE STOCK EXCHANGE. *Second Edition. Crown 8vo. 2s. 6d. net.* [Books on Business.

Duncan (S. J.) (Mrs. COTES), Author of 'A Voyage of Consolation.' ON THE OTHER SIDE OF THE LATCH. *Second Edition. Crown 8vo. 6s.*

Dunn (J. T.), D.Sc., **and Mundella (V. A.).** GENERAL ELEMENTARY SCIENCE. With 114 Illustrations. *Crown 8vo. 3s. 6d.*

Dunstan (A. E.), B.Sc. See W. T. CLOUGH.

Durham (The Earl of). A REPORT ON CANADA. With an Introductory Note. *Demy 8vo. 7s. 6d. net.*

Dutt (W. A.). NORFOLK. Illustrated by B. C. BOULTER. *Small Pott 8vo. Cloth, 3s.; leather, 3s. 6d. net.* [Little Guides.

A POPULAR GUIDE TO NORFOLK. *Medium 8vo. 6d. net.*

SUFFOLK. Illustrated by J. WYLIE. *Small Pott 8vo. Cloth, 3s.; leather, 3s. 6d. net.* [Little Guides.

THE NORFOLK BROADS. With coloured and other Illustrations by FRANK SOUTHGATE. *Large Demy 8vo. 21s. net.*

Earle (John), Bishop of Salisbury. MICRO-COSMOGRAPHIE, OR A PIECE OF THE WORLD DISCOVERED; IN ESSAYES AND CHARACTERS. *Post 16mo. 2s. net.* [Rariora.
Reprinted from the Sixth Edition published by Robert Allot in 1633.

Edwards (Clement). RAILWAY NATIONALIZATION. *Crown 8vo. 2s. 6d.* [Social Questions Series

Edwards (W. Douglas). COMMERCIAL LAW. *Crown 8vo. 2s.*
[Commercial Series.

Egan (Pierce). LIFE IN LONDON, OR THE DAY AND NIGHT SCENES OF JERRY HAWTHORN, ESQ., AND HIS ELEGANT FRIEND, CORINTHIAN TOM. With 36 Coloured Plates by I. R. and G. CRUIK-SHANK. With numerous designs on wood. *Fcap. 8vo. 4s. 6d. net.*
Also a limited edition on large Japanese paper. *30s. net.* [Illustrated Pocket Library

REAL LIFE IN LONDON, OR THE RAMBLES AND ADVENTURES OF BOB TALLYHO, ESQ., AND HIS COUSIN, the Hon. TOM DASHALL. With 31 Coloured Plates by ALKEN and ROWLANDSON, etc. *Two Volumes. Fcap. 8vo. 9s. net.*
[Illustrated Pocket Library.

THE LIFE OF AN ACTOR. With 27 Coloured Plates by THEODORE LANE, and several designs on wood. *Fcap. 8vo. 4s. 6d. net.* [Illustrated Pocket Library.

Egerton (H. E.), M.A. A HISTORY OF BRITISH COLONIAL POLICY. *Demy 8vo. 12s. 6d.*
A Colonial Edition is also published.

Ellaby (C. G.). ROME. Illustrated by B. C. BOULTER. *Small Pott 8vo. Cloth,* 3s. ; *leather,* 3s. 6d. *net.* [Little Guides.

Ellerton (F. G.). See S. J. Stone.

Ellwood (Thomas). THE HISTORY OF THE LIFE OF. Edited by C. G. CRUMP, M.A. *Crown 8vo. 6s.*

Engel (E.). A HISTORY OF ENGLISH LITERATURE: From its Beginning to Tennyson. Translated from the German. *Demy 8vo. 7s. 6d. net.*

Fairbrother (W. H.), M.A. THE PHILO-SOPHY OF T. H. GREEN. *Second Edition. Crown 8vo. 3s. 6d.*

FELISSA ; OR, THE LIFE AND OPINIONS OF A KITTEN OF SENTIMENT. With 12 Coloured Plates. *Post 16mo. 2s. 6d. net.* (5¼×3½).
From the edition published by J. Harris, 1811.

Farrer (Reginald). THE GARDEN OF ASIA. *Crown 8vo. 6s.*
A Colonial Edition is also published.

Ferrier (Susan). MARRIAGE. Edited by Miss GOODRICH FREER and Lord IDDES-LEIGH. *Two Volumes. Small Pott 8vo. Each volume, cloth,* 1s. 6d. *net; leather,* 2s. 6d. *net.* [Little Library.
THE INHERITANCE. *Two Volumes. Small Pott 8vo. Each Volume, cloth,* 1s. 6d. *net.; leather,* 2s. 6d. *net.* [Little Library.

Finn (S. W.), M.A. JUNIOR ALGEBRA EXAMINATION PAPERS. *Fcap. 8vo.* With or Without Answers, 1s.
[Junior Examination Series.

Firth (C. H.), M.A. CROMWELL'S ARMY: A History of the English Soldier during the Civil Wars, the Commonwealth, and the Potectorate. *Crown 8vo. 7s. 6d.*

Fisher (G. W.), M.A. ANNALS OF SHREWSBURY SCHOOL. With numerous Illustrations. *Demy 8vo. 10s. 6d.*

FitzGerald (Edward). THE RUB'AIYÁT OF OMAR KHAYYÁM. From the First Edition of 1859. *Second Edition. Leather,* 1s. *net.* [Miniature Library.
THE RUB'AIYÁT OF OMAR KHAY-YÁM. Printed from the Fifth and last

Edition. With a Commentary by Mrs. STEPHEN BATSON, and a Biography of Omar by E. D. ROSS. *Crown 8vo. 6s.*

EUPHRANOR: a Dialogue on Youth. *Demy 32mo. Leather,* 2s. *net.*
[Miniature Library.

POLONIUS : or Wise Saws and Modern Instances. *Demy 32mo. Leather,* 2s. *net.*
[Miniature Library.

FitzGerald (E. A.). THE HIGHEST ANDES. With 2 Maps, 51 Illustrations, 13 of which are in Photogravure, and a Panorama. *Royal 8vo. 30s. net.*

Flecker (W. H.), M.A., D.C.L., Headmaster of the Dean Close School, Cheltenham. THE STUDENTS' PRAYER BOOK. PART I. MORNING AND EVENING PRAYER AND LITANY. With an Introduction and Notes. *Crown 8vo. 2s. 6d.*

Flux (A. W.), M.A., William Dow Professor of Political Economy in M'Gill University, Montreal : sometime Fellow of St. John's College, Cambridge, and formerly Stanley-Jevons Professor of Political Economy in the Owens Coll., Manchester. ECONOMIC PRINCIPLES. *Demy 8vo. 7s. 6d. net.*

Fortescue (Mrs. G.) HOLBEIN. With 30 Illustrations. *Demy 16mo. 2s. 6d. net.*
[Little Books on Art.

Fraser (J. F.). ROUND THE WORLD ON A WHEEL. With 100 Illustrations. *Third Edition Crown 8vo. 6s.*
A Colonial Edition is also published.

French (W.), M.A., Principal of the Storey Institute, Lancaster. PRACTICAL CHEMISTRY. *Part I.* With numerous Diagrams. *Crown 8vo. 1s. 6d.*
[Textbooks of Technology.

French (W.), M.A., and **Boardman (T. H.),** M.A. PRACTICAL CHEMISTRY. *Part II.* With numerous Diagrams. *Crown 8vo. 1s. 6d.* [Textbooks of Technology.

Freudenreich (Ed. von). DAIRY BACTERIOLOGY. A Short Manual for the Use of Students. Translated by J. R. AINSWORTH DAVIS, M.A. *Second Edition. Revised. Crown 8vo. 2s. 6d.*

Fulford (H. W.), M.A. THE EPISTLE OF ST. JAMES. With Notes and Intro-duction. *Fcap. 8vo. 1s. 6d. net.*
[Churchman's Bible.

C. G., and F. C. G. JOHN BULL'S ADVENTURES IN THE FISCAL WONDERLAND. By CHARLES GEAKE. With 46 Illustrations by F. CARRUTHERS GOULD. *Second Ed. Crown 8vo. 2s. 6d. net.*

Gambado (Geoffrey, Esq.). AN ACADEMY FOR GROWN HORSEMEN : Contain-ing the completest Instructions for Walking, Trotting, Cantering, Galloping, Stumbling, and Tumbling. Illustrated with 27 Coloured Plates, and adorned with a Portrait of the Author. *Fcap. 8vo. 3s. 6d. net.*
[Illustrated Pocket Library.

Gaskell (Mrs.). CRANFORD. Edited by
E. V. Lucas.. *Small Pott 8vo. Cloth*, 1s. 6d.
net; leather, 2s. 6d. *net.* [Little Library.
Gasquet, the Right Rev. Abbot, O.S.B.
ENGLISH MONASTIC LIFE. With
Coloured and other Illustrations. *Demy 8vo.*
7s. 6d. *net.* [Antiquary's Books.
George (H. B.), M.A., Fellow of New College,
Oxford. BATTLES OF ENGLISH
HISTORY. With numerous Plans. *Fourth
Edition. Crown 8vo.* 6s.
A HISTORICAL GEOGRAPHY OF THE
BRITISH EMPIRE. *Cr. 8vo.* 3s. 6d net.
Gibbins (H. de B.), Litt.D., M.A. IN-
DUSTRY IN ENGLAND: HISTORI-
CAL OUTLINES. With 5 Maps. *Third
Edition. Demy 8vo.* 10s. 6d.
A COMPANION GERMAN GRAMMAR.
Crown 8vo. 1s. 6d.
THE INDUSTRIAL HISTORY OF ENG-
LAND. *Tenth Edition.* Revised. With
Maps and Plans. *Crown 8vo.* 3s.
[University Extension Series.
THE ECONOMICS OF COMMERCE.
Crown 8vo. 1s. 6d. [Commercial Series.
COMMERCIAL EXAMINATION
PAPERS. *Crown 8vo.* 1s. 6d.
[Commercial Series.
BRITISH COMMERCE AND COLONIES
FROM ELIZABETH TO VICTORIA.
Third Edition. Crown 8vo. 2s.
[Commercial Series.
ENGLISH SOCIAL REFORMERS.
Second Edition. Crown 8vo. 2s. 6d.
[University Extension Series.
Gibbins (H. de B.), Litt.D., M.A., and
Hadfield (R. A.), of the Hecla Works,
Sheffield. A SHORTER WORKING
DAY. *Crown 8vo.* 2s. 6d.
[Social Questions Series.
Gibbon (Edward). THE DECLINE AND
FALL OF THE ROMAN EMPIRE.
A New Edition, edited with Notes, Appen-
dices, and Maps, by J. B. Bury, M.A.,
Litt.D., Fellow of Trinity College, Dublin.
In Seven Volumes. Demy 8vo. Gilt top,
8s. 6d. *each. Also, Crown 8vo.* 6s. *each.*
MEMOIRS OF MY LIFE AND WRIT-
INGS. Edited, with an Introduction and
Notes, by G. Birkbeck Hill, LL.D.
Crown 8vo. 6s.
Gibson (E. C. S.), D.D., Vicar of Leeds.
THE BOOK OF JOB. With Introduction
and Notes. *Demy 8vo.* 6s.
[Westminster Commentaries.
THE XXXIX. ARTICLES OF THE
CHURCH OF ENGLAND. With an
Introduction. *Fourth Edition in One Vol.
Demy 8vo.* 12s. 6d. [Handbooks of Theology.
JOHN HOWARD. With 12 Illustrations.
Fcap 8vo. Cloth, 3s. 6d. *; leather*, 4s. *net.*
[Little Biographies.
Gilbert (A. R.). See W. Wilberforce.

Godfrey (Elizabeth). A BOOK OF RE-
MEMBRANCE. *Demy 16mo.* 2s. 6d. *net.*
Godley (A. D.), M.A., Fellow of Magdalen
College, Oxford. LYRA FRIVOLA.
Third Edition. Fcap. 8vo. 2s. 6d.
VERSES TO ORDER. *Second Edition.
Crown 8vo.* 2s. 6d.
SECOND STRINGS. *Fcap. 8vo.* 2s. 6d.
A new volume of humorous verse uniform
with *Lyra Frivola.*
Goldsmith (Oliver). THE VICAR OF
WAKEFIELD. With 24 Coloured Plates
by T. Rowlandson. *Royal 8vo. One
Guinea net.*
Reprinted from the edition of 1817.
[Burlington Library.
Also *Fcap. 8vo.* 3s. 6d. *net.* Also a
limited edition on large Japanese paper.
30s. *net.* [Illustrated Pocket Library.
Also *Fcap.* 32mo. With 10 Plates in Photo-
graphure by Tony Johannot. *Leather,*
2s. 6d. *net.*
Goudge (H. L.), M.A., Principal of Wells
Theological College. THE FIRST
EPISTLE TO THE CORINTHIANS.
With Introduction and Notes. *Demy 8vo.*
6s. [Westminster Commentaries.
Graham (P. Anderson). THE RURAL
EXODUS. *Crown 8vo.* 2s. 6d.
[Social Questions Series.
Granger (F. S.), M.A., Litt.D. PSYCH-
OLOGY. *Second Edition. Crown 8vo.*
2s. 6d. [University Extension Series.
THE SOUL OF A CHRISTIAN. *Crown
8vo.* 6s.
Gray (E. M'Queen). GERMAN PASSAGES
FOR UNSEEN TRANSLATION.
Crown 8vo. 2s. 6d.
Gray (P. L.), B.Sc., formerly Lecturer in
Physics in Mason University College, Bir-
mingham. THE PRINCIPLES OF
MAGNETISM AND ELECTRICITY:
an Elementary Text-Book. With 181 Dia-
grams. *Crown 8vo.* 3s. 6d.
Green (G. Buckland), M.A., Assistant
Master at Edinburgh Academy, late Fellow
of St. John's College, Oxon. NOTES ON
GREEK AND LATIN SYNTAX. *Crown
8vo.* 3s. 6d.
Green (E. T.), M.A. THE CHURCH OF
CHRIST. *Crown 8vo.* 6s.
[Churchman's Library.
Greenidge (A. H. J.), M.A. A HISTORY
OF ROME: During the Later Republic
and the Early Principate. *In Six Volumes.
Demy 8vo.* Vol. I. (133-104 B.C.). 12s. 6d.
net.
Greenwell (Dora), THE POEMS OF.
From the edition of 1848. *Leather,* 2s. *net.*
[Miniature Library.
Gregory (R. A.) THE VAULT OF
HEAVEN. A Popular Introduction to
Astronomy. With numerous Illustrations.
Crown 8vo. 2s. 6d.
[University Extension Series.

Gregory (Miss E. C.) HEAVENLY WISDOM. Selections from the English Mystics. *Pott 8vo. Cloth 2s.; leather,* 2s. 6d. net.
[Library of Devotion. Nearly Ready.

Greville Minor. A MODERN JOURNAL. Edited by J. A. SPENDER. *Crown 8vo.* 3s. 6d. net.

Grinling (C. H.). A HISTORY OF THE GREAT NORTHERN RAILWAY, 1845-95. With Illustrations. Revised, with an additional chapter. *Demy 8vo.* 10s. 6d.

Grubb (H. C.). BUILDERS' QUANTITIES. With many Illustrations. *Crown 8vo.* 4s. 6d. [Textbooks of Technology.

Guiney (L. I.). RICHARD HURRELL FROUDE. Illustrated. *Demy 8vo.* 10s. 6d. net.

Gwynn (M. L.). A BIRTHDAY BOOK. *Royal 8vo.* 12s.

Hackett (John), B.D. A HISTORY OF THE ORTHODOX CHURCH OF CYPRUS. With Maps and Illustrations. *Demy 8vo.* 15s. net.

Haddon (A. C.), Sc.D., F.R.S. HEAD-HUNTERS, BLACK, WHITE, AND BROWN. With many Illustrations and a Map. *Demy 8vo.* 15s.

Hadfield (R. A.). See H. de B. Gibbins.

Hall (R. N.) and Neal (W. G.). THE ANCIENT RUINS OF RHODESIA. With numerous Illustrations. *Second Edition, revised. Demy 8vo.* 10s. 6d. net.

Hall (R. N.). THE GREAT ZIMBABWE. With numerous Illustrations. *Royal 8vo.* 21s. net.

Hamilton (F. J.), D.D., and **Brooks (E. W.).** ZACHARIAH OF MITYLENE. Translated into English. *Demy 8vo.* 12s. 6d. net. [Byzantine Texts.

Hammond (J. L.). CHARLES JAMES FOX: A Biographical Study. *Demy 8vo.* 10s. 6d.

Hannay (D.). A SHORT HISTORY OF THE ROYAL NAVY, FROM EARLY TIMES TO THE PRESENT DAY. Illustrated. *Two Volumes. Demy 8vo.* 7s. 6d. each. Vol. I. 1200-1688.

Hannay (James O.), M.A. THE SPIRIT AND ORIGIN OF CHRISTIAN MONASTICISM. *Crown 8vo.* 6s.
THE WISDOM OF THE DESERT. *Crown 8vo.* 3s. 6d. net.

Hare, (A. T.), M.A. THE CONSTRUCTION OF LARGE INDUCTION COILS. With numerous Diagrams. *Demy 8vo.* 6s.

Harrison (Clifford). READING AND READERS. *Fcap. 8vo.* 2s. 6d.

Hawthorne (Nathaniel). THE SCARLET LETTER. Edited by PERCY DEARMER. *Small Pott 8vo. Cloth,* 1s. 6d. net; *leather,* 2s. 6d. net. [Little Library.
HEALTH, WEALTH AND WISDOM. *Crown 8vo.* 1s. net.

Heath (Dudley). MINIATURES. With many Plates in Photogravure. *Wide Royal 8vo.* 25s. net. [Connoisseurs Library.

Hedin (Sven), Gold Medallist of the Royal Geographical Society. THROUGH ASIA. With 300 Illustrations from Sketches and Photographs by the Author, and Maps. *Two Volumes. Royal 8vo.* 36s. net.

Hello (Ernest). STUDIES IN SAINT-SHIP. Translated from the French by V. M. CRAWFORD. *Fcap 8vo.* 3s. 6d.

Henderson (B. W.), Fellow of Exeter College, Oxford. THE LIFE AND PRINCIPATE OF THE EMPEROR NERO. With Illustrations. *Demy 8vo.* 10s. 6d. net.

Henderson (T. F.). A LITTLE BOOK OF SCOTTISH VERSE. *Small Pott 8vo. Cloth,* 1s. 6d. net; *leather,* 2s. 6d. net. [Little Library.
ROBERT BURNS. With 12 Illustrations. *Fcap. 8vo. Cloth,* 3s. 6d.; *leather,* 4s. net. [Little Biographies.

Henley (W. E.). ENGLISH LYRICS. *Crown 8vo. Gilt top.* 3s. 6d.

Henley (W. E.) and Whibley (C.). A BOOK OF ENGLISH PROSE. *Crown 8vo. Buckram, gilt top.* 6s.

Henson (H. H.), B.D., Canon of Westminster. APOSTOLIC CHRISTIANITY: As Illustrated by the Epistles of St. Paul to the Corinthians. *Crown 8vo.* 6s.
LIGHT AND LEAVEN: HISTORICAL AND SOCIAL SERMONS. *Crown 8vo.* 6s.
DISCIPLINE AND LAW. *Fcap. 8vo.* 2s. 6d.
THE EDUCATION ACT—AND AFTER. An Appeal addressed with all possible respect to the Nonconformists. *Crown 8vo.* 1s.

Herbert (George). THE TEMPLE. Edited, with an Introduction and Notes, by E. C. S. GIBSON, D.D., Vicar of Leeds. *Small Pott 8vo. Cloth,* 2s.; *leather,* 2s. 6d. net. [Library of Devotion.

Herbert of Cherbury (Lord), THE LIFE OF. Written by himself. *Leather,* 2s. net. From the edition printed at Strawberry Hill in the year 1764.
[Miniature Library.

Hewins (W. A. S.), B.A. ENGLISH TRADE AND FINANCE IN THE SEVENTEENTH CENTURY. *Crown 8vo.* 2s. 6d. [University Extension Series.

Heywood (W.). PALIO AND PONTE: A Book of Tuscan Games. Illustrated. *Royal 8vo.* 21s. net.

Hilbert (T.). THE AIR GUN: or, How the Mastermans and Dobson Major nearly lost their Holidays. Illustrated. *Demy 16mo.* 2s. 6d. [Little Blue Books.

Hill (Clare), Registered Teacher to the City and Guilds of London Institute. MILLINERY, THEORETICAL, AND PRACTICAL. With numerous Diagrams. *Cr. 8vo.* 2s. [Textbooks of Technology.

Hill (Henry), B.A., Headmaster of the Boy's High School, Worcester, Cape Colony. A SOUTH AFRICAN ARITHMETIC. *Crown 8vo.* 3s. 6d.
This book has been specially written for use in South African schools.

Hobhouse (Emily). THE BRUNT OF THE WAR. With Map and Illustrations. *Crown 8vo.* 6s.
A Colonial Edition is also published.

Hobhouse (L. T.), Fellow of C.C.C., Oxford. THE THEORY OF KNOWLEDGE. *Demy 8vo.* 21s.

Hobson (J. A.), M.A. PROBLEMS OF POVERTY: An Inquiry into the Industrial Condition of the Poor. *Fourth Edition. Crown 8vo.* 2s. 6d.
[Social Questions Series.
THE PROBLEM OF THE UNEMPLOYED. *Crown 8vo.* 2s. 6d.
[Social Questions Series.
INTERNATIONAL TRADE: A Study of Economic Principles. *Crown 8vo.* 2s. 6d. net.

Hodgkin (T.), D.C.L. GEORGE FOX, THE QUAKER. With Portrait. *Crown 8vo.* 3s. 6d. [Leaders of Religion.

Hogg (Thomas Jefferson). SHELLEY AT OXFORD. With an Introduction by R. A. STREATFEILD. *Fcap. 8vo.* 2s. net.

Holden-Stone (G. de). THE AUTOMOBILE INDUSTRY. *Fcap. 8vo.* 2s. 6d. net. [Books on Business.

Holdich (Sir T. H.), K.C.I.E. THE INDIAN BORDERLAND: being a Personal Record of Twenty Years. Illustrated. *Demy 8vo.* 15s. net.

Holdsworth (W. S.), M.A. A HISTORY OF ENGLISH LAW. *In Two Volumes. Vol. I. Demy 8vo.* 10s. 6d. net.

Holyoake (G. J.). THE CO-OPERATIVE MOVEMENT TO-DAY. *Third Edition. Crown 8vo.* 2s. 6d.
[Social Questions Series.

Hoppner, A LITTLE GALLERY OF. Twenty examples in photogravure of his finest work. *Demy 16mo.* 2s. 6d. net.
[Little Galleries.

Horace: THE ODES AND EPODES. Translated by A. D. GODLEY, M.A., Fellow of Magdalen College, Oxford. *Crown 8vo.* 2s. [Classical Translations.

Horsburgh (E. L. S.), M.A. WATERLOO: A Narrative and Criticism. With Plans. *Second Edition. Crown 8vo.* 5s.
SAVONAROLA. With Portraits and Illustrations. *Second Edition. Fcap. 8vo. Cloth*, 3s. 6d. ; *leather*, 4s. net.
[Little Biographies.

Horton (R. F.), D.D. JOHN HOWE. With Portrait. *Crown 8vo.* 3s. 6d.
[Leaders of Religion.

Hosie (Alexander). MANCHURIA. With Illustrations and a Map. *Second Edition. Demy 8vo.* 10s. 6d. net.

How (F. D.). SIX GREAT SCHOOLMASTERS. With Portraits. *Demy 8vo.* 7s. 6d.

Howell (G.). TRADE UNIONISM—NEW AND OLD. *Third Edition. Crown 8vo.* 2s. 6d. [Social Questions Series.

Hudson (Robert). MEMORIALS OF A WARWICKSHIRE VILLAGE. With many Illustrations. *Demy 8vo.* ~~10s. 6d.~~ 15s. *net.*

Hughes (C. E.). THE PRAISE OF SHAKESPEARE. An English Anthology. With a Preface by SIDNEY LEE. *Demy 8vo.* 3s. 6d. net.

Hughes (Thomas). TOM BROWN'S SCHOOLDAYS. With an Introduction and Notes by VERNON RENDALL. *Leather. Royal 32mo.* 2s. 6d. net.

Hutchinson (Horace G.). THE NEW FOREST. Described by. Illustrated in colour with 50 Pictures by WALTER TYNDALE and 4 by Miss LUCY KEMP WELCH. *Large Demy 8vo.* 21s. net.

Hutton (A. W.), M.A. CARDINAL MANNING. With Portrait. *Crown 8vo.* 3s. 6d.
[Leaders of Religion.

Hutton (R. H.). CARDINAL NEWMAN. With Portrait. *Crown 8vo.* 3s. 6d.
[Leaders of Religion.

Hutton (W. H.), M.A. THE LIFE OF SIR THOMAS MORE. With Portraits. *Second Edition. Crown 8vo.* 5s.
WILLIAM LAUD. With Portrait. *Second Edition. Crown 8vo.* 3s. 6d.
[Leaders of Religion.

Hyett (F. A.). A SHORT HISTORY OF FLORENCE. *Demy 8vo.* 7s. 6d. net.
HYPNEROTOMACHIA POLIPHILI UBI HUMANA OMNIA NON NISI SOMNIUM ESSE DOCET ATQUE OBITER PLURIMA SCITU SANE QUAM DIGNA COMMEMORAT. An edition limited to 350 copies on handmade paper. *Folio. Three Guineas net.*

Ibsen (Henrik). BRAND. A Drama. Translated by WILLIAM WILSON. *Third Edition. Crown 8vo.* 3s. 6d.

Inge (W. R.), M.A., Fellow and Tutor of Hertford College, Oxford. CHRISTIAN MYSTICISM. The Bampton Lectures for 1899. *Demy 8vo.* 12s. 6d. net.
LIGHT, LIFE, AND LOVE: A Selection from the German Mystics. With an Introduction and Notes. *Small Pott 8vo. Cloth* 2s. ; *leather*, 2s. 6d. net.
[Library of Devotion.

Innes (A. D.), M.A. A HISTORY OF THE BRITISH IN INDIA. With Maps and Plans. *Crown 8vo.* 7s. 6d.

Jackson (S.), M.A. A PRIMER OF BUSI-NESS. *Third Edition. Crown 8vo.* 1s. 6d. [Commercial Series.

Jackson (F. Hamilton). SICILY. With many Illustrations by the Author. *Small Pott 8vo. Cloth,* 3s.; *Leather,* 3s. 6d. *net.* [Little Guides.

Jacob (F.), M.A. JUNIOR FRENCH EXAMINATION PAPERS. *Fcap. 8vo.* 1s. [Junior Examination Series.

Jeans (J. Stephen). TRUSTS, POOLS, AND CORNERS. *Crown 8vo.* 2s. 6d. [Social Questions Series.

Jeffreys (D. Gwyn). DOLLY'S THE-ATRICALS. Described and Illustrated with 24 Coloured Pictures. *Pott 4to.* 2s. 6d.

Jenks (E.), M.A., Reader of Law in the University of Oxford. ENGLISH LOCAL GOVERNMENT. *Crown 8vo.* 2s. 6d. [University Extension Series.

Jessopp (Augustus), D.D. JOHN DONNE. With Portrait. *Crown 8vo.* 3s. 6d. [Leaders of Religion.

Jevons (F. B.), M.A., Litt.D., Principal of Hatfield Hall, Durham. EVOLUTION. *Crown 8vo.* 3s. 6d. [Churchman's Library. AN INTRODUCTION TO THE HISTORY OF RELIGION. *Second Edition. Demy 8vo.* 10s. 6d. [Handbooks of Theology.

Johnston (Sir H. H.), K.C.B. BRITISH CENTRAL AFRICA. With nearly 200 Illustrations and Six Maps. *Second Edition. Crown 4to.* 18s. *net.*

Jonés (H.). A GUIDE TO PROFESSIONS AND BUSINESS. *Crown 8vo.* 1s. 6d. [Commercial Series.

Jones (L. A. Atherley), K.C., M.P., and Bellot (Hugh H. L.). THE MINERS' GUIDE TO THE COAL MINES' REGULATION ACTS. *Crown 8vo.* 2s. 6d. *net.* [Nearly Ready.

Julian (Lady) of Norwich. REVELA-TIONS OF DIVINE LOVE. Edited by GRACE WARRACK. *Crown 8vo.* 3s. 6d.

Juvenal, THE SATIRES OF. Translated by S. G. OWEN. *Crown 8vo.* 2s. 6d. [Classical Translations.

Kaufmann (M.). SOCIALISM AND MODERN THOUGHT. *Crown 8vo.* 2s. 6d. [Social Questions Series.

Keating (J. F.), D.D. THE AGAPE AND THE EUCHARIST. *Crown 8vo.* 3s. 6d.

Keats (John), THE POEMS OF. With an Introduction by L. BINYON, and Notes by J. MASEFIELD. *Small Pott 8vo. Cloth,* 1s. 6d. *net; leather,* 2s. 6d. *net.* [Little Library.

Keats. THE POEMS OF. Edited with Introduction and Notes by E. de Selin-court, M.A. *Demy 8vo.* 7s. 6d. *net.*

Keble (John). THE CHRISTIAN YEAR. With an Introduction and Notes by W. LOCK, D.D., Warden of Keble College. Illustrated by R. ANNING BELL. *Second Edition. Fcap. 8vo.* 3s. 6d; *padded morocco,* 5s.

THE CHRISTIAN YEAR. With Intro-duction and Notes by WALTER LOCK, D.D., Warden of Keble College. *Second Edition. Small Pott 8vo. Cloth,* 2s.; *leather,* 2s. 6d. *net.* [Library of Devotion.

LYRA INNOCENTIUM. Edited, with Introduction and Notes, by WALTER LOCK, D.D., Warden of Keble College, Oxford. *Small Pott 8vo. Cloth,* 2s.; *leather,* 2s. 6d. *net.* [Library of Devotion.

Kempis (Thomas À). THE IMITATION OF CHRIST. With an Introduction by DEAN FARRAR. Illustrated by C. M. GERE *Second Edition. Fcap. 8vo.* 3s. 6d.; *padded morocco,* 5s.

THE IMITATION OF CHRIST. A Re-vised Translation, with an Introduction by C. BIGG, D.D., late Student of Christ Church. *Third Edition. Small Pott 8vo. Cloth,* 2s.; *leather,* 2s. 6d. *net.* [Library of Devotion. A practically new translation of this book which the reader has, almost for the first time, exactly in the shape in which it left the hands of the author.

THE SAME EDITION IN LARGE TYPE. *Crown 8vo.* 3s. 6d.

Kennedy (James Houghton), D.D., Assist-ant Lecturer in Divinity in the University of Dublin. ST. PAUL'S SECOND AND THIRD EPISTLES TO THE CORINTHIANS. With Introduction, Dissertations and Notes. *Crown 8vo.* 6s.

Kestell (J. D.). THROUGH SHOT AND FLAME : Being the Adventures and Ex-periences of J. D. KESTELL, Chaplain to General Christian de Wet. *Crown 8vo.* 6s.

Kimmins (C. W.), M.A. THE CHEM-ISTRY OF LIFE AND HEALTH. Illustrated. *Crown 8vo.* 2s. 6d. [University Extension Series.

Kinglake (A. W.). EOTHEN. With an Introduction and Notes. *Small Pott 8vo. Cloth,* 1s. 6d. *net; leather,* 2s. 6d. *net.* [Little Library.

Kipling (Rudyard). BARRACK-ROOM BALLADS. 73rd *Thousand. Cr. 8vo. Twentieth Edition.* 6s. A Colonial Edition is also published.

THE SEVEN SEAS. 62nd *Thousand Ninth Edition. Crown 8vo, gilt top,* 6s. A Colonial Edition is also published.

THE FIVE NATIONS. 41st *Thousand. Second Edition. Crown 8vo.* 6s. A Colonial Edition is also published.

DEPARTMENTAL DITTIES. *Sixteenth Edition. Crown 8vo. Buckram.* 6s. A Colonial Edition is also published.

Knowling (R. J.), M.A., Professor of New Testament Exegesis at King's College, London. THE EPISTLE OF S. JAMES. With Introduction and Notes. *Demy 8vo.* 6s. [Westminster Commentaries.

Lamb (Charles and Mary), THE WORKS OF. Edited by E. V. LUCAS. With Numerous Illustrations. *In Seven Volumes. Demy 8vo.* 7s. 6d. each.

THE ESSAYS OF ELIA. With over 100 Illustrations by A. GARTH JONES, and an Introduction by E. V. LUCAS. *Demy 8vo.* 10s. 6d.

ELIA, AND THE LAST ESSAYS OF ELIA. Edited by E. V. LUCAS. *Small Pott 8vo. Cloth,* 1s. 6d. *net; leather,* 2s. 6d. *net.* [Little Library.

THE KING AND QUEEN OF HEARTS: An 1805 Book for Children. Illustrated by WILLIAM MULREADY. A new edition, in facsimile, edited by E. V. LUCAS. 1s. 6d.

Lambert (F. A. H.). SURREY. Illustrated by E. H. NEW. *Small Pott 8vo, cloth,* 3s.; *leather,* 3s. 6d. *net.* [Little Guides.

Lambros (Professor). ECTHESIS CHRONICA. Edited by. *Demy 8vo.* 7s. 6d. *net.* [Byzantine Texts.

Lane-Poole (Stanley). A HISTORY OF EGYPT IN THE MIDDLE AGES. Fully Illustrated. *Crown 8vo.* 6s.

Langbridge (F.) M.A. BALLADS OF THE BRAVE: Poems of Chivalry, Enterprise, Courage, and Constancy. *Second Edition. Crown 8vo.* 2s. 6d.

Law (William). A SERIOUS CALL TO A DEVOUT AND HOLY LIFE. Edited, with an Introduction, by C. BIGG, D.D., late Student of Christ Church. *Small Pott 8vo, cloth,* 2s.; *leather,* 2s. 6d. *net.* [Library of Devotion. This is a reprint, word for word and line for line, of the *Editio Princeps.*

Leach (Henry). THE DUKE OF DEVONSHIRE. A Biography. With 12 Illustrations. *Demy 8vo.* 12s. 6d. *net.* A Colonial Edition is also published.

Lee (Captain Melville). A HISTORY OF POLICE IN ENGLAND. *Crown 8vo.* 7s. 6d.

Leigh (Percival). THE COMIC ENGLISH GRAMMAR. Embellished with upwards of 50 characteristic Illustrations by JOHN LEECH. *Post 16mo.* 2s. 6d. *net.*

Lewes (V.B.), M.A. AIR AND WATER. Illustrated. *Crown 8vo.* 2s. 6d. [University Extension Series.

Lisle (Miss F. de). BURNE-JONES. With 30 Illustrations. *Demy 16mo.* 2s. 6d. *net.* [Little Books on Art.

Littlehales (H.). See C. Wordsworth.

Lock (Walter), D.D., Warden of Keble College. ST. PAUL, THE MASTER-BUILDER. *Crown 8vo.* 3s. 6d.

JOHN KEBLE. With Portrait. *Crown 8vo.* 3s. 6d. [Leaders of Religion.

Locker (F.). LONDON LYRICS. Edited by A. D. GODLEY, M.A. *Small Pott 8vo, cloth,* 1s. 6d. *net; leather,* 2s. 6d. *net.* [Little Library.

Longfellow, SELECTIONS FROM. Edited by LILIAN M. FAITHFULL. *Small Pott 8vo, cloth,* 1s. 6d. *net; leather,* 2s. 6d. *net.* [Little Library.

Lorimer (George Horace). LETTERS FROM A SELF-MADE MERCHANT TO HIS SON. *Eleventh Edition. Crown 8vo.* 6s. A Colonial Edition is also published.

Lover (Samuel). HANDY ANDY. With 24 Illustrations by the Author. *Fcap. 8vo.* 3s. 6d. *net.* [Illustrated Pocket Library.

E. V. L. and **C. L. G.** ENGLAND DAY BY DAY : Or, The Englishman's Handbook to Efficiency. Illustrated by GEORGE MORROW. *Fourth Edition. Fcap. 4to.* 1s. *net.* A burlesque Year-Book and Almanac.

Lucian. SIX DIALOGUES. (Nigrinus, Icaro-Menippus, The Cock, The Ship, The Parasite, The Lover of Falsehood). Translated by S. T. Irwin, M.A., Assistant Master at Clifton; late Scholar of Exeter College, Oxford. *Crown 8vo.* 3s. 6d. [Classical Translations.

Lyde (L. W.), M.A. A COMMERCIAL GEOGRAPHY OF THE BRITISH EMPIRE. *Third Edition. Crown 8vo.* 2s. [Commercial Series.

Lydon (Noel S.). A JUNIOR GEOMETRY. With numerous diagrams. *Crown 8vo.* 2s. [Junior School Books.

Lyttelton (Hon. Mrs. A.). WOMEN AND THEIR WORK. *Crown 8vo.* 2s. 6d.

M. M. HOW TO DRESS AND WHAT TO WEAR. *Crown 8vo,* 1s. *net.*

Macaulay (Lord). CRITICAL AND HISTORICAL ESSAYS. Edited by F. C. MONTAGUE, M.A. *Three Volumes. Cr. 8vo.* 18s. The only edition of this book completely annotated.

M'Allen (J. E. B.), M.A. THE PRINCIPLES OF BOOKKEEPING BY DOUBLE ENTRY. *Crown 8vo.* 2s. [Commercial Series.

MacCulloch (J. A.). COMPARATIVE THEOLOGY. *Crown 8vo.* 6s. [Churchman's Library.

MacCunn (F.). JOHN KNOX. With Portrait. *Crown 8vo.* 3s. 6d. [Leaders of Religion.

McDermott, (E. R.), Editor of the *Railway News,* City Editor of the *Daily News.* RAILWAYS. *Crown 8vo.* 2s. 6d. *net.* [Books on Business

M'Dowall (A. S.). CHATHAM. With 12 Illustrations. *Fcap. 8vo. Cloth,* 3s. 6d.; *leather,* 4s. net. [Little Biographies.

Mackay (A. M.). THE CHURCHMAN'S INTRODUCTION TO THE OLD TESTAMENT. *Crown 8vo.* 3s. 6d. [Churchman's Library.

Magnus (Laurie), M.A. A PRIMER OF WORDSWORTH. *Crown 8vo.* 2s. 6d.

Mahaffy (J. P.), Litt.D. A HISTORY OF THE EGYPT OF THE PTOLEMIES. Fully Illustrated. *Crown 8vo.* 6s.

Maitland (F.W.), LL.D., Downing Professor of the Laws of England in the University of Cambridge. CANON LAW IN ENGLAND. *Royal 8vo.* 7s. 6d.

Malden (H. E.), M.A. ENGLISH RECORDS. A Companion to the History of England. *Crown 8vo.* 3s. 6d. THE ENGLISH CITIZEN: HIS RIGHTS AND DUTIES. *Crown 8vo.* 1s. 6d.

Marchant (E.C.), M.A., Fellow of Peterhouse, Cambridge. A GREEK ANTHOLOGY. *Second Edition. Crown 8vo.* 3s. 6d.

Marchant (E. C.), M.A., and **Cook (A. M.), M.A.** PASSAGES FOR UNSEEN TRANSLATION. *Second Edition. Crown 8vo.* 3s. 6d.

Marr (J. E.), F.R.S., Fellow of St John's College, Cambridge. THE SCIENTIFIC STUDY OF SCENERY. *Second Edition.* Illustrated. *Crown 8vo.* 6s. AGRICULTURAL GEOLOGY. With numerous Illustrations. *Crown 8vo.* 6s.

Marvell (Andrew). THE POEMS OF. Edited by EDWARD WRIGHT. *Small Pott 8vo, cloth,* 1s. 6d. net; *leather,* 2s. 6d. net. [Little Library.

Maskell (A.) IVORIES. With many plates in Collotype and Photogravure. *Wide Royal 8vo.* 25s. net. [Connoisseurs Library.

Mason (A. J.), D.D. THOMAS CRANMER. With Portrait. *Crown 8vo.* 3s. 6d. [Leaders of Religion.

Massee (George). THE EVOLUTION OF PLANT LIFE: Lower Forms. With Illustrations. *Crown 8vo.* 2s. 6d. [University Extension Series.

Masterman (C. F. G.), M.A. TENNYSON AS A RELIGIOUS TEACHER. *Crown 8vo.* 6s.

May (Phil) THE PHIL MAY ALBUM. *Second Edition.* 4to. 1s. net.

Mellows (Emma S.). A SHORT STORY OF ENGLISH LITERATURE. *Crown 8vo.* 3s. 6d.

Michell (E. B.) THE ART AND PRACTICE OF HAWKING. With 3 Photogravures by G. E. LODGE, and other Illustrations. *Demy 8vo.* 10s. 6d.

Millais (J.G.) THE LIFE AND LETTERS OF SIR JOHN EVERETT MILLAIS, President of the Royal Academy. With 319 Illustrations, of which 9 are in Photogravure. 2 vols. *Royal 8vo.* 20s. net.

Millais. A LITTLE GALLERY OF. Twenty examples in Photogravure of his finest work. *Demy 16mo.* 2s. 6d. net. [Little Galleries.

Millis (C. T.), M.I.M.E., Principal of the Borough Polytechnic College. TECHNICAL ARITHMETIC AND GEOMETRY. With Diagrams. *Crown 8vo.* 3s. 6d. [Textbooks of Technology.

Milne (J. G.), M.A. A HISTORY OF ROMAN EGYPT. Fully Illustrated. *Crown 8vo* 6s.

Milton, John, THE POEMS OF, BOTH ENGLISH AND LATIN, Compos'd at several times. Printed by his true Copies. The Songs were set in Musick by Mr. HENRY LAWES, Gentleman of the Kings Chappel, and one of His Majesties Private Musick.

Printed and publish'd according to Order. Printed by RUTH RAWORTH for HUMPHREY MOSELEY, and are to be sold at the signe of the Princes Armes in Pauls Churchyard, 1645.

THE MINOR POEMS OF JOHN MILTON. Edited by H. C. BEECHING, M.A., Canon of Westminster. *Small Pott 8vo, cloth,* 1s. 6d. net; *leather,* 2s. 6d. net. [Little Library.

Minchin (H. C.), M.A. A LITTLE GALLERY OF ENGLISH POETS. *Demy 16mo.* 2s. 6d. net. [Little Galleries.

Mitchell (P.Chalmers), M.A. OUTLINES OF BIOLOGY. Illustrated. *Second Edition. Crown 8vo.* 6s.

A text-book designed to cover the Schedule issued by the Royal College of Physicians and Surgeons.

Moil (A.). MINING AND MINING INVESTMENTS. *Crown 8vo.* 2s. 6d. net. [Books on Business.

Moir (D. M.). MANSIE WAUCH. Edited by T. F. HENDERSON. *Small Pott 8vo. Cloth,* 1s. 6d. net; *leather,* 2s. 6d. net. [Little Library.

Moore (H. E.). BACK TO THE LAND: An Inquiry into the cure for Rural Depopulation. *Crown 8vo.* 2s. 6d. [Social Questions Series.

Morfill (W. R.), Oriel College, Oxford. A HISTORY OF RUSSIA FROM PETER THE GREAT TO ALEXANDER II. With Maps and Plans. *Crown 8vo.* 7s. 6d.

Morich (R. J.), late of Clifton College. GERMAN EXAMINATION PAPERS IN MISCELLANEOUS GRAMMAR AND IDIOMS. *Sixth Edition. Crown 8vo.* 2s. 6d. [School Examination Series.

A KEY, issued to Tutors and Private Students only, to be had on application to the Publishers. *Second Edition. Crown 8vo.* 6s. net.

Morris (J. E.). THE NORTH RIDING OF YORKSHIRE. Illustrated by R. J. S. BERTRAM, *Small Pott 8vo, cloth,* 3s. ; *leather,* 3s. 6d. net.
[Little Guides.

Morton (Miss Anderson). See Miss Brodrick.

Moule (H. C. G.), D.D., Lord Bishop of Durham. CHARLES SIMEON. With Portrait. *Crown 8vo.* 3s. 6d.
[Leaders of Religion.

Muir (M. M. Pattison), M.A. THE CHEMISTRY OF FIRE. The Elementary Principles of Chemistry. Illustrated. *Crown 8vo.* 2s. 6d.
[University Extension Series.

Mundella (V. A.), M.A. See J. T. Dunn.

Naval Officer (A). THE ADVENTURES OF A POST CAPTAIN. With 24 coloured plates by Mr. WILLIAMS. *Fcap. 8vo.* 3s. 6d. net.
[Illustrated Pocket Library.

Neal (W. G.). See R. N. Hall.

Newman (J. H.) and others. LYRA APOSTOLICA. With an Introduction by CANON SCOTT HOLLAND, and Notes by CANON BEECHING, M.A. *Small Pott 8vo.* Cloth, 2s. ; leather, 2s. 6d. net.
[Library of Devotion.

Nichols (J. B. B.). A LITTLE BOOK OF ENGLISH SONNETS. *Small Pott 8vo.* Cloth, 1s. 6d. net ; leather, 2s. 6d. net.
[Little Library.

Nicklin (T.), M. A. EXAMINATION PAPERS IN THUCYDIDES. *Crown 8vo.* 2s.

Nimrod. THE LIFE AND DEATH OF JOHN MYTTON, ESQ. With 18 Coloured Plates by HENRY ALKEN and T. J. RAWLINS. *Third Edition. Fcap. 8vo.* 3s. 6d. net.
Also a limited edition on large Japanese paper. 30s. net.
[Illustrated Pocket Library.
THE LIFE OF A SPORTSMAN. With 35 Coloured Plates by HENRY ALKEN. *Fcap. 8vo.* 4s. 6d. net.
Also a limited edition on large Japanese paper. 30s. net.
[Illustrated Pocket Library.

Norway (A. H.), Author of 'Highways and Byways in Devon and Cornwall.' NAPLES : PAST AND PRESENT. With many Illustrations. *Crown 8vo.* 6s.

Novalis. THE DISCIPLES AT SAÏS AND OTHER FRAGMENTS. Edited by Miss UNA BIRCH. *Fcap. 8vo.* 3s. 6d.

Oliphant (Mrs.). THOMAS CHALMERS. With Portrait. *Crown 8vo.* 3s. 6d.
[Leaders of Religion.

Oman (C. W.), M.A., Fellow of All Souls', Oxford. A HISTORY OF THE ART OF WAR. Vol. II.: The Middle Ages, from the Fourth to the Fourteenth Century. Illustrated. *Demy 8vo.* 21s.

Ottley (R. L.), D.D., Professor of Pastoral Theology at Oxford and Canon of Christ Church. THE DOCTRINE OF THE INCARNATION. *Second and Cheaper Edition. Demy 8vo.* 12s. 6d.
[Handbooks of Theology.
LANCELOT ANDREWES. With Portrait. *Crown 8vo.* 3s. 6d.
[Leaders of Religion.

Overton (J. H.), M.A. JOHN WESLEY. With Portrait. *Crown 8vo.* 3s. 6d.
[Leaders of Religion.

Owen (Douglas), Barrister-at-Law, Secretary to the Alliance Marine and General Assurance Company. PORTS AND DOCKS. *Crown 8vo.* 2s. 6d. net.
[Books on Business.

Oxford (M. N.), of Guy's Hospital. A HANDBOOK OF NURSING. *Second Edition. Crown 8vo.* 3s. 6d.

Pakes (W. C. C.). THE SCIENCE OF HYGIENE. With numerous Illustrations. *Demy 8vo.* 15s.

Parkinson (John). PARADISI IN SOLE PARADISUS TERRESTRIS, OR A GARDEN OF ALL SORTS OF PLEASANT FLOWERS. *Folio.* £2, 2s. net.
Also an Edition of 20 copies on Japanese vellum. *Ten Guineas net.*

Parmenter (John). HELIO-TROPES, OR NEW POSIES FOR SUNDIALS, 1625. Edited by PERCIVAL LANDON. *Quarto.* 3s. 6d. net.

Parmentier (Prof. Léon) and Bidez (M.). EVAGRIUS. *Demy 8vo.* 10s. 6d. net.
[Byzantine Texts.

Pascal, THE THOUGHTS OF. With Introduction and Notes by C. S. JERRAM. *Small Pott 8vo.* 2s. ; leather, 2s. 6d. net.
[Library of Devotion.

Paston (George). AUTHORS AND ARTISTS OF ENGLISH COLOURED BOOKS. Illustrated. *Fcap. 8vo.* 2s. 6d. net.
ROMNEY. With many Illustrations. *Demy 16mo.* 2s. 6d. net. [Little Books on Art.

Patterson (A. H.). NOTES OF AN EAST COAST NATURALIST. Illustrated in Colour by F. SOUTHGATE. *Cr. 8vo.* 6s.

Peacock (Miss). MILLET. With 30 Illustrations. *Demy 16mo.* 2s. 6d. net.

Pearce (E. H.), M.A. THE ANNALS OF CHRIST'S HOSPITAL. With many Illustrations. *Demy 8vo.* 7s. 6d.

Peary (R. E.), Gold Medallist of the Royal Geographical Society. NORTHWARD OVER THE GREAT ICE. With over 800 Illustrations. 2 vols. *Royal 8vo.* 32s. net.

Peel (Sidney), late Fellow of Trinity College, Oxford, and Secretary to the Royal Commission on the Licensing Laws. PRACTICAL LICENSING REFORM. *Second Edition. Crown 8vo.* 1s. 6d.

Peters (J. P.), D.D. THE OLD TESTAMENT AND THE NEW SCHOLARSHIP. *Cr. 8vo.* 6s. [Churchman's Library.

Petrie (W. M. Flinders), D.C.L., LL.D., Professor of Egyptology at University College. A HISTORY OF EGYPT, FROM THE EARLIEST TIMES TO THE PRESENT DAY. Fully Illustrated. *In six volumes. Crown 8vo.* 6s. each.
VOL. I. PREHISTORIC TIMES TO XVITH DYNASTY. *Fifth Edition.*
VOL. II. THE XVIITH AND XVIIITH DYNASTIES. *Fourth Edition.*
VOL. IV. THE EGYPT OF THE PTOLEMIES. J. P. MAHAFFY, Litt.D.
VOL. V. ROMAN EGYPT. J. G. MILNE, M.A.
VOL. VI. EGYPT IN THE MIDDLE AGES. STANLEY LANE-POOLE, M.A.
RELIGION AND CONSCIENCE IN ANCIENT EGYPT. Fully Illustrated. *Crown 8vo.* 2s. 6d.
SYRIA AND EGYPT, FROM THE TELL EL AMARNA TABLETS. *Crown 8vo.* 2s. 6d.
EGYPTIAN TALES. Illustrated by TRISTRAM ELLIS. *In Two Volumes. Crown 8vo.* 3s. 6d. each.
EGYPTIAN DECORATIVE ART. With 120 Illustrations. *Crown 8vo.* 3s. 6d.

Phillips (W. A.), CANNING. With 12 Illustrations. *Fcap. 8vo. Cloth,* 3s. 6d.; *leather,* 4s. net. [Little Biographies.

Phillpotts (Eden). MY DEVON YEAR. With 38 Illustrations by J. LEY PETHYBRIDGE. *Large Crown 8vo.* 6s.

Pienaar (Philip). WITH STEYN AND DE WET. *Second Edition. Crown 8vo.* 3s. 6d.

Plautus. THE CAPTIVI. Edited, with an Introduction, Textual Notes, and a Commentary, by W. M. LINDSAY, Fellow of Jesus College, Oxford. *Demy 8vo.* 10s. 6d. net.

Plowden-Wardlaw (J.T.), B.A., King's Coll. Cam. EXAMINATION PAPERS IN ENGLISH HISTORY. *Crown 8vo.* 2s. 6d. [School Examination Series.

Pocock (Roger). A FRONTIERSMAN. *Third Edition. Crown 8vo.* 6s. A Colonial Edition is also published.

Podmore (Frank). MODERN SPIRITUALISM. *Two Volumes. Demy 8vo.* 21s. net. A History and a Criticism.

Poer (J. Patrick La). A MODERN LEGIONARY. *Crown 8vo.* 6s. A Colonial Edition is also published.

Pollard (Alice) and **Birnstingl (Ethel).** COROT. With 30 Illustrations. *Demy 16mo.* [Little Books on Art.

Pollard (A. W.). OLD PICTURE BOOKS. With many Illustrations. *Demy 8vo.* 7s. 6d. net.

Pollard (Eliza F.). GREUZE AND BOUCHER. *Demy 16mo.* 2s. 6d. net. [Little Books on Art.

Pollock (David), M.I.N.A., Author of *Modern Shipbuilding and the Men engaged in it,* etc., etc. THE SHIPBUILDING INDUSTRY. *Crown 8vo.* 2s. 6d. net. [Books on Business.

Potter (M. C.), M.A., F.L.S. A TEXTBOOK OF AGRICULTURAL BOTANY. Illustrated. *Second Edition. Crown 8vo.* 4s. 6d. [University Extension Series.

Potter Boy (An Old). WHEN I WAS A CHILD. *Crown 8vo.* 6s.

Pradeau (G.). A KEY TO THE TIME ALLUSIONS IN THE DIVINE COMEDY. With a Dial. *Small quarto.* 3s. 6d.

Prance (G.). See R. Wyon.

Prescott (O. L.). ABOUT MUSIC, AND WHAT IT IS MADE OF. *Crown 8vo.* 3s. 6d. net.

Price (L. L.), M.A., Fellow of Oriel College, Oxon. A HISTORY OF ENGLISH POLITICAL ECONOMY. *Fourth Edition. Crown 8vo.* 2s. 6d. [University Extension Series.

Primrose (Deborah). A MODERN BŒOTIA. *Cr. 8vo.* 6s. [Nearly Ready.

PROTECTION AND INDUSTRY. By various Writers. *Crown 8vo.* 1s. 6d. net.

Pugin and Rowlandson. THE MICROCOSM OF LONDON, OR LONDON IN MINIATURE. With 104 Illustrations in colour. *In Three Volumes. Small 4to.*

"Q." THE GOLDEN POMP. A Procession of English Lyrics. Arranged by A. T. QUILLER COUCH. *Crown 8vo. Buckram.* 6s.

QUEVEDO VILLEGAS, THE VISIONS OF DOM FRANCISCO DE, Knight of the Order of St. James. Made English by R. L. From the edition printed for H. Herringman, 1668. *Leather,* 2s. net. [Miniature Library.

G. R. and E. S. THE WOODHOUSE CORRESPONDENCE. *Crown 8vo.* 6s.

Rackham (R. B.), M.A. THE ACTS OF THE APOSTLES. With an Introduction and Notes. *Demy 8vo. New and Cheaper Ed.* 10s. 6d. [Westminster Commentaries.

Randolph (B. W.), D.D., Principal of the Theological College, Ely. THE PSALMS OF DAVID. With an Introduction and Notes. *Small Pott 8vo. Cloth,* 2s.; *leather,* 2s. 6d. net. [Library of Devotion.

Rannie (D. W.), M.A. A STUDENT'S HISTORY OF SCOTLAND. *Cr. 8vo.* 3s. 6d.

A 3

Rashdall (Hastings), M.A., Fellow and Tutor of New College, Oxford. DOCTRINE AND DEVELOPMENT. *Crown 8vo.* 6s.

Rawstorne (Lawrence, Esq.). GAMONIA: or, The Art of Preserving Game; and an Improved Method of making plantations and covers, explained and illustrated by. With 15 Coloured Drawings by T. RAWLINS. *Fcap. 8vo.* 3s. 6d. net.
[Illustrated Pocket Library.

A Real Paddy. REAL LIFE IN IRELAND, or The Day and Night Scenes of Brian Boru, Esq., and his Elegant Friend, Sir Shawn O'Dogherty. With 19 Coloured Plates by HEATH, MARKS, etc. *Fcap. 8vo.* 3s. 6d. net. [Illustrated Pocket Library.

Reason (W.), M.A. UNIVERSITY AND SOCIAL SETTLEMENTS. *Crown 8vo.* 2s. 6d. [Social Questions Series.

Redfern (W. B.), Author of 'Ancient Wood and Iron Work in Cambridge,' etc. ROYAL AND HISTORIC GLOVES AND ANCIENT SHOES. Profusely Illustrated in colour and half-tone. *Quarto,* £2, 2s. net.

Reynolds, A LITTLE GALLERY OF. Twenty examples in photogravure of his finest work. *Demy 16mo.* 2s. 6d. net.
[Little Galleries.

Roberts (M. E.). See C. C. Channer.

Robertson, (A.), D.D., Lord Bishop of Exeter. REGNUM DEI. The Bampton Lectures of 1901. *Demy 8vo.* 12s. 6d. net.

Robertson (C. Grant), M.A., Fellow of All Souls' College, Oxford, Examiner in the Honour School of Modern History, Oxford, 1901-1904. SELECT STATUTES, CASES, AND CONSTITUTIONAL DOCUMENTS, 1660-1832. *Demy 8vo.* 10s. 6d. net.

Robertson (Sir G. S.) K.C.S.I. CHITRAL: The Story of a Minor Siege. With numerus Illustrations, Map and Plans. *Fourth Edition. Crown 8vo.* 6s.

Robinson (A. W.), M.A. THE EPISTLE TO THE GALATIANS. With an Introduction and Notes. *Fcap. 8vo.* 1s. 6d. net.
[Churchman's Bible.

Robinson (Cecilia). THE MINISTRY OF DEACONESSES. With an Introduction by the late Archbishop of Canterbury. *Crown 8vo.* 3s. 6d.

Rochefoucauld (La), THE MAXIMS OF. Translated by DEAN STANHOPE. Edited by G. H. POWELL. *Small Pott 8vo, cloth,* 1s. 6d. net; *leather,* 2s. 6d. net. [Little Library.

Rodwell (G.), B.A. NEW TESTAMENT GREEK. A Course for Beginners. With a Preface by WALTER LOCK, D.D., Warden of Keble College. *Fcap. 8vo.* 3s. 6d.

Roe (Fred). ANCIENT COFFERS AND CUPBOARDS: Their History and Description. With many Illustrations. *Quarto.* £3, 3s. net.

Rogers (A. G. L.), M.A., Editor of the last volume of *The History of Agriculture and Prices in England.* THE AGRICULTURAL INDUSTRY. *Crown 8vo.* 2s. 6d. net. [Books on Business.

Romney. A LITTLE GALLERY OF. Twenty examples in Photogravure of his nest work. *Demy 16mo.* 2s. 6d. net.
[Little Galleries.

Roscoe (E.S.). ROBERT HARLEY, EARL OF OXFORD. Illustrated. *Demy 8vo.* 7s. 6d.
This is the only life of Harley in existence.

BUCKINGHAMSHIRE. Illustrated by F. D. BEDFORD. *Small Pott 8vo, cloth* 3s.; *leather,* 3s. 6d. [Little Guides.

Rose (Edward). THE ROSE READER. With numerous Illustrations. *Crown 8vo.* 2s. 6d. Also in 4 Parts. Parts I. and II. 6d. each; Part III. 8d.; Part IV. 10d.

Rubie (A. E.), M.A., Head Master of College, Eltham. THE GOSPEL ACCORDING TO ST. MARK. With three Maps. *Crown 8vo.* 1s. 6d.
[Junior School Books.

THE ACTS OF THE APOSTLES. *Crown 8vo.* 2s. [Junior School Books.

THE FIRST BOOK OF KINGS. With Notes. *Crown 8vo.* 1s. 6d.
[Junior School Books.

Russell (W. Clark). THE LIFE OF ADMIRAL LORD COLLINGWOOD. With Illustrations by F. BRANGWYN. *Fourth Edition. Crown 8vo.* 6s.
A Colonial Edition is also published.

St. Anselm, THE DEVOTIONS OF. Edited by C. C. J. WEBB, M.A. *Small Pott 8vo. Cloth,* 2s.; *leather,* 2s. 6d. net.
[Library of Devotion.

St. Augustine, THE CONFESSIONS OF. Newly Translated, with an Introduction and Notes, by C. BIGG, D.D., late Student of Christ Church. *Third Edition. Small Pott 8vo. Cloth,* 2s; *leather,* 2s. 6d. net.
[Library of Devotion.

'Saki' (Munro H.). REGINALD. *Fcap.* 2s. 6d. net.

Sales (St. Francis de). ON THE LOVE OF GOD. Edited by W. J. KNOX-LITTLE, M.A. *Small Pott 8vo. Cloth,* 2s.; *leather,* 2s. 6d. net. [Library of Devotion.

Salmon (A. L.). CORNWALL. Illustrated by B. C. BOULTER. *Small Pott 8vo. Cloth,* 3s.; *leather,* 3s. 6d. net. [Little Guides.
A POPULAR GUIDE TO DEVON. *Medium 8vo.* 6d. net.

Sargeaunt (J.), M.A. ANNALS OF WESTMINSTER SCHOOL. With numerous Illustrations. *Demy 8vo.* 7s. 6d.

Sathas (C.). THE HISTORY OF PSELLUS. *Demy 8vo.* 15s. net.
[Byzantine Texts.

Schmitt (John). THE CHRONICLE OF
MOREA. *Demy 8vo.* 15s. *net.*
[Byzantine Texts.
Seeley (H.G.) F.R.S. DRAGONS OF THE
AIR. With many Illustrations. *Crown
8vo.* 6s.
Sells (V. P.), M.A. THE MECHANICS
OF DAILY LIFE. Illustrated. *Crown
8vo.* 2s. 6d. [University Extension Series.
Selous (Edmund). TOMMY SMITH'S
ANIMALS. Illustrated by G. W. Ord.
Second Edition. *Fcap. 8vo.* 2s. 6d.
Settle (J. H.). ANECDOTES OF
BRITISH SOLDIERS. *Crown 8vo.*
3s. 6d. *net.*
A Colonial Edition is also published.
Shakespeare (William).
THE FOUR FOLIOS, 1623; 1632; 1664;
1685. Each *Four Guineas net*, or a com-
plete set, *Twelve Guineas net.*
The Arden Shakespeare.
Demy 8vo. 3s. 6d. *each volume.* General
Editor, W. J. Craig. An Edition of
Shakespeare in single Plays. Edited with
a full Introduction, Textual Notes, and
a Commentary at the foot of the page.
HAMLET. Edited by Edward Dowden,
Litt.D.
ROMEO AND JULIET. Edited by
Edward Dowden, Litt.D.
KING LEAR. Edited by W. J. Craig.
JULIUS CAESAR. Edited by M. Mac-
millan, M.A.
THE TEMPEST. Edited by Morton
Luce.
OTHELLO. Edited by H. C. Hart.
CYMBELINE. Edited by Edward Dowden.
TITUS ANDRONICUS. Edited by H. B.
Baildon.
THE MERRY WIVES OF WINDSOR.
Edited by H. C. Hart.
MIDSUMMER NIGHT'S DREAM.
Edited by H. Cuningham.
KING HENRY V. Edited by H. A. Evans.
TITUS ANDRONICUS. Edited by H. B.
Baildon.
ALL'S WELL THAT ENDS WELL.
Edited by W. O. Brigstocke.
THE TAMING OF THE SHREW.
Edited by R. M. Bond.
The Little Quarto Shakespeare. *Pott
16mo. Leather, price 1s. net each volume.*
TWO GENTLEMEN OF VERONA.
A COMEDY OF ERRORS.
THE TEMPEST.
THE MERRY WIVES OF WINDSOR
MEASURE FOR MEASURE.
LOVE'S LABOUR'S LOST.
A MIDSUMMER NIGHT'S DREAM.
MUCH ADO ABOUT NOTHING.
AS YOU LIKE IT.
THE MERCHANT OF VENICE.
ALL'S WELL THAT ENDS WELL.

A WINTER'S TALE.
THE TAMING OF THE SHREW.
TWELFTH NIGHT.
KING JOHN.
KING RICHARD II.
KING HENRY IV. Part I.
KING HENRY IV. Part II.
KING HENRY V.
KING HENRY VI. Part I.
KING HENRY VI. Part II.
KING HENRY VI. Part III.
KING RICHARD III.
KING HENRY VIII.
TROILUS AND CRESSIDA.
CORIOLANUS.
TITUS ANDRONICUS.
ROMEO AND JULIET.
TIMON OF ATHENS.
JULIUS CAESAR.
Sharp (A.). VICTORIAN POETS. *Crown
8vo.* 2s. 6d. [University Extension Series.
Sharp (Mrs. E. A.). REMBRANDT.
With 30 Illustrations. *Demy 8vo.* 2s. 6d.
net. [Little Books on Art.
Shedlock (J. S.). THE PIANOFORTE
SONATA: Its Origin and Development.
Crown 8vo. 5s.
Shelley (Percy B.). ADONAIS; an Elegy
on the death of John Keats, Author of
Endymion, etc. Pisa. From the types of
Didot, 1821. 2s. *net.*
Sherwell (Arthur), M.A. LIFE IN WEST
LONDON. *Third Edition.* *Crown 8vo.*
2s. 6d. [Social Questions Series.
Sichel (Walter). DISRAELI: A Study in
Personality and Ideas. With 3 Portraits.
Demy 8vo. 12s. 6d. *net.*
A Colonial Edition is also published.
BEACONSFIELD. With 12 Illustrations
Fcap. 8vo, cloth, 3s. 6d.; *leather,* 4s. *net.*
[Little Biographies.
Sime (J.). REYNOLDS. With many Illus-
trations. *Demy 16mo.* 2s. 6d. *net.*
[Little Books on Art.
Simonson (G. A.). FRANCESCO
GUARDI. With 32 Plates. *Royal folio.*
£2, 2s. *net.*
Sketchley (R. E. D.). WATTS. With
many Illustrations. *Demy 16mo.* 2s. 6d.
net. [Little Books on Art.
Skipton (H. P. R.). HOPPNER. With
numerous Illustrations. *Demy 16mo.* 2s. 6d.
net. [Little Books on Art.
Sladen (Douglas). SICILY. With over
200 Illustrations. *Crown 8vo.* 5s. *net.*
Small (Evan), M.A. THE EARTH. An
Introduction to Physiography. Illustrated.
Crown 8vo. 2s. 6d.
[University Extension Series.
Smallwood, (M. G.). VANDYCK. With
many Illustrations. *Demy 16mo.* 2s. 6d.
net. [Little Books on Art.

Smedley (F. E.). FRANK FAIRLEGH. With 28 Plates by GEORGE CRUIKSHANK. *Fcap. 8vo.* 3s. 6d. net.
[Illustrated Pocket Library.

Smith (Adam). THE WEALTH OF NATIONS. Edited with an Introduction and numerous Notes by EDWIN CANNAN, M.A. *Two volumes. Demy 8vo.* 21s. net.

Smith (Horace and James). REJECTED ADDRESSES. Edited by A. D. GODLEY, M.A. *Small Pott 8vo, cloth,* 1s. 6d. net.; *leather,* 2s. 6d. net. [Little Library.

Snell (F. J.). A BOOK OF EXMOOR. Illustrated. *Crown 8vo.* 6s.

Sophocles. ELECTRA AND AJAX. Translated by E. D. A. MORSHEAD, M.A., Assistant Master at Winchester. 2s. 6d.
[Classical Translations.

Sornet (L. A.), and Acatos (M. J.), Modern Language Masters at King Edward's School, Birmingham. A JUNIOR FRENCH GRAMMAR. *Crown 8vo.* 2s.
[Junior School Books.

South (Wilton E.), M.A. THE GOSPEL ACCORDING TO ST. MATTHEW. *Crown 8vo.* 1s. 6d. [Junior School Books.

Southey (R.) ENGLISH SEAMEN. Vol. I. (Howard, Clifford, Hawkins, Drake, Cavendish). Edited, with an Introduction, by DAVID HANNAY. *Second Edition. Crown 8vo.* 6s.
Vol. II. (Richard Hawkins, Grenville, Essex, and Raleigh). *Crown 8vo.* 6s.

Spence (C. H.), M.A., Clifton College. HISTORY AND GEOGRAPHY EXAMINATION PAPERS. *Second Edition. Crown 8vo.* 2s. 6d.
[School Examination Series.

Spooner (W. A.), M.A., Warden of New College, Oxford. BISHOP BUTLER. With Portrait. *Crown 8vo.* 3s. 6d.
[Leaders of Religion.

Stanbridge (J. W.), B.D., late Canon of York, and sometime Fellow of St. John's College, Oxford. A BOOK OF DEVOTIONS. *Second Edition. Small Pott 8vo. Cloth,* 2s.; *leather,* 2s. 6d. net. [Library of Devotion.

'Stancliffe.' GOLF DO'S AND DONT'S. *Second Edition. Fcap. 8vo.* 1s.

Stedman (A. M. M.), M.A.
INITIA LATINA: Easy Lessons on Elementary Accidence. *Sixth Edition. Fcap. 8vo.* 1s.
FIRST LATIN LESSONS. *Eighth Edition. Crown 8vo.* 2s.
FIRST LATIN READER. With Notes adapted to the Shorter Latin Primer and Vocabulary. *Sixth Edition revised.* 18mo. 1s. 6d.
EASY SELECTIONS FROM CÆSAR. The Helvetian War. *Second Edition.* 18mo. 1s.

EASY SELECTIONS FROM LIVY. Part I. The Kings of Rome. 18mo. *Second Edition.* 1s. 6d.
EASY LATIN PASSAGES FOR UNSEEN TRANSLATION. *Ninth Edition. Fcap. 8vo.* 1s. 6d.
EXEMPLA LATINA. First Exercises in Latin Accidence. With Vocabulary. *Third Edition. Crown 8vo.* 1s.
EASY LATIN EXERCISES ON THE SYNTAX OF THE SHORTER AND REVISED LATIN PRIMER. With Vocabulary. *Ninth and Cheaper Edition, re-written. Crown 8vo.* 1s. 6d. KEY, 3s. net. *Original Edition.* 2s. 6d.
THE LATIN COMPOUND SENTENCE: Rules and Exercises. *Second Edition. Crown 8vo.* 1s. 6d. With Vocabulary. 2s.
NOTANDA QUAEDAM: Miscellaneous Latin Exercises on Common Rules and Idioms. *Fourth Edition. Fcap. 8vo.* 1s. 6d. With Vocabulary. 2s. Key, 2s. net.
LATIN VOCABULARIES FOR REPETITION: Arranged according to Subjects. *Eleventh Edition. Fcap. 8vo.* 1s. 6d.
A VOCABULARY OF LATIN IDIOMS. 18mo. *Second Edition.* 1s.
STEPS TO GREEK. *Second Edition, revised.* 18mo. 1s.
A SHORTER GREEK PRIMER. *Crown 8vo.* 1s. 6d.
EASY GREEK PASSAGES FOR UNSEEN TRANSLATION. *Third Edition, revised. Fcap. 8vo.* 1s. 6d.
GREEK VOCABULARIES FOR REPETITION. Arranged according to Subjects. *Third Edition. Fcap. 8vo.* 1s. 6d.
GREEK TESTAMENT SELECTIONS. For the use of Schools. With Introduction, Notes, and Vocabulary. *Third Edition. Fcap. 8vo.* 2s. 6d.
STEPS TO FRENCH. *Sixth Edition.* 18mo. 8d.
FIRST FRENCH LESSONS. *Sixth Edition, revised. Crown 8vo.* 1s.
EASY FRENCH PASSAGES FOR UNSEEN TRANSLATION. *Fifth Edition, revised. Fcap. 8vo.* 1s. 6d.
EASY FRENCH EXERCISES ON ELEMENTARY SYNTAX. With Vocabulary. *Fourth Edition. Crown 8vo.* 2s. 6d. KEY, 3s. net.
FRENCH VOCABULARIES FOR REPETITION: Arranged according to Subjects. *Twelfth Edition. Fcap. 8vo.* 1s.
FRENCH EXAMINATION PAPERS IN MISCELLANEOUS GRAMMAR AND IDIOMS. *Twelfth Edition. Crown 8vo.* 2s. 6d. [School Examination Series.
A KEY, issued to Tutors and Private Students only, to be had on application to the Publishers. *Fifth Edition. Crown 8vo.* 6s. net.

GENERAL KNOWLEDGE EXAMINA-
TION PAPERS. *Fifth Edition. Crown
8vo. 2s. 6d.* [School Examination Series.
KEY (*Third Edition*) issued as above.
7s. net.

GREEK EXAMINATION PAPERS IN
MISCELLANEOUS GRAMMAR AND
IDIOMS. *Seventh Edition. Crown 8vo.
2s. 6d.* [School Examination Series.
KEY·(*Third Edition*) issued as above.
6s. net. '

LATIN EXAMINATION PAPERS IN
MISCELLANEOUS GRAMMAR AND
IDIOMS. *Twelfth Edition. Crown 8vo.
2s. 6d.* [School Examination Series.
KEY (*Fifth Edition*) issued as above.
6s. net.

Steel (R. Elliott), M.A., F.C.S. THE
WORLD OF SCIENCE. Including
Chemistry, Heat, Light, Sound, Magnetism,
Electricity, Botany, Zoology, Physiology,
Astronomy, and Geology. 147 Illustrations.
Second Edition. Crown 8vo. 2s. 6d.
PHYSICS . EXAMINATION PAPERS.
Crown 8vo. 2s. 6d.
[School Examination Series.

Stephenson (C.), of the Technical College,
Bradford, and **Suddards (F.)** of the York-
shire College, Leeds. ORNAMENTAL
DESIGN FOR . WOVEN FABRICS.
Illustrated. *Demy 8vo. Second Edition.
7s. 6d.*

Stephenson (J.), M.A. THE CHIEF
TRUTHS OF THE·· CHRISTIAN
FAITH. *Crown 8vo. 3s. 6d.*

Sterne (Laurence). A SENTIMENTAL
JOURNEY. Edited by H. W. PAUL.
*Small Pott 8vo. Cloth, 1s. 6d. net; leather,
2s. 6d. net.* [Little Library.

Sterry (W.), M.A. ANNALS OF ETON
COLLEGE. With numerous Illustrations.
Demy 8vo. 7s. 6d.

Steuart (Katherine). BY ALLAN WATER.
Second Edition. Crown 8vo. 6s.

Stevenson (R. L.). THE LETTERS OF
ROBERT LOUIS STEVENSON TO
HIS FAMILY AND FRIENDS.
Selected and Edited, with Notes and Intro-
ductions, by SIDNEY COLVIN. *Sixth and
Cheaper Edition. Crown 8vo. 12s.*
LIBRARY EDITION. *Demy 8vo.· 2vols. 25s. net.*
A Colonial Edition is also published. ·

VAILIMA LETTERS. With an' Etched
Portrait by WILLIAM STRANG. *Third
Edition. Crown 8vo. Buckram. 6s.*
A Colonial Edition is also published.

THE LIFE OF R. L. STEVENSON. See
G. Balfour.

Stevenson (M. I.). FROM SARANAC TO
THE MARQUESAS. Being Letters
written by Mrs. M. I. STEVENSON during
1887-8 to her sister, Miss JANE WHYTE
BALFOUR. With an Introduction by

GEORGE W. BALFOUR, M.D.; LL.D.,
F.R.S.S. *Crown 8vo. 6s. net.*
A Colonial Edition is also published.

Stoddart (Anna M.) ST. FRANCIS OF
ASSISI. With 16 Illustrations. *Fcap.
8vo. Cloth, 3s. 6d.; leather, 4s. net.*
[Little Biographies.

Stone (E. D.), M.A., late Assistant Master at
Eton. SELECTIONS FROM THE
ODYSSEY. *Fcap. 8vo. 1s. 6d.*

Stone (S. J.). POEMS AND HYMNS.
With a Memoir by F. G. ELLERTON, M.A.
With Portrait. *Crown 8vo. 6s.*

Straker (F.), Assoc. of the Institute of
Bankers, and Lecturer to the London
Chamber of Commerce. THE MONEY
MARKET. *Crown 8vo. 2s. 6d. net.*
[Books on Business.

Streane (A. W.), D.D. ECCLESIASTES.
With an Introduction and Notes. *Fcap.
8vo. 1s. 6d. net.* [Churchman's Bible.

Stroud (H.), D.Sc., M.A., Professor of Physics
in the Durham College of Science, New-
castle-on-Tyne. PRACTICAL PHYSICS.
Fully Illustrated. *Crown 8vo. 3s. 6d.*
[Textbooks of Technology.

Strutt (Joseph). THE SPORTS AND
PASTIMES OF THE PEOPLE OF
ENGLAND. Illustrated by many engrav-
ings. Revised by J. Charles Cox, LL.D.,
F.S.A. *Quarto. 21s. net.*

Stuart (Capt. Donald). THE STRUGGLE
FOR PERSIA. With a Map. *Crown
8vo. 6s.*

Suckling (Sir John). FRAGMENTA
AUREA : a Collection of all the Incom-
parable Peeces, written by. And published
by a friend to perpetuate his memory.
Printed by his own copies.
Printed for HUMPHREY MOSELEY, and
are to be sold at his shop, at the sign of the
Princes Arms in St. Paul's Churchyard,
1646.

Suddards (F.). See C. Stephenson.

Surtees (R. S.). HANDLEY CROSS.
With 17 Coloured Plates and 100 Woodcuts
in the Text by JOHN LEECH. *Fcap. 8vo.
4s. 6d. net.*
Also a limited edition on large Japanese
paper. *30s. net.*
[Illustrated Pocket Library.

MR. SPONGE'S SPORTING TOUR.
With 13 Coloured Plates and 90 Woodcuts
in the Text by JOHN LEECH. *Fcap. 8vo.
3s. 6d. net.*
Also a limited edition on large Japanese
paper. *30s. net.*
[Illustrated Pocket Library.

JORROCKS' JAUNTS AND JOLLITIES.
With 15 Coloured Plates by H. ALKEN.
Fcap. 8vo. 3s. 6d. net.
Also a limited edition on large Japanese
paper. *30s. net.*
[Illustrated Pocket Library.

ASK MAMMA. With 13 Coloured Plates and 70 Woodcuts in the Text by JOHN LEECH. *Fcap. 8vo. 3s. 6d. net.*
Also a limited edition on large Japanese paper. *30s. net.*
[Illustrated Pocket Library. NearlyReady.

Swift (Jonathan). THE JOURNAL TO STELLA. Edited by G. A. AITKEN. *Crown 8vo. 6s.*

Symes (J. E.), M.A. THE FRENCH REVOLUTION. *Second Edition. Crown 8vo. 2s. 6d.* [University Extension Series.

Syrett (Netta). A SCHOOL YEAR. Illustrated. *Demy 16mo. 2s. 6d.*
[Little Blue Books.

Tacitus. AGRICOLA. With Introduction, Notes, Map, etc. By R. F. DAVIS, M.A., late Assistant Master at Weymouth College. *Crown 8vo. 2s.*
GERMANIA. By the same Editor. *Crown 8vo. 2s.*
AGRICOLA AND GERMANIA. Translated by R. B. TOWNSHEND, late Scholar of Trinity College, Cambridge. *Crown 8vo. 2s. 6d.* [Classical Translations.

Tauler (J.). THE INNER WAY. Being Thirty-six Sermons for Festivals by JOHN TAULER. Edited by A. W. HUTTON, M.A. *Small Pott 8vo. Cloth, 2s.; leather, 2s. 6d. net.* [Library of Devotion.

Taunton (E. L.). A HISTORY OF THE JESUITS IN ENGLAND. With Illustrations. *Demy 8vo. 21s. net.*

Taylor (A. E.). THE ELEMENTS OF METAPHYSICS. *Demy 8vo. 10s. 6d. net.*

Taylor (F. G.), M.A. COMMERCIAL ARITHMETIC. *Third Edition. Crown 8vo. 1s. 6d.* [Commercial Series.

Taylor (Miss J. A.). SIR WALTER RALEIGH. With 12 Illustrations. *Fcap. 8vo. Cloth, 3s. 6d.; leather, 4s. net.*
[Little Biographies.

Taylor (T. M.), M.A., Fellow of Gonville and Caius College, Cambridge. A CONSTITUTIONAL AND POLITICAL HISTORY OF ROME. *Crown 8vo. 7s. 6d.*

Tennyson (Alfred, Lord). THE EARLY POEMS OF. Edited, with Notes and an Introduction, by J. CHURTON COLLINS, M.A. *Crown 8vo. 6s.*
IN MEMORIAM, MAUD, AND THE PRINCESS. Edited by J. CHURTON COLLINS, M.A. *Crown 8vo. 6s.*
MAUD. Edited by ELIZABETH WORDSWORTH. *Small Pott 8vo. Cloth, 1s. 6d. net; leather, 2s. 6d. net.* [Little Library.
IN MEMORIAM. Edited by H. C. BEECHING, M.A. *Small Pott 8vo. Cloth, 1s. 6d. net; leather, 2s. 6d. net.* [Little Library.
THE EARLY POEMS OF. Edited by J. C. COLLINS, M.A. *Small Pott 8vo. Cloth, 1s. 6d. net; leather, 2s. 6d. net.* [Little Library.

THE PRINCESS. Edited by ELIZABETH WORDSWORTH. *Small Pott 8vo. Cloth, 1s. 6d. net; leather, 2s. 6d. net.* [Little Library.

Terry (C. S.). THE YOUNG PRETENDER. With 12 Illustrations. *Fcap. 8vo. Cloth, 3s. 6d.; leather, 4s. net.*
[Little Biographies.

Terton (Alice). LIGHTS AND SHADOWS IN A HOSPITAL. *Crown 8vo. 3s. 6d.*

Thackeray (W. M.). VANITY FAIR. Edited by STEPHEN GWYNN. *Three Volumes. Small Pott 8vo. Each volume, cloth, 1s. 6d. net; leather, 2s. 6d. net.*
[Little Library.
PENDENNIS. Edited by STEPHEN GWYNN. *Three Volumes. Small Pott 8vo. Each volume, cloth, 1s. 6d. net; leather, 2s. 6d. net.* [Little Library.
ESMOND. Edited by STEPHEN GWYNN. *Small Pott 8vo. Cloth, 1s. 6d. net; leather, 2s. 6d. net.* [Little Library.
CHRISTMAS BOOKS. Edited by STEPHEN GWYNN. *Small Pott 8vo. Cloth, 1s. 6d. net; leather, 2s. 6d. net.* [Little Library.

Theobald (F. W.), M.A. INSECT LIFE. Illustrated. *Crown 8vo. 2s. 6d.*
[University Extension Series.

Thompson (A. H.). CAMBRIDGE AND ITS COLLEGES. Illustrated by E. H. NEW. *Small Pott 8vo. Cloth, 3s.; leather, 3s. 6d. net.* [Little Guides.

Tileston (Mary W.). DAILY STRENGTH FOR DAILY NEEDS. *Fcap. 8vo. 3s. 6d.*
Also editions in superior binding 5s. and 6s.

Tompkins (H. W.), F.R.H.S. HERTFORDSHIRE. Illustrated by E. H. NEW. *Small Pott 8vo. Cloth, 3s.; leather, 3s. 6d. net.* [Little Guides.

Townley (Lady Susan). MY CHINESE NOTE-BOOK. With 16 Illustrations. *Demy 8vo. 10s. 6d. net.*
A Colonial Edition is also published.

Toynbee (Paget), M.A., D.Litt. DANTE STUDIES AND RESEARCHES. *Demy 8vo. 10s. 6d. net.*
DANTE ALIGHIERI. With 12 Illustrations. *Second Edition. Fcap. 8vo. Cloth, 3s. 6d.; leather, 4s. net.*
[Little Biographies.

Trench (Herbert). DEIRDRE WED: and Other Poems. *Crown 8vo. 5s.*

Trevelyan (G. M.), Fellow of Trinity College, Cambridge. ENGLAND UNDER THE STUARTS. *Demy 8vo. 10s. 6d. net.*

Troutbeck (G. E.). WESTMINSTER ABBEY. Illustrated by F. D. BEDFORD. *Small Pott 8vo. Cloth, 3s.; leather, 3s. 6d. net.* [Little Guides.

Tuckwell (Gertrude). THE STATE AND ITS CHILDREN. *Crown 8vo. 2s. 6d.*
[Social Questions Series.

Twining (Louisa). WORKHOUSES AND PAUPERISM. *Crown 8vo. 2s. 6d.*
[Social Questions Series.

Tyler (E. A.), B.A., F.C.S. A JUNIOR CHEMISTRY. *Crown 8vo.* 2s. 6d.
[Junior School Books.

Tyrell-Gill (Frances). TURNER. *Demy 16mo.* 2s. 6d. net.
[Little Books on Art.

Vaughan (Henry), THE POEMS OF. Edited by EDWARD HUTTON. *Small Pott 8vo. Cloth,* 1s. 6d. net; *leather,* 2s. 6d. net.
[Little Library.

Voegelin (A.), M.A. JUNIOR GERMAN EXAMINATION PAPERS. *Fcap. 8vo.* 1s. [Junior Examination Series.

Wade (G. W.), D.D. OLD TESTAMENT HISTORY. With Maps. *Second Edition. Crown 8vo.* 6s.
This book presents a connected account of the Hebrew people during the period covered by the Old Testament; and has been drawn up from the Scripture records in accordance with the methods of historical criticism.

Wagner (Richard). *See* A. L. CLEATHER.

Wall (J. C.) DEVILS. Illustrated by the Author. *Demy 8vo.* 4s. 6d. net.

Walters (H. B.). GREEK ART. With many Illustrations. *Demy 16mo.* 2s. 6d. net. [Little Books on Art.

Walton (Izaac). and **Cotton (Charles).** THE COMPLEAT ANGLER. With 14 Plates and 77 Woodcuts in the Text. *Fcap 8vo.* 3s. 6d. net.
[Illustrated Pocket Library.
This volume is reproduced from the beautiful edition of John Major of 1824-5.
THE COMPLEAT ANGLER. Edited by J. BUCHAN. *Small Pott 8vo. Cloth,* 1s. 6d. net; *leather,* 2s. 6d. net. [Little Library.

Warmelo (D. S. Van). ON COMMANDO. With Portrait. *Crown 8vo.* 3s. 6d.

Waterhouse (Mrs. Alfred). A LITTLE BOOK OF LIFE AND DEATH. Selected. *Fourth Edition. Small Pott 8vo. Cloth,* 1s. 6d. net; *leather,* 2s. 6d. net.
[Little Library.
WITH THE SIMPLE-HEARTED : Little Homilies to Women in Country Places. *Fcap. 8vo.* 2s. net.

Weatherhead (T. C.), M.A. EXAMINATION PAPERS IN HORACE. *Crown 8vo.* 2s.
JUNIOR GREEK EXAMINATION PAPERS. *Fcap. 8vo.* 1s.
[Junior Examination Series.

Webb (W. T.). A BOOK OF BAD CHILDREN. With 50 Illustrations by H. C. SANDY. *Demy 16mo.* 2s. 6d.
[Little Blue Books.

Webber (F. C.). CARPENTRY AND JOINERY. With many Illustrations. *Third Edition. Crown 8vo.* 3s. 6d.

Wells (Sidney H.). PRACTICAL MECHANICS. With 75 Illustrations and Diagrams. *Second Edition. Crown 8vo.* 3s. 6d. [Textbooks of Technology.

Wells (J.), M.A., Fellow and Tutor of Wadham College. OXFORD AND OXFORD LIFE. By Members of the University. *Third Edition Crown 8vo.* 3s. 6d.
A SHORT HISTORY OF ROME. *Fifth Edition.* With 3 Maps. *Cr. 8vo.* 3s. 6d.
This book is intended for the Middle and Upper Forms of Public Schools and for Pass Students at the Universities. It contains copious Tables, etc.
OXFORD AND ITS COLLEGES. Illustrated by E. H. New. *Fifth Edition. Pott 8vo. Cloth,* 3s.; *leather,* 3s. 6d. net.
[Little Guides.

Wetmore (Helen C.). THE LAST OF THE GREAT SCOUTS ('Buffalo Bill'). With Illustrations. *Second Edition. Demy 8vo.* 6s.

Whibley (C.). *See* Henley and Whibley.

Whibley (L.), M.A., Fellow of Pembroke College, Cambridge. GREEK OLIGARCHIES: THEIR ORGANISATION AND CHARACTER. *Crown 8vo.* 6s.

Whitaker (G. H.), M.A. THE EPISTLE OF ST. PAUL THE APOSTLE TO THE EPHESIANS. With an Introduction and Notes. *Fcap. 8vo.* 1s. 6d. net.
[Churchman's Bible.

White (Gilbert). THE NATURAL HISTORY OF SELBORNE. Edited by L. C. MIALL, F.R.S., assisted by W. WARDE FOWLER, M.A. *Crown 8vo.* 6s.

Whitfield (E. E.). PRECIS WRITING AND OFFICE CORRESPONDENCE. *Second Edition. Crown 8vo.* 2s.
[Commercial Series.
COMMERCIAL EDUCATION IN THEORY AND PRACTICE. *Crown 8vo.* 5s. [Commercial Series.
An introduction to Methuen's Commercial Series treating the question of Commercial Education fully from both the point of view of the teacher and of the parent.

Whitehead (A. W.). COLIGNY. With many Illustrations. *Demy 8vo.* 12s. 6d. net.

Whitley (Miss). *See* Lady Dilke.

Whyte (A. G.), B.Sc., Editor of *Electrical Investments.* THE ELECTRICAL INDUSTRY. *Crown 8vo.* 2s. 6d. net.
[Books on Business.

Wilberforce (Wilfrid) and **Gilbert (A. R.).** VELASQUEZ. With many Illustrations. *Demy 16mo.* 2s. 6d. net.
[Little Books on Art.

Wilkins (W. H.), B.A. THE ALIEN INVASION. *Crown 8vo.* 2s. 6d.
[Social Questions Series.

Williamson (W.). THE BRITISH GARDENER. Illustrated. *Demy 8vo.* 10s. 6d.

Williamson (W.), B.A. JUNIOR ENGLISH EXAMINATION PAPERS. *Fcap. 8vo.* 1s. [Junior Examination Series.

A JUNIOR ENGLISH GRAMMAR. With numerous passages for parsing and analysis, and a chapter on Essay Writing. *Crown 8vo*. 2s. [Junior School Books.

A CLASS-BOOK OF DICTATION PASSAGES. *Eighth Edition*. *Crown 8vo*. 1s. 6d. [Junior School Books.

EASY DICTATION AND SPELLING. *Third Edition*. *Fcap. 8vo*. 1s.

Wilmot-Buxton (E. M.). THE MAKERS OF EUROPE. *Crown 8vo*. *Second Edition*. 3s. 6d.
A Text-book of European History for Middle Forms.

THE STORY OF THE ANCIENT WORLD. With Maps and Illustrations. *Crown 8vo*. 3s. 6d.

Wilson (Bishop). SACRA PRIVATA. Edited by A. E. BURN, B.D. *Small Pott 8vo*. *Cloth*, 2s.; *leather*, 2s. 6d. net. [Library of Devotion.

Willson (Beckles). LORD STRATHCONA: the Story of his Life. Illustrated. *Demy 8vo*. 7s. 6d.
A Colonial Edition is also published.

Wilson (A. J.), Editor of the *Investor's Review*, City Editor of the *Daily Chronicle*. THE INSURANCE INDUSTRY. *Crown 8vo*. 2s. 6d. net. [Books on Business.

Wilson (H. A.). LAW IN BUSINESS. *Crown 8vo*. 2s. 6d. net. [Books on Business.

Wilton (Richard), M.A. LYRA PASTORALIS: Songs of Nature, Church, and Home. *Pott 8vo*. 2s. 6d.
A volume of devotional poems.

Winbolt (S. E.), M.A., Assistant Master in Christ's Hospital. EXERCISES IN LATIN ACCIDENCE. *Crown 8vo*. 1s. 6d.
An elementary book adapted for Lower Forms to accompany the Shorter Latin Primer.

LATIN HEXAMETER VERSE: An Aid to Composition. *Crown 8vo*. 3s. 6d. KEY, 5s. net.

Windle (B. C. A.), D.Sc., F.R.S. SHAKESPEARE'S COUNTRY. Illustrated by E. H. NEW. *Second Edition*. *Small Pott 8vo. cloth*, 3s.; *leather*, 3s. 6d. net. [Little Guides.

THE MALVERN COUNTRY. Illustrated by E. H. NEW. *Small Pott 8vo*. *Cloth*, 3s.; *leather*, 3s. 6d. net. [Little Guides.

REMAINS OF THE PREHISTORIC AGE IN ENGLAND. With numerous Illustrations and Plans. *Demy 8vo*. 7s. 6d. net. [Antiquary's Books.

CHESTER. Illustrated by E. H. NEW. *Crown 8vo*. 3s. 6d. net. [Ancient Cities.

Winterbotham (Canon), M.A., B.Sc., LL.B. THE KINGDOM OF HEAVEN HERE AND HEREAFTER. *Crown 8vo*. 3s. 6d. [Churchman's Library.

Wood (J. A. E.). HOW TO MAKE A DRESS. Illustrated. *Third Edition*. *Cr. 8vo*. 1s. 6d. [Textbooks of Technology.

Wordsworth (Christopher), M.A., and Littlehales (Henry). OLD SERVICE BOOKS OF THE ENGLISH CHURCH. With Coloured and other Illustrations. *Demy 8vo*. 7s. 6d. net. [Antiquary's Books.

Wordsworth (W.). SELECTIONS. Edited by NOWELL C. SMITH, M.A. *Small Pott 8vo*. *Cloth*, 1s. 6d. net; *leather*, 2s. 6d. net. [Little Library.

Wordsworth (W.) and Coleridge (S. T.). LYRICAL BALLADS. Edited by GEORGE SAMPSON. *Small Pott 8vo*. *Cloth*, 1s. 6d. net; *leather*, 2s. 6d. net. [Little Library.

Wright (Arthur), M.A., Fellow of Queen's College, Cambridge. SOME NEW TESTAMENT PROBLEMS. *Crown 8vo*. 6s. [Churchman's Library.

Wright (Sophie). GERMAN VOCABULARIES FOR REPETITION. *Fcap. 8vo*. 1s. 6d.

Wylde (A. B.). MODERN ABYSSINIA. With a Map and a Portrait. *Demy 8vo*. 15s. net.

Wyndham (G.), M.P. THE POEMS OF WILLIAM SHAKESPEARE. With an Introduction and Notes. *Demy 8vo*. *Buckram, gilt top*. 10s. 6d.

Wyon (R.) and Prance (G.). THE LAND OF THE BLACK MOUNTAIN. Being a description of Montenegro. With 40 Illustrations. *Crown 8vo*. 6s.
A Colonial Edition is also published.

Yeats (W. B.). AN ANTHOLOGY OF IRISH VERSE. *Revised and Enlarged Edition*. *Crown 8vo*. 3s. 6d.

Yendis (M.). THE GREAT RED FROG. A Story told in 40 Coloured Pictures. *Fcap. 8vo*. 1s. net.

Young (Filson). THE COMPLETE MOTORIST. With many Illustrations. *Demy 8vo*. 12s. 6d. net.

Young (T. M.). THE AMERICAN COTTON INDUSTRY: A Study of Work and Workers. With an Introduction by ELIJAH HELM, Secretary to the Manchester Chamber of Commerce. *Crown 8vo*, *cloth*, 2s. 6d.; *paper boards*, 1s. 6d.

Antiquary's Books, The
General Editor, J. CHARLES COX, LL.D., F.S.A.

ENGLISH MONASTIC LIFE. By the Right Rev. Abbot Gasquet, O.S.B. Illustrated. *Demy 8vo.* 7s. 6d. net.

REMAINS OF THE PREHISTORIC AGE IN ENGLAND. By B. C. A. Windle, D.Sc., F.R.S. With numerous Illustrations and Plans. *Demy 8vo.* 7s. 6d. net.

OLD SERVICE BOOKS OF THE ENGLISH CHURCH. By Christopher Wordsworth, M.A., and Henry Littlehales. With Coloured and other Illustrations. *Demy 8vo.* 7s. 6d. net.

CELTIC ART. By J. Romilly Allen, F.S.A. With numerous Illustrations and Plans. *Demy 8vo.* 7s. 6d. net.

Business, Books on
Crown 8vo. 2s. 6d. net.

The first Twelve volumes are—

PORTS AND DOCKS. By Douglas Owen.

RAILWAYS. By E. R. McDermott.

THE STOCK EXCHANGE. By Chas Duguid. *Second Edition.*

THE INSURANCE INDUSTRY. By A. J. Wilson.

THE ELECTRICAL INDUSTRY. By A. G. Whyte, B.Sc.

THE SHIPBUILDING INDUSTRY. By David Pollock, M.I.N.A.

THE MONEY MARKET. By F. Straker.

THE AGRICULTURAL INDUSTRY. By A. G. L. Rogers, M.A.

LAW IN BUSINESS. By H. A. Wilson.

THE BREWING INDUSTRY. By Julian L. Baker, F.I.C., F.C.S.

THE AUTOMOBILE INDUSTRY. By G. de H. Stone.

MINING AND MINING INVESTMENTS. By 'A. Moil.

Byzantine Texts
Edited by J. B. BURY, M.A., Litt.D.

ZACHARIAH OF MITYLENE. Translated by F. J. Hamilton, D.D., and E. W. Brooks. *Demy 8vo.* 12s. 6d. net.

EVAGRIUS. Edited by Léon Parmentier and M. Bidez. *Demy 8vo.* 10s. 6d. net.

THE HISTORY OF PSELLUS. Edited by C. Sathas. *Demy 8vo.* 15s. net.

ECTHESIS CHRONICA. Edited by Professor Lambros. *Demy 8vo.* 7s. 6d. net.

THE CHRONICLE OF MOREA. Edited by John Schmitt. *Demy 8vo.* 15s. net.

Churchman's Bible, The
General Editor, J. H. BURN, B.D., F.R.S.E.

The volumes are practical and devotional, and the text of the Authorised Version is explained in sections, which correspond as far as possible with the Church Lectionary.

THE EPISTLE TO THE GALATIANS. Edited by A. W. Robinson, M.A. *Fcap. 8vo.* 1s. 6d. net.

ECCLESIASTES. Edited by A. W. Streane, D.D. *Fcap. 8vo.* 1s. 6d. net.

THE EPISTLE TO THE PHILIPPIANS. Edited by C. R. D. Biggs, D.D. *Fcap. 8vo.* 1s. 6d. net.

THE EPISTLE OF ST. JAMES. Edited by H. W Fulford, M.A. *Fcap. 8vo.* 1s. 6d. net.

ISAIAH. Edited by W. E. Barnes, D.D., Hulsaean Professor of Divinity. *Two Volumes. Fcap. 8vo.* 2s. net each. With Map.

THE EPISTLE OF ST. PAUL THE APOSTLE TO THE EPHESIANS. Edited by G. H. Whitaker, M.A. *Fcap. 8vo.* 1s. 6d. net.

Churchman's Library, The
General Editor, J. H. BURN, B.D., F.R.S.E.,

THE BEGINNINGS OF ENGLISH CHRISTIANITY. By W. E. Collins, M.A. With Map. *Crown 8vo.* 3s. 6d.

SOME NEW TESTAMENT PROBLEMS. By Arthur Wright, M.A. *Crown 8vo.* 6s.

THE KINGDOM OF HEAVEN HERE AND HEREAFTER. By Canon Winterbotham, M.A., B.Sc., LL.B. *Crown 8vo.* 3s. 6d.

THE WORKMANSHIP OF THE PRAYER BOOK: Its Literary and Liturgical Aspects. By J. Dowden, D.D. *Second Edition. Crown 8vo.* 3s. 6d.

EVOLUTION. By F. B. Jevons, M.A., Litt.D. *Crown 8vo.* 3s. 6d.

THE OLD TESTAMENT AND THE NEW SCHOLARSHIP. By J. W. Peters, D.D. *Crown 8vo.* 6s.

THE CHURCHMAN'S INTRODUCTION TO THE OLD TESTAMENT. Edited by A. M. Mackay, B.A. *Crown 8vo.* 3s. 6d.

THE CHURCH OF CHRIST. By E. T. Green, M.A. *Crown 8vo.* 6s.

COMPARATIVE THEOLOGY. By J. A. MacCulloch. *Crown 8vo.* 6s.

Classical Translations
Edited by H. F. FOX, M.A., Fellow and Tutor of Brasenose College, Oxford.
Crown 8vo.

ÆSCHYLUS—Agamemnon, Choephoroe, Eumenides. Translated by Lewis Campbell, LL.D. 5s.

CICERO—De Oratore I. Translated by E. N. P. Moor, M.A. 3s. 6d.

CICERO—Select Orations (Pro Milone, Pro Mureno, Philippic II., in Catilinam). Translated by H. E. D. Blakiston, M.A. 5s.

CICERO—De Natura Deorum. Translated by F. Brooks, M.A. 3s. 6d.

CICERO—De Officiis. Translated by G. B. Gardiner, M.A. 2s. 6d.

HORACE—The Odes and Epodes. Translated by A. Godley, M.A. 2s.

LUCIAN—Six Dialogues (Nigrinus, Icaro-Menippus, The Cock, The Ship, The Parasite, The Lover of Falsehood). Translated by S. T. Irwin, M.A. 3s. 6d.

SOPHOCLES—Electra and Ajax. Translated by E. D. A. Morshead, M.A. 2s. 6d.

TACITUS—Agricola and Germania. Translated by R. B. Townshend. 2s. 6d.

THE SATIRES OF JUVENAL. Translated by S. G. Owen. *Crown 8vo.* 2s. 6d.

Commercial Series, Methuen's

Edited by H. DE B. GIBBINS, Litt.D., M.A.

Crown 8vo.

COMMERCIAL EDUCATION IN THEORY AND PRACTICE. By E. E. Whitfield, M.A. 5s.
An introduction to Methuen's Commercial Series treating the question of Commercial Education fully from both the point of view of the teacher and of the parent.

BRITISH COMMERCE AND COLONIES FROM ELIZABETH TO VICTORIA. By H. de B. Gibbins, Litt.D., M.A. Third Edition. 2s.

COMMERCIAL EXAMINATION PAPERS. By H. de B. Gibbins, Litt.D., M.A. 1s. 6d.

THE ECONOMICS OF COMMERCE. By H. de B. Gibbins, Litt.D., M.A. 1s. 6d.

A GERMAN COMMERCIAL READER. By S. E. Bally. With Vocabulary. 2s.

A COMMERCIAL GEOGRAPHY OF THE BRITISH EMPIRE. By L. W. Lyde, M.A. Third Edition. 2s.

A PRIMER OF BUSINESS. By S. Jackson, M.A. Third Edition. 1s. 6d.

COMMERCIAL ARITHMETIC. By F. G. Taylor, M.A. Third Edition. 1s. 6d.

FRENCH COMMERCIAL CORRESPONDENCE. By S. E. Bally. With Vocabulary. Third Edition. 2s.

GERMAN COMMERCIAL CORRESPONDENCE. By S. E. Bally. With Vocabulary. 2s. 6d.

A FRENCH COMMERCIAL READER. By S. E. Bally. With Vocabulary. Second Edition. 2s.

PRECIS WRITING AND OFFICE CORRESPONDENCE. By E. E. Whitfield, M.A. Second Edition. 2s.

A GUIDE TO PROFESSIONS AND BUSINESS. By H. Jones. 1s. 6d.

THE PRINCIPLES OF BOOK-KEEPING BY DOUBLE ENTRY. By J. E. B. M'Allen, M.A. 2s.

COMMERCIAL LAW. By W. Douglas Edwards. 2s.

Connoisseurs Library, The

Wide Royal 8vo.　25s. net.

The first volumes are—

MEZZOTINTS. By Cyril Davenport.
MINIATURES. By Dudley Heath.

PORCELAIN. By Edward Dillon.
IVORIES. By A. Maskell.

Devotion, The Library of

With Introductions and (where necessary) Notes.

Small Pott 8vo, cloth, 2s. ; leather, 2s. 6d. net.

THE CONFESSIONS OF ST. AUGUSTINE. Edited by C. Bigg, D.D. Third Edition.

THE CHRISTIAN YEAR. Edited by Walter Lock, D.D. Second Edition.

THE IMITATION OF CHRIST. Edited by C. Bigg, D.D. Second Edition.

A BOOK OF DEVOTIONS. Edited by J. W. Stanbridge, B.D. Second Edition.

LYRA INNOCENTIUM. Edited by Walter Lock, D.D.

A SERIOUS CALL TO A DEVOUT AND HOLY LIFE. Edited by C. Bigg, D.D. Second Edition.

THE TEMPLE. Edited by E. C. S. Gibson, D.D.

A GUIDE TO ETERNITY. Edited by J. W. Stanbridge, B.D.

THE PSALMS OF DAVID. Edited by B. W. Randolph, D.D.

LYRA APOSTOLICA. Edited by Canon Scott Holland and Canon H. C. Beeching, M.A.

THE INNER WAY. Edited by A. W. Hutton, M.A.

THE THOUGHTS OF PASCAL. Edited by C. S. Jerram, M.A.

ON THE LOVE OF GOD. By St. Francis de Sales. Edited by W. J. Knox-Little, M.A.

A MANUAL OF CONSOLATION FROM THE SAINTS AND FATHERS. Edited by J. H. Burn, B.D.

THE SONG OF SONGS. Edited by B. Blaxland, M.A.

THE DEVOTIONS OF ST. ANSELM. Edited by C. J. Webb, M.A.

GRACE ABOUNDING. By John Bunyan. Edited by S. C. Freer, M.A.

BISHOP WILSON'S SACRA PRIVATA. Edited by A. E. Burn, M.A.

LYRA SACRA: A Book of Sacred Verse. Edited by H. C. Beeching, M.A., Canon of Westminster.

A DAY BOOK FROM THE SAINTS AND FATHERS. Edited by J. H. Burn, B.D.

HEAVENLY WISDOM. A Selection from the English Mystics. Edited by E. C. Gregory.

LIGHT, LIFE, AND LOVE. A Selection from the German Mystics. Edited by W. R. Inge, M.A.

Illustrated Pocket Library of Plain and Coloured Books, The

Fcap. 8vo.　3s. 6d. net to 4s. 6d. net each volume.

A series, in small form, of some of the famous illustrated books of fiction and general literature. These are faithfully reprinted from the first or best editions without introduction or notes.

COLOURED BOOKS

THE LIFE AND DEATH OF JOHN MYTTON, ESQ. By Nimrod. With 18 Coloured Plates by Henry Alken and T. J Rawlins. Third Edition. 3s. 6d. net.
Also a limited edition on large Japanese paper. 30s. net.

THE LIFE OF A SPORTSMAN. By Nimrod. With 35 Coloured Plates by Henry Alken. 4s. 6d. net.
Also a limited edition on large Japanese paper. 80s. net.

HANDLEY CROSS. By R. S. Surtees. With 17 Coloured Plates and 100 Woodcuts in the Text by John Leech. 4s. 6d. net.
Also a limited edition on large Japanese paper. 30s. net.

MR. SPONGE'S SPORTING TOUR. By R. S. Surtees. With 13 Coloured Plates and 90 Woodcuts in the Text by John Leech. 3s. 6d. net.
Also a limited edition on large Japanese paper. 30s. net.

[Continued.

THE ILLUSTRATED POCKET LIBRARY—*continued.*

JORROCKS' JAUNTS AND JOLLITIES. By R. S. Surtees. With 15 Coloured Plates by H. Alken. 3s. 6d. net.
Also a limited edition on large Japanese paper. 30s. net.
This volume is reprinted from the extremely rare and costly edition of 1843, which contains Alken's very fine illustrations instead of the usual ones by Phiz.

ASK MAMMA. By R. S. Surtees. With 13 Coloured Plates and 70 Woodcuts in the Text by John Leech. 3s. 6d. net.
Also a limited edition on large Japanese paper. 30s. net.

THE ANALYSIS OF THE HUNTING FIELD. By R. S. Surtees. With 7 Coloured Plates by Henry Alken, and 43 Illustrations on Wood. 3s. 6d. net.

THE TOUR OF DR. SYNTAX IN SEARCH OF THE PICTURESQUE. By William Combe. With 30 Coloured Plates by T. Rowlandson. 3s. 6d. net.
Also a limited edition on large Japanese paper. 30s. net.

THE TOUR OF DOCTOR SYNTAX IN SEARCH OF CONSOLATION. By William Combe. With 24 Coloured Plates by T. Rowlandson. 3s. 6d. net.
Also a limited edition on large Japanese paper. 30s. net.

THE THIRD TOUR OF DOCTOR SYNTAX IN SEARCH OF A WIFE. By William Combe. With 24 Coloured Plates by T. Rowlandson. 3s. 6d. net.
Also a limited edition on large Japanese paper. 30s. net.

THE HISTORY OF JOHNNY QUAE GENUS: the Little Foundling of the late Dr. Syntax. By the Author of 'The Three Tours.' With 24 Coloured Plates by Rowlandson. 3s. 6d. net. 100 copies on large Japanese paper. 21s. net.
Also a limited edition on large Japanese paper. 30s. net.

THE ENGLISH DANCE OF DEATH, from the Designs of T. Rowlandson, with Metrical Illustrations by the Author of 'Doctor Syntax.' *Two Volumes.* 9s. net.
This book contains 76 Coloured Plates.
Also a limited edition on large Japanese paper. 30s. net.

THE DANCE OF LIFE: A Poem. By the Author of 'Doctor Syntax.' Illustrated with 26 Coloured Engravings by T. Rowlandson. 3s. 6d. net.
Also a limited edition on large Japanese paper. 30s. net.

LIFE IN LONDON: or, the Day and Night Scenes of Jerry Hawthorn, Esq., and his Elegant Friend,

Corinthian Tom. By Pierce Egan. With 36 Coloured Plates by I. R. and G. Cruikshank. With numerous Designs on Wood. 4s. 6d. net.
Also a limited edition on large Japanese paper. 30s. net.

REAL LIFE IN LONDON: or, the Rambles and Adventures of Bob Tallyho, Esq., and his Cousin, The Hon. Tom Dashall. By an Amateur (Pierce Egan). With 31 Coloured Plates by Alken and Rowlandson, etc. *Two Volumes.* 9s. net.

THE LIFE OF AN ACTOR. By Pierce Egan. With 27 Coloured Plates by Theodore Lane, and several Designs on Wood. 4s. 6d. net.

THE VICAR OF WAKEFIELD. By Oliver Goldsmith. With 24 Coloured Plates by T. Rowlandson. 3s. 6d. net.
Also a limited edition on large Japanese paper. 30s net.
A reproduction of a very rare book.

THE MILITARY ADVENTURES OF JOHNNY NEWCOME. By an Officer. With 15 Coloured Plates by T. Rowlandson. 3s. 6d. net.

THE NATIONAL SPORTS OF GREAT BRITAIN. With Descriptions and 51 Coloured Plates by Henry Alken. 4s. 6d. net.
Also a limited edition on large Japanese paper. 30s. net.
This book is completely different from the large folio edition of 'National Sports' by the same artist, and none of the plates are similar.

THE ADVENTURES OF A POST CAPTAIN. By A Naval Officer. With 24 Coloured Plates by Mr. Williams. 3s. 6d. net.

GAMONIA: or, the Art of Preserving Game; and an Improved Method of making Plantations and Covers, explained and illustrated by Lawrence Rawstorne, Esq. With 15 Coloured Plates by T. Rawlins. 3s. 6d. net.

AN ACADEMY FOR GROWN HORSEMEN: Containing the completest Instructions for Walking, Trotting, Cantering, Galloping, Stumbling, and Tumbling. Illustrated with 27 Coloured Plates, and adorned with a Portrait of the Author. By Geoffrey Gambado, Esq. 3s. 6d. net.

REAL LIFE IN IRELAND, or the Day and Night Scenes of Brian Boru, Esq., and his Elegant Friend, Sir Shawn O'Dogherty. By a Real Paddy. With 19 Coloured Plates by Heaths, Marks, etc. 3s. 6d. net.

THE ADVENTURES OF JOHNNY NEWCOME IN THE NAVY. By Alfred Burton. With 16 Coloured Plates by T. Rowlandson. 3s. 6d. net.

PLAIN BOOKS

THE GRAVE: A Poem. By Robert Blair. Illustrated by 12 Etchings executed by Louis Schiavonetti from the Original Inventions of William Blake. With an Engraved Title Page and a Portrait of Blake by T. Phillips, R.A. 3s. 6d. net.
The Illustrations are reproduced in photogravure. Also a limited edition on large Japanese paper, with India proofs and a duplicate set of the plates. 15s. net.

ILLUSTRATIONS OF THE BOOK OF JOB. Invented and engraved by William Blake. 3s. 6d. net.
These famous Illustrations—21 in number—are reproduced in photogravure. Also a limited edition on large Japanese paper, with India proofs and a duplicate set of the plates. 15s. net.

ÆSOP'S FABLES. With 380 Woodcuts by Thomas Bewick. 3s. 6d. net.

WINDSOR CASTLE. By W. Harrison Ainsworth.

With 22 Plates and 87 Woodcuts in the Text by George Cruikshank. 3s. 6d. net.

THE TOWER OF LONDON. By W. Harrison Ainsworth. With 40 Plates and 58 Woodcuts in the Text by George Cruikshank. 3s. 6d. net.

FRANK FAIRLEGH. By F. E. Smedley. With 30 Plates by George Cruikshank. 3s. 6d. net.

HANDY ANDY. By Samuel Lover. With 24 Illustrations by the Author. 3s. 6d. net.

THE COMPLEAT ANGLER. By Izaak Walton and Charles Cotton. With 14 Plates and 77 Woodcuts in the Text. 3s. 6d. net.
This volume is reproduced from the beautiful edition of John Major of 1824.

THE PICKWICK PAPERS. By Charles Dickens. With the 43 Illustrations by Seymour and Phiz, the two Buss Plates, and the 32 Contemporary Onwhyn Plates. 3s. 6d. net.

Junior Examination Series

Edited by A. M. M. STEDMAN, M.A. *Fcap. 8vo.* 1s.

JUNIOR FRENCH EXAMINATION PAPERS. By F. Jacob, B.A.

JUNIOR LATIN EXAMINATION PAPERS. *Second Edition.* By C. G. Botting, M.A.

JUNIOR ENGLISH EXAMINATION PAPERS. By W. Williamson, B.A.

JUNIOR ARITHMETIC EXAMINATION PAPERS. By W. S. Beard. *Second Edition.*

JUNIOR ALGEBRA EXAMINATION PAPERS. By S. W. Finn, M.A.

JUNIOR GREEK EXAMINATION PAPERS. By T. C. Weatherhead, M.A.

JUNIOR GENERAL INFORMATION EXAMINATION PAPERS. By W. S. Beard.

JUNIOR GEOGRAPHY EXAMINATION PAPERS. By W. G. Baker, M.A.

JUNIOR GERMAN EXAMINATION PAPERS. By A. Voegelin, M.A.

Junior School-Books, Methuen's

Edited by O. D. INSKIP, LL.D., and W. WILLIAMSON, B.A.

A CLASS-BOOK OF DICTATION PASSAGES. By W. Williamson, B.A. *Eighth Edition. Crown 8vo.* 1s. 6d.

THE GOSPEL ACCORDING TO ST. MATTHEW. Edited by E. Wilton South, M.A. *Crown 8vo.* 1s. 6d.

THE GOSPEL ACCORDING TO ST. MARK. Edited by A. E. Rubie, M.A., Headmaster of College, Eltham. With Three Maps. *Crown 8vo.* 1s. 6d.

A JUNIOR ENGLISH GRAMMAR. By W. Williamson, B.A. With numerous passages for parsing and analysis, and a chapter on Essay Writing. *Crown 8vo.* 2s.

A JUNIOR CHEMISTRY. By E. A. Tyler, B.A., F.C.S., Science Master at Swansea Grammar School. With 73 Illustrations. *Crown 8vo.* 2s. 6d.

THE ACTS OF THE APOSTLES. Edited by A. E. Rubie, M.A., Headmaster of College, Eltham. *Crown 8vo.* 2s.

THE FIRST BOOK OF KINGS. Edited by A. E. Rubie, M.A. *Crown 8vo.* 1s. 6d.

A JUNIOR FRENCH GRAMMAR. By L. A. Sornet and M. J. Acatos, Modern Language Masters at King Edward's School, Birmingham. *Cr. 8vo.* 2s.

ELEMENTARY EXPERIMENTAL SCIENCE. PHYSICS by W. T. Clough, A.R.C.S. CHEMISTRY by A. E. Dunstan, B.Sc. With 2 Plates and 154 Diagrams. *Crown 8vo.* 2s.

A JUNIOR GEOMETRY. By Noel S. Lydon. With 239 Diagrams. *Crown 8vo.* 2s.

Leaders of Religion

Edited by H. C. BEECHING, M.A., Canon of Westminster. *With Portraits.* Crown 8vo. 3s. 6d.

A series of short biographies of the most prominent leaders of religious life and thought of all ages and countries.

CARDINAL NEWMAN. By R. H. Hutton.

JOHN WESLEY. By J. H. Overton, M.A.

BISHOP WILBERFORCE. By G. W. Daniell, M.A.

CARDINAL MANNING. By A. W. Hutton, M.A.

CHARLES SIMEON. By H. C. G. Moule, D.D.

JOHN KEBLE. By Walter Lock, D.D.

THOMAS CHALMERS. By Mrs. Oliphant.

LANCELOT ANDREWES. By R. L. Ottley, M.A.

AUGUSTINE OF CANTERBURY. By E. L. Cutts, D.D.

WILLIAM LAUD. By W. H. Hutton, M.A.

JOHN KNOX. By F. MacCunn.

JOHN HOWE. By R. F. Horton, D.D.

BISHOP KEN. By F. A. Clarke, M.A.

GEORGE FOX, THE QUAKER. By T. Hodgkin D.C.L.

JOHN DONNE. By Augustus Jessopp, D.D.

THOMAS CRANMER. By A. J. Mason, D.D.

BISHOP LATIMER. By R. M. Carlyle and A. J. Carlyle, M.A.

BISHOP BUTLER. By W. A. Spooner, M.A.

Little Biographies

Fcap. 8vo. Each volume, cloth, 3s. 6d. ; leather, 4s. net.

DANTE ALIGHIERI. By Paget Toynbee, M.A., D.Litt. With 12 Illustrations. *Second Edition.*

SAVONAROLA. By E. L. S. Horsburgh, M.A. With 12 Illustrations. *Second Edition.*

JOHN HOWARD. By E. C. S. Gibson, D.D., Vicar of Leeds. With 12 Illustrations.

TENNYSON. By A. C. Benson, M.A. With 9 Illustrations.

WALTER RALEIGH. By J. A. Taylor. With 12 Illustrations.

ERASMUS. By E. F. H. Capey. With 12 Illustrations.

THE YOUNG PRETENDER. By C. S. Terry. With 12 Illustrations.

ROBERT BURNS. By T. F. Henderson. With 12 Illustrations.

CHATHAM. By A. S. M'Dowall. With 12 Illustrations.

ST. FRANCIS OF ASSISI. By Anna M. Stoddart. With 16 Illustrations.

CANNING. By W. A. Phillips. With 12 Illustrations.

BEACONSFIELD. By Walter Sichel. With 12 Illustrations.

GOETHE. By H. G. Atkins. With 12 Illustrations.

Little Blue Books, The

General Editor, E. V. LUCAS.

Illustrated. Demy 16mo. 2s. 6d.

1. THE CASTAWAYS OF MEADOWBANK. By T. Cobb.
2. THE BEECHNUT BOOK. By Jacob Abbott. Edited by E. V. Lucas.
3. THE AIR GUN. By T. Hilbert.
4. A SCHOOL YEAR. By Netta Syrett.
5. THE FEELES AT THE CAPITAL. By Roger Ashton.

[Continued.

THE LITTLE BLUE BOOKS—*continued.*

6. THE TREASURE OF PRINCEGATE PRIORY. By T. Cobb.
7. MRS. BARBERRY'S GENERAL SHOP. By Roger Ashton.

8. A BOOK OF BAD CHILDREN. By W. T. Webb.
9. THE LOST BALL. By Thomas Cobb.

Little Books on Art

Demy 16mo. 2s. 6d. *net.*

GREEK ART. H. B. Walters.
BOOKPLATES. E. Almack.
REYNOLDS. J. Sime.
ROMNEY. George Paston.
WATTS. Miss R. E. D. Sketchley.
LEIGHTON. Alice Corkran.
VELASQUEZ. Wilfrid Wilberforce and A. R. Gilbert.
GREUZE AND BOUCHER. Eliza F. Pollard.
VANDYCK. M. G. Smallwood.

TURNER. F. Tyrell-Gill.
DURER. Jessie Allen.
HOFFNER. H. P. K. Skipton.
HOLBEIN. Mrs. G. Fortescue.
MILLET. Miss N. Peacock.
BURNE-JONES. Miss F. de Lisle.
REMBRANDT. Mrs. E. A. Sharp.
COROT. Alice Pollard and Ethel Birnstingl.

Little Galleries, The

Demy 16mo. 2s. 6d. *net.*

A LITTLE GALLERY OF REYNOLDS.
A LITTLE GALLERY OF ROMNEY.

A LITTLE GALLERY OF HOFFNER.
A LITTLE GALLERY OF MILLAIS.

A LITTLE GALLERY OF ENGLISH POETS.

Little Guides, The

Small Pott 8vo, cloth, 3s.; leather, 3s. 6d. net.

OXFORD AND ITS COLLEGES. By J. Wells, M.A. Illustrated by E. H. New. *Fourth Edition.*
CAMBRIDGE AND ITS COLLEGES. By A. Hamilton Thompson. Illustrated by E. H. New.
THE MALVERN COUNTRY. By B. C. A. Windle, D.Sc., F.R.S. Illustrated by E. H. New.
SHAKESPEARE'S COUNTRY. By B. C. A. Windle, D.Sc., F.R.S. Illustrated by E. H. New. *Second Edition.*
SUSSEX. By F. G. Brabant, M.A. Illustrated by E. H. New.
WESTMINSTER ABBEY. By G. E. Troutbeck. Illustrated by F. D. Bedford.
NORFOLK. By W. A. Dutt. Illustrated by B. C. Boulter.
CORNWALL. By A. L. Salmon. Illustrated by B. C. Boulter.
BRITTANY. By S. Baring-Gould. Illustrated by J. Wylie.
HERTFORDSHIRE. By H. W. Tompkins, F.R.H.S. Illustrated by E. H. New.

THE ENGLISH LAKES. By F. G. Brabant, M.A. Illustrated by E. H. New. 4s.; *leather,* 4s. 6d. *net.*
KENT. By G. Clinch. Illustrated by F. D. Bedford.
ROME. By C. G. Ellaby. Illustrated by B. C. Boulter.
THE ISLE OF WIGHT. By G. Clinch. Illustrated by F. D. Bedford.
SURREY. By F. A. H. Lambert. Illustrated by E. H. New.
BUCKINGHAMSHIRE. By E. S. Roscoe. Illustrated by F. D. Bedford.
SUFFOLK. By W. A. Dutt. Illustrated by J. Wylie.
DERBYSHIRE. By J. Charles Cox, LL.D., F.S.A. Illustrated by J. C. Wall.
THE NORTH RIDING OF YORKSHIRE. By J. E. Morris. Illustrated by R. J. S. Bertram.
HAMPSHIRE. By J. C. Cox. Illustrated by M. E. Purser.
SICILY. By F. H. Jackson. With many Illustrations by the Author.

Little Library, The

With Introductions, Notes, and Photogravure Frontispieces.

Small Pott 8vo. *Each Volume, cloth,* 1s. 6d. *net ; leather,* 2s. 6d. *net.*

VANITY FAIR. By W. M. Thackeray. Edited by S. Gwynn. *Three Volumes.*
PENDENNIS. By W. M. Thackeray. Edited by S. Gwynn. *Three Volumes.*
ESMOND. By W. M. Thackeray. Edited by S. Gwynn.
CHRISTMAS BOOKS. By W. M. Thackeray. Edited by S. Gwynn.
SELECTIONS FROM GEORGE CRABBE. Edited by A. C. DEANE.
JOHN HALIFAX, GENTLEMAN. By Mrs. Craik. Edited by Annie Matheson. *Two Volumes.*
PRIDE AND PREJUDICE. By Jane Austen. Edited by E. V. Lucas. *Two Volumes.*
NORTHANGER ABBEY. By Jane Austen. Edited by E. V. Lucas.

THE PRINCESS. By Alfred, Lord Tennyson. Edited by Elizabeth Wordsworth.
MAUD. By Alfred, Lord Tennyson. Edited by Elizabeth Wordsworth.
IN MEMORIAM. By Alfred, Lord Tennyson. Edited by H. C. Beeching, M.A.
THE EARLY POEMS OF ALFRED. LORD TENNYSON. Edited by J. C. Collins, M.A.
A LITTLE BOOK OF ENGLISH LYRICS. With Notes.
THE INFERNO OF DANTE. Translated by H. F. Cary. Edited by Paget Toynbee, M.A., D.Litt.
THE PURGATORIO OF DANTE. Translated by H. F. Cary. Edited by Paget Toynbee, M.A., D.Litt.
THE PARADISO OF DANTE. Translated by H. F. Cary. Edited by Paget Toynbee. M.A., D.Litt.

[*Continued.*

THE LITTLE LIBRARY—*continued.*

A LITTLE BOOK OF SCOTTISH VERSE. Edited by T. F. Henderson.
A LITTLE BOOK OF LIGHT VERSE. Edited by A. C. Deane.
A LITTLE BOOK OF ENGLISH SONNETS. Edited by J. B. B. Nichols.
POEMS. By John Keats. With an Introduction by L. Binyon, and Notes by J. Masefield.
A complete Edition.
THE MINOR POEMS OF JOHN MILTON. Edited by H. C. Beeching, M.A.
THE POEMS OF HENRY VAUGHAN. Edited by Edward Hutton.
SELECTIONS FROM WORDSWORTH. Edited by Nowell C. Smith.
SELECTIONS FROM THE EARLY POEMS OF ROBERT BROWNING. Edited by W. Hall Griffin, M.A.
THE ENGLISH POEMS OF RICHARD CRASHAW. Edited by Edward Hutton.
SELECTIONS FROM WILLIAM BLAKE. Edited by M. Perugini.
SELECTIONS FROM THE POEMS OF GEORGE DARLEY. Edited by R. A. Streatfeild.
LYRICAL BALLADS. By W. Wordsworth and S. T. Coleridge. Edited by George Sampson.
SELECTIONS FROM LONGFELLOW. Edited by Lilian M. Faithfull.
SELECTIONS FROM THE ANTI-JACOBIN; with George Canning's additional Poems. Edited by Lloyd Sanders.
THE POEMS OF ANDREW MARVELL. Edited by Edward Wright.
A LITTLE BOOK OF LIFE AND DEATH. Edited by Mrs. Alfred Waterhouse. *Fourth Edition.*
A LITTLE BOOK OF ENGLISH PROSE. Edited by Mrs. P. A. Barnett.
EOTHEN. By A. W. Kinglake. With an Introduction and Notes.

CRANFORD. By Mrs. Gaskell. Edited by E. V. Lucas.
LAVENGRO. By George Borrow. Edited by F. Hindes Groome. *Two Volumes.*
THE ROMANY RYE. By George Borrow. Edited John Sampson.
THE HISTORY OF THE CALIPH VATHEK. By William Beckford. Edited by E. Denison Ross.
THE COMPLEAT ANGLER. By Izaak Walton. Edited by J. Buchan.
MARRIAGE. By Susan Ferrier. Edited by Miss Goodrich-Freer and Lord Iddesleigh. *Two Volumes.*
THE INHERITANCE. By Susan Ferrier. Edited by Miss Goodrich-Freer and Lord Iddesleigh. *Two Volumes.*
ELIA, AND THE LAST ESSAYS OF ELIA. By Charles Lamb. Edited by E. V. Lucas.
THE ESSAYS OF ABRAHAM COWLEY. Edited by H. C. Minchin.
THE ESSAYS OF FRANCIS BACON. Edited by Edward Wright.
THE MAXIMS OF LA ROCHEFOUCAULD. Translated by Dean Stanhope. Edited by G. H. Powell.
A SENTIMENTAL JOURNEY. By Laurence Sterne. Edited by H. W. Paul.
MANSIE WAUCH. By D. M. Moir. Edited by T. F. Henderson.
THE INGOLDSBY LEGENDS. By R. H. Barham. Edited by J. B. Atlay. *Two Volumes*
THE SCARLET LETTER. By Nathaniel Hawthorne. Edited by P. Dearmer.
REJECTED ADDRESSES. By Horace and James Smith. Edited by A. D. Godley, M.A.
LONDON LYRICS. By F. Locker. Edited by A. D. Godley, M.A.
A reprint of the First Edition.

Miniature Library, Methuen's

EUPHRANOR: a Dialogue on Youth. By Edward FitzGerald. From the edition published by W. Pickering in 1851. *Demy 32mo. Leather, 2s. net.*
POLONIUS: or Wise Saws and Modern Instances. By Edward FitzGerald. From the edition published by W. Pickering in 1852. *Demy 32mo. Leather, 2s. net.*
THE RUBAÍYAT OF OMAR KHAYYAM. By Edward FitzGerald. From the 1st edition of 1859. *Second Edition. Leather, 1s. net.*

THE LIFE OF EDWARD, LORD HERBERT OF CHERBURY. Written by himself. From the edition printed at Strawberry Hill in the year 1764. *Medium 32mo. Leather, 2s. net.*
THE VISIONS OF DOM FRANCISCO DE QUEVEDO VILLEGAS, Knight of the Order of St. James. Made English by R. L. From the edition printed for H. Herringman, 1668. *Leather, 2s. net.*
POEMS. By Dora Greenwell. From the edition of 1848. *Leather, 2s. net.*

School Examination Series

Edited by A. M. M. STEDMAN, M.A.   *Crown 8vo.   2s. 6d.*

FRENCH EXAMINATION PAPERS. By A. M. M. Stedman, M.A. *Twelfth Edition.*
A KEY, issued to Tutors and Private Students only, to be had on application to the Publishers. *Fifth Edition. Crown 8vo. 6s. net.*
LATIN EXAMINATION PAPERS. By A. M. M. Stedman, M.A. *Twelfth Edition.*
KEY (*Fourth Edition*) issued as above. 6s. net.
GREEK EXAMINATION PAPERS. By A. M. M. Stedman, M.A. *Seventh Edition.*
KEY (*Second Edition*) issued as above. 6s. net.
GERMAN EXAMINATION PAPERS. By R. J. Morich. *Fifth Edition.*
KEY (*Second Edition*) issued as above. 6s. net.

HISTORY AND GEOGRAPHY EXAMINATION PAPERS. By C. H. Spence, M.A., Clifton College. *Second Edition.*

PHYSICS EXAMINATION PAPERS. By R. E. Steel, M.A., F.C.S.

GENERAL KNOWLEDGE EXAMINATION PAPERS By A. M. M. Stedman, M.A. *Fourth Edition.*
KEY (*Third Edition*) issued as above. 7s. net.

EXAMINATION PAPERS IN ENGLISH HISTORY. By J. Tait Plowden-Wardlaw, B.A.

Social Questions of To-day
Edited by H. DE B. GIBBINS, Litt.D., M.A.
Crown 8vo.   2s. 6d.

TRADE UNIONISM—NEW AND OLD. By G. Howell. *Third Edition.*

THE CO-OPERATIVE MOVEMENT TO-DAY. By G. J. Holyoake. *Second Edition.*

PROBLEMS OF POVERTY. By J. A. Hobson, M.A. *Fourth Edition.*

THE COMMERCE OF NATIONS. By C. F. Bastable, M.A. *Third Edition.*

THE ALIEN INVASION. By W. H. Wilkins, B.A.

THE RURAL EXODUS. By P. Anderson Graham.

LAND NATIONALIZATION. By Harold Cox, B.A.

A SHORTER WORKING DAY. By H. de B. Gibbins and R. A. Hadfield.

BACK TO THE LAND: An Inquiry into Rural Depopulation. By H. E. Moore.

TRUSTS, POOLS, AND CORNERS. By J. Stephen Jeans.

THE FACTORY SYSTEM. By R. W. Cooke-Taylor.

THE STATE AND ITS CHILDREN. By Gertrude Tuckwell.

WOMEN'S WORK. By Lady Dilke, Miss Bulley, and Miss Whitley.

SOCIALISM AND MODERN THOUGHT. By M. Kauffmann.

THE HOUSING OF THE WORKING CLASSES. By E. Bowmaker.

THE PROBLEM OF THE UNEMPLOYED. By J. A. Hobson, M.A.

LIFE IN WEST LONDON. By Arthur Sherwell, M.A. *Third Edition.*

RAILWAY NATIONALIZATION. By Clement Edwards.

WORKHOUSES AND PAUPERISM. By Louisa Twining.

UNIVERSITY AND SOCIAL SETTLEMENTS. By W. Reason, M.A.

Technology, Textbooks of
Edited by PROFESSOR J. WERTHEIMER, F.I.C.
Fully Illustrated.

HOW TO MAKE A DRESS. By J. A. E. Wood. *Third Edition. Crown 8vo. 1s. 6d.*

CARPENTRY AND JOINERY. By F. C. Webber. *Third Edition. Crown 8vo. 3s. 6d.*

PRACTICAL MECHANICS. By Sidney H. Wells. *Second Edition. Crown 8vo. 3s. 6d.*

PRACTICAL PHYSICS. By H. Stroud, D.Sc., M.A. *Crown 8vo. 3s. 6d.*

MILLINERY, THEORETICAL AND PRACTICAL. By Clare Hill. *Crown 8vo. 2s.*

PRACTICAL CHEMISTRY. By W. French, M.A. *Crown 8vo.* Part I. *Second Edition. 1s. 6d.* Part II.

TECHNICAL ARITHMETIC AND GEOMETRY. By C. T. Millis, M.I.M.E. With Diagrams. *Crown 8vo. 3s. 6d.*

BUILDER'S QUANTITIES. By H. C. Grubb. With many Illustrations. *Crown 8vo. 4s. 6d.*

Theology, Handbooks of

THE XXXIX. ARTICLES OF THE CHURCH OF ENGLAND. Edited by E. C. S. Gibson, D.D. *Third and Cheaper Edition in One Volume. Demy 8vo. 12s. 6d.*

AN INTRODUCTION TO THE HISTORY OF RELIGION. By F. B. Jevons, M.A., Litt.D. *Second Edition. Demy 8vo. 10s. 6d.*

THE DOCTRINE OF THE INCARNATION. By R. L. Ottley, M.A. *Second and Cheaper Edition. Demy 8vo. 12s. 6d.*

AN INTRODUCTION TO THE HISTORY OF THE CREEDS. By A. E. Burn, B.D. *Demy 8vo. 10s. 6d.*

THE PHILOSOPHY OF RELIGION IN ENGLAND AND AMERICA. By Alfred Caldecott, D.D. *Demy 8vo. 10s. 6d.*

A HISTORY OF EARLY CHRISTIAN DOCTRINE. By J. F. Bethune-Baker, M.A., Fellow of Pembroke College, Cambridge. *Demy 8vo. 10s. 6d.*

University Extension Series
Edited by J. E. SYMES, M.A.,
Principal of University College, Nottingham.
Crown 8vo.   Price (with some exceptions) 2s. 6d.

A series of books on historical, literary, and scientific subjects, suitable for extension students and home-reading circles. Each volume is complete in itself, and the subjects are treated by competent writers in a broad and philosophic spirit.

THE INDUSTRIAL HISTORY OF ENGLAND. By H. de B. Gibbins, Litt.D., M.A. *Tenth Edition.* Revised. With Maps and Plans. *3s.*

A HISTORY OF ENGLISH POLITICAL ECONOMY. By L. L. Price, M.A. *Third Edition.*

VICTORIAN POETS. By A. Sharp.

THE FRENCH REVOLUTION. By J. E. Symes, M.A.

PSYCHOLOGY. By F. S. Granger, M.A. *Second Edition.*

THE EVOLUTION OF PLANT LIFE: Lower Forms. By G. Massee. Illustrated.

AIR AND WATER. By V. B. Lewes, M.A. Illustrated.

THE CHEMISTRY OF LIFE AND HEALTH. By C. W. Kimmins, M.A. Illustrated.

THE MECHANICS OF DAILY LIFE. By V. P. Sells, M.A. Illustrated.

ENGLISH SOCIAL REFORMERS. By H. de B. Gibbins, Litt.D., M.A. *Second Edition.*

ENGLISH TRADE AND FINANCE IN THE SEVENTEENTH CENTURY. By W. A. S. Hewins, B.A.

THE CHEMISTRY OF FIRE. By M. M. Pattison Muir, M.A. Illustrated.

A TEXT-BOOK OF AGRICULTURAL BOTANY. By M. C. Potter, M.A., F.L.S. Illustrated. *Second Edition. 4s. 6d.*

THE VAULT OF HEAVEN. A Popular Introduction to Astronomy. By R. A. Gregory. With numerous Illustrations.

METEOROLOGY. By H. N. Dickson, F.R.S.E., F.R. Met. Soc. Illustrated.

A MANUAL OF ELECTRICAL SCIENCE. By George J. Burch, M.A., F.R.S. Illustrated. *3s.*

THE EARTH. An Introduction to Physiography. By Evan Small, M.A. Illustrated.

INSECT LIFE. By F. W. Theobald, M.A. Illustrated.

ENGLISH POETRY FROM BLAKE TO BROWNING. By W. M. Dixon, M.A. *Second Edition.*

ENGLISH LOCAL GOVERNMENT. By E. Jenks, M.A.

THE GREEK VIEW OF LIFE. By G. L. Dickinson. *Third Edition.*

Westminster, Commentaries The

General Editor, WALTER LOCK, D.D., Warden of Keble College,
Dean Ireland's Professor of Exegesis in the University of Oxford.

THE BOOK OF GENESIS. Edited with Introduction and Notes by S. R. Driver, D.D., Canon of Christ Church, and Regius Professor of Hebrew at Oxford. *Second Edition. Demy 8vo.* 10s. 6d.

THE BOOK OF JOB. Edited by E. C. S. Gibson, D.D. *Demy 8vo.* 6s

THE ACTS OF THE APOSTLES. Edited by R. B. Rackham, M.A. *Demy 8vo. Second and Cheaper Edition.* 10s. 6d.

THE FIRST EPISTLE OF PAUL THE APOSTLE TO THE CORINTHIANS. Edited by H. L. Goudge, M.A. *Demy 8vo.* 6s.

THE EPISTLE OF ST. JAMES. Edited by R. J. Knowling, M.A. *Demy 8vo.* 6s.

PART II.—FICTION

Marie Corelli's Novels.
Crown 8vo   6s. *each.*

A ROMANCE OF TWO WORLDS. *Twenty-Fourth Edition.*

VENDETTA. *Twentieth Edition.*

THELMA. *Thirtieth Edition.*

ARDATH: THE STORY OF A DEAD SELF. *Fifteenth Edition.*

THE SOUL OF LILITH. *Twelfth Edit.*

WORMWOOD. *Thirteenth Edition.*

BARABBAS: A DREAM OF THE WORLD'S TRAGEDY. *Thirty-Ninth Edition.*
'The tender reverence of the treatment and the imaginative beauty of the writing have reconciled us to the daring of the conception. This "Dream of the World's Tragedy" is a lofty and not inadequate paraphrase of the supreme climax of the inspired narrative.'—*Dublin Review.*

THE SORROWS OF SATAN. *Forty-Eighth Edition.*
'A very powerful piece of work. . . . The conception is magnificent, and is likely to win an abiding place within the memory of man. . . . The author has immense command of language, and a limitless audacity. . . . This interesting and remarkable romance will live long after much of the ephemeral literature of the day is forgotten. . . . A literary phenomenon . . . novel, and even sublime.'—W. T. STEAD in the *Review of Reviews.*

THE MASTER CHRISTIAN.
                          [165th *Thousand.*
'It cannot be denied that "The Master Christian" is a powerful book; that it is one likely to raise uncomfortable questions in all but the most self-satisfied readers, and that it strikes at the root of the failure of the Churches—the decay of faith—in a manner which shows the inevitable disaster heaping up. . . . The good Cardinal Bonpré is a beautiful figure, fit to stand beside the good Bishop in "Les Misérables." It is a book with a serious purpose expressed with absolute unconventionality and passion . . . And this is to say it is a book worth reading.'—*Examiner.*

TEMPORAL POWER: A STUDY IN SUPREMACY.   [150th *Thousand.*
'It is impossible to read such a work as "Temporal Power" without becoming convinced that the story is intended to convey certain criticisms on the ways of the world and certain suggestions for the betterment of humanity. . . . If the chief intention of the book was to hold the mirror up to shams, injustice, dishonesty, cruelty, and neglect of conscience, nothing but praise can be given to that intention.'—*Morning Post.*

GOD'S GOOD MAN: A SIMPLE LOVE STORY.

Anthony Hope's Novels.
Crown 8vo   6s. *each.*

THE GOD IN THE CAR. *Ninth Edition.*
'A very remarkable book, deserving of critical analysis impossible within our limit; brilliant, but not superficial; well considered, but not elaborated; constructed with the proverbial art that conceals, but yet allows itself to be enjoyed by readers to whom fine literary method is a keen pleasure.'—*The World.*

A CHANGE OF AIR. *Sixth Edition.*
'A graceful, vivacious comedy, true to human nature. The characters are traced with a masterly hand.'—*Times.*

A MAN OF MARK. *Fifth Edition.*
'Of all Mr. Hope's books, "A Man of Mark" is the one which best compares with "The Prisoner of Zenda."'—*National Observer.*

THE CHRONICLES OF COUNT ANTONIO. *Fifth Edition.*
'It is a perfectly enchanting story of love and chivalry, and pure romance. The Count is the most constant, desperate, and

modest and tender of lovers, a peerless gentleman, an intrepid fighter, a faithful friend, and a magnanimous foe.'—*Guardian.*

PHROSO. Illustrated by H. R. MILLAR. *Sixth Edition.*
'The tale is thoroughly fresh, quick with vitality, stirring the blood.'—*St. James's Gazette.*

SIMON DALE. Illustrated. *Sixth Edition.*
'There is searching analysis of human nature, with a most ingeniously constructed plot. Mr. Hope has drawn the contrasts

of his women with marvellous subtlety and delicacy.'—*Times.*

THE KING'S MIRROR. *Fourth Edition.*
'In elegance, delicacy, and tact it ranks with the best of his novels, while in the wide range of its portraiture and the subtilty of its analysis it surpasses all his earlier ventures.'—*Spectator.*

QUISANTE. *Fourth Edition.*
'The book is notable for a very high literary quality, and an impress of power and mastery on every page.'—*Daily Chronicle.*

THE DOLLY DIALOGUES.

W. W. Jacobs' Novels
Crown 8vo   3s. 6d. each.

MANY CARGOES. *Twenty-Seventh Edition.*
SEA URCHINS. *Tenth Edition.*
A MASTER OF CRAFT. Illustrated. *Sixth Edition.*
'Can be unreservedly recommended to all who have not lost their appetite for wholesome laughter.'—*Spectator.*
'The best humorous book published for many a day.'—*Black and White.*

LIGHT FREIGHTS. Illustrated. *Fourth Edition.*
'His wit and humour are perfectly irresistible. Mr. Jacobs writes of skippers, and mates, and seamen, and his crew are the jolliest lot that ever sailed.'—*Daily News.*
'Laughter in every page.'—*Daily Mail.*

Lucas Malet's Novels
Crown 8vo.   6s. each.

COLONEL ENDERBY'S WIFE. *Third Edition.*
A COUNSEL OF PERFECTION. *New Edition.*
LITTLE PETER. *Second Edition.* 3s. 6d.
THE WAGES OF SIN. *Fourteenth Edition.*
THE CARISSIMA. *Fourth Edition.*
THE GATELESS BARRIER. *Fourth Edition.*
'In "The Gateless Barrier" it is at once evident that, whilst Lucas Malet has preserved her birthright of originality, the artistry, the actual writing, is above even the high level of the books that were born before.'—*Westminster Gazette.*

THE HISTORY OF SIR RICHARD CALMADY. *Seventh Edition.* A Limited Edition in Two Volumes. *Crown 8vo.* 12s.
'A picture finely and amply conceived. In the strength and insight in which the story has been conceived, in the wealth of fancy and reflection bestowed upon its execution, and in the moving sincerity of its pathos throughout, "Sir Richard Calmady" must rank as the great novel of a great writer.'—*Literature.*
'The ripest fruit of Lucas Malet's genius. A picture of maternal love by turns tender and terrible.'—*Spectator.*
'A remarkably fine book, with a noble motive and a sound conclusion.'—*Pilot.*

Gilbert Parker's Novels
Crown 8vo.   6s. each.

PIERRE AND HIS PEOPLE. *Fifth Edition.*
'Stories happily conceived and finely executed. There is strength and genius in Mr. Parker's style.'—*Daily Telegraph.*
MRS. FALCHION. *Fourth Edition.*
'A splendid study of character.'—*Athenæum.*
THE TRANSLATION OF A SAVAGE. *Second Edition.*
THE TRAIL OF THE SWORD. Illustrated. *Eighth Edition.*

'A rousing and dramatic tale. A book like this is a joy inexpressible.'—*Daily Chronicle.*
WHEN VALMOND CAME TO PONTIAC: The Story of a Lost Napoleon. *Fifth Edition.*
'Here we find romance—real, breathing, living romance. The character of Valmond is drawn unerringly.'—*Pall Mall Gazette.*
AN ADVENTURER OF THE NORTH: The Last Adventures of 'Pretty Pierre.' *Third Edition.*

'The present book is full of fine and moving stories of the great North.'—*Glasgow Herald.*

THE SEATS OF THE MIGHTY. Illustrated. *Thirteenth Edition.*
'Mr. Parker has produced a really fine historical novel.'—*Athenæum.*
'A great book.'—*Black and White.*

THE BATTLE OF THE STRONG: a Romance of Two Kingdoms. Illustrated. *Fourth Edition.*
'Nothing more vigorous or more human has come from Mr. Gilbert Parker than this novel.'—*Literature.*

THE POMP OF THE LAVILETTES. *Second Edition.* 3s. 6d.
'Unforced pathos, and a deeper knowledge of human nature than he has displayed before.'—*Pall Mall Gazette.*

Arthur Morrison's Novels

Crown 8vo. 6s. each.

TALES OF MEAN STREETS. *Sixth Edition.*
'A great book. The author's method is amazingly effective, and produces a thrilling sense of reality. The writer lays upon us a master hand. The book is simply appalling and irresistible in its interest. It is humorous also; without humour it would not make the mark it is certain to make.'—*World.*

A CHILD OF THE JAGO. *Fourth Edition.*
'The book is a masterpiece.'—*Pall Mall Gazette.*

TO LONDON TOWN. *Second Edition.*
'This is the new Mr. Arthur Morrison, gracious and tender, sympathetic and human.'—*Daily Telegraph.*

CUNNING MURRELL.
'Admirable. . . . Delightful humorous relief . . . . a most artistic and satisfactory achievement.'—*Spectator.*

THE HOLE IN THE WALL. *Third Edition.*
'A masterpiece of artistic realism. It has a finality of touch that only a master may command.'—*Daily Chronicle.*
'An absolute masterpiece, which any novelist might be proud to claim.'—*Graphic.*
'"The Hole in the Wall" is a masterly piece of work. His characters are drawn with amazing skill. Extraordinary power.' —*Daily Telegraph.*

Eden Phillpotts' Novels

Crown 8vo. 6s. each.

LYING PROPHETS.

CHILDREN OF THE MIST. *Fifth Edition.*

THE HUMAN BOY. With a Frontispiece. *Fourth Edition.*
'Mr. Phillpotts knows exactly what school-boys do, and can lay bare their inmost thoughts; likewise he shows an all-pervading sense of humour.'—*Academy.*

SONS OF THE MORNING. *Second Edition.*
'A book of strange power and fascination.'—*Morning Post.*

THE STRIKING HOURS. *Second Edition.*
'Tragedy and comedy, pathos and humour, are blended to a nicety in this volume.'—*World.*
'The whole book is redolent of a fresher and ampler air than breathes in the circumscribed life of great towns.'—*Spectator.*

THE RIVER. *Third Edition.*
'"The River" places Mr. Phillpotts in the front rank of living novelists.'—*Punch.*
'Since "Lorna Doone" we have had nothing so picturesque as this new romance.' *Birmingham Gazette.*
'Mr. Phillpotts's new book is a masterpiece which brings him indisputably into the front rank of English novelists.'—*Pall Mall Gazette.*
'This great romance of the River Dart. The finest book Mr. Eden Phillpotts has written.'—*Morning Post.*

THE AMERICAN PRISONER. *Third Edition.*

S. Baring-Gould's Novels

Crown 8vo. 6s. each.

ARMINELL. *Fifth Edition.*
URITH. *Fifth Edition.*
IN THE ROAR OF THE SEA. *Seventh Edition.*
CHEAP JACK ZITA. *Fourth Edition.*
MARGERY OF QUETHER. *Third Edition.*

THE QUEEN OF LOVE. *Fifth Edition.*
JACQUETTA. *Third Edition.*
KITTY ALONE. *Fifth Edition.*
NOÉMI. Illustrated. *Fourth Edition.*
THE BROOM-SQUIRE. Illustrated. *Fourth Edition.*
DARTMOOR IDYLLS.

THE PENNYCOMEQUICKS. *Third Edition.*
GUAVAS THE TINNER. Illustrated. *Second Edition.*
BLADYS. Illustrated. *Second Edition.*
DOMITIA. Illustrated. *Second Edition.*
PABO THE PRIEST.

WINIFRED. Illustrated. *Second Edition.*
THE FROBISHERS.
ROYAL GEORGIE. Illustrated.
MISS QUILLET. Illustrated.
LITTLE TU'PENNY. *A New Edition.* 6d.
CHRIS OF ALL SORTS.
IN DEWISLAND.

Robert Barr's Novels

Crown 8vo. 6s. each.

IN THE MIDST OF ALARMS. *Third Edition.*
'A book which has abundantly satisfied us by its capital humour.'—*Daily Chronicle.*
THE MUTABLE MANY. *Second Edition.*
'There is much insight in it, and much excellent humour.'—*Daily Chronicle.*

THE COUNTESS TEKLA. *Third Edition.*
'Of these mediæval romances, which are now gaining ground "The Countess Tekla" is the very best we have seen.'—*Pall Mall Gazette.*
THE LADY ELECTRA.

Albanesi (E. Maria). SUSANNAH AND ONE OTHER. *Fourth Edition. Crown 8vo.* 6s.
THE BLUNDER OF AN INNOCENT. *Crown 8vo.* 6s.
CAPRICIOUS CAROLINE. *Crown 8vo.* 6s.
LOVE AND LOUISA. *Crown 8vo.* 6s.
PETER, A PARASITE. *Crown 8vo.* 6s.
Anstey (F.), Author of 'Vice Versâ.' A BAYARD FROM BENGAL. Illustrated by BERNARD PARTRIDGE. *Third Edition. Crown 8vo.* 3s. 6d.
Bacheller (Irving), Author of 'Eben Holden.' DARREL OF THE BLESSED ISLES. *Third Edition. Crown 8vo.* 6s.
Bagot (Richard). A ROMAN MYSTERY. *Third Edition. Crown 8vo.* 6s.
Balfour (Andrew). VENGEANCE IS MINE. Illustrated. *Crown 8vo.* 1s. net.
Balfour (M. C.). THE FALL OF THE SPARROW. *Crown 8vo.* 6s.
Baring-Gould (S.). See page 34 and 1s. Novels.
Barlow (Jane). THE LAND OF THE SHAMROCK. *Crown 8vo.* 6s.
FROM THE EAST UNTO THE WEST. *Crown 8vo.* 1s. net.
Barr (Robert). See page 35 and 1s. Novels.
Begbie (Harold). THE ADVENTURES OF SIR JOHN SPARROW. *Crown 8vo.* 6s.
Belloc (Hilaire) MR. BURDEN, DEALER IN HARDWARE. With 36 Illustrations by G. K. CHESTERTON. *Crown 8vo.* 6s.
Benson (E. F.). DODO: A Detail of the Day. *Crown 8vo.* 6s.
THE CAPSINA. *Crown 8vo.* 1s. net.
Benson (Margaret). SUBJECT TO VANITY. *Crown 8vo.* 3s. 6d.
Besant (Sir Walter). A FIVE YEARS' TRYST, and Other Stories. *Crown 8vo.* 1s. net.

Bowles (C. Stewart). A STRETCH OFF THE LAND. *Crown 8vo.* 6s.
Bullock (Shan. F.). THE SQUIREEN. *Crown 8vo.* 6s.
THE RED LEAGUERS. *Crown 8vo.* 6s.
Burton (J. Bloundelle). THE YEAR ONE: A Page of the French Revolution. Illustrated. *Crown 8vo.* 6s.
DENOUNCED. *Crown 8vo.* 6s.
THE CLASH OF ARMS. *Crown 8vo.* 6s.
ACROSS THE SALT SEAS. *Crown 8vo.* 1s. net.
THE FATE OF VALSEC. *Cr. 8vo.* 6s.
A BRANDED NAME. *Crown 8vo.* 6s.
Capes (Bernard), Author of 'The Lake of Wine.' THE EXTRAORDINARY CONFESSIONS OF DIANA PLEASE. *Crown 8vo.* 6s.
Chesney (Weatherby). THE BAPTIST RING. *Crown 8vo.* 6s.
THE TRAGEDY OF THE GREAT EMERALD. *Crown 8vo.* 6s.
THE MYSTERY OF A BUNGALOW. *Crown 8vo.* 6s.
Clifford (Hugh). A FREE LANCE OF TO-DAY. *Crown 8vo.* 6s.
Cobb (Thomas). A CHANGE OF FACE. *Crown 8vo.* 6s.
Cobban (J. Maclaren). THE KING OF ANDAMAN: A Saviour of Society. *Crown 8vo.* 6s.
WILT THOU HAVE THIS WOMAN? *Crown 8vo.* 6s.
THE ANGEL OF THE COVENANT. *Crown 8vo.* 6s.
Corbett (Julian). A BUSINESS IN GREAT WATERS. *Crown 8vo.* 6s.
Corelli (Marie). See page 32.
Cotes (Mrs. Everard). See S. J. Duncan.
Crane (Stephen) and **Barr (Robert).** THE O'RUDDY. *Crown 8vo.* 6s.
Crockett (S. R.), Author of 'The Raiders,' etc. LOCHINVAR. Illustrated. *Second Edition. Crown 8vo.* 6s.
THE STANDARD BEARER. *Cr. 8vo.* 6s.

Croker (B. M.). ANGEL. *Third Edition. Crown 8vo. 6s.*
PEGGY OF THE BARTONS. *Fifth Edition. Crown 8vo. 6s.*
A STATE SECRET. *Third Edition. Crown 8vo. 3s. 6d.*
JOHANNA. *Second Edition. Cr. 8vo. 6s.*
THE HAPPY VALLEY. *Crown 8vo. 6s.*

Doyle (A. Conan), Author of 'Sherlock Holmes,' 'The White Company,' etc.
ROUND THE RED LAMP. *Ninth Edition. Crown 8vo. 6s.*

Duncan (Sara Jeannette) (Mrs. Everard Cotes), Author of 'A Voyage of Consolation.' THOSE DELIGHTFUL AMERICANS. Illustrated. *Third Edition. Crown 8vo. 6s.*
THE PATH OF A STAR. Illustrated. *Second Edition. Crown 8vo. 6s.*
THE POOL IN THE DESERT. *Crown 8vo. 6s.*
A VOYAGE OF CONSOLATION. *Cr. 8vo. 3s. 6d.*

Fenn (G. Manville). AN ELECTRIC SPARK. *Crown 8vo. 6s.*
A DOUBLE KNOT. *Crown 8vo. 2s. 6d.*

Findlater (J. H.). THE GREEN GRAVES OF BALGOWRIE. *Fourth Edition. Crown 8vo. 6s.*
A DAUGHTER OF STRIFE. *Crown 8vo. 1s. net.*

Findlater (Mary). OVER THE HILLS. *Second Edition. Crown 8vo. 6s.*
BETTY MUSGRAVE. *Second Edition. Crown 8vo. 6s.*
A NARROW WAY. *Third Edition. Crown 8vo. 6s.*
THE ROSE OF JOY. *Second Edition. Crown 8vo. 6s.*

Fitzstephen (Gerald). MORE KIN THAN KIND. *Crown 8vo. 6s.*

Fletcher (J. S.). THE BUILDERS. *Crown 8vo. 6s.*
LUCIAN THE DREAMER. *Crown 8vo. 6s.*
DAVID MARCH. *Crown 8vo. 6s.*

Francis (M. E.). MISS ERIN. *Second Edition. Crown 8vo. 1s. net.*

Fraser (Mrs. Hugh). Author of 'The Stolen Emperor.' THE SLAKING OF THE SWORD. *Crown 8vo. 6s.*

Gallon (Tom), Author of 'Kiddy.' RICKERBY'S FOLLY. *Crown 8vo. 6s.*

Gaunt (Mary). DEADMAN'S. *Crown 8vo. 6s.*
THE MOVING FINGER. *Crown 8vo. 3s. 6d.*

Gerard (Dorothea), Author of 'Lady Baby.' THE CONQUEST OF LONDON. *Second Edition. Crown 8vo. 6s.*
HOLY MATRIMONY. *Second Edition. Crown 8vo. 6s.*

THINGS THAT HAVE HAPPENED. *Crown 8vo. 6s.*
MADE OF MONEY. *Crown 8vo. 6s.*
THE BRIDGE OF LIFE *Cr. 8vo. 6s.*

Gerard (Emily). THE HERONS' TOWER. *Crown 8vo. 6s.*

Gilchrist (R. Murray). WILLOW-BRAKE. *Crown 8vo. 6s.*

Gissing (George), Author of 'Demos,' 'In the Year of Jubilee,' etc. THE TOWN TRAVELLER. *Second Edition. Crown 8vo. 6s.*
THE CROWN OF LIFE. *Crown 8vo. 6s.*

Glanville (Ernest). THE DESPATCH RIDER. *Crown 8vo. 3s. 6d.*
THE INCA'S TREASURE. Illustrated. *Crown 8vo. 3s. 6d.*

Gleig (Charles). BUNTER'S CRUISE. Illustrated. *Crown 8vo. 3s. 6d.*

Goss (C. F.). THE REDEMPTION OF DAVID CORSON. *Third Edition. Crown 8vo. 6s.*

Harrison (Mrs. Burton). A PRINCESS OF THE HILLS. Illustrated. *Crown 8vo. 6s.*

Herbertson (Agnes G.). PATIENCE DEAN. *Crown 8vo. 6s.*

Hichens (Robert), Author of 'Flames,' etc. THE PROPHET OF BERKELEY SQUARE. *Second Ed. Crown 8vo. 6s.*
TONGUES OF CONSCIENCE. *Second Edition. Crown 8vo. 6s.*
FELIX. *Fourth Edition. Crown 8vo. 6s.*
THE WOMAN WITH THE FAN. *Fifth Edition. Cr. 8vo. 6s.*
BYEWAYS. *Crown 8vo. 3s. 6d.*
THE GARDEN OF ALLAH. *Crown 8vo. 6s.*

Hobbes (John Oliver), Author of 'Robert Orange.' THE SERIOUS WOOING. *Crown 8vo. 6s.*

Hope (Anthony). See page 32.

Hough (Emerson). THE MISSISSIPPI BUBBLE. Illustrated. *Crown 8vo. 6s.*

Housman (Clemence). SCENES FROM THE LIFE OF AGLOVALE. Illustrated. *Crown 8vo. 6s.*

Hunt (Violet). THE HUMAN INTEREST. *Crown 8vo. 6s.*

Hyne (C. J. Cutcliffe), Author of 'Captain Kettle.' MR. HORROCKS, PURSER. *Third Edition. Crown 8vo. 6s.*

Jacobs (W. W.). See page 33.

James (Henry), Author of 'What Maisie Knew.' THE SOFT SIDE. *Second Edition. Crown 8vo. 6s.*
THE BETTER SORT. *Crown 8vo. 6s.*
THE AMBASSADORS. *Second Edition. Crown 8vo. 6s.*
THE GOLDEN BOWL. *Crown 8vo. 6s.*

Janson (Gustaf). ABRAHAM'S SACRIFICE. *Crown 8vo. 6s.*

Lawless (Hon. Emily). TRAITS AND CONFIDENCES. *Crown 8vo.* 6s.
MELCHO. *Crown 8vo.* 1s. *net.*

Lawson (Harry), Author of 'When the Billy Boils.' CHILDREN OF THE BUSH. *Crown 8vo.* 6s.

Linden (Annie). A WOMAN OF SENTIMENT. *Crown 8vo* 16s.

Linton (E. Lynn). THE TRUE HISTORY OF JOSHUA DAVIDSON, Christian and Communist. *Twelfth Edition. Medium 8vo.* 6d.

Long (J. Luther), Co-Author of 'The Darling of the Gods.' MADAME BUTTERFLY. *Crown 8vo.* 6s.
SIXTY JANE. *Crown 8vo.* 6s.

Lorimer (Norma). MIRRY ANN. *Crown 8vo.* 6s.
JOSIAH'S WIFE. *Crown 8vo.* 6s.

Lyall (Edna). DERRICK VAUGHAN, NOVELIST. *42nd Thousand. Crown 8vo.* 3s. 6d.

M'Carthy (Justin H.), Author of 'If I were King.' THE LADY OF LOYALTY HOUSE. *Crown 8vo.* 6s.

Mackie (Pauline Bradford). THE VOICE IN THE DESERT. *Crown 8vo.* 6s.

Macnaughtan (S.). THE FORTUNE OF CHRISTINA MACNAB. *Third Edition. Crown 8vo.* 6s.

Malet (Lucas). See page 33.

Mann (Mrs. M. E.). OLIVIA'S SUMMER. *Second Edition. Crown 8vo.* 6s.
A LOST ESTATE. *A New Edition. Crown 8vo.* 6s.
THE PARISH OF HILBY. *A New Edition. Crown 8vo.* 6s.
THE PARISH NURSE. *Crown 8vo.* 6s.
GRAN'MA'S JANE. *Crown 8vo.* 6s.
MRS. PETER HOWARD. *Cr. 8vo.* 6s.
A WINTER'S TALE. *Crown 8vo.* 6s.
THERE WAS ONCE A PRINCE. Illustrated. *Crown 8vo.* 3s. 6d.
WHEN ARNOLD COMES HOME. Illustrated. *Crown 8vo.* 3s. 6d.

Marriott, (Charles), Author of 'The Column.' GENEVRA. *Crown 8vo.* 6s.

Marsh (Richard). MARVELS AND MYSTERIES. *Crown 8vo.* 6s.
THE TWICKENHAM PEERAGE. *Second Edition. Crown 8vo.* 6s.
A METAMORPHOSIS. *Crown 8vo.* 6s.
GARNERED. *Crown 8vo.* 6s.
A DUEL. *Crown 8vo.* 6s.

Mason (A. E. W.), Author of 'The Courtship of Morrice Buckler,' 'Miranda of the Balcony,' etc. CLEMENTINA. Illustrated. *Crown 8vo. Second Edition.* 6s.

Mathers (Helen), Author of 'Comin' thro' the Rye.' HONEY. *Fourth Edition. Crown 8vo.* 6s.
GRIFF OF GRIFFITHSCOURT. *Crown 8vo.* 6s.
THE FERRYMAN. *Crown 8vo.* 6s.

Meade (L. T.). DRIFT *Crown 8vo.* 6s.
RESURGAM. *Crown 8vo.* 6s.

'Miss Molly' (The Author of). THE GREAT RECONCILER. *Crown 8vo.* 6s.

Mitford (Bertram). THE SIGN OF THE SPIDER. Illustrated. *Sixth Edition. Crown 8vo.* 3s. 6d.
IN THE WHIRL OF THE RISING. *Second Edition. Crown 8vo.* 6s.

Montresor (F. F.), Author of 'Into the Highways and Hedges.' THE ALIEN. *Third Edition. Crown 8vo.* 6s.

Morrison (Arthur). See page 34.

Nesbit (E.). (Mrs. E. Bland). THE RED HOUSE. Illustrated. *Fourth Edition. Crown 8vo.* 6s.
THE LITERARY SENSE. *Cr. 8vo.* 6s.

Norris (W. E.). THE CREDIT OF THE COUNTY. Illustrated. *Second Edition. Crown 8vo.* 6s.
THE EMBARRASSING ORPHAN. *Crown 8vo.* 6s.
HIS GRACE. *Third Edition. Cr. 8vo.* 6s.
THE DESPOTIC LADY. *Crown 8vo.* 6s.
CLARISSA FURIOSA. *Crown 8vo.* 6s.
AN OCTAVE. *Second Edition. Crown 8vo.* 6s.
NIGEL'S VOCATION. *Crown 8vo.* 6s.
JACK'S FATHER. *Crown 8vo.* 2s. 6d.
LORD LEONARD THE LUCKLESS. *Crown 8vo.* 1s. *net.*

Oliphant (Mrs.). THE TWO MARYS. *Crown 8vo.* 6s.
THE LADY'S WALK. *Crown 8vo.* 6s.
THE PRODIGALS. *Crown 8vo.* 1s. *net.*

Ollivant (Alfred). OWD BOB, THE GREY DOG OF KENMUIR. *Sixth Edition. Crown 8vo.* 6s.

Oppenheim (E. Phillips). MASTER OF MEN. *Third Edition. Crown 8vo.* 6s.

Oxenham (John), Author of 'Barbe of Grand Bayou.' A WEAVER OF WEBS. *Crown 8vo.* 6s.

Pain (Barry). THREE FANTASIES. *Crown 8vo.* 1s.
LINDLEY KAYS. *Crown 8vo.* 6s.

Parker (Gilbert). See page 33.

Pemberton (Max). THE FOOTSTEPS OF A THRONE. Illustrated. *Second Edition. Crown 8vo.* 6s.
I CROWN THEE KING. With Illustrations by Frank Dadd and A. Forrestier. *Crown 8vo.* 6s.

Penny (Mrs. F. E.). A MIXED MARRIAGE. *Crown 8vo.* 1s. *net.*

Phillpotts (Eden). See page 34.

Pickthall (Marmaduke). SAID THE FISHERMAN. *Fourth Edition. Crown 8vo.* 6s.

Pryce (Richard). THE QUIET MRS. FLEMING. *Crown 8vo.* 3s. 6d.

'Q.' Author of 'Dead Man's Rock.' THE WHITE WOLF. *Second Edition. Crown 8vo.* 6s.

Queux (W. le). THE HUNCHBACK OF WESTMINSTER. *Second Edition. Crown 8vo. 6s.*
THE CLOSED BOOK. *Crown 8vo. 6s.*

Rhys (Grace). THE WOOING OF SHEILA. *Second Edition. Crown 8vo. 6s.*
THE PRINCE OF LISNOVER. *Crown 8vo. 6s.*

Rhys (Grace) and Another. THE DIVERTED VILLAGE. With Illustrations by DOROTHY GWYN JEFFREYS. *Crown 8vo. 6s.*

Ridge (W. Pett). LOST PROPERTY. *Second Edition. Crown 8vo. 6s.*
SECRETARY TO BAYNE, M.P. *Crown 8vo. 6s.*
ERB. *Second Edition. Crown 8vo. 6s.*
A SON OF THE STATE. *Crown 8vo. 3s. 6d.*
A BREAKER OF LAWS. *Cr. 8vo. 3s. 6d.*
MRS. GALER'S BUSINESS. *Crown 8vo. 6s.*

Ritchie (Mrs. David G.). THE TRUTHFUL LIAR. *Crown 8vo. 6s.*

Roberts (C.G.D.). THE HEART OF THE ANCIENT WOOD. *Crown 8vo. 3s. 6d.*

Russell (W. Clark). MY DANISH SWEETHEART. Illustrated. *Fourth Edition. Crown 8vo. 6s.*
ABANDONED. *Second Edition. Crown 8vo. 6s.*

Sergeant (Adeline). Author of 'The Story of a Penitent Soul.' THE MASTER OF BEECHWOOD. *Crown 8vo. 6s.*
BARBARA'S MONEY. *Second Edition. Crown 8vo. 6s.*
ANTHEA'S WAY. *Crown 8vo. 6s.*
THE YELLOW DIAMOND. *Second Edition. Crown 8vo. 6s.*
UNDER SUSPICION. *Crown 8vo. 6s.*
THE LOVE THAT OVERCAME. *Crown 8vo. 6s.*
THE ENTHUSIAST. *Crown 8vo. 6s.*
ACCUSED AND ACCUSER. *Crown 8vo. 6s.*
THE PROGRESS OF RACHEL. *Cr. 8vo. 6s.*

Shannon (W. F.). THE MESS DECK. *Crown 8vo. 3s. 6d.*
JIM TWELVES. *Second Edition. Crown 8vo. 3s. 6d.*

Sonnichsen (Albert). DEEP SEA VAGABONDS. *Crown 8vo. 6s.*

Strain (E. H.). ELMSLIE'S DRAG-NET. *Crown 8vo. 6s.*

Stringer (Arthur). THE SILVER POPPY. *Crown 8vo. 6s.*

Sutherland (Duchess of). ONE HOUR AND THE NEXT. *Third Edition. Crown 8vo. 1s. net.*

Swan (Annie). LOVE GROWN COLD. *Second Edition. Crown 8vo. 1s. net.*

Swift (Benjamin). SIREN CITY. *Crown 8vo. 6s.*

Tanqueray (Mrs. B. M.). THE ROYAL QUAKER. *Crown 8vo. 6s.*

Thompson (Vance). SPINNERS OF LIFE. *Crown 8vo. 6s.*

Waineman (Paul). A HEROINE FROM FINLAND. *Crown 8vo. 1s. net.*
BY A FINNISH LAKE. *Crown 8vo. 6s.*
THE SONG OF THE FOREST. *Crown 8vo. 6s.*

Watson (H. B. Marriott). ALARUMS AND EXCURSIONS. *Cr. 8vo. 6s.*
CAPTAIN FORTUNE. *Cr. 8vo. 6s.*

Wells (H. G.) THE SEA LADY. *Crown 8vo. 6s.*

Weyman (Stanley), Author of 'A Gentleman of France.' UNDER THE RED ROBE. With Illustrations by R. C. WOODVILLE. *Eighteenth Edition. Crown 8vo. 6s.*

White (Stewart E.), Author of 'The Blazed Trail.' CONJUROR'S HOUSE. A Romance of the Free Trail. *Second Edition. Crown 8vo. 6s.*

Williamson (Mrs. C. N.), Author of 'The Barnstormers.' PAPA. *Second Edition. Crown 8vo. 6s.*
THE ADVENTURE OF PRINCESS SLYVIA. *Crown 8vo 3s. 6d.*
THE WOMAN WHO DARED. *Crown 8vo. 6s.*
THE SEA COULD TELL. *Second Edition. Crown 8vo. 6s.*

Williamson (C. N. and A. M.). THE LIGHTNING CONDUCTOR : Being the Romance of a Motor Car. Illustrated. *Sixth Edition. Crown 8vo. 6s.*
THE PRINCESS PASSES. *Cr. 8vo. 6s.*

Yeats (S. Levett). ORRAIN. *Crown 8vo. 6s.*

Boys and Girls, Books for

Crown 8vo.   3s. 6d.

THE ICELANDER'S SWORD. By S. Baring-Gould.

ONLY A GUARD-ROOM DOG. By Edith E. Cuthell.

THE DOCTOR OF THE JULIET. By Harry Collingwood.

MASTER ROCKAFELLAR'S VOYAGE. By W. Clark Russell.

SYD BELTON : Or, the Boy who would not go to Sea. By G. Manville Fenn.

THE RED GRANGE. By Mrs. Molesworth.

A GIRL OF THE PEOPLE. By L. T. Meade.

HEPSY GIPSY. By L. T. Meade. *2s. 6d.*

THE HONOURABLE MISS. By L. T. Meade.

Dumas, The Novels of Alexandre

Price 6d.—Double Volume, 1s.

THE THREE MUSKETEERS. With a long Introduc-
tion by Andrew Lang. Double volume.
THE PRINCE OF THIEVES. *Second Edition.*
ROBIN HOOD. A Sequel to the above.
THE CORSICAN BROTHERS.
GEORGES.
CROP-EARED JACQUOT.
TWENTY YEARS AFTER. Double volume.
AMAURY.
THE CASTLE OF EPPSTEIN.
THE SNOWBALL.
CECILE; OR, THE WEDDING GOWN.
ACTÉ.
THE BLACK TULIP.
THE VISCOMTE DE BRAGELONNE.
THE CONVICT'S SON.
THE WOLF-LEADER.
NANON; OR, THE WOMEN'S WAR.
PAULINE; MURAT; AND PASCAL BRUNO.
THE ADVENTURES OF CAPTAIN PAMPHILE.
FERNANDE.
GABRIEL LAMBERT.
THE REMINISCENCES OF ANTONY.
CATHERINE BLUM.
THE CHEVALIER D'HARMENTAL.

CONSCIENCE

Illustrated Edition.

THE THREE MUSKETEERS. Illustrated in Colour
by Frank Adams.
THE PRINCE OF THIEVES. Illustrated in Colour by
Frank Adams.
ROBIN HOOD THE OUTLAW. Illustrated in Colour
by Frank Adams.
THE CORSICAN BROTHERS. Illustrated in Colour
by A. M. M'Lellan.
FERNANDE. Illustrated in Colour by Munro Orr.
THE BLACK TULIP. Illustrated in Colour by A. Orr.
ACTÉ. Illustrated in Colour by Gordon Browne.
GEORGES. Illustrated in Colour by Munro Orr.
THE CASTLE OF EPPSTEIN. Illustrated in Colour
by A. Orr.
TWENTY YEARS AFTER. Illustrated in Colour by
Frank Adams.
THE SNOWBALL AND SULTANETTA. Illustrated
in Colour by Frank Adams.
THE VICOMTE DE BRAGELONNE. Illustrated in
Colour by Frank Adams.
AMAURY. Illustrated in Colour by Gordon Browne.
CROP-EARED JACQUOT. Illustrated in Colour by
Gordon Browne.

Methuen's Universal Library

EDITED BY SIDNEY LEE. *In Sixpenny Volumes.*

MESSRS. METHUEN are preparing a new series of reprints containing both books of classical repute, which are accessible in various forms, and also some rarer books, of which no satisfactory edition at a moderate price is in existence. It is their ambition to place the best books of all nations, and particularly of the Anglo-Saxon race, within the reach of every reader. All the great masters of Poetry, Drama, Fiction, History, Biography, and Philosophy will be represented. Mr. Sidney Lee will be the General Editor of the Library, and he will contribute a Note to each book.

The characteristics of METHUEN'S UNIVERSAL LIBRARY are five:—

1. SOUNDNESS OF TEXT. A pure and unabridged text is the primary object of the series, and the books will be carefully reprinted under the direction of competent scholars from the best editions. In a series intended for popular use not less than for students, adherence to the old spelling would in many cases leave the matter unintelligible to ordinary readers, and, as the appeal of a classic is universal, the spelling has in general been modernised.

2. COMPLETENESS. Where it seems advisable, the complete works of such masters as Milton, Bacon, Ben Jonson and Sir Thomas Browne will be given. These will be issued in separate volumes, so that the reader who does not desire all the works of an author will have the opportunity of acquiring a single masterpiece.

3. CHEAPNESS. The books will be well printed on good paper at a price which on the whole is without parallel in the history of publishing. Each volume will contain from 100 to 350 pages, and will be issued in paper covers, Crown 8vo, at Sixpence net.

4. CLEARNESS OF TYPE. The type will be a very legible one.

5. SIMPLICITY. There will be no editorial matter except a short biographical and bibliographical note by Mr. Sidney Lee at the beginning of each volume.

Where it is possible, each separate book will be issued in one volume, but the longer ones must be divided into several volumes. The volumes may also be obtained in cloth at One Shilling net, and where a single book is issued in several Sixpenny volumes it may be obtained in cloth in a double or treble volume. Thus GIL BLAS may be bought in two Sixpenny volumes, or in one cloth volume at 1s. 6d. net, and SHAKESPEARE will be given in ten Sixpenny volumes, or in five cloth volumes at 1s. 6d. each.

The Library will be issued at regular intervals after the publication of the first six books, all of which will be published together. Due notice will be given of succeeding issues. The order of publication will be arranged to give as much variety of subject as possible, and the volumes composing the complete works of an author will be issued at convenient intervals.

The early Books are in the Press

Novelist, The

MESSRS. METHUEN are issuing under the above general title a Monthly Series of Novels by popular authors at the price of Sixpence. Each number is as long as the average Six Shilling Novel. The first numbers of 'THE NOVELIST' are as follows:—

1. DEAD MEN TELL NO TALES. By E. W. Hornung.
2. JENNIE BAXTER, JOURNALIST. By Robert Barr.
3. THE INCA'S TREASURE. By Ernest Glanville.
4. A SON OF THE STATE. By W. Pett Ridge.
5. FURZE BLOOM. By S. Baring-Gould.
6. BUNTER'S CRUISE. By C. Gleig.
7. THE GAY DECEIVERS. By Arthur Moore.
8. PRISONERS OF WAR. By A. Boyson Weekes.
9. A FLASH OF SUMMER. By Mrs. W. K. Clifford.
10. VELDT AND LAAGER : Tales of the Transvaal. By E. S. Valentine.
11. THE NIGGER KNIGHTS. By F. Norreys Connel.
12. A MARRIAGE AT SEA. By W. Clark Russell.
13. THE POMP OF THE LAVILETTES. By Gilbert Parker.
14. A MAN OF MARK. By Anthony Hope.
15. THE CARISSIMA. By Lucas Malet.
16. THE LADY'S WALK. By Mrs. Oliphant.
17. DERRICK VAUGHAN. By Edna Lyall.
18. IN THE MIDST OF ALARMS. By Robert Barr.
19. HIS GRACE. By W. E. Norris.
20. DODO. By E. F. Benson.
21. CHEAP JACK ZITA. By S. Baring-Gould.
22. WHEN VALMOND CAME TO PONTIAC. By Gilbert Parker.
23. THE HUMAN BOY. By Eden Phillpotts.
24. THE CHRONICLES OF COUNT ANTONIO. By Anthony Hope.
25. BY STROKE OF SWORD. By Andrew Balfour.
26. KITTY ALONE. By S. Baring-Gould.
27. GILES INGILBY. By W. E. Norris.
28. URITH. By S. Baring-Gould.
29. THE TOWN TRAVELLER. By George Gissing.
30. MR. SMITH. By Mrs. Walford.
31. A CHANGE OF AIR. By Anthony Hope.
32. THE KLOOF BRIDE. By Ernest Glanville.
33. ANGEL. By B. M. Croker.
34. A COUNSEL OF PERFECTION. By Lucas Malet.
35. THE BABY'S GRANDMOTHER. By Mrs. Walford.
36. THE COUNTESS TEKLA. By Robert Barr.
37. DRIFT. BY L. T. Meade.
38. THE MASTER OF BEECHWOOD. By Adeline Sergeant.
39. CLEMENTINA. By A. E. W. Mason.
40. THE ALIEN. By F. F. Montresor.
41. THE BROOM SQUIRE. By S. Baring-Gould.
42. HONEY. By Helen Mathers.
43. THE FOOTSTEPS OF A THRONE. By Max Pemberton.
44. ROUND THE RED LAMP. By A. Conan Doyle.
45. LOST PROPERTY. By W. Pett Ridge.
46. THE TWICKENHAM PEERAGE. By Richard Marsh.
47. HOLY MATRIMONY. By Dorothea Gerard.
48. THE SIGN OF THE SPIDER. By Bertram Mitford.
49. THE RED HOUSE. By E. Nesbit.
50. THE HOLE IN THE WALL. By A. Morrison.
51. A ROMAN MYSTERY. By Richard Bagot.
52. THE CREDIT OF THE COUNTY. By W. E. Norris.
53. A MOMENT'S ERROR. By A. W. Marchant.
54. PHROSO. By Anthony Hope.
55. I CROWN THEE KING. By Max Pemberton.
56. JOHANNA. By B. M. Croker.
57. BARBARA'S MONEY. By Adeline Sergeant.
58. A NEWSPAPER GIRL. By Mrs C. N. Williamson.
59. THE GODDESS. By Richard Marsh.
60. MRS. PETER HOWARD. By M. E. Mann.

Sixpenny Library

THE MATABELE CAMPAIGN. By Major-General Baden-Powell.
THE DOWNFALL OF PREMPEH. By Major-General Baden-Powell.
MY DANISH SWEETHEART. By W. Clark Russell.
IN THE ROAR OF THE SEA. By S. Baring-Gould.
PEGGY OF THE BARTONS. By B. M. Croker.
THE GREEN GRAVES OF BALGOWRIE. By Jane H. Findlater.
THE STOLEN BACILLUS. By H. G. Wells.
MATTHEW AUSTIN. By W. E. Norris.
THE CONQUEST OF LONDON. By Dorothea Gerard.
A VOYAGE OF CONSOLATION. By Sara J. Duncan.
THE MUTABLE MANY. By Robert Barr.
BEN HUR. By General Lew Wallace.
SIR ROBERT'S FORTUNE. By Mrs. Oliphant.
THE FAIR GOD. By General Lew Wallace.
CLARISSA FURIOSA. By W. E. Norris.
CRANFORD. By Mrs. Gaskell.
NOEMI. By S. Baring-Gould.
THE THRONE OF DAVID. By J. H. Ingraham.
ACROSS THE SALT SEAS. By J. Bloundelle Burton.
THE MILL ON THE FLOSS. By George Eliot.
PETER SIMPLE. By Captain Marryat.

MARY BARTON. By Mrs. Gaskell.
PRIDE AND PREJUDICE. By Jane Austen.
NORTH AND SOUTH. By Mrs. Gaskell.
JACOB FAITHFUL. By Captain Marryat.
SHIRLEY. By Charlotte Brontë.
FAIRY TALES RE-TOLD. By S. Baring Gould.
THE TRUE HISTORY OF JOSHUA DAVIDSON. By Mrs. Lynn Linton.
A STATE SECRET. By B. M. Croker.
SAM'S SWEETHEART. By Helen Mathers.
HANDLEY CROSS. By R. S. Surtees.
ANNE MAULEVERER. By Mrs. Caffyn.
THE ADVENTURERS. By H. B. Marriott Watson.
DANTE'S DIVINE COMEDY. Translated by H. F. Cary.
THE CEDAR STAR. By M. E. Mann.
MASTER OF MEN. By E. P. Oppenheim.
THE TRAIL OF THE SWORD. By Gilbert Parker.
THOSE DELIGHTFUL AMERICANS. By Mrs. Cotes.
MR. SPONGE'S SPORTING TOUR. By R. S. Surtees.
ASK MAMMA. By R. S. Surtees.
GRIMM'S FAIRY STORIES. Illustrated by George Cruikshank.
GEORGE AND THE GENERAL. By W. Pett Ridge.
THE JOSS. By Richard Marsh.
MISER HOADLEY'S SECRET. By A. W. Marchmont.

SD - #0029 - 010822 - C0 - 229/152/21 - PB - 9780331322040 - Gloss Lamination